Human Behavior
in the
Social Environment

Human Behavior in the Social Environment

Vimala Pillari
Norfolk State University

Brooks/Cole Publishing Company
Pacific Grove, California

Brooks/Cole Publishing Company
A Division of Wadsworth, Inc.

© 1988 by Wadsworth, Inc., Belmont, California, 94002. All rights reserved. No part of this book may be reproduced, stored in a retrieval system, or transcribed, in any form or by any means—electronic, mechanical, photocopying, recording, or otherwise—without the prior written permission of the publisher, Brooks/Cole Publishing Company, Pacific Grove, California 93950, a division of Wadsworth, Inc.

Printed in the United States of America
10 9 8 7 6 5 4 3 2

Library of Congress Cataloging in Publication Data
Pillari, Vimala.
    Human behavior in the social environment / by Vimala Pillari
      p. cm.
    Includes bibliographies and index.
    ISBN 0-534-09060-5
    1. Life cycle, Human—Psychological aspects.   2. Human behavior.
3. Social interaction.   4. Developmental psychology.   5. Helping
behavior.   I. Title.
HM251.P535 1988
302—dc19
                                                88-14539
                                                  CIP

Sponsoring Editor: *Claire Verduin*
Marketing Representative: *Dawn Beke*
Editorial Assistant: *Linda Ruth Wright, Gay Bond*
Production Editor: *Linda Loba*
Production Assistant: *Nancy Shammas*
Manuscript Editor: *Carey Charlesworth, Meredy Amyx*
Permissions Editor: *Carline Haga*
Interior Design: *Vernon Boes*
Cover Design: *Flora Pomeroy*
Art Director: *Katherine Minerva*
Typesetting: *TCSystems, Inc., Shippensburg, PA*
Cover Printing: *Lehigh Press, Inc. Pennsauken, NJ*
Printing and Binding: *The Maple-Vail Book Manufacturing Group, York, PA*

Dedicated to my son,
Kapil,
whose evolving self in constant interaction
with different environments of wonderment
never ceases to amaze, capture, and teach me.

Preface

I am rushing through the streets of New York City to the library. It's cold and there is a tremendous amount of old snow clinging grudgingly to the sidewalks. An old woman, bent with age, is trying hard to step off the curb and cross the street. I, like the rest of the passersby, notice the old woman, but rush past her in a hurry. But, something in me protests: My family background and upbringing are in the forefront of my mind and they stop me from walking away. I walk back to the old woman, offer her a hand, and help her across the street. She looks up at me, her large, warm, grey eyes startling me as she smiles pleasantly and says, "I like it here, people always help me." I am amazed at her inner strength and her belief in people. Her personality comes through to me and as I walk away, she waves at me and says, "Have a good day."

Seventeen-year-old Chris, an extremely well-behaved student, suddenly is in trouble because he lost his temper with his classmate, beat him badly, and was suspended from school.

John and Wendy, who apparently had been "happily married," obtained a divorce after their youngest child left home.

Why do people behave the way they do? The main purpose of this book is to help readers understand human behavior and the various factors that cause people to behave the way they do.

This is a text for students who want to understand human behavior in the social environment. It is especially prepared for graduate and undergraduate students in social-work programs and fulfills the requirements of the Council on Social Work Education. The Council recommends that the course on human behavior in the social environment encompass the psychological, socio-cultural, and biological aspects of development, so that students are able to understand these dimensions of social work, as well as offer help through constructive interventions.

Organization of the Book

There are two ways of writing and teaching a course on human behavior in the social environment: the topical approach and the chronological approach. In the topical approach, only one aspect of development is traced through the lifespan. For instance, moral development is traced from childhood through old age. I have chosen to use the chronological approach, which looks at the functioning of all aspects of development in various stages of life, from conception to old age. I also chose the chronological approach in accordance with the desires of my students, who found it to be more meaningful and easier to relate to than the topical approach.

The multifaceted aspects of development are presented in the nine chapters of this text: A Life-Span View of Human Development and Behavior; Conception, Pregnancy, and Childbirth; Infancy; Preschool Years; Middle Childhood; Adolescence; Early Adulthood; Middle Adulthood; and The Older Years. Each chapter discusses various theories of development, along with the biological, social, and psychological factors that influence development. Case studies, highlighting racial, ethnic, socio-class, or gender factors, are presented from a social worker's perspective to illustrate a point or explain a concept.

Every chapter deals with the implications of practice, so that students of social work can understand the roles they can play in helping people during various stages of their lives.

Acknowledgments

I thank my students whose desire and interest started me on this venture. To Dr. Isaac Alcabes, my colleague at the State University of New York, who read the initial chapters and critiqued them.

To my colleagues at Norfolk State University for their support. A special thanks to LaVerne Anderson, librarian at Norfolk State University. My deep gratitude to Dean Moses Newsome, Jr., whose constant encouragement, support, understanding, concern, and interest made this project easier to do.

I thank my reviewers whose constructive criticism helped to add new dimensions to this book: Professor Anna Bowman, Goshen College, Indiana; Professor Betty P. Broadhurst, Colorado State University; Professor Betty Brown Chappell, University of Chicago; Dr. Frank W. Clark, University of Montana; Dr. Genevieve DeHoyos, Brigham Young University, Utah; Associate Professor Karen Kirst-Ashman, University of Wisconsin; Professor Phylis Peterman, Rutgers University, New Jersey; and Professor Doreen Portner, Chapman College, California.

My special thanks to the Brooks/Cole family: Claire Verduin, for her support and masterful guidance through the project; to Linda Loba who worked closely with me throughout this project.

My sincere and special thanks to Thanga. My heartfelt thanks to Steve for his understanding and caring patience.

Vimala Pillari

Contents

Chapter 1
A Life-Span View of
Human Development and Behavior 1

Introduction 2
The Study of Development and Behavior 3
Determinants of Human Development 4
Social Development and Behavior 5
Science and Theories of Human Behavior 7
The Ego and Its Functions 9
Ego Theorists 11
The Environment 16
The Life-Span Development Perspective 16
Implications for Research 19
The Life Span 27
Chapter Summary 31
References 33

Chapter 2
Conception, Pregnancy, and Childbirth 36

Psychosocial Context of Pregnancy 37
Prenatal Development 39
Genetic Influences 44
Environmental Influences in the Prenatal Stage 49
The Birth Experience 54
The Special Circumstances of the Newborn 58
Parent–Infant Relationships 61
Developmental Abnormalities 62
Implications for Social Work Practice 64
Chapter Summary 65
References 67

Chapter 3
Infancy   69

Principles of Infant Development   70
Major Theorists on Infancy   78
Critical Issues for the Child in Its Environment   85
Implications for Social Work Practice   97
Chapter Summary   99
References   100

Chapter 4
Preschool Years   103

Physical Growth   104
New Skills   105
Cognitive Development   107
Language Development   109
The Psychosocial Environment   112
Moral Development   115
The Social Environment   118
Child-Rearing Practices and Patterns   122
Divorce   126
The Impact of Television   127
Implications for Social Work Practice   128
Chapter Summary   129
References   130

Chapter 5
Middle Childhood   132

Physical Development   133
Cognitive Development   136
Moral Development   139
Socialization and the School Setting   144
The Psychosocial Environment   149
Parenting   156
Peer Influences on Personality   160
Learning Disabilities   165
Implications for Social Work Practice   170
Chapter Summary   171
References   172

Chapter 6
Adolescence   178

Physical Changes   180
Cognitive Development   183
Value Systems   186
Identity   190
Competence   195
Family Relationships   197
Sex-Role Identity   201
Peer Relationships   203
Minority-Group Culture   205
Critical Issues   205
Implications for Social Work Practice   215
Chapter Summary   216
References   218

Chapter 7
Early Adulthood   224

Changes in Adulthood   225
Psychosocial Environment   226
Cognitive Development   226
Erikson: Intimacy versus Isolation   228
Identity and Self   232
The Role of Work for the Adult   232
Household and Family Patterns   236
Sexuality and Intimacy   242
Parenthood   251
Implications for Social Work Practice   256
Chapter Summary   257
References   259

Chapter 8
Middle Adulthood   263

Character of the Middle Years   264
Physical Changes   267
Cognitive Processes   270
The Psychosocial Environment   273
Tasks of Middle Age   278
Changing Patterns of the Family   279
Career Adjustments   287

Implications for Social Work Practice   292
Chapter Summary   294
References   296

Chapter 9
The Older Years   300

Models and Theories of Aging   303
Physical Aging and Disease   305
Personal Adaptation to Aging   308
Myths of Aging   311
Erikson: Integrity versus Despair   312
Cognitive Functioning   313
Social Aspects of Aging   316
Social Issues and Problems   324
Death   329
Implications for Social Work Practice   336
Chapter Summary   337
References   339

Index   343

Human Behavior
in the
Social Environment

1

A Life-Span View of Human Development and Behavior

Introduction

The Study of Development and Behavior

Determinants of Human Development

Social Development and Behavior

Science and Theories of Human Behavior

The Ego and Its Functions

Ego Theorists

The Environment

The Life-Span Development Perspective

Implications for Research

The Life Span

Chapter Summary

References

Introduction

Human behavior is fascinating as well as perplexing. People's behavior can make us laugh, cry, be angry, or be reasonable. We learn to distinguish that John has a "nice" sense of humor and Tom's humor is "dry." Why do people behave in different ways? What influences one person to become a preacher and another a murderer? What kind of a person are you? Why is it that you are different from your parents' best friends' children? Answers to such questions can be found through the study of human behavior and social environment in the life-span perspective.

By understanding how people develop from conception to old age, we learn more about ourselves as well as about other people. This knowledge becomes useful to us, as social work practitioners, when we try to deal with problem situations, whether created by persons or by situational circumstances. An understanding of people equips practitioners to help both individuals and society to fulfill their potential.

This book views human development and behavior within the social environment from a life-span developmental perspective. A hallmark of this approach indicates that development occurs at all points of a person's life cycle, from conception to death. Traditional views of human development have emphasized maturation and growth during infancy, childhood, and adolescence; stability during adulthood; and degeneration and decline during old age. The life-span view of human development attempts to describe, explain, and optimize intra-individual change in behavior. It also attempts to describe and explain inter-individual differences in such change throughout life in interaction with the environment. This book rejects the traditional notion that children flower in childhood, stop abruptly at the end of adolescence, remain static in early adulthood, and begin at midlife a steady and irreversible withering. Instead, it reflects the conviction that growth and change take place in all age levels at various points in a person's life.

To understand the life-span developmental perspective, you should be aware of certain terms. In his book *A Theory of Data*, Coombs (1964) distinguishes the terms *behavior, raw data,* and *data*. Behavior is described as everything that is potentially observable about a person or event. Raw data are the bits of information that are selected and constructed by the investigator as empirical facts for further analysis. "Data" refers to a body of facts that have already undergone interpretation according to the investigator's chosen method. Coombs reveals two dimensions in scientific activities: (1) the discovery, selection, and construction of raw data out of the total pool of behavior and (2) the mapping of raw data—that is, the procedures used for empirical verification and falsification (Baltes & Cornelius, 1977). Theorists constantly use data to support their points of view. In this book, we draw upon the theories that add to and support the life-span perspective, enabling us to enrich and better understand human development and behavior in the social environment.

The Study of Development and Behavior

Before we proceed further, the term *development* has to be explained. In development, changes take place. There is some consensus that "development" refers to change—but not all changes are developmental ones. An accident in a house can bring about changes in people's lives, but these are nondevelopmental changes: random, unorganized, and unsystematic.

Nondevelopmental changes could also be called *nonnormative life events;* for example, the death of a child or a young parent or the birth of a child with congenital defects. Nonnormative changes could also include happy events such as unexpected opportunities in a foreign country or a sudden financial inheritance. Such an event causes more stress than a developmental event. If the person has not expected it and therefore was not prepared for it, the person may need special help in adapting. Human beings have tremendous potential to create their own positive nonnormative events and be active participants in their own development.

In contrast, developmental changes are systematic, organized changes, and the entity or thing that changes could be a culture, a society or group, or an individual. In an individual, systematic changes take place when a person passes from childhood to adulthood to old age. Developmental changes in individuals are multidirectional.

Heinz Werner (1957), a major theorist, described development as a process that is characterized by increasing differentiation and hierarchical integration. Differentiation implies that human organisms change during development from simple, general forms to more complex, specific forms. During the first few weeks following conception, cells are undifferentiated; that is, they do not perform any specialized function. But after a few weeks they become differentiated into skeletal cells, digestive cells, circulatory cells, and so on. This process of differentiation applies to behavioral as well as psychological functioning. In the first year of life, for example, the gross, reflexive motor actions of the newborn change into more complex, specialized, and voluntary patterns of behavior. In the same manner, a person's notions of what is acceptable and what is unacceptable become clearer as the person ages and develops.

"Hierarchical integration" refers to the manner in which differentiated parts and functions of the individual become increasingly coordinated into organized systems during development. When a child begins to walk, the individual motor responses of the young infant become integrated into a complex, coordinated motor system that results in walking. Hierarchical integration implies that as development proceeds, the more primitive and psychological systems of an individual become subordinated to a more sophisticated system. Although the developmentally less advanced behaviors remain with the individual, they are overshadowed and controlled by more sophisticated psychological systems (Brodzinsky, Gormly, & Ambron, 1986). When 15-year-old Johnny is pestered by his 8-year-old sister, he is able to understand and overlook it as her way of getting attention. However, when he is tired after a tough day at school, or when he has to prepare for an exam, he gets angry with her annoying behavior and stomps out of the room. Like a large number of us, Johnny, has the capacity to control expression of immature cognitive, emotional, and behavioral responses, and in most cases he does. Occasionally, however, the usually effective mechanisms may fail or are purposely put aside. It is during these times that developmentally less advanced behaviors emerge.

The processes of differentiation and hierarchical integration characterize, in a general way, the manner in which people change over the course of a life span. Changes in adulthood occur in different directions, some abilities increasing and others diminishing. For example, older people may continue to expand their vocabular but experience a decrease in their reaction time or their ability to perform physical work. As they grow older, some people develop new abilities. Winston Churchill took up painting in his later years.

Determinants of Human Development

Every one of us is unique. Our thoughts, feelings, attitudes, and behavior are like no one else's. What makes us the way we are? How do we follow a specific developmental path that is uniquely our own? Our differences are based on two major factors: heredity and environment. "Heredity" refers to the genes that are passed on from parents to children at the time of conception. Briefly, "environment" refers to the wide array of experiences to which an individual is exposed from the time of conception to death. (A detailed discussion of environments is presented later in this chapter.)

Historically, there has been a controversy about the relative importance of heredity and environment in the development of a person. By contrast, most recent research shows that development can be understood only in terms of the interaction between genetic and experiential forces (Anastasi, 1958). However, it should not be assumed that each of these factors plays an equal role in all aspects of development. Some behaviors such as walking can best be explained by the process of maturation, which is guided by a genetic blueprint. Other behaviors, such as which kinds of outdoor or indoor games interest us, are explained by the influence of individuals we meet and the society we encounter. Thus the critical question concerning development is not which factor—heredity or environment—is responsible for our behaviors but how these two factors interact so as to propel us along our unique developmental roads.

Experiences that we face could be biological in nature, such as inadequate nutrition or exposure to disease or drugs, or they could be primarily social, such as the interactions one has within the family, among peers, in school, through media, and within the specific community and culture in which one lives. All these factors intertwined with heredity influence the way we grow, feel, act, and behave.

Social Development and Behavior

Social development is the process by which individuals adopt behaviors that are customary and acceptable to the standards of their reference group.

Learning of Roles

Every group has expectations of its members according to situation, sex role, and life stage. Children learn social roles under various circumstances. Within each of these roles it is necessary for children as well as adults to learn different kinds of approved behavior that are accepted as appropriate by their own reference group. Next they must develop appropriate attitudes toward their reference group, permitting interaction in social settings and creating opportunities that are necessary for social self-image, self-esteem, and reinforcement. Finally, individuals learn to participate in social interactions and become sociable persons; however, people exhibit varying degrees of sociability, depending on their upbringing, lifestyle, and personality. Although few people conform to all expectations of their group, gaining social approval in important matters requires most people to reconcile their needs with group expectations. Thus, a well-socialized individual will eventually become skilled at knowing how far ahead of the group one can be and still be perceived as a leader or a fashion setter rather than a deviant.

The term *social* is used for a person who has mastered the processes just mentioned. A gregarious person is a sociable, outgoing person who has mastered the social aspects and has also received much reinforcement. An unsocial person is someone who has not mastered the social processes and is likely to spend time alone. An antisocial person is aware of the reference group's expectations and has developed an antagonistic attitude toward the group. A nonsocial person is one who has not experienced the processes of socialization.

Many traits developed by children as part of the socialization process remain stable throughout life. However, depending on the culture, social norms, and expectations of the social group, changes take place in response to the pressures and expectations of adult life (Neugarten & Datan, 1973). It is not unusual for an individual's coping style to require gradual adjustment in old age. Such changes could take place due to the result of stereotypes of age-appropriate behavior that have been imposed on the elderly by themselves and younger people.

Role learning is an important aspect of an individual's development. Children learn social roles early in life; young children are not allowed to assume a variety of roles that are appropriate to older children and adults. As young children grow, they become socialized through acquiring verbal skills and through role-playing. Children who have good verbal skills will be comfortable in role enactment. Children not only learn their own roles but also learn to ascribe roles to their peers, often simplistic ones such as "crybaby" or "bully."

Within the family, too, children learn to differentiate between the roles of father and mother and follow some specific sex roles. Similarly, they learn roles related to ethnic group and social class. Roles learned in the home are modified as children move through nursery as well as formal school education. There are at least five types of identity that children begin to follow as they grow up (Gordon, 1976):

1. sexual identity, which is consistently reinforced and is the most pervasive identity
2. ethnic identity, which influences personal values, association patterns, and often the choice of marriage partner
3. occupational identity, which relates to the adult's role in the workplace as well as at home
4. membership identity, which is seen as the link between formal and informal organizational life of the community
5. political identity, which describes a person's membership in a political party as a leader, loser, or peacemaker.

Transmission of Norms

Throughout the life-span, socialization also means the transmission of norms. Although there is popular talk about the "generation gap," research suggests that cultural as well as behavioral norms continue to be transmitted from one generation to another. Sociologists describe three elements of the transmission mechanisms that maintain intergenerational solidarity: association or objective interaction between generations, affect or the degree of sentiment among family members, and consensus or agreement on values and opinions (Bengston, 1976). Clearly the transmission of norms can occur only if there is continuous closeness among generations at many points in life. In spite of our great mobility, such propinquity does occur. Shanas, Townsend, Wedderburn, Friis, Milhoj, and Stehouwer (1968) reported that 84% of the elderly in three industrial societies live within an hour's travel from at least one child, and 85% of those surveyed said that they had seen their children during the week preceding the survey. Evidence provided by a study of three-generation families (Shanas et al., 1968) shows that there is affective solidarity.

The continuity of norms between generations seems apparent within families even when a younger individual moves into adult status and encounters life transitions already experienced by an older role model. Norms with intergenerational similarities persist despite ideological differences arising from the younger generation's peer interactions (Hill & Aldous, 1969).

Although there is continuity of norms, change is as much an aspect of the human life-span as constancy. On the basis of the belief that change is predictable, developmental theorists continue with their research in order to get a better understanding of life. As people develop, they learn norms and values of behavior that are acceptable to their social groups.

Change is physical as well as psychological and social. What gives the body and its organs stability in the face of chemical and structural turnover? For instance, a scar from a childhood accident can be part of a person throughout life. The cells of the nervous system that integrate life do not divide and increase after the fetal stage (Birren, 1969). These cells grow larger, but they do not increase in number to replace dead cells. As the cells of certain systems accumulate experience, we can recognize the uniqueness of our own history in comparison with others'. There is memory in the immunological system as well; when we recover from an infectious disease, the system may impart immunity if we encounter that disease in the future. Knowledge about the laws of change in the human organism over its life span is by no means a finished business. Much information remains to be discovered at the psychological as well as biological level; an appreciation of the mechanisms and limits of change would lead to a more enlightened society.

Science and Theories of Human Behavior

Science is a social enterprise; it is not private and cannot be understood exclusively in terms of criteria that are internal to the scientific method. Scientific pursuits should also be related to the social-psychological context of cultural and scientific developments. Thus, far from representing a unity of thought, science reveals a multiplicity of viewpoints (Baltes & Willis, 1977). According to scientist Weimer (1979), it is not different data but different arguments that scientists encounter in the constructive rhetoric and rational criticism of their colleagues. To deliver this rhetoric fruitfully, scientists have to rely on either some explicit social-proof structures (White, 1977) or some shared, tacit structures of social proof that are learned through scientists' own devices in order to develop their own theories (Weimer, 1979). A theory can be described as a set of interrelated statements about a phenomenon.

What is basic human nature? Are human beings driven by passions, or are we rational and goal oriented? How can we both as educators and students develop knowledge? Can knowledge be accumulated through insight in small sequential steps, or are we motivated by reward, punishment, curiosity, and inner pain? What is a conscience, and how can it be developed? Can we look at developmental psychology for answers to these basic questions? The answers differ in accordance with various theories of human development and the corresponding sets of assumptions about behavior on which those theories are based. Social scientists formulate significant questions by which to select as well as to organize their data in order to understand the data within a larger framework. Without a theory, we would be overwhelmed by a large amount of unusable data. To test a theory, a researcher must test its predictions about human behavior.

All of us, educators as well as students, have our own theories about the issues that will be discussed in this book. Often we will find ourselves leaning toward one kind of explanation rather than another. For instance, juvenile delinquency can be viewed as a problem that young, irresponsible people create for themselves or as a problem due to the environment; that is, delinquent young people could either be viewed as deviants or perpetrators, or seen as victims suffering from lack of training in their families. Likewise, some parents may feel that 5-year-old children are capable of making their own decisions about what to study at school, and other parents may not. We find that we have broad assumptions about the degree to which individuals are responsible for their behavior and the degree to which human rationality can be relied on to direct human actions.

In some settings, social work practitioners are free to follow the theories of human behavior that they personally espouse; in others, they may have to adopt the theories accepted by their agency settings. Different theories may be suited to different clients or to different aspects of behavior. Therefore practitioners need to be familiar with a number of theoretical approaches.

There are various theories about human behavior and development. For instance, Mischel (1970) has suggested that one may study human behavior with emphasis on the effects of either environmental conditions or phenomenological factors (such as affects and thoughts) on mediating personal variables such as competencies, expectations, values, and rules. At a more general level, Reese and Overton (1970; Overton & Reese, 1973) compared the mechanistic and organismic paradigms and their respective notions of what constitutes relevant raw data.

The mechanistic view indicates that people are not qualitatively different from other phenomena that exist in the natural world. People are governed by the same forces that control all natural phenomena. At the most basic level, all natural phenomena are made up of atoms and molecules, and all that is necessary for the attainment of knowledge is to understand the mechanical workings of physics and chemistry. Scientists who view people in this manner are said to have a mechanistic world view (Bertalanffy, 1962; Lerner, 1976).

The basic metaphor of the mechanistic model is a machine. In the mechanistic view, complex phenomena are reduced to elementary parts of their relationships. The whole is viewed as the sum of its parts. For the mechanist, the movements of parts depend on the application of outside forces, which results in a chainlike sequence of events. Thus forces are conceptualized not only as being external to individuals but also as preceding an event (Lerner & Hultsch, 1983).

Application of the mechanistic view to the study of human behavior yields a reactive model of development. People are seen as essentially passive organisms who react only to events. The individual is inherently at rest, and activity is the result of external forces. Therefore change can be explained by such forces. Change is viewed as quantitative rather than qualitative. Complex activities such as expression of emotions and solving of problems could be reduced ultimately to simple elements—for example, stimulus–response behavior.

In the organismic view, the person is seen as being an active organism. Opposing the mechanistic view, the organismic view indicates that people cannot be reduced to atoms and molecules as studied by physicists and chemists. This theory emphasizes that when combined, the constituent parts possess characteristics that they lack when viewed in isolation. The essence of this model is that one must study the whole person (Bertalanffy, 1933; Reese & Overton, 1970). To organismic researchers, people resemble other biological organisms rather than machines. A person is seen as a complex, organized system of interrelated parts. The whole is equal to more than the sum of its parts because complex phenomena cannot be reduced to elementary parts and their relationships. The components of the organism have meaning only as they are considered in the context of which they are a part. Individuals are viewed as dynamic, in a constant state of activity. The manner in which parts move depends upon the activity of the organism and its action on environments. Any change that takes place is explained by the organism's action on the environment. Change is seen as qualitative rather than quantitative. In both the mechanistic and the organismic view, raw data are analyzed in ways consistent with a particular philosophical way of viewing people.

The contrast between the mechanistic and the organismic views shows that human behavior can be studied from any conceptual framework. The type of perspective used dictates the questions that will be asked, as well as the manner of interpreting the data. Therefore, in making use of research it is important to take the researcher's perspective into account.

The content of this book is presented in terms of a life-span perspective. The choice of this framework does not signify its inherent superiority to other perspectives. This framework permits the author to explain some of the issues and puzzles interwoven through human development and behavior, but the color and flavor of the author's understanding come from professional practice.

There is no one theory that is universally accepted by all practitioners; each has its dedicated adherents and its impassioned critics. Whereas some practitioners would align themselves with a single body of thought, most thoughtful students of human behavior will find that each theory contributes something to their understanding without being sufficient in itself. When practitioners employ theories to understand human development and behavior, it becomes easier to devise a number of interventions that are likely to succeed in dealing with the clients and their problems. In this book we will discuss and evaluate ego and cognitive theories of human development with emphasis on the influence of social environments, examining them from a life-span perspective. We will not attempt a thorough analysis of every theory in all its aspects. However, strengths and weaknesses of each theory will be presented as developmental life events are discussed. Various types of therapies offered to people are based upon these and other theories of behavior.

The Ego and Its Functions

In order to comprehend the transactions between the ego and the environment and its significance for the life-span perspective, it is necessary to understand the ego and its functions.

In tracing the development of Freud's thinking about the ego, Hartmann (1964) pointed out that Freud defined it as an organism with constant cathexis—the concentration of psychic energy on a particular person, thing, idea or aspect of life—and assigned to it such functions as defense, reality testing, perception, memory, attention, and judgment. Hartmann regarded the ego as synonymous with the conscious mind and defined it as a sense organ for perception, for thought processes, and thus for the reception of external and internal stimuli. Heinz Hartmann is regarded as the father of ego psychology. His work is a direct outcome of the introduction of structural theory in Freud's revised concept of the ego. This theory opened up many questions about the development of the ego and its functions.

Hartmann presented his first paper on ego psychology in Vienna in 1937. Historically, it represents a turning point in the development of modern psychoanalytic theory. The paper is considered to be a natural sequel to Freud's previous formulations of the structural hypothesis and his contributions to psychoanalytic thought, and it continues to modify our ideas about people and their functioning. Concepts that originated with Hartmann—the undifferentiated phase, the conflict-free ego sphere, conflict-free ego development, and primary and secondary autonomy—give evidence of the tremendous impact of his theories.

Hartmann discusses the conflict-free ego sphere as the ensemble of functions that at any given time exert their effects outside the region of mental conflicts. He indicates that people are born with a preadaptation to an average expectable environment and are equipped with an innate apparatus for establishing relationships with their environments. Thus Hartmann views the individual as having biologically endowed potentialities, and as emerging able to develop a response to the realities encountered in the environment. According to Hartmann, the organism not only adapts to the environment but also is capable of changing the environment in a creative process of mutual adaptation. This task of the ego is more or less closely related to the tasks of reality mastery.

The ego performs a number of functions, which can be classified as perceptive, cognitive, adaptive and protective, object-relationship, and executive and integrative functions. The ego's perceptive functions include perception of self (based on self-awareness, self-image, and body image), perception of others in relation to self, and reality testing. Cognitive functions include remembering and the ability to associate, to differentiate, and to select behaviors on the basis of anticipated outcomes and logical thinking. They also include communicating verbal and nonverbal information. Adaptive and protective functions of the ego are the utilization of adaptive defensive mechanisms in order to obtain satisfaction of needs as well as to handle related feelings. Ego defense mechanisms protect the ego from anxiety and reduce anxiety. They are essential for the maintenance of balance. Usually people are called well adapted if their productivity, their ability to enjoy life, and their mental equilibrium are undisturbed. What does it mean to say that a person has adapted meaningfully? What makes a person succeed or fail in a given situation? A person's degree of adaptiveness is determined with reference to environmental situations—that is, average expectable, typical situations or unexpected, atypical situations (Hartmann, 1964).

The object-relationship functions of the ego deal with affect, capacity for intimacy, nurturance, and the capacity for extended social relationships. The executive and integrative functions of the ego include:

1. planning and establishing priorities in relation to goals, interests, and motives
2. decision making—that is, making choices that involve consideration of both negative and positive consequences
3. social functioning—that is, delay of gratification and goal-directed behavior, which are means of carrying out social roles and responsibilities
4. problem solving and the capacity to learn, to relearn, and to integrate new learning
5. the ability to reach a compromise between what one wants and what one can realistically get or achieve
6. maintaining a sense of balance and wholeness and at the same time modifying one's behavior through making changes in oneself or through transactions with the environment.

In order to function effectively, all people need to cope and adapt themselves to their life situations, dealing with such life phases as infancy, childhood, adolescence, adulthood, marriage, employment, old age, retirement, and death and bereavement. At times, they need to deal with unusual life situations such as war and other crises.

Ego Theorists
Erik Erikson

Erik Erikson, a psychoanalyst, extended the Freudian notion of the ego and was interested in the influence of the environment on the development of the individual. Erikson (1980) classified the development of a person into eight different stages of life, each having a characteristic concern:

Infancy	Basic trust versus basic mistrust
Early childhood	Autonomy versus doubt and shame
Play age	Initiative versus guilt
School age	Industry versus inferiority
Adolescence	Identity versus role confusion
Young adulthood	Intimacy versus isolation
Middle adulthood	Generativity versus stagnation
Old age	Ego integrity versus despair

Erikson specified that the successful resolution of a turning point or crisis at every stage leads to meaningful development. A crisis or a critical period is the time when a given event would have the most important impact on a person. Psychoanalysts have emphasized the concept of critical periods. Freud believed that the experiences a child undergoes before the age of five have a serious impact on the child's development. Erikson believes that in every stage of life there is a critical period for emotional as well as social development.

According to Erikson's theory, an individual undergoes a major conflict at every stage of development. The ultimate personality of the individual depends on whether or not these conflicts have been successfully resolved. In Erikson's theory there is an emphasis on the influence of social and cultural factors that affect the development of an individual's personality.

An advantage in utilizing Erikson's theory is that it covers the entire life span. One of the important criticisms that has been aimed at Erikson (which will be discussed as we study the various stages) is his lack of emphasis on women's development. He has been accused of an antifemale bias for failing to take into consideration the social and cultural factors that influence the attitudes and behaviors of the sexes. According to another criticism, it is not easy to assess some of his concepts objectively and use them as the basis of follow-up research.

Robert White

Another theorist who moved away from Freudian thinking and developed his own school of thought is Robert White. In addition to the concept of the ego, White stresses the notion of competence. Competence means fitness or ability to carry on transactions with the environment that result in a person's self-maintenance, growth, and flourishing. There is some modification in current psychoanalytical thought about the role of the ego. In the current view, the ego assigns motives to the ego proper (White, 1960), whereas the traditional view says that all motivations of the ego are derivatives of motives that serve the id. According to White, the ego begins to master reality even when a child is very young. For instance, a child who wishes to break a vase may hesitate because of the consequences. Many times, a child may give in to impulses because he or she does not know what else to do; but as the ego increases in strength and rational thought processes intervene, the child spends more time deliberating before taking action. The ego learns to avoid failure or punishment by identifying situations that are associated with it.

White underscores competence as a major driving force in life. All people strive to master their circumstances. A child learns to care for himself or herself by mastering simple skills, later extending that competence to school work and small chores around the home. Still later, the person trains for some kind of job. Cutting across all these forms of competence seeking are the social skills that the person must master. Successful living is highly contingent on a person's competence. White's theory is an exciting one because it emphasizes potentials in individuals, as well people's ability to grow and change, based on the competence drive.

White suggests that careful study of children's exploratory play, even at 1 year of age, shows the characteristics of directiveness, selectivity, and persistence. White proposes that selective manipulation and exploration are both aspects of competence, and he assumes that one general motivational principle lies behind them. He calls this motive *effectance* because its most characteristic feature is the production of effects on the environment. At first, those effects could consist of any changes in sensory input that follow activity or exertion, but before long the child is able to intend particular changes and to be content only with these. White has designated the experience that goes with producing such changes as the feeling of *efficacy* (White, 1960).

White presents his ideas of development in the classification originated by Freud:

the oral stage
the anal stage
the phallic stage
the latency stage
adolescence

These stages will be discussed in appropriate chapters.

Jean Piaget

Jean Piaget (1896–1980) was an important advocate of the organismic theory. A great deal of the information we have about children comes from this great Swiss psychologist.

The organismic perspective. The organismic perspective sees people as active organisms who, through their own actions, can bring about their own development. Organismic theory is interested more in the process than in the product. Unlike the psychoanalysts, organismic theorists do not focus on the underlying motivational forces of which a child is not aware. This theory emphasizes a view of the child as a doer and an actor—someone who actively constructs his or her own world. Organismic theory concerns itself with the qualitative changes (the nature of what has changed) rather than the quantitative changes (the leaps from one stage of development to another). Organismic theorists often describe development as occurring in a set of sequences of qualitatively different, discontinuous stages, so that later behaviors cannot be predicted from earlier ones. They do not attach importance, as other theorists do, to the fact that reinforcements given by people or other forces shape a child's responses.

The world of the child. Piaget explored the various aspects of children's thoughts in terms of stages, each of which represents a qualitative change in type of thought or behavior. According to his stage theory, all persons have to go through the same stages in the same order, even though the actual timing varies from one person to another, making any age demarcation only approximate. Thus each stage builds on the one that went before and lays the foundation for the next stage. Every stage has many facets to it.

According to Piaget, the child's cognitive world develops through a scheme—an individual's representation of the world—that becomes increasingly complex and more abstract. Thus cognitive development happens through a two-step process of expanding ideas to include this new knowl-

Chapter 1

Developmental Stages According to Piaget (1970)

Infancy	Sensorimotor—the knowledge that external objects exist
2 to 7 years	Sensorimotor/preoperational Preoperational—mentally representing absent objects and using symbols to represent objects
7 to 11 years	Concrete operational—reversibility of actions; thoughts limited to objects that have a concrete real existence
11 through adulthood*	Formal operational (beginning to develop for some)—all possible combinations of elements of a problem to find a solution, real or imaginary

* Ages are author's approximation.

edge. The two-step process of cognitive development arises from the action of the organism on the environment and from the action of the environment on the organism.

Piaget's stages will be discussed in great detail in upcoming chapters.

Recognized as the world's authority on how children think, Piaget developed a meaningful theory of how children grow intellectually. He established a unique way of evaluating the development of logical thinking. Piaget has brought about more research than any other theorist of the past few decades, and he has also stimulated many practical innovations in the education of young children.

Piaget has not escaped the critics. Some critics charge that he primarily discusses the "average" child's abilities and does not take into consideration such influences on performance as education and culture. He says very little about emotional and personality development, except as it relates to a person's cognitive development. One of the chief criticisms has concerned his study of subjects. Many of his ideas about cognitive growth emerged from his highly personal observations of his own three children and from his own idiosyncratic way of interviewing children.

Lawrence Kohlberg

The thinking of Lawrence Kohlberg, a theorist who has emphasized the moral development of individuals, has been profoundly inspired by Piaget. Kohlberg developed a moral stage theory: people go from premoral to moral development.

Kohlberg's theory is very comprehensive and develops in a definite sequential pattern. He builds on Piaget's thinking that moral development is related to cognitive development. By finding the reasons for people's choices, Kohlberg has uncovered a great deal about the thinking that underlies moral judgment. He has also accelerated research by others and inspired many classroom programs on morality. These are the levels and stages in the revised version of Kohlberg's theory of moral reasoning (adapted from Kohlberg, 1976):

Level 1: Preconventional
    Stage 1: Heteronomous morality
    Stage 2: Individualism, instrumental purpose, and exchange
Level 2: Conventional
    Stage 3: Mutual interpersonal expectations, interpersonal con-
        formity and relationships
    Stage 4: Social systems and conscience
Level 3: Postconventional or principled
    Stage 5: Social contract or utility and individual rights.

In the present version of the theory (Colby, 1978; Kohlberg, 1976, 1978), as in the first version, there are three levels of moral-reasoning development. However, in this new version the first two levels each have two stages and the last level includes only one stage. The major change in the theory is in the definition of these five stages, representing the person's social perspective as moving toward increasingly greater scope, which includes more people and institutions, and greater abstraction—that is, one moves from physicalistic reasoning (preoccupation with bodily matters) to reasoning about values, rights, and implicit contracts.

Kohlberg's theory has been criticized for two limitations. It concerns itself only with moral thinking, as opposed to behavior, not accounting for the fact that a person's moral thinking and behavior may contradict one another. And his view of morality is narrow in that it focuses on a sense of justice, omitting other aspects of morality, such as compassion and integrity.

Carol Gilligan

Carol Gilligan's insightful theory of women's development and the differences between men and women will be discussed in later chapters. Her theory about women's moral development in relation to men's moral development is enlightening and helps to place Kohlberg's perspective on moral development in a realistic context.

Gilligan (1982) believes that psychology has consistently and systematically misunderstood women—that is, misunderstood their motives, their moral commitments, the course of their psychological growth, and their sense of what is important in life. A number of developmental theorists have built their theories on the observation of men's lives. Gilligan attempts to correct misconceptions about women and refocus psychology's view of the female life cycle. Her thinking is rooted not only in research but in good common sense, contributing to a more meaningful understanding of human experience. When life-cycle theorists, using her theory, divide their attention and begin to observe the lives of women as they have those of men, their vision encompasses the experiences of both sexes and their theories become correspondingly more fertile.

Men and women complement each other. In order to understand them and offer constructive help, it is necessary to understand their respective emotions, sense of self, and development. Both male and female practitioners would gain in therapeutic skill from an understanding of the differences and similarities between men's and women's development. Therefore our discussion will incorporate the thinking of such psychologists as J. B. Miller, N. Chodorow, D. Dinnerstein, M. Greenspan, and others who have productively researched women's development.

The Environment

The notion of studying an environment, particularly with reference to human behavior, is complex; it is difficult to distinguish between inner and outer environment. Leaving aside philosophical as well as scientific issues, a conceptualization of the environment would take into account physical and social aspects and culture. The physical environment comprises the built world as well as the natural world. The social environment comprises the network of human relations at various levels of organization. Both the physical and the social environment are affected by the cultural values, norms, knowledge, and beliefs that pattern social interaction and determine how we use and react to the physical environment (Germain, 1979). In short, the structure of behavior is based on people's abilities and motivations, the process of development is based on person–environment transactions and "goodness-of-fit," and the goals of behavior are based on task mastery and social competence.

As life advances and experiences increase, both internal and external phases of behavior and growth change consistently. Human beings follow the universal laws of growth and development. For instance, the maturational process, the stages of development, and the directions of growth are fundamental to people everywhere. Although the physical principles of maturational development unfold naturally, they are subject to change according to the rate and extent of development, which in turn depend on environmental influences. For instance, a child seriously malnourished on account of poor environmental conditions might develop an ineffective intellectual system. The notion of environmental influences on people's development will be discussed at appropriate points in the book.

The Life-Span Development Perspective
Definition

This book uses the life-span perspective as a framework to introduce the student of human development and behavior to the study of the human life span (birth to death). By looking at the development of a person from birth to death, we begin to understand how each period of development and behavior has its own challenges and frustrations and how it relates to other periods of development. The infant and the preschooler learn how to control their behavior and develop a sense of self in relation to the world of family and play. The schoolchild adjusts to a new environment (school) and a new adult (teacher) while learning to read, write, and develop friendships with peers.

The adolescent comes to grips with himself or herself in terms of the world of work, career, and social development. The young adult further clarifies vocational direction and lifestyle and may begin intimate social or family relationships. The middle-aged adult consolidates self-growth and development by generating activities that support and strengthen career, social, and family associations. Finally, the aging adult faces the prospect that life will be over and that death is inevitable.

As the life-span view suggests, behaviors as well as behavioral changes are generally influenced by a number of incidental and formal causes. Thus, to look for a single determinant of behavior is highly illusory and futile. From a conceptual perspective, the status of a particular determinant can be categorized as necessary or sufficient and then must be seen in relation to the broader spatio-temporal context of determinants in which it is embedded. The context is subject to historical changes as well (Labouvie, 1982). Thus, the task in using the life-span perspective is not only to identify a particular determinant as necessary and sufficient but to specify the contexts in which a single determinant or a multiple set of determinants is (1) sufficient and necessary, (2) necessary but not sufficient, (3) sufficient and not necessary, or (4) neither necessary nor sufficient in reference to occurrence or form of behavioral changes that are being studied (Labouvie, 1982).

The life-span view of human development and behavior has several attributes, one of the most important being that any one portion of life is just part of the entire life span. Another attribute is its multidisciplinary approach to understanding and working with human beings. The life-span perspective incorporates knowledge from a number of academic disciplines that study human development and behavior. Information presented in this book is taken from psychology, social work, sociology, history, biology, anthropology, medicine, and law.

Now let us look at the components of the life-span perspective.

Differences in Inter-individual and Intra-individual Changes

A life-span perspective or orientation for studying human development deals with long-term sequences and patterns of change in human behavior. These sequences and patterns can be viewed in the context of either inter-individual changes (changes in relationships among individuals) or intra-individual changes (changes within an individual). A focus on intra-individual change emphasizes specificity. It is person centered. In contrast, a focus on inter-individual change emphasizes generality along the person dimension. It is group centered.

When the life-span perspective focuses on changes in inter-individual differences, which it often does, this focus reflects constructed change patterns and sequences in either of two forms: (1) differences and trends in group frequencies as well as group means or (2) a group of simultaneously occurring, auto- and cross-lagged correlations or covariances. By connecting inter-individual differences at any point in time to differences at other points in time via means-average or correlations-covariance techniques, inter-individual differences become what are constructed and interpreted, rather than intra-individual change (Labouvie, 1982). Neither approach is necessarily better; preference depends on one's purposes and goals.

Issues

Life-span developmentalists usually focus on three tasks: description, explanation, and optimization (Baltes, 1973). First, all the changes that characterize development must be described. Second, they must be explained; one must show how antecedent or current events make behavior take the form that it does over time. Third, once development has been described and explained, it should be optimized; one should attempt to prevent unhealthy development and foster change as helpfully as possible. For instance, during adolescence and young adulthood, males as well as females choose roles—socially defined forms of behavior that will influence their adult lives. Our study of life development shows that males and females do not commonly enter roles of equal status in areas such as vocation. Males usually enter higher-status vocations than females (Tangri, 1972). Studying this disparity, the life-span developmentalists would want to describe antecedent childhood-role-related behaviors and their relation to consequent adult-role-related behaviors. The psychology and development of women, as well as their mental outlook as it differs from men's, would be highlighted through the presentation of ideas of such theorists as Carol Gilligan and Jean Baker Miller. The life-span developmentalists would attempt to promote higher-status role choices in females and thus enhance or optimize their development. They would also explain why the antecedent and current events in the lives of older people reflect how they behaved in adolescence and young adulthood and show how such behavior shapes the rest of a person's adult life.

It can be said that the life-span developmental approach and its relevant issues are emerging especially when we study long-term sequences of change in continuously changing historical contexts. The life-span developmental theories cannot develop without considering issues that involve the choice of explanatory paradigms and the construction and explanations of the paradigms, the selection and construction of concepts and measures, and the choice of representational modes for construction and description of change itself. Each of these issues is multifaceted, and discussions elsewhere have focused on some facets more than others. Illumination of as many facets as possible helps both to refine the objectives of the life-span developmental approach and to document its usefulness.

From the life-span developmental perspective, development is seen as involving multiple patterns of change for different behaviors and different persons at different points in time.

Some Organizing Principles

Chronological age. Chronological age is a dimension in which behavior changes are recorded. Chronological age is useful as a tool for describing change patterns that are homogeneous enough to exhibit a high correlation between age and behavior change (Baltes & Willis, 1977). If there are large between-person differences in these patterns, then the use of a chronological dimension is likely to be unproductive.

Cohort.   "Cohort" can be defined as a group of persons experiencing some event in common, such as year of birth (Schaie, 1965). Someone born in 1952 would belong to the 1952 cohort. The specific range of time involved is arbitary. For example, Nesselroade, Schaie, and Baltes (1972) analyzed measures of dimensions of intelligence obtained from members of eight birth cohorts taken at two points in time (1956 and 1963). It was found that 59-year-olds measured in 1963 (1904 cohort) scored higher than 59-year-olds measured in 1956 (1897 cohort). It was reported that cohort differences were as large as age differences, if not larger. Such cohort differences reflect not only biological but also environmental influences, which are also referred to as *normative history-graded influences*. The latter include the worldwide economic depression of the 1930s, the political turmoil of the 1960s and 1970s caused by the Vietnam war, and the major famines in Africa in the 1980s. They include cultural factors as well, such as the changing role of women and the impact of the computer on the younger generation.

Life transitions.   Life transitions could be defined by reference to normative life events such as marriage, the birth of children, and retirement. Although not all people experience these events, they are sufficiently normative to serve as a potentially useful organizing variable.

Throughout the life span, from conception and birth to death, the developmental tasks that individuals face are innumerable. It is impossible to list or study the growth responsibilities encountered by one person in a lifetime. Yet there are general categories of tasks that allow us to catalog the common developmental tasks within a culture. Different cultures make different demands on their members. In most cultures of today, the developmental tasks of each generation may also differ from those of its predecessors. As they grow up, all individuals face developmental tasks that are peculiar to their time and place. Each individual moves from a state of helpless dependence as an infant through varying degrees of independence as an adolescent to a mature level of interdependence with others as an adult. This mature level is the product of the environmental conditions and the body–mind factors that contribute to a person's holistic growth and development, which continue throughout adulthood.

Implications for Research

The study of human behavior is a complex one. A great deal of information is gathered from a diverse array of sources, as well as from different disciplines, and the information is interpreted. Any study of people's behavior should be governed by a commitment to the scientific method, an approach by which researchers examine the phenomena of the world. To understand human behavior in a scientific manner is to develop knowledge based not on speculation but on facts obtained through systematic observation and through a scientific search for material, formulating conclusions based on data. This approach distinguishes science from philosophy. In order to understand human behavior, researchers must examine, question, interview, and observe people methodically. They cannot rely just on what they believe or wish to believe about human behavior. The procedures by which researchers make observations and collect and examine data are called *research methods.*

As Kerlinger (1973) put it, the purpose of research is to examine the relationships among variables. One might say that the goal of research, in human behavior or any other field, is simply to reduce the degree of error in stating relationships among variables. Research methods consist of a set of rules and procedures that help researchers make valid inferences about phenomena.

Issues in Data Collection

In planning a questionnaire for data collection, a social work researcher has to consider some important questions: Are the subjects being surveyed representative of the total population? Are the respondents' answers on the questionnaire consistent from one testing to another? Does the questionnaire accurately reflect reality? These three questions arise from the concepts of sampling, reliability, and validity.

Sampling.   "Sampling" refers to the method of choosing sample subjects for study. Researchers frequently employ the principles of random selection to ensure that every member of the population being studied has the same chance of being chosen for the study. A random sample is an unbiased sample of the population that may be representative of the entire group.

For example, in a study of methods for helping children develop their problem-solving skills, the researcher uses some incentive, such as social praise, to reward success. Children in the randomly selected sample will possess a wide range of skills in proportion to that of the population of young children as a whole. If researchers manipulate a variable like social praise to note its effects on problem solving, they can then assume that its effect would be similar if measured in the larger population of children. Thus, using random-sampling principles allows researchers to generalize their results beyond a relatively small number of subjects.

Reliability.   Reliability is the degree of consistency with which a test or scale measures something. If the researcher measures a phenomenon today, tomorrow, and again next week and gets approximately the same results each time, the measuring instrument is reliable. "Reliability" also refers to the amount of agreement among individuals who are observing the same kind of behavior. An important question to bear in mind is whether observer 1 and observer 2 are measuring the same thing. Both measurement instruments and data-collection procedures must be reliable if the data gathered in a study are to be accurate.

Validity. "Validity" refers to the degree to which a test or scale measures what it is supposed to measure. Internal validity pertains to the adequacy with which a relationship between two variables has been identified or interpreted. The internal validity of a study could be affected if there are alternative interpretations, which could be due to the presence of a third variable.

For example, to permit repairs in a residential home for physically handi-capped people, the inmates are sent to their relatives' homes. When the repairs have been completed, the inmates return, and they appear to be happy and satisfied. There is a correlation between improvements in their housing and a dramatic increase in their morale. Is a third variable present to account for the inmates' happiness? Yes, for visiting relatives could have had a positive effect on the inmates. As a result, there is no way to determine which of the two plausible explanations is accurate (Lerner & Hultsch, 1983).

External validity has to do with generalizability of findings. If the observa-tions made in a subset of a population are statistically predictive of that population, then they are externally valid. External validity does assume the existence of internal validity. Just as with internal validity, there are many potential threats to external validity. It is essential to note that the issue of external validity involves more than generalization across a sample of persons to a population of persons. As Baltes, Reese, and Nesselroade (1977) indicated, external validity applies to inferences made from a sample of observations to a population of potential observations. Every single observa-tion represents a unique combination of person, place, measurement, treat-ment, and historical time variable (Lerner & Hultsch, 1983).

Current Research Methods

Can we predict how people behave at various points in their development? Yes, to some degree, on the basis of two kinds of study. People can be observed as they go about their daily lives and they could be studied under planned conditions. The three principal techniques used to study people are naturalistic, clinical, and experimental.

Naturalistic studies. Naturalistic studies depend on observation. Research-ers observe people in their natural habitats, making no effort to alter sub-jects' behavior. Such studies provide the practitioner with normative infor-mation—information about the average times when various kinds of behavior occur among normal people. These data may be based on average groups of people or could be derived from individual case studies. Naturalistic studies commonly take the form of either baby biographical studies or naturalistic observations.

Baby biographical studies usually consist of observing babies from the time they are born. Typically the researcher studies one baby, as did Charles

Darwin, who in 1877 published notes about his son and advocated better understanding of our species through long-term study of babies and children (Dennis, 1936). Another such researcher was Piaget (1952), who based his highly original theories on his meticulous day-to-day observations of his own three children.

Biographies offer useful information about normative development although they give us a glimpse of but a single child's personality. However, this type of research does have some shortcomings. Many such studies record information but do not explain behavior. Usually studies of babies are done by parents, who may suffer from observer bias: the recorder emphasizes certain aspects of behavior over others. Parents tend to downplay a child's negative behavior. Moreover, isolated biographies tell a lot about a particular child, but such information cannot be applied to children in general (Papalia & Olds, 1986).

In naturalistic observations, researchers observe vast numbers of people and record information about their development at various ages to derive average ages for the appearance of various skills and behaviors and formulate other growth measures (Papalia & Olds, 1986).

One technique of naturalistic research is time sampling. Researchers record the occurrence of a certain type of behavior, such as aggression, babbling, or crying, during a given time period. One researcher used this technique to study the ways infants and their parents act with each other. The researcher went into the homes of 40 15-month-old babies and observed the lives of those children two hours a day for two days. He watched the parents and children interact without giving them any instructions. Throughout each two-hour session, he observed and recorded during alternating 15-second periods using a checklist he had drawn up of 15 parent behaviors and 8 infant behaviors (Belsky, 1979). The conclusion he reached was that fathers and mothers are more alike than different in the ways they treat their babies. Parents showed a slight preference for paying attention to a child of the same sex as themselves. Parents interacted more with their babies when they were alone than when both parents were present. Babies were found to be more sociable when they were alone with one parent.

Clinical studies.   Clinical studies come in two types: the clinical method and the interview method. The clinical method was developed by Piaget, who combined careful observation with individualized questioning. Tailoring the test situation to the individual who is being questioned, so that no two persons are questioned in the same manner, is a flexible way of assessing thought. This open-ended, individualized method is different from standardized testing, which makes the testing situation as similar as possible for all respondents. With the clinical method, a researcher can probe the meaning underlying what a subject says. However, there are biases in the clinical method. Its flexibility requires the interviewer's ability to ask the right questions as well as to draw the right inferences. The only possible check on this method is comparison of the results of a large number of researchers who have varying points of view (Papalia & Olds, 1986).

The interview method is used to understand one or more aspects of people's lives. Studies using the interview method have focused on family relationships, occupational aspirations, and other areas of significance to researchers, such as the effects of family myths on family members' behavior toward each other (Pillari, 1986). Some interviews are combined with intellectual tests and personality matching. One of the drawbacks of this type of research is that the information is obtained mainly from the interviewee's memory, which is often faulty. Some interviewees have forgotten certain events, and others may distort their replies to make them more acceptable to the interviewers or to themselves.

Experimental studies.   There are three principal types of experiments: those conducted in the laboratory, those conducted in the field (a setting that is part of the subject's everyday life), and those that make use of naturally occurring experiences, such as hospitalization, which we call *natural experiments* or *natural studies.*

In laboratory experiments, subjects are brought into the laboratory and their reactions to certain controlled conditions are recorded. Their behavior may be contrasted with the same individuals' behavior under different conditions or with the behavior of other individuals who are subjected to the same or a different set of laboratory conditions. In the first case, parents and children might be brought into the laboratory together in order to measure the strength of parent–child attachment. Researchers compare what happens when a parent leaves the child with what happens when a stranger leaves the child. In the second case, an experiment might be constructed in which some children see a person behaving aggressively while other children do not, and then both groups are measured to determine the degree to which they act aggressively.

In field experiments, researchers introduce a change into a familar setting, such as school or home or workplace. A field experiment might offer an enrichment program to some young children in a daycare center but not to others in the center and measure the effects on some variable.

Natural experiments are studies that do not manipulate behavior. Natural studies compare two groups of subjects whose exposure or nonexposure to a certain life experience represents the variable the researcher is studying. Natural experiments might measure the effects of certain life calamities, which for ethical reasons cannot be replicated. Examples include hospitalization, malnutrition, teenage pregnancy, and divorce.

Experimental versus Naturalistic Approach

Performing experiments has some advantage over conducting naturalistic studies. Naturalistic studies are co-relational; they do not inform the researcher about cause-and-effect relationships. Usually co-relational studies can tell the researcher only about the direction and magnitude of a relationship between variables; for example, that two variables are related in a positive direction (as one increases, the other also increases). A researcher might ask if there is a positive correlation between the number of hours a person spends in swimming and the swimmer's performance in a competition: the more hours, the better the performance. There might also be a negative correlation between the number of hours a person swims and the amount of anxiety the person feels about competition, measured by a test just before entering the competition: the more hours of preparatory swimming, the less anxiety.

"Magnitude" refers to the degree of correlation, which is measured numerically. A perfect positive (or direct) relationship is a correlation of +1.0. A perfect negative (or inverse) relationship is a correlation of −1.0. The higher the number (from 0.0 to 1.0), the stronger the relationship (Papalia & Olds, 1986).

Having found a positive correlation between specific recreational activities and a relaxed attitude in people, a researcher cannot safely conclude that the recreational activities cause a relaxed attitude. The researcher can only conclude that the two variables are related in a positive way. A conclusion about cause and effect would require an experiment that manipulates exposure to the recreational activities.

Good experiments are tightly regimented and carefully described so that they can be replicated and the results corroborated by other researchers. Repetitive studies with different groups of subjects also help to check the reliability of results. Many experiments are designed to look at only one or two facets of development at a time. By focusing so narrowly, however, they sometimes miss general knowledge about people's lives. Therefore researchers have to be careful not to miss the forest while looking at the trees.

Within the category of experiments, the three types vary in degree of experimenter control. Laboratory experiments are the most rigidly controlled, but in field experiments the experimenter also maintains a high degree of control. Natural studies are controlled only in the way the experimenter collects and uses the data.

Another difference among the three types of experimental study lies in the degree to which findings can be generalized, or applied to a broad range of people. The degree of generalizability is in inverse proportion to the degree of control; that is, laboratory experiments, which have the most control, are typically the least generalized. Because laboratory studies are carried out in artificial settings, researchers are not sure that their results can be applied to real-life situations.

To make better use of research in the study of human development and behavior, it would be meaningful to combine naturalistic with experimental approaches. As Papalia and Olds (1986) have suggested, researchers should first observe people in their everyday lives, determine the apparent co-relations that exist, and then use that information to design experimental studies that will zero in on some of the apparent relationships.

Methods of Data Collection

Most of the data cited in this book pertain to an individual's development and behavior in the social environment. The designs commonly used for developmental research are longitudinal, cross-sectional, and time-lag studies. Sequential strategies combine some features of the first two.

Longitudinal design. In a longitudinal study, the same group of people is studied more than once to ascertain similarities and differences in behavior and development. Without longitudinal observations of the same people, a researcher would not learn how a given behavior seen in a person early in life tends to be expressed by the same person later in life. Just a few longitudinal studies of human behavior have been done because they are expensive as well as time consuming (Livson & Peskin, 1980; Thomas & Chess, 1977).

One of the advantages of longitudinal studies is that they provide a good picture of development within individuals and not just an overview of differences among age groups. Moreover, by following the development of a specific behavior over a period of time, researchers are able to answer questions about its developmental stability. Often they can determine what earlier conditions or experiences influenced development of the behavior in question (Schaie and Herzog, 1983).

Longitudinal studies have problems as well as advantages. Samples tend to be small because few people are willing to participate in this type of study. Some people drop out. Some people's awareness of or familarity with the tests influences their behavior, thus biasing the study.

Cross-sectional design. In cross-sectional studies, different groups of people are studied at one time, and observations can be completed relatively quickly. A study of the development of social relationships might use the cross-sectional method. Instead of observing one group of people every year for 20 years, the researcher would observe groups of individuals in each age group from 2 to 20. To compare the levels of moral reasoning of 25- and 50-year-olds, a social worker might interview subjects in those age categories within a relatively short period, perhaps a week or two. If the 25-year-olds demonstrated higher levels of moral reasoning than the 50-year-olds, the researcher might conclude that young adults are morally more sensitive than older adults. The researcher might further hypothesize that adults lose their ability to draw moral conclusions as they age.

Cross-sectional studies are quick and relatively inexpensive, and they give the researcher a good overview of the developmental phenomenon under investigation. Yet this type of research also has limitations. It is difficult to fully and adequately control all variables that affect behavior differently. One may not be certain whether differences among the various age groups reflect real age changes or merely reflect the fact that the groups are not identical to begin with. The researcher has to match the individuals on a number of important variables other than age (for example, race, father's or mother's education, background, income level, or type of housing) in order to make sure that there is some degree of compatibility. However, full comparability is hard to achieve.

One might expect cross-sectional studies to yield results that are comparable to those obtained from studying the same group of people over time and just as efficient. However, it has been found that the results of cross-sectional and longitudinal studies are rarely consistent (Schaie & Strother, 1968).

Time-lag design. In contrast to the one-cohort or one-time measurement, time-lag studies allow the researcher to see the differences in behavior that are associated with particular ages at various times in people's history. For instance, if the focus of research is to discern characteristics associated with particular age groups—say, 20—at different times of measurement, the researcher might compile data from 1960, 1970, and 1980. The time-lag design is not used in research as frequently as longitudinal or cross-sectional designs.

Sequential strategies. In order to overcome some of the drawbacks of both the longitudinal and the cross-sectional design, a number of sequential strategies have been designed. A cross-sequential study is one example: people in a cross-sectional sample are tested more than once and the results are analyzed to determine how various groups differ over time. Sequential techniques have been employed to understand intellectual functioning in adulthood. These techniques provide a more realistic assessment than either cross-sectional studies, which tend to overestimate a drop in intellectual functioning in later years, or longitudinal studies, which tend to underestimate it. Because of factors such as selective dropout, the sample at the end of a longitudinal study is different from and more capable than the original sample (Papalia & Olds, 1986).

Ethical Issues in Research

The methods of research, manipulation of variables, and other aspects of study and experimentation imply interactions between people—that is, between the investigator and participants. The American Psychological Association (1981) has developed ethical principles to govern those interactions:

1. Individuals cannot be involved in research without their knowledge or consent.
2. The participants should be informed of the nature of the research study.
3. Participants should not be misinformed about the true nature of research.
4. The researcher should not coerce individuals to participate in research.
5. The researcher should not fail to honor promises or commitments to participants.
6. The participants should not be exposed to undue physical or mental stress.
7. The researcher should not cause physical or psychological harm to participants.
8. The researcher cannot invade the participant's privacy without the participant's permission.
9. The researcher has to maintain confidentiality of information received and should not withhold benefits for participation in control groups.

Ethical problems can arise not because the researcher is uncaring but because of the kinds of variables involved and the nature of people themselves. It is important to weigh the cost of research against its benefits. For example, it would be difficult to study a significant event like death of a spouse without exposing subjects to mental stress. Before agreeing to participate, bereaved subjects should be informed of the nature of the mental stress that they may have to deal with while discussing the topic. Severe stress, however, is never justified. The knowledge derived from research is valuable, but sometimes its cost in human terms would be too great; the end does not always justify the means.

The Life Span

The life-span perspective views human behavior in terms of developmental tasks that characterize various stages of growth. Thus, although the life span is a continuum, the life-span perspective tends to look at it in definable segments: gestation and birth, infancy, the preschool years, later childhood, adolescence, young adulthood, middle adulthood, and old age. The remaining chapters of this book correspond to those stages.

Pregnancy (Chapter 2) begins with conception and continues while the fetus develops in the mother's uterus. Pregnancy usually arouses new feelings in the parents and confers new roles and responsibilities, as well as involving plans for the expectant mother. The months of anticipation culminate in the baby's birth, uniting the new baby, the new mother, and the new father into a new family.

The birth of the baby appears to be an important transition for the parents. About 120 couples were studied during various stages of new parenthood: when the wife was in midpregnancy, when the baby was 6 weeks old, and when the child was 8 months old. Some of the negative experiences that they reported were fatigue, loss of sleep, extra work, and demands on the mother's time. Husband–wife relationships were strained, and the emotional costs of parenthood included awesome responsibility, uncertainty about parental competence, anxiety, frustration, and depression, as well as resentment and restriction of adult activities, finances, and careers. On the other hand, these parents mentioned that the child's upbringing brought them a sense of fulfillment and a new meaning in life, strengthening the husband–wife relationship and family cohesiveness (Miller & Sollie, 1980).

The tasks of infancy (Chapter 3) represent the beginnings of independence. By the end of infancy, average children have usually acquired some autonomy and are feeding themselves solid food. They have usually begun to walk and, after mastering a few steps, are becoming increasingly adept at walking. All the tasks that infants have to achieve represent many hours of practice, accomplished through play as well as through hours of real work. At this point in an infant's life, the parents are solely responsible for the child's well-being. Children need early stimulation, and parents need resources for parenting skills (Duvall & Miller, 1985).

Children begin preschool development (Chapter 4) between the ages of $2\frac{1}{2}$ and 6. Preschool children who are within the average range develop according to predictable principles of human development. They attain more autonomy, as well as making some notable advances in initiative and imagination. During the preschool period, most children become toilet trained, and they are greatly impressed with a sense of their own bodies. They get around easily and communicate freely with words as well as symbols. They like to know how to do things such as working with blocks, playing with utensils, and riding a bicycle.

Most of the child's development occurs through exposure to social interaction and to a physical environment that allows experimentation with competence. Enrollment in a preschool that offers programs to encourage children to test their skills is of immeasurable value to the child. Most middle-class homes cannot furnish enough educational toys and activities to provide the same enrichment. There are also nursery schools geared to underprivileged children—to stimulate their perception of the world around them as well as their development of a sense of meaningful transaction with their immediate environment and an enthusiasm for learning. These children have the opportunity to make new discoveries, to think, and to reason, and as they grow older they develop the ability to concentrate on an activity for longer and longer periods of time.

Later childhood (Chapter 5) is represented as a period of stable physical growth from age 6 to 12. During this fascinating period, elementary school children proceed through a wide range of normal physical, mental, and social development. They enter school as little children and emerge seven years later in various stages of puberty. Growth in height is steady until 9 to 12 years of age. Weight increases slowly, and there is a more mature distribution of fat in most children of this age than in younger children. Appetite varies from poor to ravenous, and digestion is usually good. The school years are vigorous, healthy, and meaningful for most children. In this age group, children are in a latency period and are easy to deal with. However, theorists do observe and describe various dimensions in different ways.

During this period parents or chief caretakers still provide overall care of the children. Children lead a less hectic life and grow at a slower rate than they did as infants or preschoolers. They are generally satisfied with their relationships with their parents and are involved to a considerable degree in family activities.

Adolescence (Chapter 6) is a period of physical, cognitive, and emotional change from childhood to adulthood. Adolescence is difficult to define. A person in adolescence is not just reaching reproductive maturity but is also making changes that are biological, social, cultural and historical. The developmental tasks of adolescents were originally formulated from intensive longitudinal studies. Young people often have to identify their own developmental tasks; their ethnic, racial, and social-class identities influence the priorities they set, and the manner in which they would accomplish them. It was found that lower- and lower-middle-class teenagers strive for upward mobility and set tasks for themselves accordingly, not content with continuing the patterns of the past. Similarly, some middle, upper-middle, and upper-class young people, unwilling to live up to the traditions of their families, may rebel and become downwardly mobile by adopting the behaviors and goals of lower-class people. Of teenagers who drop out of school only about 15% to 20% are from impoverished homes. Usually children with poor grades have the highest dropout rates. More than 27% of the dropouts are either unemployed or so dissatisfied with their jobs that they are looking for other work, according to a recent two-year study (National Center for Education Statistics, 1984).

Some underprivileged boys tend to give their primary loyalty to their peers; before the end of their teen years, many have become delinquent. Often, authors and researchers appear to get caught up in the discussion of the strength of peer relationships in adolescence. However, in this period adolescents also need their parents. The teen years appear to create a strain on both parents and children. As young people emancipate themselves from their parents, they tend to become very critical of them, to the point of disrespect and defiance. At the same time, adolescents feel undervalued and not respected by parents. Studies show that parents as well as high school students exaggerate the power that adolescents have in the family, but they agree on the degree of closeness to one another (Jessop, 1981).

The task of the adolescent stage is to forge a coherent sense of self, to verify an identity that can span the discontinuity of puberty as well as make possible an adult capacity for love and for work. Our discussion of adolescence emphasizes ego and sex identity because this is the period when young people start to develop an identity with which they are comfortable, moving toward a lifestyle in which ego identity overlaps with sexual identity. Some young people make a commitment to a specific lifestyle at this time, whereas others wait until they reach their early twenties or so.

For the first two decades of life, the young person lives within a system of expectations of age and grades. In young adulthood (Chapter 7) the person emerges from the norms of the age/grade system into a future of his or her making. A person's success as an adult depends on how the person plans and chooses for his or her own future. Face to face with an adult world, the young person is eager to learn as well as to perform. As we know, formal or theoretical education offers little guidance in making life's most crucial decisions.

Young adulthood is in some ways the most individualistic part of a person's life. Important tasks are handled with a minimum of social attention and assistance (Havighurst, 1972). In this period, young people have to grow with a sense of purpose. They have a feeling of directionality, of moving toward the future. This constellation of thoughts moves young people as they enter the prime time of their lives. For many, the self-imposed command is, "I will make it, now."

People in middle adulthood (Chapter 8) have been called the "sandwich generation" because it is at this period in life that people develop new responsibilities and are simultaneously developing new and different ways of responding to grown children and aging parents. People over 40 are different from those who are younger. They have to learn to accept limitations, make compromises with reality, and go on. The husband and wife who are in their midfifties and midsixties may enter the postparental years, and retirement takes them into the final stage of the family life cycle. Through their middle years, the husband and wife form the nuclear family and maintain their husband–wife interaction as a central interpersonal relationship. At this time, each occupies a variety of positions in the family: spouse, parent, grand-parent, mother- or father-in-law, and daughter or son of aging parents. Husband and wife in their middle years form the bridging generation between younger and older members of the family, who look to them for strength and support from time to time.

The departure of children from their parents' homes establishes their independence and is the turning point in the life of the family; new pat-terns must be established and former habits abandoned as inappropriate. Neugarten (1970) observes that when the empty-nest stage comes at an expected time it is dealt with meaningfully. However, when the children leave at an unexpected time, the timing becomes important and the parents have to make more adjustments to the normal aspect sequences of the life cycle.

The difficulty of this developmental stage for the older woman who stayed home and took care of children depends on how she brought them up. It is usually harder for the woman who clings to her children and refuses to let them go. A mother can encourage the children to become autonomous by seeking other outlets for her need to provide nurturance or by throwing herself into other projects, into her career, or into community service. Parents who accept their children as adults and respect their independence are better able to accept the children's autonomous lifestyles and continue their own lives.

The tasks of middle adulthood are to give up the completed responsibility of taking care of a child and to deal with the changing patterns and ways of living in middle age. Physical changes may affect health as well as cognitive processes. Both parents and children have to make intergenerational adjustments, and divorce or widowhood may occur. Sometimes career adjustments create a new work environment that becomes important and consuming.

Aging adults (Chapter 9) represent the last part of life-span development. Most Americans are living longer than their predecessors; life expectancy has increased dramatically since the turn of the 20th century. Life expectancy for both men and women is 73 years of age (Butler, 1981), and many individuals live longer. The number and percentage of older people in the nation's population will double by the end of the 21st century. Death rates for people over 65 years of age, particularly women, have fallen considerably over the past 40 years; the over-65 population grew twice as fast as the nation's total population between 1960 and 1980. The fastest-growing population is that of the 85-and-over group, up 165% in the past 22 years. Longevity is not the only cause of the current growth of the over-65 population. Millions of people born in the baby-boom years of the 1950s will be in their seventies by the year 2020, and they will account for the exceptionally large number of elderly in the population (U.S. Bureau of the Census, 1983). As old age becomes commonplace in the United States, families will have to come to terms with their aging family members.

There are still some developmental tasks that aging couples have to face. By that time, most children have become established adults with concerns for the well-being of their aging parents, and many of them are participants in the plans being laid by and for the aging couple. If an aging couple lives for a long period of time, their developmental tasks are intertwined as they face the rest of their lives together. Both must adjust to the common task of developing a lifestyle that is meaningful to each of them.

Widowhood or divorce may end the marriage, but most older couples continue together as long as they live, carrying out the final stage of the family life cycle through their joint developmental tasks. Those involve adjusting to retirement income, making satisfactory living arrangements, and adjusting to changes in both their bodies and their minds. Maintaining their marital relationships, maintaining contact with their own families, keeping active and involved, and finding meaning in life are all important for older people. Another important aspect of aging is reminiscing, which is not a sign of senile adjustment but the basis for making a life review. Reminiscing makes it easier for older people to adjust to difficult situations and contributes to a perspective in which life makes sense.

Later in life, many vigorous or demanding life activities are no longer possible, but religious faith and practice have no age limits. Many older people who are religiously inclined may stop going to church because of failing health, reduced income, or feelings of being unappreciated or being pushed out of the church by younger generations. Older people wish not merely to live longer but to live more fulfillingly. They also have to deal with the concept of death and dying. Older people who have accepted the idea of death are better able than others to communicate with their families about their fears and sometimes their desire to die. Old age is not something that springs upon people suddenly; it happens gradually. Old age is part of a continuum and an evolution. Older people who are kind and caring did not become that way overnight, and neither did those who are quarrelsome, angry, and troublesome. Temperament in old age is only a result of what people have done with their lives over the years. Integrity of personality is really a conservation of one's lifestyle—that is, the consolidation, protection, and retention of the ego integrity one has accrued over a lifetime, despite loss and divestment of usual roles and functions.

Chapter Summary

The study of human development and behavior is scientific and is based on quantitative and qualitative changes that take place over time. Changes that take place in people could be classified as developmental and nondevelopmental changes. Nondevelopmental changes are nonnormative life events like the death of a child, opportunities in a foreign country, and birth of a child with congenital defects. Developmental changes are normative changes that are systematic and organized. They could include systematic changes in a society, a culture, or an individual. Although we look separately at various aspects of development—that is, physical, social, and intellectual—they do not occur in isolation; one affects the other. Social development, role learning, and continuation of social norms are important aspects of growth.

The functions of the ego and the transactions that take place between the ego and the environment play a crucial part in the process of human development. Theorists Erik Erikson and Robert White originally developed their thinking in the psychoanalytical school but branched away and differ markedly in some aspects of their theories.

Organismic theory presents people as active contributors to their own growth and development. Theorists of this orientation, among them Jean Piaget and Lawrence Kohlberg, view development as occurring in a series of qualitatively different stages. Differences between men and women in life-cycle events are the focus of the thinking of Carol Gilligan.

The notion of environment includes the physical, social/emotional, and intellectual environments that play a role in the development of people.

The life-span perspective, which forms the conceptual framework for this book, is defined as an orientation to lifelong human development. It deals with long-term sequences and patterns of change in human behavior. Practitioners of the life-span development perspective focus on three tasks: description, explanation, and optimization of development. Organizing principles in this discussion of the life-span perspective are chronological age, cohort, and life transitions, or normative life events.

The life-span perspective has implications for research in human behavior. Issues in data collection include sampling, reliability, and validity. Random sampling is a way of ensuring that every member of a given population has the same chance to be selected for the study. Reliability describes the degree of consistency with which a test or scale measures something. Validity is the degree to which a test or scale measures what it is supposed to measure.

There are three research methods available for studying people: naturalistic studies, which are subdivided into baby biographies and naturalistic observations; clinical studies, which include the clinical and the interview methods; and experimental studies, which include laboratory, field, and natural experiments. The designs commonly used for human-development studies are longitudinal, cross-sectional, and time-lag designs and sequential strategies. In a longitudinal design, each person is studied more than once. In a cross-sectional study, different groups of people are studied at one time, and observations can be completed relatively quickly. The time-lag design allows the researcher to see the differences in behavior that are associated with particular ages at various times in people's history. Sequential strategies involve testing subjects more than once to determine the differences that show over time for different groups of people.

The stages in the human life span are pregnancy and birth of a child, infancy, preschool years, later childhood, adolescence, young adulthood, middle adulthood, and old age. Each stage is characterized by developmental tasks that confront each individual.

References

American Psychological Association. (1981). *Manual of ethical principles*. Washington, DC: Author.

Anastasi, A. (1958). Heredity, environment and the question "how?" *Psychological Review, 65*, 197–208.

Baltes, P. B. (1973). Prototypical paradigms and questions in lifespan research on development and aging. *Gerontologist, 13*.

Baltes, P. B., & Cornelius, S. W. (1977). The status of dialectics in developmental psychology: Theoretical orientation versus scientific method. In N. Datan & H. W. Reese (Eds.), *Life-span developmental psychology: Dialectical perspectives on experimental research*. New York: Academic Press, 1977.

Baltes, P. B., Reese, H. W., & Nesselroade, J. R. *Lifespan Developmental Psychology: Introduction to Research Methods*. Monterey, CA: Brooks/Cole, 1977.

Baltes, P. B., & Willis, S. L. (1977). Toward psychological theories of aging and development. In J. E. Birren & K. W. Schaie (Eds.), *Handbook of psychology of aging*. Belmont, CA: Wadsworth.

Belsky, J. (1979). Mother–father–infant interaction: A naturalistic observational study. *Developmental Psychology, 15*, 601–607.

Bengston, V. L. (1976). The "generation gap" of aging family members. In E. Olander & A. Haddad (Eds.), *Time, self and roles in old age*. New York: Behavioral Publications.

Bertalanffy, L. von. (1933). *Modern theories of development*. London: Oxford University Press.

Bertalanffy, L. von. (1962). *Modern theories of development*. London: Oxford University Press.

Birren, J. E. (1969). The principles of research on aging. In J. E. Birren (Ed.), *Handbook of aging and the individual*. Chicago: University of Chicago Press.

Brodzinsky, D. M., Gormly, A. V., & Ambron, S. R. (1986). *Lifespan human development*. New York: Holt, Rinehart & Winston.

Butler, R. N. (1981, August 24). Interview: Latest on extending the human lifespan. *U.S. News and World Report*.

Colby, A. (1978). Evolution of a moral-developmental theory. *New Directions in Child Development, 2*, 89–104.

Coombs, C. H. (1964). *A theory of data*. New York: Wiley.

Dennis, W. (1936). The bibliography of baby biographies. *Child Development, 7*, 71–73.

Duvall, E. M., & Miller, B. C. (1985). *Marriage and family development*. New York: Harper & Row.

Erikson, E. H. (1980). *Identity and the life cycle*. New York: Norton.

Germain, C. B. (1979). *People and environments*. New York: Columbia University Press.

Gilligan, C. (1982). *In a different voice*. Boston: Harvard University Press.

Gordon, C. (1976). Development of evaluated role identities. *Annual Review of Sociology, 2*, 112–115.

Hartmann, H. (1964). *Essays on ego psychology*. New York: International Universities Press.

Havighurst, R. J. (1972). *Developmental tasks and education* (3rd ed.). New York: David McKay.

Hill, R., & Aldous, J. (1969). Socialization for marriage and parenthood. In D. Goslin (Ed.), *Handbook of socialization theory research*. Chicago: Rand McNally.

Jessop, D. J. (1981). Family relations as viewed by parents and adolescents: A specification. *Journal of Marriage and the Family, 43*, 95–106.

Kerlinger, F. N. (1973). *Foundations of behavioral research.* New York: Holt, Rinehart & Winston.

Kohlberg, L. (1976). Moral stages and moralization: The cognitive-developmental approach. In T. Luckona (Ed.), *Moral development and behavior.* New York: Holt, Rinehart & Winston.

Kohlberg, L. (1978). Revisions in the theory and practice of moral development. *New Directions for Child Development, 2.*

Labouvie, E. W. (1982). Issues in lifespan development. In B. B. Wolman, G. Stricker, S. J. Ellman, & P. Keith-Spigel (Eds.), *Handbook of developmental psychology.* New Jersey: Prentice-Hall.

Lerner, R. M. (1976). *Concepts and theories of human development.* Reading, MA: Addison-Wesley.

Lerner, R. M., & Hultsch, D. F. (1983). *Human development.* New York: McGraw-Hill, 1983.

Livson, N., & Peskin, H. (1980). Perspectives on adolescence from longitudinal research. In J. Adelson (Ed.), *Handbook of adolescent psychology.* New York: Wiley.

Miller, B. C., & Sollie, D. L. (1980). Normal stresses during transition to parenthood. *Family Relations, 29,* 459–465.

Mischel, W. (1970). Sex typing and socialization. In P. H. Mussen (Ed.), *Carmichael's manual of child psychology* (Vol. 2). New York: Wiley.

National Center for Education Statistics. (1984). *The condition for education* (Publication No. NCES84-401). Washington, DC: U.S. Government Printing Office.

Nesselroade, J. R., & Baltes, P. B. (1974). Adolescent personality development and historical changes: 1970–1972. *Monographs of the Society for Research in Child Development, 39* (Whole No. 154).

Nesselroade, J. R., Schaie, K. W., & Baltes, P. B. (1972). Ontogenetic and generational components of structured and quantitative change in adult behavior. *Journal of Gerontology, 27,* 222–228.

Neugarten, B. L. (1970). Dynamics of transition from middle age to old age: Adaptation and the life cycle. *Journal of Geriatric Psychiatry, 4,* 71–87.

Neugarten, B. L., & Datan, N. (1973). Sociological perspectives on the life cycle. In P. B. Baltes & K. W. Schaie (Eds.), *Life-span developmental psychology: Personality and socialization.* New York: Academic Press.

Overton, W. F., & Reese, H. W. (1973). Models of development: Methodological implications. In J. R. Nesselroade & H. W. Reese (Eds.), *Lifespan developmental psychology: Methodological issues.* New York: Academic Press.

Papalia, D. E., & Olds, S. W. (1986). *Human development.* New York: McGraw-Hill.

Piaget, J. (1952). *The child's conception of number.* London: Routledge & Kegan Paul.

Piaget, J. (1970). Piaget's theory. In P. H. Mussen (Ed.), *Carmichael's manual of child psychology* (Vol. 1). New York: Wiley.

Pillari, V. (1986). *Pathways to family myths.* New York: Brunner/Mazel.

Reese, H. W., & Overton, W. F. (1970). Models of development and theories of development. In L. R. Goulet & P. B. Baltes (Eds.), *Lifespan developmental psychology: Research and theory.* New York: Academic Press.

Schaie, K. W. (1965). A general model for the study of developmental problems. *Psychological Bulletin, 64,* 92–107.

Schaie, K. W., & Herzog, C. (1983). A fourteen-year cohort sequential analysis of adult intellectual development. *Developmental Psychology, 19,* 531–543.

Schaie, K. W., & Strother, C. R. (1968). A cross-sequential analysis of adults in intellectual development. *Developmental Psychology, 70,* 671–680.

Shanas, E., Townsend, P., Wedderburn, D., Friis, H., Milhoj, P., & Stehouwer, J. (1968). *Old people in three industrial societies.* New York: Atherton.

Tangri, S. S. (1972). Determinants of occupational role innovation in college women. *Journal of Social Issues, 28,* 177–199.

Thomas, A., & Chess, S. (1977). *Temperament and development.* New York: Brunner/Mazel.

U.S. Bureau of the Census. (1983). Population of the United States, 1970–2050. *Current Population Reports,* Series P-25, Nos. 917 and 922.

Weimer, W. B. (1979). *Notes on the methodology of scientific research.* Hillsdale, N.J.: Erlbaum.

Werner, H. (1957). The concept of development from a comparative and organismic point of view. In D. Harris (Ed.), *The concept of development: An issue in the study of human behavior.* Minneapolis: University of Minnesota Press.

White, R. W. (1960). Competence and the psychosexual stages of development. In *Nebraska Symposium on Motivation.* Lincoln: University of Nebraska Press.

White, S. H. (1977). Social proof structures: The dialectic of method and theory in the work of psychology. In N. Datan & H. W. Reese (Eds.), *Lifespan developmental psychology: Dialectical perspectives on experimental research.* New York: Academic Press.

2

Conception, Pregnancy, and Childbirth

Psychosocial Context of Pregnancy

Prenatal Development

Genetic Influences

Environmental Influences in the Prenatal Stage

The Birth Experience

The Special Circumstances of the Newborn

Parent–Infant Relationships

Developmental Abnormalities

Implications for Social Work Practice

Chapter Summary

References

Psychosocial Context of Pregnancy

Like any other developmental period in a person's life, pregnancy has both personal and social aspects. A sound understanding of it requires a theoretical foundation. Human behavior is the direct result of one's definition of the situation, and each person functions within a uniquely conceived reality. In every person's life the present is defined in terms of the past and the future, and the past is constantly being redefined in terms of the present. Individuals rely on past experiences to make sense of the world around them and select behaviors that are appropriate to their interpretations of the day-to-day events of their lives (Darling, 1983).

The human capacity for adjustment is almost infinite. When people are prepared in advance for noncrisis situations that they may face in life, usually they adjust relatively smoothly. Even if expectant parents are not prepared for a pregnancy, they usually learn to accept it in time.

Miller (1977) suggests that pregnancy as a social role does not really begin until suspicions of pregnancy are confirmed by an informed medical authority. Thus the physican establishes the theme "going to have a baby." The meaning of this theme varies for prospective parents, depending on whether the pregnancy was wanted or unwanted, whether it is the couple's first pregnancy, and what the prevailing definitions of pregnancy are in the expectant couple's social world.

The processes of pregnancy and childbearing entail stress and continual coping and adapting. From conception to adulthood of the child, and sometimes beyond, the parents have to deal constantly with an enormous variety of situations, some expected and others unexpected. Pregnancy itself is affected by the woman's and man's genetic endowments, the woman's age and general health, the intrauterine environment, the presence or absence of such complications as toxemia, anoxia, Rh incompatibility, drugs, alcohol, reduction of hormones, stress, and the prevailing family environment.

Rossa (1977) argues that a couple's first pregnancy creates a crisis and is a potential strain on the marital relationship. Conversely, Doering, Entwistle, and Quinlan (1982) claim that a first pregnancy is not likely to threaten an otherwise stable marriage.

Both women in their first pregnancies and experienced parents feel concern over the health of the unborn child (Darling, 1983). A childless couple who have experienced one or more miscarriages or stillbirths have to cope with a tremendous amount of stress. As one first-time mother commented, " 'I had two miscarriages before I became pregnant with Ricky . . . I thought maybe I had bad genes or something . . . . it was in the back of my mind through the whole pregnancy' " (Darling, 1983).

Different views of pregnancy are colored by the definitions received from friends, relatives, and neighbors. Rosengren (1962) notes that reactions to pregnancy vary by social class. Lower-class people are more likely to define pregnancy in terms of temporary sickness, whereas upper-class people view the gestation period as a time of normalcy. Whether or not the prenatal period is defined in terms of illness, once labor begins, medical definitions and medically based authority nearly always prevail.

Some of the following case situations specify ethnic or racial factors. Because social work practitioners work with diverse groups of people, we have brought as much diversity as possible to our illustrations.

> Brenda, a 16-year-old student, is pregnant. She comes from a lower-middle-class family and is not married but plans to keep the baby. Her parents are concerned, and so is her grandmother, who is a single parent herself. As time passes, Brenda observes her body changing, and the tension surrounding her pregnancy builds up; there is an uneasy atmosphere in the family.

> Mary and John have been married for 12 years and they do not have any children. In an effort to conceive, they visited a number of clinics and took various medications. At last Mary was expecting her first child, and there was an air of pleasant expectancy in the family. They had enough savings to provide for this new member of the family.

> Jim and Kim have been married for 14 years, and have seven children. Kim is expecting their eighth child. This family is overburdened with financial problems. They live in a crowded three-bedroom apartment and they cannot afford to move to a better dwelling. Kim suffers from high blood pressure. Another child will be an additional burden to the family.

In each of these different situations, the family's reactions and attitudes to pregnancy depend on the problems it faces and the uniqueness of the pregnant woman. An impending birth affects the entire family and is influenced by the family's income, health, age, religious background, and marital status. Social and economic factors are strong determinants of whether medical services of any sort will be used (Watkins & Johnson, 1979). Prenatal care and advice are closely linked to ethnic, cultural, and racial differences. Expectant mothers are more likely to follow professional advice on prenatal care if the health care providers' attitudes reflect an understanding and acceptance of the family's cultural patterns. For instance, the recommendation of a high-protein diet, such as steak and vegetables, may shock and confuse a new immigrant from Mexico who is used to spicy food, or a Black person who is used to "soul food" or a White middle-class college graduate who is a strict vegetarian.

What happens to the pregnant woman is unique to herself. Not all pregnant women react to their physiological changes in the same way; some of them experience a sense of personal fulfillment and maintain a positive self-image, whereas others experience discomfort during pregnancy, due to weight gain and other complications. Some women respond positively and others respond negatively to pregnancy. Many of these factors may affect the attitude of the mother toward her unborn child.

No child is born in a vacuum. Almost from the moment of conception the child becomes a part of a psychosocial as well as physical environment. Later in this chapter, we will present the effects of environmental influences on the fetus and discuss the biological and maturational aspects of the prenatal periods.

What is the role of the social worker in the early stages of pregnancy? Consider the case of Tina.

> Tina is a young, pregnant teenager. She wanted this baby despite the protests of her parents and her boyfriend. Though determined to have the child she is frightened and angry because she does not receive any support from her family, is confused about herself, and does not understand the sudden nausea and giddiness she experiences. She imagines she is losing her mind and her self-control. A social worker at the women's health center educates Tina through counseling, and shares simple literature on what it is to be a parent.

Social workers could be asked to participate in either family planning or crisis intervention, including decisions about abortion. Practitioners should be knowledgeable enough to participate effectively in any such social action.

Prenatal Development
Conception

When a new life is conceived, a process begins in the mother that leads toward the development of a new human being, unique, possessing qualities all his or her own. One person grows tall, and another is short. One is shy and another domineering. Human beings are the products of both their heredity and their life experiences.

How does creation of a human being with unique characteristics begin? Once every 28 days, in an average woman, an ovum (egg) ripens in one of the two ovaries and is discharged into one of the fallopian tubes, which lead to the uterus. The ovum is one of the largest cells in the human body. The sperm, which comes from the man, is one of the smallest cells in the human body, only 0.05 millimeters in diameter. Egg and sperm cells are called *gametes*. The mature ovum survives for only two to three days. A man's sperm, deposited in a woman's vagina during intercourse, can survive for as long as three days. Of the 300 million spermatozoa deposited in the vagina, it takes only one traveling from the uterus to the fallopian tube to fertilize the ovum at this critical period. If not fertilized, the ovum continues down the tube to the uterus, where it disintegrates and is flushed from the body during menstruation. However, when the sperm penetrates and fertilizes the ovum while it is traveling to the uterus, a new life begins. The fertilized egg is called the *zygote*. The zygote represents a special combination of genetic potential, half from the father and half from the mother. Its sex is determined by the sperm; all ova carry an X chromosome, whereas a sperm cell has an equal probability of carrying either an X or a Y chromosome. When X and Y chromosomes are paired, the child will be a male. An XX combination becomes a female.

Within 48 hours after fertilization the new cell has duplicated its nucleus and divided into two identical cells, then in a geometric pattern the two cells become four, the four cells become eight and so forth. This process of reproduction is called *mitosis*. The cluster of cells is nourished by the yolk of the ovum. The cell cluster continues to divide itself. The process known as *differentiation* is about to begin: the cells will separate into groups according to their future roles. At this point, the cluster is a *blastocyst*, a hollow ball of cells. Half of this ball consists of two distinct layers of cells, and this half will eventually become the baby. The other half contains only a single layer of cells. This forms the housing and life-support systems for the fetus: the placenta, the umbilical cord, and the amniotic sac.

The blastocyst, which at first floats in the uterus, will implant itself in the uterine wall. This is an important step in gestation; if the blastocyst does not implant itself properly at the right time and place, the cell mass will die before it can reach the embryonic stage. If everything goes well, the blastocyst will be firmly implanted about two weeks after conception.

Though it appears as if fertilization could take place easily, and it often happens accidentally, at least 10% of married couples face infertility (Guttmacher, 1973). This is more commonly identified as a problem among older couples. Medical specialists can often help in identifying the causes of infertility and aid the couple in becoming parents through a variety of medical, surgical, and educational techniques.

> Harry and Elaine, both in their midthirties, went to the Planned Parenthood clinic because they had tried to have a baby for a long time and felt cheated by their failure. The couple received counseling for their apparent lack of self-esteem, particularly Elaine's. They seemed to have fears, doubts, and anxieties about trying anything new, so they were encouraged to think about several options. Since the basic problem seemed to be Harry's low sperm count, the counselor suggested artificial insemination as a possible alternative, as well as adoption of a hard-to-place child. They discussed the risks and expenses involved, and the couple were given emotional support and help in making a decision.

Another and more common problem that social workers in similar clinics confront is unwanted pregnancy, especially among the younger population. At a women's health center in a suburb of New York City, more than fifty per day is typical. A missed menstrual period frequently brings young women to the door of a family health clinic. Sometimes the cause of the missed period is illness or emotional stress, but many of those young women are pregnant and need help in coping with their feelings and planning their lives, as well as requiring prenatal medical care.

A definitive diagnosis of pregnancy can be made two to eight weeks after conception. However, special pregnancy tests, called *serum tests*, are available to doctors and provide reliable answers as early as a few days after a missed period (Mussen, Conger, Kagan, & Gewitz, 1979). Recent technology has yielded such products as EPT (Early Pregnancy Test) and Answer, which women can buy in any drugstore to find out if they are pregnant one day after they have missed a period. These tests take 10 to 30 minutes and suggest retesting for reliability.

Alternatives to Conventional Pregnancy

Revolutionary methods are now available to couples who have problems either in conceiving or in successfully completing a pregnancy. On July 25, 1984, Louise Brown was born in England to very delighted parents. Her mother had been able to produce eggs but could not conceive due to a blockage in her fallopian tubes that prevented fertilization. Her doctors perfected a surgical procedure by which they removed a ripened ovum from Mrs. Brown's body, transferred it to a special culture, and then fertilized it with sperm obtained from her husband (Lenard, 1981). This procedure is called *in vitro* (meaning "in glass," or test tube) *fertilization*. When the fertilized ovum had grown into an embryo, they transferred it to the uterus, where it attached itself and continued to grow.

In another case, a woman was not producing eggs, so an ovum was taken from a donor and fertilized with the woman's husband's sperm. The embryo was successfully implanted into the woman's body. Two-and-a-half months earlier, the woman had been given hormone treatment to prepare her body to receive the fertilized ovum. After the embryo was successfully implanted, she was treated with additional hormones to maintain a normal pregnancy.

Another kind of pregnancy that has been happening in the United States and other countries involves a surrogate mother. A donor who is willing to bear the child for the couple is artificially inseminated with sperm from the husband. The surrogate mother signs a legal document promising to give the child to the natural parents. The donor-sperm and the donor-egg techniques have created greater possibilities for couples with infertility problems; however, the legal, psychological, and ethical issues of such pregnancies are very complex.

The Embryonic Period

During the embryonic period, the embryo grows to the length of more than 1 inch. Many bodily functions take place during this period, and the embryo develops the appearance of a human being. Hetherington and Parke (1979) note that from the time of conception to the end of the embryonic period the organism increases in size 2 million %. As the cells multiply, they become differentiated into three distinct layers. The outer layer of cells is termed the *ectoderm*. The skin, nervous system, hair, and nails will eventually develop from this layer of cells. The middle layer of cells, called the *mesoderm*, will eventually make up the muscles and bones of the body. The inner layer of cells is called the *endoderm*. These cells will develop into important components of the gastrointestinal system, the liver, lungs, several glands, and the adipose tissue.

In the embryonic period, which lasts for approximately six weeks, the life support systems—the placenta, the umbilical cord and the amniotic sac—are refined. The part of the embryo attached to the uterine wall becomes the placenta. The placenta is a blood-filled, spongy mass which supplies the embryo with all its nutrients and carries its waste matter. The embryo is linked to the placenta through the umbilical cord. The umbilical cord is a tough, hoselike structure made up of two arteries and one vein surrounded by a jelly-like substance. The placenta continues to grow in size during pregnancy and has two sets of blood vessels connected to it. One set goes to the developing baby through the umbilical cord and the other goes to the mother's circulatory system. There is no direct link between these two blood systems. The semi-permeable membrane in the vessels permits an exchange of nutrients and other elements small enough to pass through the blood vessel walls. It is through this indirect passage that the embryo receives oxygen, proteins and other important ingredients for growth and exchanges waste products of carbon dioxide. The embryo is basically a parasite on the mother's body (Brodzinsky, Gormly, & Ambron, 1986).

By the end of the third week, the embryo's heart beats, and its nervous system is forming rapidly. After eight weeks of rapid growth, all the major body organs are present. During this period, the liver begins making blood cells and the kidneys remove waste matter. At this time the embryo is easily affected by chemicals, including hormones and drugs, and viruses in the mother's system.

It is estimated that 30% of all embryos are spontaneously aborted (Mussen et al., 1979). A spontaneous abortion or miscarriage is the expulsion from the uterus of an embryo that is unable to survive outside the womb. The embryo is sensitive and interacts with a number of environmental conditions. If there are deficiencies in the mother's system, such as poor diet or inadequate hormone levels, or the presence of drugs or viruses, the embryo may be affected. About 3 out of 4 miscarriages occur within the first trimester and affect an estimated 30% to 50% of all pregnancies (Gordon, 1975).

Twenty-nine-year-old Sonia looked emaciated. She had undergone three spontaneous abortions. She wanted a child very much, but, overwhelmed by the fear that she might again lose her unborn child, she was afraid to get pregnant again. A discussion of her lifestyle revealed that she worked at three different jobs and used liquor as a form of relaxation; she also took prescription painkillers to get rid of her aches and pains. Her relationship with her husband was strained because he worked at seasonal jobs and was unemployed most of the year. This couple needed marital counseling to improve their relationship before having a family. This meant cutting down the number of hours Sonia worked and changing their lifestyle. Although those adjustments would not be easy to accomplish, at least the visible problems had been pinned down with the social worker.

Most miscarriages result from abnormal pregnancies. Chromosomal abnormalities could be present in half of all spontaneous abortions (Ash, Vennart, & Carter, 1977). Other possible causes include defective ovum or sperm, unfavorable conditions for implantation, breakdown in supplies of oxygen or nourishment due to abnormal development of the umbilical cord, and physiological abnormalities of the mother (Papalia & Olds, 1986).

The Fetal Period

From the end of the second month until birth, the developing organism is called a *fetus*. The rate of growth reaches its highest peak during the early fetal period and then slowly declines. During the fourth or fifth month, the mother starts to feel spontaneous fetal movements. The fetus can open and close its mouth and make certain head movements (Ambron & Brodzinsky, 1979). By the fourth month, the fetus has increased in length to about 6 inches from head to buttocks. Limbs become sensitive to touch, and parts such as hair, nails, and external sex organs become differentiated. Further changes in the existing structures include changes in body proportions and increases in function.

During this second trimester (three-month period), qualitative changes also take place. Kicking appears to be on the increase, and squirming decreases slowly. The presence or absence of reflexes becomes a guide in evaluating neurological development, since there is a definite timetable for the development and dropping out of most reflexes. At the end of the embryonic period and the beginning of the fetal period, the fetus responds to strong, direct stimulation of its muscles. The response consists of a local contraction, called the *myogenic response*, which is a muscle response and does not involve the nervous system (Ambron & Brodzinsky, 1979).

At about 8 to 9 weeks, the fetus responds behaviorally when a fine hair is drawn across its lips (Hofer, 1981). When the fetus is 11 to 17 weeks of age, it develops an increasing variety of responses in the limbs and in the trunk. This is the time when the facial muscles first respond to outside stimuli, and the body movements are flowing and graceful. At 16 weeks the fetus reveals spontaneous movements that are varied, including squirming movements and jerks and thrusts. All these movements are felt by the mother, beginning when the fetus is about 7 inches long (Hofer, 1981). Other patterns of behavior, like wriggling, reaching, and kicking, are also present, and facial grimacing and pouting occur during this period.

When the fetus is about 17 to 18 weeks old, an extraordinary change takes place. The movements of the fetus slow down and finally become stilled. The movements that can be elicited are sluggish, and spontaneous activity is limited to levels reached a month before. The fetus regresses to an earlier level of functioning. This phase is called the *period of inhibition* and *the period of discontinuities in behavior development*. It is also called the *period of acquiescence* (Hofer, 1981). The discontinuities do not appear simultaneously in all parts of the fetus, but rather one at a time. Inhibition lasts until the fetus is 24 weeks old. It is assumed that the fetus might be subjected to partial anoxia (oxygen deficiency) during this period. Responsiveness reappears at the end of the quiescent period, when the fetus begins to respond as it had originally, beginning with the head and neck and progressing to the arms and finally to the lower limbs.

It is important to note that after the end of the second trimester the fetus is able to survive outside the mother's body if it is placed in an incubator and given special care.

Restrictive abortion laws handed down in 1973 by the Supreme Court differentiate among trimesters by giving unrestricted legal right to an abortion during the first trimester, imposing some restrictions during the second, and prohibiting abortion during the last trimester unless continuation of pregnancy represents a threat to the mother's life or health. In 1977, the Court held that the government is not required to fund elective abortions for the financially needy, but there are still debates regarding this decision, which many believe discriminates against the poor (Specht & Craig, 1982).

Infants born before 8 months have a survival rate of 70% (Rugh & Shettles, 1971). The risks they face will be discussed later in this chapter.

In the ninth month, the fetus continues to grow and begins to take a head-down position in preparation for the trip through the birth canal. From one to two weeks before birth, the fetus "drops" as the uterus settles lower into the pelvis area. At this time, the mother's muscles and uterus may move sporadically. The fetus does not gain weight easily any more, the cells of the placenta begin to disintegrate, and all is ready for birth. From conception to birth takes about 266 days. Having begun with two cells at conception, the child at birth has as many as 200 billion cells.

Genetic Influences

This section deals with the mechanisms of inheritance, genetic defects, and the relatively new field of genetic counseling.

Mechanisms of Inheritance

Half of an individual's genetic material comes from the mother and half from the father when the sperm fertilizes the ovum, uniting to form a unique combination of genetic potentialities. In the fertilized egg, or *zygote,* are the materials that bear the pattern of a new person who is different from his or her parents, yet somewhat like them. What are these materials? Inside the zygote there are 46 chromosomes—23 that were originally in the egg and the additional 23 brought by the sperm (Ambron & Brodzinsky, 1979). Each chromosome contains about 20,000 genes, each of which is composed of a chemical called *deoxyribonucleic acid,* or DNA. DNA is made up of a special sugar, phosphoric acid, and two alternative nitrogen bases: pyridine, which is in the form of cytosine and thymine, or purine, in the form of adenine and guanine (Ambron & Brodzinsky, 1979). DNA is the molecule of heredity; it contains the genetic code that determines what is passed from one generation to the next.

Nearly all of an individual's tens of thousands of genes occur in pairs, one inherited from the mother and the other from the father. Alternate forms of the same gene pair are called *alleles.* Each person carries two alleles for the same trait, one from the father and one from the mother. Sometimes, both alleles give the same direction for the determination of the trait, and in this case the individual is said to be homozygous for that trait. For example, if the trait in question is eye color, and both of an individual's eye-color alleles call for blue eyes, then the individual is homozygous for eye color. A person whose alleles both call for brown eyes is also homozygous.

When one of a person's alleles calls for brown eyes and the other for blue eyes, the individual is said to be heterozygous for eye color. Such an individual will have brown eyes because the allele for brown eyes is dominant over the allele for blue eyes.

In some exceptional cases, the dividing zygote cells become separated into two masses and develop into two individuals. These two individuals are called *identical twins*, or *monozygotic twins*. Fraternal twins develop from two different zygotes—two eggs, each fertilized by a different sperm.

Monozygotic twins are more closely related than fraternal twins throughout the prenatal period. They usually develop together in one amniotic sac, both bathed by the same amniotic fluid, whereas fraternal twins usually have separate amniotic sacs (Ambron & Brodzinsky, 1979). Most traits result not from a single gene pair but from a combination of many gene pairs. Genetic sources of individuality take three forms: (1) genetic determinants of the rate of development, (2) genetic determinants for individual traits, and (3) genetic determinants of defective traits.

Most significant characteristics, such as weight, height, blood group, and skin color, are controlled by the combined action of several genes. However, it is important to remember that genetic individuality does not provide the final script but merely supplies the early elements of the relationship. For instance, when compared with identical twins reared together, identical twins reared apart show greater differences in such traits as weight and intelligence. This finding shows that some variables are more susceptible to environmental influences than others. Gene pairs may interact in various ways: one gene pair may either allow the expression of another gene pair or inhibit it.

Genetic Defects

Chromosomal abnormalities. A missing or extra chromosome or a gross chromosomal abnormality is usually dangerous to the fetus. Often the defective gene has been in the family for generations, passed from parent to child. Down's syndrome, or mongolism, is a well-known genetic disorder that causes a person to be born with a limited mental capacity due to the presence of an extra chromosome or part of it. Mothers who give birth to such children are usually either over 40 or extremely young. Down's syndrome is found in one out of every 500 babies born in the United States (Ambron & Brodzinsky, 1979).

For most parents, the birth of a defective child is an unanticipated and traumatic event. The majority of parents have little or no knowledge of birth defects before the child is born. Even childbirth preparation classes present only the situation of having a normal baby, and the parent's prior experience with birth defects is usually minimal. The following comments were made by parents of congenitally handicapped children (Darling, 1983):

> "I never heard of Down's . . . mental retardation wasn't something you talked about in the house . . . there wasn't much exposure."
>
> "I heard mongoloid—something I had read in passing in a book or something. Just a freak of nature. I remember thinking, before I got married, it would be the worst thing that could ever happen to me."

Most parents enter the birth situation with the expectation that events will proceed normally and they will take home a normal infant. Giving birth to a defective child can create feelings of meaninglessness, powerlessness, and helplessness.

Sex-linked genetic defects. A dramatic example of a sex-linked genetic abnormality is hemophilia, or bleeder's disease. In hemophilia, an element of blood plasma needed for normal clotting is deficient. A hemophiliac could bleed to death from a small wound that would normally clot within a few minutes. Internal bleeding, if not noticed, can lead to death. Hemophilia is sex-linked, carried as a recessive gene only on the X chromosome. Because the Y (male) chromosome is much shorter than the X chromosome, it has no site for a corresponding gene to pair with it. In the absence of a countering gene, any male who inherits the gene for hemophilia or any other such sex-linked traits will express it, regardless of whether the gene is dominant or recessive (Specht & Craig, 1982). (Females have two matching X chromosomes.)

Other hereditary defects include sickle-cell anemia, cystic fibrosis, Tay-Sachs disease, and a predisposition to diabetes. Certain disorders occur almost exclusively among specific national, racial, or ethnic groups. For example, Tay-Sachs disease appears primarily among Eastern European Jews, cystic fibrosis occurs among Caucasians, and sickle-cell anemia is found among Africans, Black Americans, and some Mediterranean populations (Specht & Craig, 1982).

Discovering that they are carrying "bad" genes is a scary experience for most people. Should they marry? Should they have children? Most people who harbor potentially lethal genes are not even aware of them. A number of recessive and non–sex-linked genes will not be expressed. Still, when the need arises, people can find out about their genetic inheritance and that of their potential marital partners.

Genetic Counseling

Genetic counseling is one way of protecting the next generation from genetic defects. Genetic counseling is a newly available resource that can help individuals become aware of their own genetic risks, as well as assisting them in making intelligent decisions about those risks. Families who feel that they might carry hereditary defects may decide to have their genealogy studied in order to learn whether they are likely to carry genes that could transmit defects to their offspring. For instance, a woman who is aware that congenital blindness has occurred in her family can find out the likelihood of her carrying the gene. The presence of some defective genes can be determined by biological tests. In the process of genetic counseling, the woman can find out if her gene alone can transmit blindness to her children or whether the defect could occur only if her husband also carried the gene. This information helps the couple to decide if their chance of having a healthy child warrants their taking a risk and beginning a pregnancy.

Social workers engaged in adoptions, family planning, and services to the physically or mentally handicapped see many clients who might benefit from genetic counseling. Schild (1977) indicates that only 5% of the population expecting a child actually take advantage of such services. Unless directly affected themselves, most people have great difficulty in deciding on the best course when genetic defects are involved, particularly when the statistical probability of occurrence of a particular defect in their own children is remote.

Diagnosis. Techniques for possible diagnosis of the genetic defects of an unborn child include the use of ultrasound pictures, amniocentesis, and fetoscopes. Using ultrasound, a technique by which some types of gross defect can be identified, doctors scan the uterus with extremely high-level sound waves to get a picture of the skeleton of the fetus. The presence of twins can be detected in this manner. Pictures obtained by ultrasound mapping reveal the location of the placenta, position of the fetus, size of the fetal skull, and characteristics of the fetal heartbeat. Ultrasound would disclose anencephaly, a rare and fatal defect in which parts of the brain are missing or malformed (Ambron & Brodzinsky, 1979).

If a pregnant woman who is over 35 years of age fears that she may give birth to a child with a genetic defect, she can undergo a procedure called *amniocentesis,* which allows for testing of the fetus's general makeup. This test is done when the woman is in her 14th week of pregnancy, by which time the child's basic systems are all functioning. A hollow needle is inserted through the woman's abdomen and a small amount of the amniotic fluid that surrounds the fetus is removed. This fluid contains loose cells and other things that have been discarded by the fetus. The cells are separated from the fluid, grown in a culture, and examined for evidence of any suspected defect. If there are no fetal defects, the mother is spared many months of unnecessary anxiety. If defects are found, the parents must decide whether to have an abortion or to go ahead with the pregnancy in the hope that the child will lead a fairly normal life in spite of the problem. Parental planning and adjustment to the child's condition can then begin before the child is born.

A fetoscope is a long hollow needle with a small lens and a light source at its end. Inserted into the mother's uterus, it enables the doctor to observe the developing fetus and look for any abnormal conditions.

A genetic counselor prepares a family history of the prospective parents and their relatives and determines the risks of abnormality in the offspring. This type of prenatal diagnosis has not gained much acceptance and is used most often by middle-class people and those with more than average education (National Center for Health Statistics, 1978). Sometimes the counselor's findings are certain, such as when an abnormal chromosomal arrangement is found in a developing fetus. Or the odds of having a defective child can be isolated within a low range. A couple with an abnormal child whose problem was not of genetic origin can be reassured that the risks of having another abnormal child are minimal.

Public issues. Surrounding genetic counseling are a number of public issues that have yet to be handled. Although it is possible to prevent the birth of many fetuses known to be defective, the social worker who deals with programs of genetic counseling or screening must be aware of the development of public policies for the prevention of genetic defects. The least controversial programs call for low-cost, low-risk mass screening to prevent birth defects that might otherwise require costly institutionalization; for instance, compulsory screening in almost all states for phenylketonuria. But there are controversies over abortion of fetuses who reveal symptoms of Down's syndrome and other genetic defects and over questions like whether people who are severely retarded should be sterilized.

> Twenty-three-year-old Sally is severely retarded, and her mother is retarded as well. The family is preoccupied with its financial and day-to-day problems. Sally spends a lot of time with men and has mothered two severely retarded children who have been institutionalized. If Sally gets pregnant a third time, should the state have a say in whether or not she bears the child?

Some of the tricky questions that need to be answered involve the rights of the newborn, the rights of the family, the financial costs to the community of lifetime care for the severely disabled, and the potential impact on future generations. How does society deal with its "defective" members? Should those who are "unfit" be sterilized, or should they be offered a full range of social services in the belief that all people are entitled to quality care? Our current policies fall between these two extremes. Through research, lobbying, and social action, social workers should be able to make a significant contribution to the difficult task of establishing and monitoring these policies (Specht & Craig, 1982).

> Kathleen and Michael, both strict Catholics, are extremely troubled because they have two children who are mentally retarded, one of whom is also congenitally blind, and Kathleen is pregnant again. Her pregnancy is an accident. They see a social worker for genetic counseling. After the family history and genetic screening are done, it is obvious that the next child's chances of being normal are pretty low. The social worker presents the facts and offers emotional support. Although he personally favors abortion in that situation, he is careful not to push the couple toward a particular decision, in tune with the great importance that social workers place on respecting the client's right to self-determination.

Today, increasing numbers of hospitals test pregnant women for genetic defects, but gene therapy—the manipulation of individual genes to correct certain defects—is still in its infancy. Important advances are being made in basic genetic engineering. New knowledge may help us to predict and alter genetic characteristics. However, these techniques are concerned only with heredity. There are also important sociopsychological factors that influence the total development of an individual.

Environmental Influences in the Prenatal Stage

The fetal environment is simple compared to the complex outside world, yet there are variations in the prenatal environment, and they can result in significant psychological and physical differences in infants. The ability to produce a child usually begins one and a half years after menarche (onset of menstruation) and ends at climacteric (menopause). Women between the ages of 18 and 35 tend to provide a better uterine environment and give birth to children with fewer complications than do women who are under 18 or over 35 (Mussen et al., 1979).

Annually, 5% to 8% of the children born in North America have some type of birth defect. Some are due to hereditary defects and others are due to environmental causes. The study of developmental abnormalities is called *teratology,* and a teratogen is the specific agent that disturbs the development of the fetus. For many years, it was believed that the infant in the uterus was completely insulated from all outside influences, but now we are aware that this is not true. Environmental influences ranging from radioactivity to drugs, chemicals, and viruses in the mother's bloodstream can affect prenatal development. Even though the placenta acts as a filter and keeps the mother's blood and the blood of the fetus from mixing, a number of dangerous substances can pass through. Exaggerated emotional stress during pregnancy may also bring about chemical changes and cause muscular tensions that can affect the environment of the developing fetus (Ambron & Brodzinsky, 1979).

Each fetal part or system has a critical period of development. In the mother's womb, the fetus first undergoes a phase of rapid multiplication of cells. In the second stage, the body parts and organ systems are growing most rapidly, both in cell number and size. If an environmental factor such as a chemical or virus interferes with growth during this critical period, development could be permanently damaged. An organ does not have a second chance to develop. The effects of environmental influences vary in accordance with the stage of prenatal development in which the influences are encountered.

Sula came from a Muslim family that was extremely superstitious. Her parents had married when they were barely out of high school, and Sula did the same. She and her new husband lived in a run-down neighborhood and had financial difficulties. He was an alcoholic, had lost his job, and was on welfare. Sula believed that the conception of a child had brought them ill luck, and she appeared to have a negative feeling for the unborn child. This belief was reinforced when her father got involved in a bad mugging incident.

At the Social Service Center, Sula told the worker that the unborn child could be defective because of the negative things that had happened in her life, including having been frightened by a black cat in the night. The worker had to help Sula understand that frightening and negative incidents in her own and family members' lives would not affect the baby, but that the attitude she developed toward the child was important. The worker spent a few sessions educating Sula about her responsibility as a parent, as well as relieving many of her fears about the child. Malnutrition also appeared to be a problem with her. Besides administering multivitamins, the worker gave Sula both advice and educative material about eating inexpensive but nutritious food.

Maternal Diet

Pregnant women should have an adequate diet in order to maintain their own general good health as well as to deliver a healthy infant. Researchers (Restak, 1979) found that mothers who followed a well-balanced diet had fewer complications such as anemia and toxemia and suffered fewer miscarriages, stillbirths, and premature deliveries. Mothers who were on a well-balanced diet were generally healthier after childbirth than mothers not on a well-balanced diet. It was also found that mothers with nutritionally sound diets had babies who were less likely to contract bronchitis, pneumonia, or colds during early infancy, and their babies' bones and teeth were well developed.

Toxemia

Toxemia is a disorder of pregnancy that is characterized by high blood pressure (hypertension); edema, or waterlogging of tissues; and the presence of proteins in the urine (proteinuria). It appears in the last three months of pregnancy in 5% to 10% of pregnant women (Vander Zanden, 1978). Toxemia ranks as the second or third cause of maternal mortality. Toxemia creates a chemical environment in the mother's body that interferes with the proper functioning of the placenta. A fetus's chance of surviving toxemia is 50% (Jones & Smith, 1973). If untreated, toxemia can be fatal both to mother and infant. The common treatment for toxemia is the administration of magnesium sulfate to control convulsions, enforced bedrest, and reduction of the woman's blood pressure with appropriate medication.

Anoxia

Toxemia is one of several diseases that could cause anoxia (oxygen deficiency or starvation) in a fetus. Of the various body cells, the cells of the brain are the most vulnerable to the lack of oxygen. They can be destroyed by an insufficient supply of oxygen, and once they are destroyed they are not capable of regenerating themselves. By contrast, skin cells can be renewed after a cut or laceration. Thus anoxia is a potentially serious complication.

When labor is difficult, infants may suffer gross oxygen deprivation. Severe damage or even death may occur. Lesser degrees of oxygen starvation may lead to mental retardation, cerebral palsy, learning disorders, and behavior disorders. At least 10% of American children have learning disabilities related to anoxia (Vander Zanden, 1978). If the damage to the brain is not too severe, it may be possible to compensate for the disorder to some degree. For instance, epilepsy can be controlled with drugs, and many victims of cerebral palsy can gain some control of their affected muscles through medication.

The Rh Factor

An incompatibility of blood type between mother and baby is commonly called the *Rh factor*. When the unborn child's blood contains a certain protein substance and the mother's blood does not, antibodies in the mother's blood may attack the fetus and can result in spontaneous abortion, stillbirth, heart defects, anemia, mental retardation, and even death. How does this happen?

All blood is either Rh positive or Rh negative. Each blood factor is transmitted genetically in accordance with Mendelian rules, and usually Rh positive is dominant. Normally the maternal and fetal blood supplies are separated by the placenta. When an Rh negative woman is carrying an Rh positive offspring it is possible for some fetal blood to escape the placenta and enter her blood system. The mother's body will then produce Rh antibodies. Usually the production of these antibodies does not pose a threat to the first baby because of the low level of antibodies produced. However, as time passes the mother's body produces more Rh antibodies and the child of a subsequent pregnancy may be affected with fetal erythroblastosis (when the maternal antibodies cross the placenta and attack the fetal red blood cells). It is found that out of 3.3 million births in the United States each year, 260,000 result in the birth of an Rh positive child to an Rh negative mother. About 10% are afflicted with some degree of Rh disease (Brodzinsky, Gormly, & Ambron, 1986).

Drugs

Different drugs have different effects on the developing fetus. Their effects also vary depending on the stage of pregnancy. A drug may have one kind of effect on the mother and another kind of effect on the fetus. Furthermore, the fetal system cannot handle a drug as efficiently as the maternal system can.

Infants born to narcotics users may suffer serious distress during withdrawal, with the severity of the symptoms depending on the degree of the mother's addiction, the size of her doses, and how close to the time of delivery she took the last dose (Best & Taylor, 1955). Babies born to addicts tend to have low body weight and suffer withdrawal symptoms such as extreme irritability, vomiting and shaking, and faulty temperature control.

Many infants suffer from disturbed sleep, poor appetite, and lack of weight gain (Best & Taylor, 1955).

> Denise was a drug addict and an inmate in a prison. When her baby was born it was practically impossible to mother responsively. Denise saw the child at regular intervals but the baby was highly irritable and cried all the time. This angered Denise and she started abusing the child whenever she handled it. The social worker who offered counseling to this young mother advised that the child be placed in foster care until Denise had served her prison sentence. Meanwhile, special efforts were made to find the child a home where appropriate parenting could be offered to an infant affected by drugs.

In the early seventies it was found that chronic drinking has an effect on the fetus. The symptoms of fetal alcohol syndrome include eye and ear problems, heart defects, extra fingers and toes, and disturbed sleep. There is an increased risk of fetal alcohol syndrome in babies of mothers who drink two or more ounces of hard liquor every day, or the equivalent in beer or wine. It is estimated that 6000 infants born every year in the United States suffer from fetal alcohol syndrome (Hall, 1970).

Radiation

Radiation in early pregnancy from repeated X rays and from radium treatment for cancer have produced marked effects on prenatal development. One or two X-ray photographs have not been found to be harmful, but larger amounts of exposure have been associated with physical and mental abnormalities (Hall, 1970).

Venereal Disease

Venereal diseases can cause the unborn child to suffer from mental deficiency, blindness, or deafness. AIDS (acquired immune deficiency syndrome) is a relatively new venereal disease that is common among homosexuals and intravenous drug users in North America. However, it has found its way into the heterosexual community as well and is readily transmitted from an infected mother to her fetus.

Stress

Although there are no direct connections between the nervous system of the mother and the fetus, it has been said that the mother's emotional state does influence the fetus because emotions release hormones and other chemicals into the fetal bloodstream. When a mother's stress level is high for a prolonged period, fetal activity during the entire period is increased. Hall (1970) notes that spontaneous abortions occurred as a result of emotional turmoil in the lives of patients. Researchers found that psychological support helped women to have safe deliveries—even women who had earlier experienced a number of spontaneous abortions. Women faced with emotionally upsetting events had experienced toxen vomiting. Later research showed that the mother's affected the fetus; fast music led to more fetal movement to reduced movement. This effect was apparently con mother's heart activity, which accordingly affected the flow o umbilical cord (Hall, 1970).

Rosen (1955) found that 54 pregnant women who faced intense li experienced more vomiting and nausea than others and had long labor comparative group of mothers who were relatively free of emotional stres gave birth to babies more easily. Studies of the effects of stress on the newborn show that both sudden shock and prolonged chronic stress can influence fetal development. Scott (1971) has made connections between psychological stress during pregnancy (including marital problems, death in the family, serious injury, and ill health) and congenital malformation and mental retardation in the offspring. McDonald (1968) concluded that the mother's emotional state is a relevant and powerful dimension in influencing the young fetus. Increases in the production of epinephrine and norepineph-rine can alter the fetal environment by producing more rapid heartbeat, constriction of blood vessels, and increased uterine contractions. The produc-tion of excess hormones can be assumed to carry an abundance of epineph-rine and norepinephrine to the fetus through the placenta, directly influenc-ing fetal activity, tension, and emotionality. The child born under such conditions has more chances of being a vulnerable child; excessive adrenal hormone produces fear and emotional arousal that interfere with the new-born's ability to relax. Factors such as the mother's sleeplessness and indigestion also affect the fetus (Ambron & Brodzinsky, 1979).

Excessive stress in the seventh to tenth week of pregnancy may be a factor in the formation of cleft palate and harelip in the fetus, for this is the period when the roof of the mouth and the bones of the upper jaw are forming (Greene & Lowe, 1975). In the later stages of pregnancy, however, stress is less likely to cause physical abnormalities. If a mother faces prolonged stress and has not adapted to it by the time her child is born, then the new demands of parenting will exacerbate her stressful state, in turn recycling the maternal–fetal tension initiated in the uterus.

The Family Environment

The greatest miracle in life is not the explosion of knowledge or the transplanting of an organ from one human being to another but the creation, development, and birth of a new life. This new life is born into a mosaic of physical, psychological, and cultural surroundings that determine how much of the new person's potential becomes realized.

Various factors may influence a woman's decision to become pregnant: pressure from parents or peers, early sex-role identifications with her parents, delight in relating to young children, and a desire to procreate. Accidental pregnancy is most common among teenagers; an increasing number of sexually active girls are becoming pregnant (Feldman, 1971).

Pregnancy affects not only the physical appearance of the woman but also

d wife. Research studies (Specht &
experience stress for as long as six
tressful factors may include sleepless-
oping with child care, interruptions in
tion with the infant, and differences of
ild. For many new parents, the birth of
ment, in the sense that couples have to
s. Thus pregnancy could be viewed as a
The extent to which the situation appears
of the marriage, family organization, the
and certain social background factors and
number of years married. After the first
s of other children also become important
born to single women, who often belong to
ind do not follow a traditional lifestyle; and
there is an increas_   er of 30- and 40-year-old professional women
who are becoming single mothers. Single mothers have fewer support
systems, and they tend to face more stresses in childbirth and after.

The decision to have a baby (or having one by accident), the social
experience of pregnancy, the particular style of help that is available for
delivery of the baby, the care given to mother and baby after delivery, and the
attitudes toward them are components of family lifestyles and cultural
patterns of a community.

The Birth Experience

Prenatal development leads to childbirth and the development of the baby.
During the first month of its development, the newborn infant is called a
neonate. A fairly new branch of medicine, termed *perinatology*, considers
childbirth as beginning with conception and extending through the prenatal
period to delivery of the child and the first few years of life (Norr, Block,
Charles, Meyering, & Meyers, 1977). This is a multifaceted approach involving obstetricians, biochemists, and pediatricians. Social workers contribute a
special awareness of the impact of medical problems on the family and
community, and they can recommend and implement social programs
needed to help families in coping with any difficulties that arise.

Chin Lee and Susie were a Vietnamese refugee couple who had come to
the United States with great difficulty. While expecting her first child,
Susie had not been on a good, nutritious diet, nor had she received
prenatal care, and she was under considerable emotional stress. The
baby was delivered weak, tiny, and hardly able to cry. Chin Lee was
petrified. Communication was difficult. He could hardly speak English,
and to be confronted with a life-and-death situation for his wife and child
was mind-boggling. In his own culture, members of the extended family
would have been able to take care of the new mother, but here he was on
his own. The social worker on the ward tried to interpret the complicated

realities to Chin and at the same time reassure him that the situation was hopeful. Help could be provided by the hospital's medical staff, the dietitian, and the social worker herself. The social worker provided emotional support both verbally and nonverbally, holding Chin's hands to reassure him. This case did have a happy ending; Susie and her new daughter recovered. However, we cannot overemphasize the role of the social worker, who provides information as well as help in coordinating services.

The following section presents a general discussion of childbirth. Neither parents nor researchers agree on the best way to deliver a child; therefore, various methods are presented without favoring any.

By the time of labor, most expectant parents have had some anticipatory socialization in childbirth. The attitudes of a family are affected by its members' experiences with childbirth, as well as by the culture of their particular community. Those who have taken courses in prepared childbirth do appear to have a definite set of expectations about the events and procedures that will occur. Other parents have heard stories or read about childbirth.

Several studies show that the birth process is more meaningful and consequently more enjoyable for those who have taken classes in prepared childbirth. According to Norr et al. (1977), those who have prepared for childbirth in this manner are likely to be better educated families with less traditional sex-role attitudes and a close marriage.

The stress and crisis of childbirth build when the pregnant woman is admitted to the hospital. Overwhelmed with feelings of powerlessness by the admissions procedures that have to be followed, the pregnant woman is stripped of her clothing, possibly her pubic hair is shaved and she is administered an enema. Irrespective of her relationship with her obstetrician, the woman who is to give birth has almost no say in how she is handled in the labor and delivery rooms.

A study of middle-class mothers who had attended prenatal classes revealed a number of complaints about situations of labor and delivery. There were complaints about the lack of congeniality in the physical setting of the hospital, lack of interest or conflicting advice from professionals, and an insensitivity to their feelings (Norr et al., 1977). Even if the mother is prepared, and the birth is uncomplicated, these events are meaningful, and the mother experiences a sense of powerlessness.

Process of Birth

The process of childbirth can be divided into three stages. The first stage, labor, is the period during which the cervix of the uterus dilates, through the involuntary contractions of the uterine muscles, to allow the passage of the baby. The average time for first labor is 14 hours; for later labor, 8 hours (Danziger, 1979). The uterine contractions serve two important functions: effacement and dilation. *Effacement* refers to the shortening of the cervical canal, and *dilation* refers to the gradual enlargement of the cervix from an opening only a millimeter wide to a diameter of 10 centimeters (without the deliberate efforts of the mother). Once the cervix has been fully enlarged, the mother can assist in the birth of the infant by exerting pressure on the abdominal walls around the uterus.

Delivery is the second stage. About 95% of babies are born with their head emerging first, in what is called *vertex presentation*. This type of birth is normal, and delivery is spontaneous (Danziger, 1979). About 3% of babies are born with their buttocks and feet emerging first, and this position is called *breech birth*. Such births require special attention and are generally more difficult. In most cases there is a satisfactory delivery. If the baby is disproportionately large or the mother's pelvic opening is small, the physician may advise a caesarean birth. This is a surgical delivery: an incision is made in the abdominal wall and the uterus and the child is removed. The incision is then carefully sewn. About one out of every 50 babies is delivered in this manner (Danziger, 1979). A forceps, or instrument, delivery becomes necessary when the uterine contractions weaken or stop during delivery, so that for some physiological reason the baby is not pushed through the birth canal. In such situations, obstetricians use forceps, which are curved, tonglike instruments shaped to fit each side of the baby's head. In an emergency procedure, a high forceps delivery is made during the first stage of labor or early in the second stage. A low forceps delivery is one made at the time of natural delivery and does not involve much risk (Ambron & Brodzinsky, 1979).

The third stage of childbirth is called *afterbirth;* the placenta, the umbilical cord, and related tissues are expelled from the mother's body. This stage is more or less painless and generally occurs approximately 20 minutes after the child is born. The mother helps in the process by bearing down. With delivery of the placenta, the birth process is complete. After the expulsion, the placenta and the umbilical cord are checked for imperfections that might signal damage to the newborn.

Delivery of the Infant

Two medications frequently used today to relieve childbirth pains are Demerol® and Valium®. There are also amnesics, which obliterate all sensations. Recently, researchers have begun to look at the possible effect of these drugs on newborn infants, especially in light of the extreme danger of some drugs taken in early pregnancy. A review of various studies (Ambron & Brodzinsky, 1979) explains that most of the medication administered during labor diffuses through the placenta to the fetus. No study found that these medications had long-term effects on the baby, but they did find sluggish movements in babies whose mothers had taken certain medications. Visual attentiveness, weight gain, general brain activity, and sucking behavior were generally affected for a few weeks.

Findings such as these have prompted more and more mothers to experience childbirth in an atmosphere free from the unnecessary impositions of the hospital regimen. Advocates of natural childbirth methods emphasize that hospitals treat childbirth as an illness, whereas natural childbirth implies maternal preparation, limited medication, and participation. As early as 1953, Dick-Read felt that the important factor in preparation for childbirth, particularly in Euro-American cultures, is to help women overcome their exaggerated fear of childbirth, which leads to muscular tension that makes labor more painful than necessary. Dick-Read attempted to teach mothers about the birth process so that they could participate in each stage and be more relaxed during labor, experiencing less pain through the use of breathing techniques and therefore requiring little or no medication. Moreover, he taught that participation in childbirth by both husband and wife could be an exciting experience, with the child born alert and responsive to alert and exhausted but responsive parents.

There are several types of natural childbirth. One, using techniques developed by Fernand Lamaze (1970), involves the participation of both parents. In six- to eight-session courses, the mother is taught exercises in relaxation, breathing, and muscle strengthening, while the father learns to serve as an active coach.

French obstetrician Frederick Leboyer (1976) developed a method of childbirth that is thought to be less traumatic for the child. He formulated his approach in agreement with and in response to the thinking of Otto Rank, who indicated that the dramatic expulsion of the neonate from the safe, comfortable environment of the uterus creates the first basic trauma in a child's life. Leboyer proposed a reorganization of hospital procedures so that an infant could be born in a quiet, dimly lit room, placed immediately on the mother's abdomen, and later bathed in warm water.

Many hospitals have now become more accommodative to the wishes of the parents. Facilities commonly called *alternative birth centers* permit the inclusion of family members in the total birthing experience. Some hospitals encourage rooming-in, an arrangement whereby the mother keeps the baby with her in her room rather than in the hospital nursery and feeds the baby on demand. Not all expectant mothers prefer these options—some, for instance, want the nursery staff to care for the baby while they get extra rest (Specht & Craig, 1982)—but they are becoming increasingly available.

Besides their options in type of hospital birthing experience, parents have the option of home delivery. In choosing this alternative, however, parents must make sure they have an emergency plan in case hospitalization is required. Home deliveries are a common phenomenon in Sweden, Finland, and Japan, where highly trained nurses are used as midwives. Although until the early 20th century home deliveries were the norm in the United States, the rate of home births has remained at 1% since 1975. Though midwives could be a valuable addition to the medical team, there has been very little integration of midwifery into the general medical care in the United States. The home birth of babies in poor rural American families has been associated with high mortality rates and failure to discover early disorders in the infant (Specht & Craig, 1982).

The Special Circumstances of the Newborn

For some couples, parenthood is so romanticized that there is little effective preparation for parental roles. Shereshefsky, Liebenberg, and Lockman (1973) quote a first-time mother who had not really been prepared for motherhood "because you read in books and you talk with people and you think that all of a sudden there is going to be this motherly surge of love, which is not true. . . . I had this colicky baby that spit up and we had to stay home. It took me a long time. . . ." Dyer (1963) notes that 80% of both husbands and wives studied admitted that things were not as they expected them to be after the child was born.

> At 17, Melissa decided to leave home and live with her boyfriend Tom because she was expecting his child. Both of them were excited at the prospect of becoming parents. However, reality struck them as a rude shock. Tom was not prepared to see his girlfriend spending all her time with the baby. He became resentful and angry with the baby for being demanding. Melissa feared that he might hurt the baby. With the help of a social worker, Melissa's mother and aunts intervened to help the two of them adjust to their new roles as parents.

Eiduson (1980) has made a study of a variety of family lifestyles that reflect the pluralistic development of the family in the United States today. These families included 50 single-mother households, 50 social-contract (rather than legal-contract) couples, and 50 communities or living groups, including religious and charismatic-leader groups, triads, and domestic, rural, and urban communities. His comparison group consisted of 50 traditional, nuclear two-parent families. After an intensive study he concluded that single mothers brought up their children differently from two-parent families; couples living together brought up their children differently, depending on their socioeconomic status (along with other factors); and those who were members of religious communities raised children differently from the traditional two-parent families. Thus Eiduson found that different lifestyles have different effects on the upbringing of children.

Bigner (1979) indicates that whether parenthood is viewed as a crisis situation or merely as a transitional event for parents is only a semantic difference. In either case, it is a true turning point in the family's lifestyle, structure, and relationships.

For most couples, the stress of giving birth to a normal child appears to be short-lived. Feelings of powerlessness and helplessness that at first overwhelmed the parents are reduced as the child interacts with his or her parents and responds to parental handling. Social support from significant others is also helpful. As the child becomes less dependent and more familiar with the routine, the parents' feelings of chronic exhaustion simply fade away.

> Anne stayed awake until late in the night because her newborn daughter did not sleep well at night. Her husband had to leave for work early in the morning and could not offer any support at nighttime. Anne was constantly exhausted, tired, and angry and wondered what had hap-

pened to the bundle of joy that they had lo
breastfeeding a drag and was envious of he
home and go to work. However, soon her da
her with smiles. That made Anne happy
daughter became more attached to each othe
to feeding and playing with the child. Chron
with new energy and an enthusiasm for work

Chapter 2   60   the biological raw
the birth orde
background
that resu
that p

Bonding

Just like other species, human beings must acco
natural settings. Besides the physical environme
people have to adapt themselves to cultural systems. As these cultural
systems grow out of human action, they create their own restrictions, limiting
and shaping the direction of change. The relationship between parent and
child is influenced by the culture of the family.

The parent–child relationship is a special one. Bonding is the process of
establishing strong emotional ties between a parent and a child. In an
important early study, Klaus, Kennell, Plumb, and Zuehlke (1970) reported
that early mother–child skin-to-skin contact appeared to facilitate bonding.
Klaus and Kennel (1976) describe bonding as a possibly biochemical process
that ties the mother closely to the child in the first hours after birth. Other
research suggests that bonding begins before the birth of the child. The
amount of bonding that occurs seems to depend more on social-system
reinforcement than on the behavior of the fetus itself. However, fetal
behavior could also affect bonding. The fetus's kicks and its heartbeats, which
can be heard through the stethoscope and later on by ear, contribute to the
reinforcement of the bond.

Bonding increases with the birth of a child, and this increase is conso-
nant with the environmental reinforcements available to the parents. At
birth, reinforcements increase substantially; there is a recognizable visual
stimulus—the baby is more than a swelling in the mother's abdomen or a
giver of kicks. For many women, the birth process is an exhilarating
experience. After birth the child can be touched; touching appears to be a
critical component in relating (Klaus & Kennell, 1976) and an important
reinforcer. Touching is an essential part of early feeding, early comforting,
and many other positive transactional contacts. The child can now make eye
contact, track voices, make noise, and calm down with comforting. Through
birth the infant has increased its potential to reinforce its parents. Flowers,
visits from friends and relatives, and congratulatory cards and gifts are also
reinforcers. Thus the social environment plays a part in intensifying the
infant's contact with its new parents.

The arrangements that are made between a newborn infant and its parents
vary from culture to culture. In many cultures of the world the mother and
child are placed together immediately after birth, but in our North American
culture, the infant is often separated from its chief caretaker, at least for the
first few days of its life. Thus culture and environment, the family background, and the birth experience shared by parent and child begin to shape

material toward its own unique development. According to
, age, socioeconomic status, and in some cases, the religious
of the parents, transactions take place between parents and child
t in an upbringing appropriate to the needs, desires, and outlook of
rticular family in a specific culture.

The Neonate

This period is a time of adjustment for the newborn, having just left the closed, protective environment of the mother's womb and entered the outside world. In many ways, the first month is the period of recovery from the birth process, as well as a period of adjustment to the body's respiration, circulation, feeding, crying, sleeping, and body-heat regulation.

The weight of the neonate at birth typically ranges between $5\frac{1}{2}$ and $9\frac{1}{4}$ pounds, and the height ranges from 19 to 22 inches. The newborn commonly arrives with puffy eyelids, an absent gaze, and blood spots in the eyes, lasting for a few days, due to the pressure experienced during delivery. The nose may also suffer temporary distortion from being pressed down during birth, and the head has not yet assumed its normal shape. The neonate's appearance comes as a surprise to first-time parents, but it will soon change for the better.

It has been found that the rate of infant mortality in the first year of life is 55% higher for non-Whites than for Whites (National Center for Health Statistics, 1978). The non-White infants who survive have a higher risk of developmental defects.

Assessment. It is necessary to detect any problems in infants as soon as they are born. Using a standard scoring system developed by Virginia Apgar in 1953, hospitals are able to evaluate an infant's condition quickly by observing pulse, breathing, muscle tone, general reflex response, and (for White babies) color of skin or (for non-White babies) the mucous membranes, palms, and soles (Apgar, 1953). A few days after a baby is born, hospitals provide a neurological examination and a behavioral assessment. Most states require a mass screening for phenylketonuria (PKU) since prompt introduction of a special diet can prevent it from causing retardation.

In the average newborn neonate, behavior can be classified into three broad categories: sleeping, crying, and feeding and eliminating. The neonate has a number of complex impulses that can disappear by the age of 3 to 4 months. Crying in the newborn is an unlearned, involuntary response but is readily shaped; it is an infant's first adaptive technique for interacting with the environment. Other useful reflexes include the rooting reflex. When one cheek is touched, a baby "roots," or moves the mouth toward the stimulus, seeking the nipple. The infant's vision is blurred and it cannot see beyond from 7 to 20 inches, but vision improves slowly as weeks pass.

Individual differences. Neonates develop at their own individual rates. They are born with their own temperament, and they manifest their uniqueness almost immediately. Some infants are born more irritable than others. Some protest while lying naked on their backs to be changed. Some may show little tolerance for stomach upsets and as a result cry more than others. In a short time, the infant begins to display its individual temperament in interaction with the environment. Family members react to the child's behavior in a variety of ways. Interaction with the family is as important in influencing the child as its inborn temperament.

Psychologists interested in understanding how personality is formed concentrate their energies on the child's early environment. Thomas, Chess, and Birch (1970) found that children could be grouped by three clusters of characteristics: those children who were "easy" and biologically regular and rhythmical, "difficult" babies who withdrew from new stimuli and adapted more slowly to change, and those who were "slow to warm up"—that is, children who withdrew from activities quietly and who showed interest in new situations only if they were allowed to do so gradually, without pressure. About 35% of the children studied could not be classified under any of the three types. In the others, some of the characteristics became less prominent as they developed and adapted to circumstances.

The investigators found that any demand that conflicted strongly with a child's temperament placed the child under tremendous stress. Those parents who understand the child's temperament and recognize what the child can and cannot do may be in a position to avoid many problems in development as well as in behavior. There are personality differences between parent and infant, and parents need time and patience in order to become acquainted with the child's unique personality and develop a relationship. How the parent–child relationship affects the neonate's development will be discussed in the following section.

Pat was a quiet, timid teenage parent who had expected to give birth to an infant that she could take care of like a doll. Baby Nina had other ideas. She cried noisily and demanded constant attention. The only technique that seemed to calm Nina was to pick her up and rock her rhythmically. However, Pat did not like this at all—after all, her child was supposed to be quiet. She started to neglect this 1-month-old baby out of disgust, turning to her own mother for help, support, and the nurturing of Nina. At that point, the worker assigned to Nina met with them and discussed the differences in babies, underscoring the need for Pat to understand and accept the baby as she was and work at creating a mutually satisfying relationship.

Parent–Infant Relationships

Social workers, psychologists, and psychiatrists have emphasized the profound influence that parents and extended families have in shaping an infant's personality. Recently, social behavioral scientists have begun to recognize that in the socialization process children are not only being influenced, but are in turn influencing the caretakers, as we saw in the case of

Pat and Nina. The characteristics of an infant elicit various types of responses from adults. A cuddly baby, a crying baby, and a squirming baby each bring out different responses in adults.

We cannot minimize the importance of the infant's constitutional characteristics in creating the initial pattern of mother–infant interaction, but it is clear that the mother and the baby are caught up in an interacting spiral. The behavior of each influences the responses of the other. Because of these spiral effects, it is difficult to distinguish what negative or positive variables belong to a person's makeup; they blend together as part of a continuum and an expansive spiral.

Children do play a significant role in determining the form and direction of parental behavior. Lewis & Rosenblum (1974) indicate that even young infants undertake to control their chief caretakers' actions. For example, suppose that a mother and child are looking at each other. If the infant looks away and then turns back, it may find it has lost its mother's gaze. When this happens, the infant starts to fuss and whimper, stopping as soon as it has regained the mother's gaze. Infants swiftly learn elaborate means for securing and maintaining a caretaker's attention. Thus socialization is a two-way process: a reciprocal relationship that involves both parent and child.

Researchers also note that the child's sex and position in the family may play a part in influencing parental behavior. Brown, Bakerman, Snyder, Fredrickson, Morgan, & Hepler (1976) studied a group of urban Black mothers and found that they rubbed, patted, kissed, rocked, and talked more to their male newborns than to their female newborns. Mothers of firstborn children spent more time in feeding their babies than mothers of later-born children. The behavior of each parent while interacting with the child was affected by the presence of the other. All this research shows that, very early in the developing relationship, different styles of interaction between parent and child become established, and both parent and child contribute to its patterning.

The environment initially created varies from home to home. It includes physical surroundings, other people, and the myriad social and cultural forces that influence the family. Human babies depend on others for sustenance. If babies are not fed or protected they will die. Through nourishment and nurturing, as well as by observation and imitation, children acquire the language, customs, attitudes, and skills of their group. Each cultural group has its own social heritage, derived from the history of its people and from other cultures. A culture shapes the children brought up in it, who develop their attitudes, concepts, and modes of thinking on the basis of that physical, sociocultural environment.

Developmental Abnormalities

A child may have any of a number of defects. Defects influence the attitude of the parents toward the children and vice versa. For example, children of overprotective parents may become overdependent. When parents reject a child, the child may in turn withdraw from them.

All expectant parents are concerned about the possibility of having children with birth defects. Research shows that 20% of birth defects are due to heredity and about 20% are caused by environmental factors such as drugs, medicine, viral infections, and vitamin deficiencies. The remaining 60% of the defects result from interaction between environmental factors and genetic predisposition (Darling, 1983).

Prematurity and Low Birth Weight

The term *premature* refers to the length of gestation and is applicable to a baby born more than three weeks ahead of schedule. Usually such children have a very low birth weight, are anemic, and may require blood transfusions. A premature baby is more than normally susceptible to infection and requires careful medical supervision. Seven percent of all births are premature. Prematurity is more common among boys than among girls. It is also more common in the lower socioeconomic class and among non-Whites than among Whites (Vander Zanden, 1978).

Sudden Infant Death Syndrome

Sudden, unexpected death of an infant within two to four months after birth is called *sudden infant death syndrome* (SIDS), or *crib death*. It appears to be more common among premature babies and babies of teenage mothers than among other groups. Research reveals that crib deaths are due to a variety of reasons, such as (1) overwhelming infection by an unknown virus, (2) an unknown error in the infant's metabolism, (3) abnormalities in the central nervous system that lead to sporadic closure of the larynx or failure of the cardiac system, and (4) apnea—that is, cessation of breathing for brief periods while sleeping. Two pediatricians mentioned in the report of the Foundation of the American Medical Association that crib-death babies were almost invariably found lying flat in a horizontal position, either on their stomachs or on their backs. The doctors advised that a baby's head should be raised 2 inches to a 10-degree angle of elevation from the crib mattress. For twenty minutes after feeding the baby should be kept upright in a baby carrier rather than placed in a crib.

Our culture is uncomfortable with death, particularly that of an infant. Today infant death is viewed as a failure of medical technology. The immediate reaction of the family is shock, disbelief, and anger (Helmrith & Sternitz, 1978). The anger may be directed toward health-care professionals, one's spouse, or oneself for allowing the death to occur, toward God for taking the child, and sometimes toward the infant for dying. While dealing with their guilt feelings, parents have to face the external problems of interacting with friends and relatives. Dealing with other people has always been the most difficult part of the grieving process. Most people do not know how to respond to parents experiencing a child's demise; Helmrith and Sternitz (1978) have referred to this aspect as the "conspiracy of silence."

How long does the grief last? Responses to the loss of an infant appear to mirror the effects of other forms of grief. Although the death is never forgotten, the acute stages of grief subside after a period of months, and by the end of a year most parents have been reintegrated into normal behavior patterns. This analysis was validated by De Frain and Ernst (1978), who studied 50 parents at various times following their infants' deaths. The study also reflects parents' tremendous potential for coping with a crisis situation and eventually adapting to a loss. Dealing with the death and dying of young children is another area in which social workers play an important role, especially in helping parents to move ahead with their lives and not remain obsessed with blaming anyone.

Implications for Social Work Practice

Social workers must know about the early phase of human life in order to deal with problems such as infertility, unwanted pregnancy, birth defects, and difficult situations like child neglect and abuse. An awareness of family factors such as lifestyle, socioeconomic status, ethnicity, and race plays a role in understanding a family's attitudes and child-rearing practices.

Social workers are also members of families with points of view based on life experiences of their own. However, in order to work with other families and individuals, social workers must be able to understand the behavior of other people based on their lifestyles. This means that social workers need to have self-awareness and a capacity for self-development. Self-awareness includes self-perception, an awareness of one's own needs, values, attitudes, feelings, experiences, expectations, and expertise.

While dealing with pregnant women, practitioners need to be aware of their particular needs. Many pregnant women are without support systems. They may need to belong to groups that provide information about emotional and physical aspects of labor and childbirth. Group sessions could also teach special exercises for mothers-to-be and allow them to share with others the many problems that arise in pregnancy. Joining a group helps the expectant mother to move from her passive role into an active one and thus become a meaningful participant in her own labor and childbirth.

Pregnancy, childbirth, and child rearing are viewed differently in different parts of the world. A look at the lifestyle that was prevalent in Samoa when the famous anthropologist Margaret Mead (1973) did her study in the early 1920s illustrates cultural differences. Margaret Mead writes:

> The expectant mother goes home laden with food gifts and when she returns to her husband's family, her family provide her with the exact equivalent in mats and bark cloth as a gift to them. At the birth itself the father's mother or sister must be present to care for the new-born baby while the midwife and the relatives care for her. There is no privacy about a birth. Convention dictates that the mother should neither writhe nor cry, nor wail against the presence of twenty or thirty people in the house who sit up all night if need be, laughing, joking and playing games. The midwife cuts the cord with a fresh bamboo knife and then all wait eagerly for the cord to fall off, the signal for a feast. If the baby is a girl, the cord is buried under a paper mulberry tree (the tree from which the bark cloth is

made) to ensure her growing up to be industrious at household tasks; for a boy it is thrown into the sea that he may be a skilled fisherman, or planted under a taro plant to give him industry in farming. When the visitors go home, the mother rises and goes about her daily tasks, and the new baby ceases to be of much interest to anyone. The day, the month in which it was born is forgotten.

Its first steps or first word are remarked without exuberant comment, without ceremony. It has lost all ceremonial importance and will not regain it until after puberty; in most Samoan villages a girl is ignored until she is married. Even the mother remembers only that Losa is older than Pupu and her sister's little boy, Fale, is younger than her brother's child, Vigo. Relative age is of great importance, for the elders may always command the younger—until the positions of adult life upset the arrangement—but the actual age will be forgotten.

Although labor and childbirth are common events, they are as diverse and complex as the people involved. Different life and birth patterns, rituals, child-rearing practices, and family interactions—in short, different cultures—add different flavor, color, and texture to human behavior. The social worker needs to have sufficient awareness to deal comfortably with diversity.

As a teenager Alice gave birth to a premature baby and decided to keep it. Though she was firm in her decision to keep the infant, she had great difficulty relating to the child, who did not respond with smiles or crying. The young mother in turn attempted to reject the unresponsive child by purposeful neglect. Fortunately, she was in a setting that provided help. The young mother was given information about prematurity and its effects on the response level of the infant and about the necessity for proper care if the child was to develop into a caring adult. Alice was encouraged to discuss her needs and fears, as well as her anger toward the child for not being "normal." Three months of supportive therapy helped the young mother in the difficult task of parenting this child. Alice's family was enlisted as a support system; her mother and her sisters helped to sustain Alice's ability to care for her child.

In Alice's case, the practitioner used the potential of the family as a support system, which enhanced Alice's ability to cope and adapt to her new role as a parent, alleviating some stress. She learned to care for the child, feeding it, changing its diapers, and so forth. Positive reinforcement of such actions led Alice to feel efficient and competent despite minimal reward from the premature infant; meaningful actions combined with family support led to a sense of accomplishment and greater self-esteem. The practitioner's timing in offering help and his knowledge of the developmental life cycle set the stage for the positive result.

Chapter Summary

Human development and behavior begin with the fertilization of the ovum, when the genetic material from the ovum combines with the genetic material of a single sperm. This fertilized ovum undergoes cell division and is called the *zygote*. The zygote embeds itself in the uterine wall. This process takes a couple of weeks and is followed by the embryonic period, which lasts until the end of the second month after conception. The fetal period follows and lasts until birth. The embryo develops within the amniotic sac and receives oxygen and nourishment through the placenta. By the time the fetus is ready for birth, all its organs are functional and it can respond to sound and touch.

Through the development of new technology, babies have been conceived in test tubes with the sperm and ova of their parents. Surrogate motherhood is an alternative by which a woman bears a child for a couple following artificial insemination with the husband's sperm.

Every infant is influenced by both genetic and environmental factors. An individual's genetic potentialities are inherited from both parents, but the combination of genes a person receives is unique. A gene is the part of a chromosome that directs the formation of a single trait. Each chromosome carries thousands of genes, which are in turn made up of DNA molecules. Inheritance is transmitted through the pairing of 23 chromosomes from each parent.

The study of developmental abnormalities is called *teratology*. Genetic counseling can help parents in understanding and dealing with genetic risks. Some genetic defects are due to a missing or extra chromosome; for instance, Down's syndrome is the outcome of chromosomal abnormality, and hemophilia is a sex-linked genetic disorder.

Environmental factors that affect the fetus include the diet of the mother, drugs, radiation, and toxemia and other maternal conditions.

The prenatal period has psychological, social, and cultural significance for the family as well as for the new family member.

The birth experience consists of labor, birth, and afterbirth. During labor the involuntary contractions of the uterus help prepare the mother for the birth contractions. At birth, uterine contractions expel the child through the dilated cervix. In the afterbirth stage, the placenta is expelled from the mother's system.

Anesthesia or drugs may be used to relieve pain in childbirth, or the mother may follow a "natural" childbirth method such as that of Lamaze or Leboyer. Since any birth could involve complications, planning for a natural childbirth at home should include emergency provisions.

Infants are called *neonates* during the first month after birth. That month can be a high-risk period, especially for children born prematurely. Though not common, sudden infant death syndrome is one risk. The Apgar score provides a quick neonatal assessment.

The neonate has a large number of reflexes, but a good deal of learning also takes place during the early period. Researchers have found that the relationship between the chief caretaker and the infant is reciprocal.

Knowledge of the early phase of development is especially valuable for social work practitioners who deal with problems such as infertility, unwanted pregnancies, and birth defects. Their client population may represent diverse socioeconomic, ethnic, racial, religious, and age groups.

References

Ambron, S. R., & Brodzinsky, D. (1979). *Lifespan human development*. New York: Holt, Rinehart & Winston.

Apgar, V. (1953). A proposal for a new method of evaluation of the newborn infant. *Anesthesia and Analgesia, 32*, 260–267.

Ash, P., Vennart, J., & Carter, C. (1977, April). The incidence of hereditary disease in man. *Lancet*, 849–851.

Best, C. H., & Taylor, N. B. (1955). *The physiological basis of medical practice*. Baltimore: Williams & Wilkins.

Bigner, J. J. (1979). *Parent–child relations: An introduction to parenting*. New York: Macmillan.

Brodzinsky, D. M., Gormly, A. V., & Ambron, S. R. (1986). *Lifespan human development*. New York: Holt, Rinehart & Winston.

Brown, J. V., Bakerman, R., Snyder, P. A., Fredrickson, W. T., Morgan, S. T., & Hepler, R. (1976). Interactions of Black inner city mothers with their newborn infants. *Child Development, 46*, 677–686.

Danziger, S. K. (1979). Treatment of women in childbirth: Implications for family beginnings. *American Journal of Public Health, 69*, 521–555.

Darling, R. B. (1983). The birth defective child and the crisis of parenthood: Redefining the situation. In E. J. Callahan & K. A. McClusky (Eds.), *Life-span developmental psychology*. New York: Academic Press.

De Frain, J. D., & Ernst, L. (1978). The psychological effects of sudden infant death syndrome on surviving family members. *Journal of Family Practice, 6* (5), 985–989.

Dick-Read, G. (1953). *Childbirth without fear*. New York: Harper & Row.

Doering, S. G., Entwistle, D. R., & Quinlan, D. (1982). *Modeling the quality of women's birth defects in society*. St. Louis: C. V. Mosby.

Dyer, E. D. (1963). Parenthood as crisis: A re-study. *Marriage and Family Living, 25*, 196–201.

Eiduson, B. T. (1980). Child development in emergent family styles. In M. Bloom (Ed.), *Life span development*. New York: Macmillan.

Feldman, A. (1971). The effects of children on the family. In A. Michael (Ed.), *Family issues of employed women in Europe and America*. The Netherlands: E. F. Brell.

Gordon, J. (1975). Nutritional individuality. *American Journal of Diseases of Children, 129*(4), 422–424.

Greene, C. P., & Lowe, S. J. (1975). Teenage pregnancy: A major problem of minors. Zero Population Growth. *National Reporter*, p. 3.

Guttmacher, A. (1973). *Pregnancy, birth and family planning*. New York: Viking Press.

Hall, R. E. (Ed.) (1970). *Abortion in a changing world* (Vol. 1). New York: Columbia University Press.

Helmrith, T. A., & Sternitz, E. M. (1978). Death in an infant: Parental grieving and the failure of social support. *Journal of Family Practice, 6*, 943–949.

Hetherington, E. M., & Parke, R. D. (1979). *Child psychology: A contemporary viewpoint*. New York: McGraw-Hill.

Hofer, M. A. (1981). *The roots of human behavior*. San Francisco: W. H. Freeman.

Jones, K. L., & Smith, D. W. (1973). Recognition of fetal alcohol syndrome in early infancy. *Lancet, 2*, 999.

Klaus, M. H., & Kennell, J. H. (1976). *Maternal and infant bonding*. St. Louis, C. V. Mosby. Vol. 46, 187–192.

Klaus, M. H., Kennell, J. H., Plumb, N., & Zuehlke, S. (1970). Human maternal behavior at first contact with her young. *Pediatrics, 46,* 187–192.

Lamaze, F. (1970). *Painless childbirth: The Lamaze method.* Chicago: Regnery.

Leboyer, F. (1976). *Birth without violence.* New York: Knopf.

Lenard, I. (1981, August). High tech babies. *Science Digest,* pp. 86–89, 116.

Lewis, M., & Rosenblum, L. A. (Eds.). (1974). *The effect of the infant on its caregiver.* New York: Wiley.

McDonald, R. L. (1968). The role of emotional factors in obstetrics complications: A review. *Psychosomatic Medicine, 30,* 222–237.

Mead, M. (1973). *Coming of age in Samoa* (2nd ed.). New York: Morrow.

Miller, R. S. (1977). The social construction and reconstruction of physiological events: Acquiring the pregnant identity. In N. Denzin (Ed.), *Studies in symbolic interaction.* Greenwich, CT: Jai Press.

Mussen, P. H., Conger, J. J., Kagan, J., & Gewitz, J. L. (1979). *Psychological Development.* New York: Harper & Row.

National Center for Health Statistics. (1978, March). U.S. Department of Health, Education and Welfare, *Monthly vital statistics reports* (Series 26, No. 10).

Norr, K. L., Block, C. R., Charles, A., Meyering, S., & Meyers, E. (1977). Explaining pain and enjoyment in childbirth. *Journal of Health and Social Behavior,* p. 18.

Papalia, D. E., & Olds, S. W. (1986). *Human development.* New York: McGraw Hill.

Restak, R. M. (1979, January 21). Birth defects and behavior: A new study suggests a link. *The New York Times,* p. C7.

Rosen, S. (1955). Emotional factors—nausea and vomiting in pregnancy. *Psychiatric Quarterly, 29,* 112–115.

Rosengren, W. R. (1962). The sick role during pregnancy: A note on research in progress. *Journal of Health and Human Behavior, 3,* 217–229.

Rossa, L. (1977). *Conflict and power in marriage.* Beverly Hills, CA: Sage Publications.

Rugh, R., & Shettles, L. B. (1971). *From conception to birth: The drama of life's beginnings.* New York: Harper & Row.

Schild, S. (1977, February). Social work with genetic problems. *Health and Social Workers, 2*(1). Cited in Specht, R., & Craig, G. J. (1982).

Scott, D. H. (1971). The child's hazards in utero. In J. B. Howells (Ed.), *Modern perspectives in international child psychiatry.* New York: Brunner/Mazel.

Shereshefsky, P. M., Liebenberg, B., & Lockman, R. F. (1973). Maternal deprivation. In P. M. Shereshefsky & L. J. Yarrow (Eds.), *Psychological aspects of a first pregnancy and early post-natal adaptation.* New York: Wiley.

Specht, R., & Craig, G. J. (1982). *Human development.* Englewood Cliffs, NJ: Prentice-Hall.

Thomas, A., Chess, S., & Birch, H. (1970, August). The origin of personality. *Scientific American, 233,* 102–109.

Vander Zanden, J. W. (1978). *Human development.* New York: Knopf.

Watkins, E. L., & Johnson, A. E. (Eds.). (1979). *Removing cultural and ethnic barriers to healthcare.* Chapel Hill, NC: University of North Carolina Press.

Infancy

Principles of Infant Development

Major Theorists on Infancy

Critical Issues for the Child in Its Environment

Implications for Social Work Practice

Chapter Summary

References

At 8 months of age, Anton was a beautiful baby with a ready smile. He was placid and content to play with his toys. He cried only when his diaper needed changing but otherwise he showed no symptoms of temper. At 2 years of age Anton continued to be easygoing and gentle. He had very little fear of strangers and was outgoing and friendly. He had reliable eating habits.

Within a few days after birth, Sean had revealed that he was a fussy baby. By the time he was 6 months old, he was having violent temper tantrums. He had distinct preferences for food, toys, and people. At 18 months Sean was independent and active. His sleep could be disturbed by small noises, so his parents had to be careful. He would get up in the middle of the night howling and crying. By the age of 2, Sean's expressions of joy, fear, and anger were intense. His parents worried, for by nature they were calm, quiet people.

Infancy is a period of rapid growth, a time when children become aware of themselves and the world around them. They learn to communicate and represent things symbolically. They also begin to discriminate among people, places, tastes, and sounds.

The case illustrations reveal how different children can be from one another. Their individual temperaments are unique. Although there are norms of growth and behavior at various ages, individual styles will persist throughout the life span.

Principles of Infant Development

A hallmark of the first two years of life—the period called *infancy*—is the child's tremendous expenditure of energy in exploring, learning about, and becoming competent in its environment (Vander Zanden, 1977). Few characteristics of infants are more revealing than their relentless pursuit of competence. They constantly begin activities by which they can interact effectively with the environment. Healthy children are active creatures who seek stimulation from the world around them and who, in turn, act upon it. Although a newborn baby appears to play a relatively passive role, it provides social stimulus for its parents. The infant uses crying and smiling as elementary ways of interacting socially.

During infancy, rapid growth and achievement take place in all areas of development. This rapidity discloses some of the general principles that govern human development at all stages of life: (1) there is a characteristic growth rate, (2) there is a characteristic direction that growth follows, (3) there is a characteristic pattern of differentiation, and (4) there is integration of a characteristic developmental sequence (Vander Zanden, 1977).

As a result of physical growth, motor development, and perceptual development, four developmental tasks take place during infancy: the development of (1) primary motor functions such as early eye–hand coordination, reaching, sitting, crawling, standing, and walking, (2) a sense of the permanence of objects, (3) a behavioral, though not conceptual, understanding of the relationship between means and ends, and (4) social attachment. The rest of this section presents four categories of developmental principles that are characteristic of infancy: physical development, perceptual development, language development, and psychosocial development.

Physical Development

The holistic principle. Biological characteristics and environmental factors cooperate in order to enhance optimal development. Any negative interference from the "inside," such as neurological problems or hormonal imbalance, or from the "outside," such as improper diet or lack of stimulation, can turn the positive growth cycle into a negative one.

> Eighteen-month-old Tanya was afraid of people. As an infant she had been abused by her parents and ill fed. Whenever Tanya put out her hand to touch something, she experienced physical pain. At her young age, Tanya exhibited withdrawal behavior; when touched she would shrivel up like a snail.

> Mothers don't respond to children who have delayed language and verbal abilities the same way that mothers of normal children do. Lugo and Hershey (1979) and others found that delayed preschoolers generally spent more time in solitary play, initiated fewer interactions, and responded less frequently to maternal interactions and questions. Their mothers gave more commands, initiated fewer positive interactions, and were less likely to respond positively to their children's interactions, play activities, and cooperative behaviors.

From mass activity to specific activity. In the beginning stages, infants typically exhibit mass activity. A pinprick may affect not only the finger but also the hands and arms and the movements of the head and shoulders. If excited, an infant moves its whole body around—its head, arms, fingers, legs, toes, and torso. As the infant grows older, mass activity is replaced by specific activity, which is a specific, individualized, and coordinated response.

Differentiation and integration. The means by which specific activity replaces mass activity is called *differentiation*. Once a certain degree of differentiation has been reached, the infant moves toward integration: small units of behavior combine and become coordinated into larger, more functional units. The child follows a sequential behavior for the purpose of obtaining nourishment. It could take the form of crying, searching for food, or reaching toward the bottle or breast (if within reach) and placing it in the mouth (Vander Zanden, 1977).

The cephalocaudal and proximodistal principles. Infant development also follows the cephalocaudal and the proximodistal principles (Vander Zanden, 1977). According to the cephalocaudal principle, growth proceeds from head to feet. Improvements in function and structure also follow the same order, occurring first in the head region, then in the trunk, and finally in the leg region. At birth, the head is disproportionately large, making up $\frac{1}{4}$ of the body, whereas in adults it is only $\frac{1}{10}$ to $\frac{1}{12}$ of the body. In contrast, the legs and arms of the newborn are disproportionately short compared with those of an adult.

Motor development also follows the cephalocaudal principle of proceeding from head to foot. Infants learn to contract the muscles of the head and neck, then of the arms and abdomen, and finally of their legs. When they begin to crawl, infants use their upper body to propel themselves and drag their feet passively behind. As they grow older and stronger they begin to use their legs as an aid in crawling.

The proximodistal principle indicates that growth proceeds from near to far, from head and torso toward the extremities. In early infancy, babies learn to move their heads and trunks. As they grow older, they learn to use their legs and arms independently. Control over the movements travels down the arms as children become increasingly able to perform precise and sophisticated grasping and other manual operations. Children learn large-muscle control before fine-muscle control. Thus an infant can walk, jump, climb, run, and perform other activities that require the use of the larger muscles before developing the ability to draw or write, which involve the smaller muscles. Thus movements proceed from mass to specific activity.

Rates of physical growth.   A group of psychologists (Vander Zanden, 1977) evolved normative standards for evaluating a child's developmental progress in relation to an average child in the same age group. There are broad similarities in people's sequences of developmental change although individuals' rates of maturing may differ. A person's growth may be rapid, slow, or uneven during the first 20 years of life. In general, however, growth in the first 3 years is rapid and slows down between the ages of 3 and 5. After the age of 5, the rate of growth is slow and steady until puberty, during which period there is a rapid acceleration of growth called the *adolescent growth spurt.*

Even in the young infant, all parts of the system do not grow at the same speed. The nervous system develops more rapidly than others. At birth, the brain is already 25% of its adult weight; at 6 months, nearly 50%; at $2\frac{1}{2}$ years, 75%; at 5, 90%; and at age 10 it is nearly 95%. Unlike the brain, the reproductive system grows slowly until adolescence, and then there is a spurt in growth.

As children are growing up physically, they need to follow a routine. There is a time for eating and a time for sleeping. A schedule creates a tempo, rhythm, and balance in the infant's life that eventually become a pattern. Other physical factors that affect the infant are weather, type of clothing worn (overdressed or underdressed babies are uncomfortable), type of living arrangements made for the child, and its ordinal position in the family.

Feeding schedule.   Infants' feeding schedules are based on various schools of thought. Some parents adhere to a strict schedule, believing that an infant should be encouraged to drink a given amount at every feeding, calculated according to the height and weight of the baby. Others believe that babies should be fed on a demand schedule: whenever the baby is hungry, it is permitted to drink as much or as little as it wants. Some infants are fed more often than others, their feeding schedules based on stomach size and the constitution of the infant. An infant's feeding schedule is also affected by the lifestyle of the parents. Not all infants have the advantage of a feeding schedule.

At 24, Maria was the mother of five children. Her welfare check was not sufficient to meet all her needs. She fed her children as best she could, but poverty was always close at hand. To feed her older children as well as possible, she deprived the infant. This child's constant crying eventually became pitiful, sporadic whining. Maria did not like her youngest because its father was an alcoholic who had treated her badly. However, she gave the child at least one full meal a day, whenever it suited her convenience.

As a child grows older, his or her stomach can hold larger amounts, accounting for longer intervals between feedings. One of the common problems that an infant could face at this point is digestive disorders.

Digestive disorders. Colic is a digestive disorder in which the abdomen becomes distended with gas, producing severe pain. This usually happens when the child is a few weeks old, particularly if the child is the firstborn. Tension in the mother does not help the situation, but usually colic disappears by itself and does not require medical attention (Kaluger & Kaluger, 1979).

Rosa became a single parent at 31. She had read a number of books and really wanted to be an excellent parent. To her it did not matter if the child had a father present or not. She had chosen a lifestyle that offered her the greatest fulfillment. She was in for a bad shock, however—her baby cried incessantly, and there was no one around to help her. Rosa did not understand the problem and called the doctor frequently. The child was found to have colic. Rosa's anxious state of mind was relieved only when the colic condition disappeared.

Sleep patterns. The amount of sleep a child requires varies with age. At birth, full-term babies sleep 50% to 60% of the time; premature babies sleep about 80% of the time (Kaluger & Kaluger, 1979). Young infants need more sleep than toddlers. As a child's abilities increase and experiences widen, the child resists bedtime, and slowing down for bedtime becomes more and more difficult.

The quality of sleep that a child needs also changes dramatically. During the early months sleep is relatively shallow, and the infant awakens whenever hungry or wet. Often the infant awakens with sharp cries. But as children grow older, they learn to sleep more peacefully.

Sensorimotor skills. Infancy is a period of tremendous motor growth. The term *motor* refers to muscular movements. Motor development is dependent on the child's overall physical growth. The infant cannot grasp, crawl, walk,

or climb before reaching a certain degree of skeletal and muscular development. General mass movements and reflex actions of the neonate are replaced
by specific muscular control that permits voluntary coordinated responses to
take place. Besides muscle development, muscle control makes use of sensory
acuity and awareness, perceptual discrimination, and adequate sensorimotor
integration and coordination.

The infant's maturational forces are of primary importance in developing
motor coordination. Maturation is measured in rate, level of readiness, and
pattern of early motor responses. Progress in motor development is influenced by environmental factors, such as opportunities to practice motor
skills, and by the child's attitude toward learning the skills, which reflects
encouragement or lack of encouragement from adults or siblings, as well as
physiological inhibition to learning. The process of development follows a
predictable sequence unless negative internal or external conditions interfere.

During infancy the child gains two complex abilities: (1) upright postural
control and locomotion and (2) manipulation and prehension (the ability to
reach with the hand and grasp and manipulate objects) (Kaluger & Kaluger,
1979).

Postural control and locomotion.   Despite variation among infants in time of
occurrence, there is a progressive regularity in the sequence that leads to
walking. According to Kaluger and Kaluger (1979), there are five basic stages:

1. gaining the postural control to sit with support
2. gaining the postural control to sit alone
3. making active efforts toward locomotion
4. creeping and walking with support
5. walking alone.

By the seventh month, most children have begun to crawl, having the
abdomen in contact with the floor, and to maneuver by twisting their bodies
and pulling and tugging with their arms. They also creep, moving on their
hands and knees with the body parallel to the floor.

By the age of 8 months, infants are constantly moving and resemble
perpetual motion machines. When infants pull themselves to a standing
position, they also have no difficulty sitting down. Their desire to be
competent is so powerful that they practice constantly. Falls, hurts, and
obstacles are viewed only as temporary hindrances; the infant keeps moving,
determined to succeed.

Infants begin to walk when they are between 11 and 15 months of age.
There are, of course, late learners and early learners, but the average child
will follow this approximate timetable.

Manual skills.   An infant's development of manual skills proceeds in accordance with the proximodistal principle—that is, from the center of the body
toward the periphery. At about 2 months, infants make a swiping movement
toward an object with the upper body and arms, but they do not attempt to
grasp the object. At 3 months, their reaching consists of clumsy shoulder and

elbow movements, but their aim is poor and their hands are still closed fists. By 4 months they approach an object with open hands. At about 5 months, they are capable of touching an object in one quick, direct motion of the hands, and once in a while they may succeed in grasping it in an awkward manner. By 6 months, they employ a corralling and swooping approach with the palm and fingers. By the time they are 7 months of age, they begin to oppose the thumb to the palm and the other fingers. At 8 months, they are able to coordinate their grasp with the tips of the thumb and forefinger. Eventually, at 12 months, they master a more sophisticated forefinger grasp (Vander Zanden, 1977).

Perceptual Development

During the first six months of the baby's life there is a discrepancy between the infant's vast sensory capabilities and its relatively sluggish motor development. The sensory apparatus yields perceptual input that far exceeds the baby's ability to use it. During this period infants have the capacity to extract information from the environment at a phenomenal level. When the perceptual and motor abilities are used in concert, beginning at about the seventh month, the child develops in an awesome fashion. Between 11 and 18 months the child becomes an accomplished social being, calling out to parents with "dada" and "mama" and using expressions like "bye-bye." It performs imitative actions, such as talking on the telephone, reading a magazine, and sweeping the floor.

Language Development

As infants grow older, language becomes an important and intimate part of their development. There is a difference between language development and speech development. "Language development" refers to words, their pronunciation, and methods of combining them. Language development concerns the length and patterns of sentence structure. "Speech" refers to vocalization, the development of units of speech sound—the phonemes—and maturation toward proper articulation of the sounds (Kaluger and Kaluger, 1979).

Speech. Infant speech is important to observers because it provides them with a new avenue of access to the child's mental processes and a better clue to understanding the child's way of thinking. Baby talk serves the expressive function of permitting the child to communicate needs and interests through means other than tears, smiles, shouts, and gestures. Thus infant speech becomes a vehicle of self-expression and communication as well as of mental development. From a transactional perspective, it helps to strengthen the infant's bonds with people. By talking, the child becomes more than just a small presence—it can ask for attention.

The infant moves quickly from vocalizing to babbling and talking. Infants do make sounds from the time they are born. By the time an infant is 2 months old, its parents can distinguish a variety of cries and smiles, as well as sounds of contentment.

Phonemes and culture.   By the age of 1 year, children are already favoring the sounds peculiar to the language of their caretakers. This pattern of selective phonemic learning reveals the significance of culture-specific linguistic systems. At this age, the child's speech is holophrastic, consisting of one-word utterances having more than literal meaning. The child's manner of expression enlarges the meaning of the word, conveying delight, dismay, or the thrill of a fresh discovery. Later the child moves on to telegraphic speech, made up of two- or three-word utterances with simple grammar. The child achieves effective communication using only key words in phrases like "where dada" and "there dada" (Braine, 1963).

The way in which a child learns to speak depends upon the socioeconomic background of the family. According to Tulkin and Kagan (1972), social-class differences in language become evident at a very young age as a result of the way caretakers interact with their offspring. Benedict (1975) notes that mothers talk differently to their babies than to older children or adults. They use shorter sentences, fewer words, simpler grammar, and a lot of repetition.

Psychosocial Development

Human infants are born into a social environment. From birth they take their place in that environment. To be human is to be a social product.

Emotions.   Emotions are a natural part of an infant's life. Infants interact with the environment and create the beginnings of a social world for themselves.

The term *emotion* implies a system of feelings. Many psychologists agree that emotion is, first of all, affective: an element of feeling or awareness is present in it. Second, the central nervous system and the autonomic system are involved, providing characteristic motor, glandular, and visceral activities. Third, emotion is in some way related to motivation as an energizer of behavior. Fourth, emotion can be classified into various types of phenomena, such as fear, anger, joy, disgust, pity, and affection.

An infant's emotions are simple, spontaneous, and transitory but more frequently expressed than those of adults. As soon as an infant's emotion passes, it is forgotten, and the infant is free from strain and stress until new conditions arise that evoke an emotional response. There is a definite relationship between emotional states and organismic needs. Needs and emotions are simple when the child is young. The chief caretakers provide the emotional environment. Warmth, caring, and bodily satisfactions are equivalent to love for both the baby and the parent.

One of the infant's chief emotions is excitement. Another is distress, which can be observed by the end of the second month. Between 3 and 6 months of age, infants show anger, disgust, and fear. As maturation and learning take place, complex interactions come into play. The chief caretakers have much to do with the emotional development of the infant.

Social interaction.   Like adults, children depend upon their social environment (which for infants usually consists of adults and siblings) for their existence. The social group and available networks not only supply the infant's needs but to a great extent determine what kind of individual the infant will become. The first social group with which a normal child interacts is its immediate family, which could consist of two parents, a single parent, or an extended family including siblings. The family plays an important part in establishing the child's attitudes and habits. As the infant becomes an adolescent and then an adult, his or her social networks change and expand, and reliance on the family decreases.

Infants make their first social responses to adults. By the age of 4 weeks, they stare at faces that are close by and appear to enjoy following the movements of objects and people. They begin to coo and babble. By the end of their third month, infants interact with people by responding to voices, turning their head or eyes in the direction of the sound. At 5 months, they can respond to a person's smile by smiling in return. This stage marks the beginning of mutuality and reciprocity.

As infants' perceptive powers increase, they interact more with whatever is in the immediate environment. By 7 months, they learn to play peekaboo or hide-your-face. They enjoy the attention they receive from familiar adults but are afraid of strangers. Between 8 and 10 months, infants begin to display aggressive behavior (Tulkin & Kagan, 1972). They may pull adults' hair or grab their noses. They also learn to imitate some vocal sounds.

By the time children are 1 year old they enjoy social give and take. They slowly come to understand that other people besides the family can be friendly. Playthings no longer hold their attention because they enjoy being chased while they try to creep away. At 18 months, infants are into everything. Most of them can walk and enjoy being on their feet. They enjoy exploring and develop a great interest in household things and activities. During this period children are responsive to adults and are aware of social approval, which is an important aspect of their lives.

At 18 months, Nicholas lives in a crowded city with his mother, his mother's intermittently resident boyfriend, a couple of aunts, his grandmother, and six older siblings. Home life is chaotic; there are no rules for behavior, and the older the child, the greater the freedom. Alcohol and drugs are common features of family life. Nicholas is constantly neglected by his mother, who is attempting to maintain the family on her meager welfare check and the income from drug trafficking. The real nurturer and caretaker in the family is the grandmother. In his mother's presence, Nicholas's behavior is quiet and withdrawn. But when his grandmother enters the house, Nicholas babbles loudly and smiles easily, and she responds with affection. Thus nurturing and social approval stimulate Nicholas's social behavior.

Major Theorists on Infancy
Erikson: Acculturation and Developmental Stages

One of the pioneers of developmental theory, Erik Erikson carefully noted and described how human potentials are adapted to culture. He highlights psychosocial rather than psychosexual development through the life cycle and classifies its phases into eight stages of life. His work on the life cycle is impressive, a carefully woven tapestry of biological, psychological, personal, cultural, historical, and political factors in the human life span.

Trust versus mistrust. As the first component of normal personality Erikson nominates the concept of basic trust versus mistrust (Erikson, 1980). Basic trust involves a positive orientation toward oneself, the world, and others, and mistrust is shown in negative feelings, insecurities, and fears.

Once outside the womb, the infant remains completely dependent on the care of nurturing adults. The infant who is well cared for, in terms of nourishment, contact, and attention, develops a sense of contentment. A psychosocial crisis at this stage indicates tension between the developmental needs of the individual and the social expectations of the culture. An infant seeks warmth, consistency, and stimulation from its caretaker. Trust is an experiential phenomenon for the nonverbal child. If its needs are met, the infant feels valued and develops confidence in its surroundings. Trust can be inferred from an infant's ability to delay gratification and from the warmth and happiness it reveals in interacting with adults.

When infants' needs are not recognized or when they are treated inconsistently, they can develop feelings of mistrust. When a crying infant is sometimes cuddled, sometimes ignored, and sometimes pushed around harshly, even a tiny infant may conclude that it is not important to get attention. Such infants simply view their world as being unfriendly and see themselves as worthless persons.

Basic mistrust is soon revealed in behavior. Infants whose physical needs, such as for nourishment and physical caring, are not satisfied react with prolonged crying. Ainsworth (1973) found that the amount and frequency of infants' crying really reflected the degree of responsiveness that the parents had shown the child. Poor parental response increased the infant's crying episodes. Such infants believe that no one will come to them (Ainsworth, 1973).

Once infants adopt the orientation of mistrust, the environment works to reinforce it. In time, the child's caretakers come to view the child as a cranky one who simply cannot be attended to. The infant is scolded and is picked up only in a desperate attempt to quiet it. Basic mistrust leads to self-defeating behavior, with a reduced sense of self-esteem and an inability to deal positively with others. Once entrenched, this transactional pattern between adults and infants affects the emotional development of the infant and the emotional responses of the adults.

Every culture inculcates its general rules through its child-rearing practices. The child's basic needs are satisfied by the adult caretakers, and in the process a social interchange takes place between child and parent. Caretakers are influenced by their own socialization, cultural norms, environmental influences, and vision of an ideal parent. By receiving, the child learns how to become the giver, and thus mutuality and reciprocity are established.

According to Erikson, if everything does not go well in one stage of development, an individual does possess the ability to compensate for the setback by reworking the conflict during that period or at a later point in life. The child's sense of identity gradually evolves in the recognition of mutual caretaker–child relationships.

> Jane was a sad child. Neglected and abused, she was placed in a foster home at 18 months of age. She habitually withdrew from all human contact and shrieked when touched. The foster parent learned to approach Jane by cooing and babbling in a soft voice, which seemed to puzzle but not provoke the child. Jane's behavior continued to reveal lack of trust, but as time passed and she was fed and cared for with affection, Jane began to break through her fears in small degrees and to respond to the new parenting differently, without fear and pain.

Jane's case proves two points: first, that the damage was not permanent; the child was removed from her harmful environment at a crucial time in her life and began to compensate and grow positively; second, that the interplay of person and environment is of obvious importance.

Infancy and ritualization. Erikson discusses ritualization and its effects on the infant and the caretaker. A daily ritual takes place between the infant and the chief caretaker. From the moment of waking, the infant evokes in the chief caretaker a whole repertoire of verbal, emotional, and manipulative behavior. The caretaker approaches the child with a smiling or a worried look, is either happy or anxious, and voices his or her opinions accordingly while commencing the morning routine. By feeling, seeing, and smelling, the caretaker determines whether the baby is comfortable or uncomfortable and offers such services as changing, feeding, or rearranging the infant's position or picking it up. The caretaker feels obliged, if not a little pleased, to repeat a performance that arouses a predictably positive response in the infant, which in turn encourages the parent's agreeable behavior. Thus daily events between the chief caretaker and the child become ritualized. This ritualization is highly individualized between a particular parent and a particular child.

Ritual also takes place when a child is given a name. Name-giving ceremonies are usually considered significant by parents, extended family, and the community. The child also learns special designations for referring to its caretakers. This arrangement has a special meaning in human ritualization; it is based on the mutuality of the physical and emotional needs of infant and caretaker, which becomes the fundamental basis for assimilation of culture (Erikson, 1977).

Autonomy versus doubt and shame. As identified by Erikson (1980), the second stage of development in the life cycle is characterized by the quest for autonomy. As the muscles of the infant mature, the child moves toward three new activities: walking, achieving bowel and bladder control, and talking. Muscle control allows the child to engage his or her will in "holding on" and "letting go"—the mechanics of retention and elimination. These activities empower the child with a sense of autonomy. It is during this period that children become aware of their separateness. Through a number of experiences they learn that their parents do not always know what children want and do not always understand their feelings. This insight leads to a feeling of delight in the sense of self.

Toilet-training experience is an important factor in the development of autonomy. If a child's parents are restrictive, rigid, and punitive about toilet training, the child may rebel by refusing to exercise the necessary control over bladder and bowel movements. Unfortunately, children defeat their own purposes through this tactic, for they thereby deny themselves the growing sense of autonomy that accompanies control. As Erikson (1980) put it, children are faced with a "double rebellion and a double defeat." Such children cannot be sure of themselves.

Bowel and bladder control is an important milestone for both infants and their parents. However, other kinds of experience also figure in the child's struggle for autonomy. In the early phases, children use primitive devices to explore their independence. For instance, they learn to say no to everything offered to them, whether they like it or not. This behavior is typical of the period called *the terrible twos*. Later in the development of autonomy, the emphasis changes from a somewhat rigid, nay-saying, ritualized, unreasonable style to an independent, energetic, persistent style of action. The older child's behavior is characterized by the phrase "I can do it myself." If children are allowed to experiment with autonomy, they develop a strong foundation of self-confidence and a delight in behaving independently.

The establishment of a sense of autonomy during childhood requires not only tremendous effort by the child but also extreme patience and supportiveness from significant others. The parents have to learn to cajole, teach, absorb insults, wait, and praise. At times, parents allow children to try things that they are not yet able to do. Only with constant encouragement from the parents does the child continue to engage in new tasks, gaining a sense of competence when he or she succeeds. Some parents constantly discourage and criticize a child, whose feelings of self-confidence and self-worth are then replaced by constant self-doubt.

Developing an overwhelming sense of shame and self-doubt to cope with stress is the negative resolution of the psychosocial crisis of childhood. Young children who arrive at this resolution lack confidence in their ability to perform, and they expect to fail at what they do. Shame is the end result of such feelings. The experience of shame is extremely unpleasant, and in order to avoid it children may refrain from participating in all kinds of new activities. Thus learning new skills becomes a difficult task.

Two-year-old Neal and his parents had a number of problems. His father was an alcoholic, and his mother spent a lot of time away from home working at odd jobs. Neal's older sister, scarcely 8 years old, took care of his needs. All family members were unnecessarily strict and harsh with Neal. At his young age, Neal had learned how to get his family's attention—he wet himself. It made his sister and his parents angry, but it got him their negative attention. The more they revealed their disapproval of him, the more wetting he did. Toilet training became a game to him.

When children take on new tasks and fail in them, it is important that they be helped to understand that failure is not utter disaster—that they can safely take a chance and try again. This lesson has to be learned in all areas of development and reaffirmed throughout adult life.

White: The Competence Model

Robert White (1963) applies the competence model to the normal development of the child. In their early dealings with the environment, says White, children have to learn to cope with and adapt to their new surroundings. Infants' lives are dominated by imperatives such as hunger, and by acute discomforts such as wetness. Infants attempt to cope with the stress by improving their ability to do what they do well—crying and sucking. These actions produce consequences. The arrival of the nipple and the more rapid intake of milk may be presumed to give the infant a feeling of efficacy. Having been swamped by hunger, the infant's feelings of efficacy are impossible to disentangle from those of gratification, so gains in competence, if they occur, must be attributed to the transaction as a whole. In this transaction, the infant deals with stress by coping and adapting in meaningful ways that offer it satisfaction and gratification (White, 1963).

During the oral period, development is seen in terms of feeding and its effects on the personality of the infant. White indicates that as infants get older, they find meals increasingly entertaining. They investigate the utensils, explore the behavior of spilled food, and play with toys. These different behaviors affect their personalities positively and they develop competency.

Playtime is also an important factor in development. Gesell's (1940) typical day for an infant shows an hour of play before breakfast, two hours before lunch, two hours during the afternoon, and maybe an hour of play before bedtime. Thus, when infants are 1 year old they are spending as much as six hours a day in play, not to mention play during meals and bath. What happens during playtime? At first, visual exploration is the most concentrated form of activity, although babbling and gross motor movements are also present. Halfway through the first year, the child learns to grasp and is eagerly intent on playing. Moving into the realm of social competence, children participate in social play because they have the opportunity to do something interesting with the environment. White's competence model is represented by children's exploratory play: their active interactions with their surroundings start as fun but contribute steadily to the attainment of adult competence.

What types of competence does the child achieve through interacting with the environment? Consider locomotion: children start as awkward toddlers, but by the middle of the second year they have become restless and get into everything. They experiment with their prowess by such stunts as walking backward or pushing their own carriages. Children's first upright steps may have been applauded, but their locomotor accomplishments soon become cause for parental despair and seem to continue without benefit of social reward. By their third birthday, children may display their astonishing gains by playing quite happily by themselves for long stretches of time. The child engages in constant activity, carrying objects about, filling and emptying containers, tearing things apart and fitting them together, lining up blocks and eventually building with them, and digging and constructing in sand-boxes. Such play may look meaningless to an adult, but it brings about a tremendous increase in the child's ability to deal with the physical world.

Because of their practiced maturing of general coordination and verbal capacity, children at 2 years reach a critical juncture in their ability to interact with their social environment. They attempt to exploit possibilities to increase their sense of social competence. At first their attempts appear to be somewhat crude and uncompromising. In their inexperience, children challenge rather forcefully their parents' sense of competence. These challenges are trying for parents. The temptation to prevail at all costs is powerful, not only for parents who would like to exercise authority but also for apostles of permissiveness who are startled to find such tyranny emerging in the young. In provoking these crises, how much sense of social competence can the child preserve? The child's first efforts to measure his or her efficacy against that of other people may leave quite a lasting impression on his or her confidence.

White views toilet training as another model for developing competence. During the anal period, and in some cases toward the end of it, children develop stubbornness, parsimony, and orderliness, which are necessary to prevent their being pushed around. These qualities emerge when they do because they depend on certain developmental achievements; namely, a sense of the constancy of objects and a continuity of play interests from day to day.

Piaget: Cognitive Learning

The work of Jean Piaget (Flavell, 1963) concentrates on the cognitive development of children. His initial work was based on observations of his own children, following a variant of the case-study method. Children achieve cognitive learning by coping with and adapting to words, language, and nonverbal communication.

"Cognition" means knowing. As young people grow older, "knowing" comes to mean something more definite, more certain and lasting than immediate sense perception. Sometimes "cognition" can refer to all of mental life. Kaluger and Kaluger (1979) define cognition as including imagination, perception, thought, reasoning, reflection, problem solving, and all verbal behavior. In infancy, cognition is well developed and is practically inseparable from the development of the senses.

Piaget suggests that the child's cognitive development can be described in four main periods: the sensorimotor period (infancy, or from birth to 2 years), the preoperational period (2 to 7 years of age), the period of concrete operations (ages 7 to 11), and the period of formal operations (11 and on through to adulthood).

Piaget views the child as both an active and an interactive organism, whose behavior can be understood only in terms of the way it adapts to the world around it. Piaget emphasizes that the infant uses the processes of both assimilation and accommodation in making its adaptation (Flavell, 1977). The development of assimilation and accommodation during the sensorimotor period has been cast into six successive stages, to which descriptive labels have been added.

Stage I: Beginning of systematic use of natural reflexes.   Estimated to begin during the first month of life, Stage I involves the increasingly smooth and systematic use of natural reflexes. The infant engages in the "reflex exercise," such as blinking the eyes. For example, during the first few days of life, the infant gains increasing competence in the sucking reflex, finding the nipple more readily when it slips out of its mouth. This improvement is called *functional assimilation;* it leads to what is called *generalized assimilation* (the infant sucks on all kinds of objects) and *recognitive assimilation* (the baby recognizes the nipple as being different from other objects).

Stage II: Primary circular reaction.   During Stage II, the 4-month-old infant develops the habit of voluntarily putting its thumb into its mouth and keeping it there. This behavior is different from the reflexive thumb sucking seen in neonates; the child now recognizes thumb sucking as a nursing activity. Systematic thumb sucking is a primary circular reaction—"primary" because the actual content of behavior has a biological base, and "circular" because the response is repetitive and appears to produce reinforcement.

Stage III: Secondary circular reaction.   The secondary circular reaction begins when the child is between 4 and 8 months of age. The child learns to make combinations or derivatives of primary reactions developed separately at an earlier time. For instance, shaking a rattle to hear the noise is a secondary circular reaction. The child has previously performed the reaching and grasping aspects of this activity, as well as the response of listening. Now the child learns to amalgamate these separate activities into a new and more complex behavioral sequence.

Stage IV: Threshold of intelligent behavior.   During Stage IV, infants are at the threshold of intelligent behavior. Piaget notes that between 8 and 12 months infants seem to acquire truly instrumental behavior. He experimented with his son Laurent, who was then 7 months and 13 days old. Piaget placed a toy in a visible location in front of the child and then covered it with a red pillow, which barred the child from reaching it. Piaget found that visibility was not essential to the child's locating the toy; Laurent found it under the red pillow. After some time, Piaget arranged two pillows, one red and one blue, and hid a toy under the red pillow while Laurent watched. Later he removed the toy, showed it to the child, and placed it under the blue pillow while the child watched. Then he asked Laurent to find the toy. Although the child had seen his father place the toy under the blue pillow, he looked only under the red pillow. The response of looking under a pillow represented the beginning of intelligent behavior, whereas the incorrect choice revealed the child's inability to recognize the continuous processes involved in his environment. His consequent repetition of specific acts that had been successful in the past suggests that certain cognitive processes had not yet developed. The appropriate competence appears when the child is 12 to 18 months of age.

Stage V: Tertiary circular reaction.   Between 12 and 18 months of age, infants begin to search for new means to reach objects. For example, the child sees an object on the rug and pulls on a near corner of the rug, drawing the object within reach. The child discovers that the movement of the rug also produces movement in the desired object. The discovery and use of this possibility are the milestone of Stage V. The basic idea may be discovered quite by accident, but the child then begins to experiment with the situation again and again. Repetition is neither absolutely stereotyped nor simply arbitrary. Instead the child seems to try out, in a more or less systematic way, variations in the newly discovered act to observe the effects they have (Specht & Craig, 1982).

One of the most important accomplishments that generally occurs within this period is the infant's gradual gaining of the perceptual and mental ability to understand object permanence—the realization that objects are the same from one occasion to another. At first, infants believe that when objects are out of sight they do not exist, but this idea disappears as the child grows older. Lack of the concept of object permanence explains the excitement and delight of young children playing peekaboo. When they cover their eyes, what they have been looking at no longer exists. Uncovering their eyes, they are thrilled and happy to see the object again. This game appears to be the most fun for children who have not developed the concept of object permanence—the object's reappearance is not totally predictable. The attainment of the concept of object permanence frees the young child from total reliance on what it can see. This ability to hold the image of an object in the mind is the first step toward the beginning of complex representational thinking. The concept of object permanence is the fundamental building block of logical thought (Specht & Craig, 1982).

Stage VI: Stage of schemata.   Stage VI begins when the child is about 18 months old and lasts until its second year. The stage is characterized by an ability to combine various sorts of possibilities mentally, to reach new and different solutions. During this period, the young child has begun to develop what Piaget refers to as *schemata*—miniature frameworks that enable the child both to fit and to manipulate new pieces of information and hence assimilate and accommodate to the environment. At this time, the child's performance may be seen as the integration and completion of sensorimotor coordination; that is, as the rudiments of intelligence. The appearance of insightful behavior in infants marks the conclusion of one sort of cognitive development and the beginning of another—mental representation. Now the road for conceptual thinking is opened (Flavell, 1963).

Piaget stresses the organizing capacity of the intellect and uses it as an organizing principle in his theory of the personality. The cognitive theory of Piaget concerns itself with the central organizing principles in higher animals and recognizes the partial autonomy of these principles, in the sense that a person interacts with, rather than simply reacts to, his or her environment. In contrast, Erikson and White view the ego as organizer, controlling motility and perception of both the outer world and the self. The ego serves as a protective barrier against excessive external and internal stimuli. Collectively these theorists provide a balanced way of viewing the interactions of the ego and the environment.

Critical Issues for the Child in Its Environment

Attachment

The basic social relatedness of the human organism is explained through the development of attachment. Attachment takes place between an infant and significant others in the infant's life when they create a mutual and reciprocal relationship.

Defining the concept. It is clear from the literature on attachment that the term *attachment* eludes definition. Cohen (1974) and Weinraub, Brooks, and Lewis (1977) have persuasively challenged most of the frequently preferred components of attachment definitions, and it has aptly been said that defining *attachment* is like trying to reach a platonic ideal. To illustrate some of these problems, we note that Ainsworth (1963) distinguishes, on the one hand, among attachment, dependency, and object relations and, on the other, between attachment and attachment behavior. She stresses that the hallmark of attachment is behavior that promotes proximity to or contact with the specific figure or figures to whom a person is attached. Ainsworth's concept of attachment appears markedly similar to what others call *dependency* (see Maccoby & Masters, 1970). In fact, Maccoby and Masters believe that the term *dependency* has a technical meaning that includes the same kind of behaviors that other authors like Bowlby (1969) would term *attachment*.

The definition of attachment used throughout the remainder of this book represents an integration of diverse conceptions of attachment to form a definitional consensus. The definition has five components. Proceeding from the top, each successive component has progressively less consensus in the literature. "Attachment" refers to behavior having the following characteristics (Bowlby, 1969):

1. It is proximity- and/or contact-seeking and/or -maintaining behavior.
2. This behavior is shown to one or a few specific persons.
3. It elicits reciprocal behaviors in, or secures the presence of, these others.
4. The absence of reciprocal behaviors produces an aversive state (shown through distress behavior) for the person emitting the attachment behavior.
5. The aversive state may lead the attached person to seek alternative attachment opportunities among his or her broader social network.

When the term *attachment* is applied to infants by psychologists and social workers, it usually means that the infant directs most of its behavior—touching, reaching to be picked up, holding on, and clinging—toward a particular person, the chief caretaker (in most instances, the mother).

Attachment behavior and preferences. There is a distinction between attachment and affiliative behaviors (Lamb, 1977). Affiliative behaviors occur at a distance; for example, smiling, looking, talking, showing, or pointing. Unlike attachment, they are independent of physical contact. For infants, attachment and not affiliative behavior reduces stress, a difference that, to Lamb, proves that the distinction is real. Ainsworth (1973) views these two classes of behavior as reflecting different qualities of attachment and not as distinct kinds of social behavior.

Kotelchuck (1972) exposed various groups of infants, ranging in age from 6 to 21 months, to 13 different episodes involving father, mother, or stranger, alone or in combination, in a modified "strange situation" procedure (an unfamiliar situation). Kotelchuck focused on the effects of the departure of an adult on the infant's playing, crying, and touching. For all measures, the infants at 6 months and 9 months showed essentially no differences in behavior as a result of who left the room, implying that in this situation they had no attachment preferences for father, mother, or stranger. A clear pattern appeared with 12-month-old infants: they showed more distress when their mothers left than when fathers left and relief when the stranger left. For example, play increased and crying decreased when the stranger left, but the opposite happened when the mother or father left. All attachment measures were at a maximum at either 15 or 18 months and all showed a decline thereafter (Kotelchuck, 1972).

Studies done by Cohen and Campos (1974) with 10-, 13-, and 16-month-old infants of White middle-class families attained results that were consistent with Kotelchuck's. Studies by Dunn (1976) showed that 1-year-olds exhibited greater attachment to their mothers than to their fathers, but by 2½ years of age this difference had disappeared.

From the above studies, it can be concluded that in the age range between 6 and 9 months infants show no attachment preferences for parents or strangers. By 10 months, they prefer mothers to fathers and fathers to strangers. These strong preferences reach a maximum when the child is between 15 and 18 months of age. At 2 years old, infants showed essentially equal attachment behaviors toward parents, preferring both to strangers. These conclusions were based on group averages; in every experiment, some 10-month-old infants preferred their father to their mother.

Being separated from its chief caretaker makes the child feel distressed, particularly in unfamiliar environments. When the child is reunited with its mother, it usually calms down. The infant is unlikely to become scared when it is with its chief caretaker and is also more easily soothed. It is more likely to seek attachment when it is hungry, tired, bored, or afraid.

Is there a critical period for attachment and a specific time during infancy when the infant develops a strong, well-differentiated preference for one person? Soon after the infant's birth, the parent's attachment to the infant becomes specific: the parents would not be willing to replace their own child with any other child of similar age. When does the infant make this type of commitment to the parent? Yarrow (1964) observed 100 infants who had been transferred from foster parents to adoptive parents. Babies who had been separated from their parents when they were 6 months old or younger displayed minimal distress, but older infants showed strong negative reactions that included angry protest and withdrawal. This negative reaction revealed that babies found the disruption of their earlier relationship very stressful.

Quite appropriately, the research on maternal attachment has brought about an increased interest in the behavior of fathers. Greenberg, Morris, and Lind (1973) have used the term *engrossment* (absorption, preoccupation, and interest) to describe the powerful impact of a newborn child on its father. They have identified several specific aspects of the father's developing bond to his newborn, ranging from his attraction to the infant and his perception of the newborn as perfect to extreme elation and an increased sense of self-esteem.

Parke (1974) observed parents in three different situations: the mother and father each alone with the 2- to 4-day-old infant and the father, mother, and infant together (triadic interaction) in the mother's hospital room. The most striking finding is that Parke's studies have not revealed any significant behavioral differences between fathers alone with their infants and mothers alone with their infants. In a triadic situation, the father tends to hold the infant nearly twice as much as the mother, vocalizes more, touches the infant slightly more, and smiles significantly less than the mother. When both parents are present, the father plays the more active role, in contrast to the cultural stereotype of the father as a passive participant (Parke, 1974).

Cultural factors. Although studies have generally researched the ideal two-parent families, there are other family lifestyles. In single-parent families, the bonding takes place essentially between one parent and the child. In extended families having more than one caretaker, the child may become attached to an adult who is not its parent but its chief caretaker.

Most of the research evidence is drawn from studies of middle-class Euro-American families. Their infants are typically raised in nuclear families and taken care of primarily by a single person, the mother.

Klaus, Kennell, Mata, Sosa, and Urrutia (Klaus & Kennell, 1976) studied infants' attachment behavior toward mothers and fathers in families of the Ladino culture of Guatemala. Ladinos belong to Spanish-speaking cultures of Indian-European stock. The families in this experiment lived in a small city and were of low socioeconomic status. The infants studied varied in age—9, 12, 18, and 24 months. Basically the infants' play behavior, crying, closeness, and searching were observed following the comings and goings of any adult.

Infants of all ages played more with either parent when present than with strangers. Crying increased when parents departed and decreased when strangers departed. Moreover, just as the North American data showed, infants at 24 months exhibited few differences in attachment to the three adults but marked differences at 18 months. Two major discrepancies between the North American and Ladino data stand out. First, unlike the North American infants studied, 9-month-old Ladino babies showed attachment. Further findings suggest that this could be true because Ladino babies are much less frequently separated from their mothers than are American infants. Second, Ladino infants were not as strongly attached to their fathers as were American infants. Findings note that Ladino fathers spend much less time with their infants than do American fathers.

In a study of attachment behavior among the children of Israeli kibbutzim, or collective farms (Fox, Aslin, Shea, & Dumais, 1980), the infants were either 8 to 10, 12 to 15, or 21 to 24 months of age. Besides their mothers, there was a chief caretaker called the *metapelet*. All the infants had been cared for by metapelets for at least four months prior to testing. In the kibbutz, infants were brought to an "infant house" four days after birth, where they were placed in the care of the metapelet. Mothers spent as much time as possible there for the first six weeks and then gradually returned to work. As the mothers spent less time with their infants, the metapelet spent more. When the infants reached 3 or 4 months, they were placed with another metapelet, who cared for them until they reached the age of 3. During that period children had a daily three-hour visit with both parents at their home. There was a high rate of turnover among the metapelets due to job training and maternity leave. Thus there was some variability in the amount of time the infants had been cared for by a particular metapelet.

This situation provided a good opportunity for studying the attachment behavior of infants toward adults. The researchers found few differences in behavior toward the three adults for 21- to 24-month-old infants, marked differences for 12- to 15-month-olds, and small differences for 8- to 10-month-olds. During separation, infants displayed equivalent levels of attachment to mother and metapelet, both substantially greater than toward a stranger. During reunion, infants showed greater attachment to their mothers than toward the metapelet, and greater toward either than toward the stranger.

It can be concluded from these studies that infants reared in environments that are normal for a particular culture reveal attachment behavior toward their primary caretakers. The extent of the attachment depends on how enjoyable and extensive their interactions have been. Cuddling, hugging, and playing with the infant contribute to the enjoyment.

no significant cultural difference

Mutuality. Attachment develops at various periods of a person's lifetime, but the first relationship appears to create the groundwork for future development. The infant–caretaker bond is described as a strong prototypical relationship. Attachment behavior in the first year of life has been well chronicled by Bowlby. Attachment behavior depends on infants' perceptual range and on their ability to understand the events in their world, which lead to changes in the manner in which attachment takes place (Bowlby, 1958).

How does attachment behavior begin? It can be said that attachment behavior between two people is mutual. The chief caregiver feeds the baby, changes its diapers, and satisfies its other physical needs. Infants appear to invite nurturant responses from the caregiver. Some researchers have suggested that during the first few days after birth the caregiver and infant are highly receptive to cues from one another and that their early interactions determine the type of future relationship they will have.

Early mutuality may thus lay the foundation for long-term patterns of interaction. For instance, caregivers who respond promptly and consistently to infants in the first few months of life are likely to have infants who cry less than others by the end of the first year. Another result is the degree of confidence babies develop in the effectiveness of their communications. With inconsistent care, infants do not develop confidence and become inconsistent and less responsive themselves. When the caretaker creates a secure relationship, the infant develops a basis for establishing other competencies, such as active exploration, early mastery in play, and meaningful relationships with others in the immediate environment.

Touching and responses to it, eye-to-eye contact, odor, body heat and body movements, and voice tones are all reciprocal behaviors that result in attachment. Bowlby (1958) explained a child's attachment to its mother in terms of a tendency he called *monotropy:* the tendency of instinctual responses to be directed toward a particular person or group of individuals and not promiscuously toward many people.

How do adults become attached to their infants? For 12 months Klaus and Kennell (1976) studied factors that led to parents' attachment to an infant and came up with seven principles that are crucial components in the process of attachment.

1. There is a sensitive period in the first minutes and hours after the child is born. The process of attachment is so structured that the parents should have close contact then with their neonate for later development to be optimal.

2. There appears to be a species-specific response to the infant in the human mother and father (caretakers) when they are first given their infant.

3. The process of attachment is so structured that parents will become optimally attached to one child at a time. (Bowlby stated this principle in the other direction and termed it monotropy.)

4. During the process of the mother's attachment to her infant, it is important that the infant respond to the mother by some signal, such as body or eye movements. As Klaus and Kennell put it, "You cannot love a dishrag."

5. Individuals who witness the birth process become strongly attached to the infant.

6. For some persons it is difficult to go through the processes of attachment and detachment simultaneously; that is, to develop an attachment to one person while mourning the loss or threatened loss of the same or another person. Therefore the timing of birth in relation to other events may have long-lasting effects.

7. Anxiety about the well-being of a baby with a temporary disorder in the first day of life may result in enduring concerns that cast long shadows and adversely shape the development of the child.

No form of behavior is accompanied by stronger feelings than attachment behavior. The people toward whom it is directed are loved, and they are greeted with signs of happiness and joy. Loss of the attachment, or threat of loss, creates anxiety; actual loss causes sorrow and often anger. These responses are explored under the topic of separation.

Separation

When a child has developed a close relationship with a caretaker, separation from the caretaker causes a three-stage reaction in the child: protest, despair, and detachment (Bowlby, 1980). During the protest period, children may refuse to be separated from the person to whom they are attached. They reveal their tension by crying, kicking, and banging their heads. Second, children lose all hope and cry monotonously with despair but not anger. As children lose hope, they become very quiet. As time passes, separated children proceed to the third stage, accepting attention from all people who are part of their environment, and show no special attraction to a former primary caretaker who visits them. Instead, they may react to this person with disinterest or detachment. Bowlby views detachment as a form of defense mechanism that is a regular constituent of mourning at any stage in the life cycle.

The duration of a child's detachment from the mother correlates highly and significantly with the length of separation. A child who has been separated from the mother for a long period of time does not respond to the chief caretaker when the reunion takes place. Many mothers returning after separation are puzzled and wounded by this reaction; even when hurt, the child does not attempt to seek her comfort.

We can conclude that long-term detachment of an infant from its chief caretaker has negative effects on the infant, which reverberate to the caretaker. Furthermore, the relationship between caretaker and infant is based on mutuality and reciprocity; each needs feedback from the other to maintain a meaningful relationship.

Twenty-four-year-old Betty, a woman from the inner city, was arrested for selling drugs. Betty had a number of problems, and her only source of joy was her 18-month-old, Kristie. The day of her arrest, everything had gone wrong. Her boyfriend beat her up. When she went home to her mother's, where she had continued to live off and on, her stepfather, who had previously attempted to seduce her, beat her up on the pretext that she had been on the streets the whole day. Her only love was Kristie, but before she could make any attempt to see the child, her stepfather threw her out. In a short while she was arrested for prostitution. Nobody bothered to bail her out. One month passed. She missed her baby, but nobody heard her pleas. She told her story again and again, begging to see her child. Eventually, with the help of the jail's social worker, she did get an opportunity to vent her feelings. After a month and a half, she got out and went home. Her greatest pain and disappointment in the experience came when Kristie looked through her mother as if she did not exist. This separation had affected the mother–child relationship.

Separation is not always something planned. Illness, unforeseen circumstances, or accidents could bring about separation. The infant's failure to understand can cause tremendous pain on both sides.

Parental Roles

All parental actions play a part in shaping a child's personality. Infants cope, adapt, and develop in response to adults' actions toward them, whether the actions are purposeful or unintentional. The warmth or hostility of the parent–child relationship can be understood with reference to acceptance or rejection, the control or autonomy of the disciplinary approach (that is, restrictiveness or permissiveness), and the parents' disciplinary consistency.

Mothers. The newborn child is seen by society as an extension of the mother. The mother has to live up to certain expectations of society. Mothers are usually judged by the extent to which their children follow the normative expectations of growth and behavior. The mother is expected to anticipate, elicit, and respond to phase-specific behavior of the child, and to do so intuitively. During the first few months, the mother is expected to respond to every need of the child. She is the object of a symbiotic relationship: she is expected to shield the baby, mediate between the baby and excessive stimulation, and reciprocate the child's first efforts at playing and taking the initiative. After the sixth month, she is expected to accept both the assertiveness of the baby and the demands that she alone can meet.

The common assumption is that the mother's role comes naturally to all women. In reality, this is not true; not all women can automatically become model mothers. Mothering is a trial-and-error process in which the mother learns to understand and take care of the baby. Some women find this role self-actualizing and others do not.

Broussard and Hartner (1971) have reported pioneering work on the effect of maternal expectations on the psychological development of the infant. They found that negative maternal perceptions of the behavior of 1-month-old infants were highly predictive of social and emotional problems in these young children when they were $4\frac{1}{2}$ and 10 years old.

Some studies of temperament have explored the relationship between maternal behavior and maternal ratings of a child's temperamental "difficultness." Kelly (1976) found that maternal ratings of difficult temperament were related to negative mother–infant interactions. However, a study by Bates (1977) found no significant relationship between maternal ratings of "difficultness" and maternal behavior.

In a recent study on the relationship between maternal perception and maternal behavior in a "normal" group of 9-month-old infants and their mothers, Nover, Shore, Timberlake, and Greenspan (1984) found that the mothers tended to perceive their babies accurately and responded appropriately to their cues. Nevertheless, certain distortions did appear between perceptions and behavior, as a consequence of which the mothers' behavior became less responsive and more interfering. This maternal response correlated with the anxiety level of the mothers; in addition, those distortions were associated with sleeping difficulties among the children. This study suggests that there is a range of normal behavior between mothers and infants. It is clear that some perceptual distortion, due to the presence of feelings, is inherent in normal interpersonal interactions. Future research may help to identify the point at which maternal misperceptions become pathological and the differences, if any, in the nature of distortions among pathological and normal groups.

A study was made of maternal stress and social support and their effects on maternal–infant relationships from the infant's birth to the age of 18 months. Social support is generally considered to encompass several dimensions, among them instrumental assistance, information provision, and emotional empathy and understanding. Henderson, Byrne, and Duncan-Jones (1981) proposed that social support to reduce maternal stress operates on a number of ecological levels, including intimate relationships, friendships, and less formal neighborhood or community contacts. Having such a support framework theoretically indicates that the individual is cared for, loved, valued, and is a member of a network of mutual obligation.

Cochran and Brassard (1979) have specifically suggested that social support networks outside the nuclear family influence parental attitudes and behavior and, in turn, have both direct and indirect effects on child development.

Crnic, Greenberg, Ragazin, Robinson, and Basham (1983) studied an initial sample of 105 mother–infant pairs. Of the 105 infants, 52 were premature (born after less than 38 weeks of gestation and having a birth weight of less than 1800 grams) and 53 were full term (39 to 42 weeks of gestation and birth weight greater than 2500 grams). None of the infants revealed any gross neurological or physical impairment. Infants were case matched for family ethnicity and mother's education; there was no significant difference between the groups in mother's marital status, type of delivery, or child's sex or birth order. Mothers' perceived levels of stress and social support were found to be significant predictors of maternal attitudes and of the quality of interaction with their infants when measured concurrently across an 18-month period. However, long-term predictions were poor; maternal stress and support factors were only moderately stable. The quality of the infants' interactional behavior was also affected by levels of maternal stress and support, but only during the early measurement periods of 1 to 4 months.

Fathers.   Most research on child development has focused on the relationship between mother and child, paying little attention to the relationship between father and child. Research evidence shows that children who have frequent and regular contact with their fathers do form early attachments to them. The stronger the attachment, the more influence the father has over the child. There is a strong continuity between father–child interaction in infancy and in later childhood. Fathers who are accessible to their infants may find it easy to establish strong emotional ties later. In our culture, the father is often viewed as the secondary caregiver, but he does play an important role in the complex family interaction. A study by Clarke-Stewart (1978) of three-way patterns in families showed that the mother's influence on the child is direct, whereas the father's influence is indirect, through the mother. The child influences both parents directly. Studies show that fathers tend to be physical and spontaneous with their infants, and play between fathers and children occurs in cycles of high excitement and attention followed by periods of minimal activity.

When fathers become primary caretakers in our society, they tend to act more as mothers do. They smile more at their infants, imitate their facial expressions, and vocalize with them more than secondary fathers do.

> Tom was a 27-year-old single parent. He had won a custodial court battle with his estranged wife, a drug addict. He was a caring, loving father. At 2 years of age, the child developed pneumonia, and Tom panicked. Overly anxious about the child, as well as fearful that his former wife would use the situation against him, he became unable to function as a "normal" parent. The social worker at the Family and Child Center reassured him through emotional support, while emphasizing that if a child is sick all that a parent can do is to take care of the child. If problems arose with his former wife, he would need to deal with them as they appeared and not spend time anticipating trouble.

Child-Care Centers

In 1976, 6.5 million children had working mothers, and since then the trend for women to enter the job market has increased tremendously. As the number of women in the work force has grown, more and more mothers have turned to daycare centers for the care of their children. A daycare center's effect on a child depends on the quality of the program, the amount of time the child spends at the center, and the interactions between parent and child when they stay home together.

Kagan, Kearsley, and Zalazo (1978), of Tufts University Medical Center, set up a daycare facility for 40 children from middle- and working-class homes in Boston's South End. Children entered the center at 4 months of age and left at 29 months. The caretakers were chosen on the basis of their nurturing qualities, and the ratio of teachers to children was 1 : 3 or 1 : 4. These children were compared with home-reared children of the same age, social class, and ethnic background. Kagan and his associates found that daycare children were no more or less attached to their mothers than children raised at home. However, home-raised youngsters were more sociable at 29 months of age than daycare children.

Multiple Mothering

In the United States the usual environment for raising children is the nuclear family, which consists of two parents and their children. The concept that mothering should be provided by one individual has been underscored by most professionals as the key to mental health. But this view has been found to be a culture-bound perspective, for throughout the world children are cared for in situations of multiple mothering, an arrangement in which responsibility for a child's care is distributed among a number of people. Children reveal a remarkable resilience, and they do cope with and adapt to multiple mothering. In the Israeli agricultural economy a collective form of social and economic life is the kibbutzim. From early infancy children in Israeli kibbutzim are reared in a nursery with other children by two or three professional caretakers. The responsibility for disciplining and punishment falls upon professional caretakers (Devereux, Shouval, Bronfenbrenner, Rodgers, Veneki, Keely, & Kenson, 1974), but the children's affectional needs are usually satisfied by their mothers.

Shared parenting is an egalitarian arrangement whereby each parent works part time and takes care of the child part time. The child is consistently and alternately in the charge of two caring adults who have a lot in common in terms of family living. The child learns to accept and become part of this two-parent rearing pattern.

Child Abuse and Neglect

Child abuse can be described as nonaccidental physical attack on or injury to children by an older individual. Called by doctors the *battered child syndrome*, a pattern of such mistreatment of a child, typically by a caretaker, results in abrasions, burns, fractures, concussions, and bruises. Neglect can be described as the absence of adequate emotional, social, and physical care. Steele and Pollack (1968) found that, without exception, abusive parents were raised in an authoritarian atmosphere, which they recreate for their own children. Abusive parents come from all segments of the population: all socioeconomic strata, all levels of education and intelligence, and most religious and ethnic groups. Abusers do not fall into a single psychiatric diagnostic category but represent an entire spectrum of emotional disorders that can be seen in any clinical population.

The topic of child abuse and neglect is depressing, particularly so because the practice is self-perpetuating. Children learn how to love from their parents, but if they are unloved and abused they often become abusive or unloving parents. Kempe, Silverman, Steele, Droegenmueller, and Silver (1962) found that about 80% of abusive parents could be helped so that they no longer physically punish their children. Both short-term and long-term help are widely available. Many cities have hot lines for parents to call when they are losing control, and some areas offer around-the-clock crisis nurseries to relieve parents in need of a few hours of peace. Long-term help, in the form of individual and family therapy, is also offered to caretakers who seek it or are mandated by the family courts to receive it.

Nationwide attention to child abuse has made people aware of the problem and in some ways has effectively curbed it.

Teresa, a Puerto Rican, was a single parent from a lower socioeconomic group. Among her varied problems, she had little money, no steady job, and no place to call home. She had left Puerto Rico with the hope of finding a job and making it big in New York. But the reality was that her boyfriend deserted her a few months after they arrived in New York, leaving her pregnant with Juan. She could not forgive the child for being born; he was definitely unwanted. Her stress, already high, increased every time she faced rejection in a place of prospective employment. By the time Juan was 6 months old, she could not stand him. Her impulse control was minimal, and so she began battering him. She felt tremendously guilty after each episode and would attempt to make it up to the child. Eventually Juan wound up in the hospital. The social worker saw Teresa as a lonely, lost young woman who even had difficulty communicating in the English language. The worker attempted to help Teresa secure a job and gave her information about where to leave her child if she needed a few hours of rest and time away from him. Thus with the help of an extremely empathetic worker, Teresa learned to make use of the center for temporary daycare services.

The Institutionalized Child

The first large-scale study of institutionalized children was done by R. A. Spitz (1945; 1946), an Austrian psychoanalyst-physician. He compared two groups of infants during their first year of life, one group in a foundling home and the other group in a prison nursery. In the foundling home, the children were well fed and physically well cared for by the overworked nursery personnel. The babies in the prison nursery spent most of their time with their mothers and received individual care.

Spitz found that children who were raised by their own mothers made better progress in development than the babies in the foundling home who, despite their impeccable care, were susceptible to infection and illness. He also found that the infants in the foundling home tended toward severe mental and motor retardation. As Spitz interpreted his results, the impairment of the mother–child relationship during the first year of life inflicts permanent damage on a child.

A study by Wayne Dennis (1973) also emphasized the retarding effects of institutional life upon infants. However, Dennis found the cause not in the absence of mother–child contact but in the absence of adequate cognitive experiences. In the 1950s and 1960s Dennis studied infants in a foundling home. Because of a shortage of staff, children were taken out of their cribs only for short periods of time, to be bathed or changed. Children who were 2 or 3 years of age spent a large amount of time in their playpens and cribs. They had little opportunity to walk and creep on the floor. Infants under 1 year of age could not sit alone, crawl, or creep and the children who were 2 years of age could not walk. Dennis conducted intelligence tests and found that the 2-year-olds averaged an IQ score of 53, which classified them as mentally retarded. But those foundlings who had been adopted by the age of 2 showed rapid increase in capabilities, and they quickly reached an IQ of approximately 100. The test scores of children adopted after they reached 2 years of age did not reveal much development beyond the mental age of those children who remained in the foundling home.

The Spitz and Dennis studies have been criticized for faulty design and interpretation (Biehler, 1976). It was observed that most of the serious decline evident in the foundling home studied by Spitz predated the infants' separation from their mothers. In both of the studies, some of the children were placed in foster care during their first year, raising the question of whether the unadopted or unplaced children were in some way less desirable and hence unrepresentative. Those children had been twice screened and twice rejected; first their parents could not establish a home for them and then prospective foster parents had selected another child (Jersild, Telford, & Sawrey, 1975).

Development of Personality

A concept of self begins to develop in infancy, when the child begins to differentiate himself or herself from the environment. By the age of 1, most infants indicate genuine interest in self-recognition. This often shows up in mirror play. As thought and self-awareness develop, the child comes to think of himself or herself as being tall or strong or talkative or healthy or slow or dull or awkward or dirty. Obviously the child makes these self-references because of his or her earlier learning experiences.

Another way of understanding self-awareness in a child is to assess the child's use of personal pronouns: I, my, and so forth. Observing children in the age groups between 13 and 24 months, Kagan (1981) found a significant increase in 19- to 24-month-olds both in the use of self-referent words and in the use of words to accompany action. For example, while climbing onto a tall chair, a little girl described her actions by saying "Up." In a recent study of 2-year-old boys, Levine (1983) found that those who had a more advanced sense of self (which was measured by mirror and pronoun use) interacted more positively with other 2-year-olds than those who had a less mature view of themselves. Levine concluded that the possessiveness of a 2-year-old actually may reflect the child's attempt to interact socially with another child, and thus develop greater self-awareness. The sense of self that develops in infancy increases in complexity with cognition and social maturity. As the child grows older, he or she becomes more self-assertive.

Implications for Social Work Practice

Infancy is a significant period in a child's life. To maximize their understanding of its developmental issues, social workers need to be aware of factors such as child-rearing practices in various North American cultures. Parents' expectations regarding children's autonomy and self-discipline vary with their lifestyle and background. For instance, studies show that working-class families tend to do less talking and explaining to their children and to use more physical methods of discipline than do middle-class parents. They expect a greater degree of compliance from their children (Miller & Swanson, 1966). Behind this type of discipline is the assumption that it teaches children the most effective behaviors for the bureaucratic and technological world they will be entering. Middle-class parents usually pass on to children their verbal and negotiating skills, which they themselves value, believing that they will be rewarding as the child grows older.

Disciplinary techniques also vary according to ethnic and racial background. Native American children are usually disciplined in a nonverbal manner, by a stern look or occasional teasing (Miller, 1979). Some Black children may learn in their families that it is dangerous to challenge White authority openly or ask a number of questions. Researchers also note that there are social-class differences in child rearing within minority groups (Boutlette, 1978; Scanzoni, 1971).

In assessing a family, the social worker should take into account the number of children and caregivers in the family, as well as the degree of flexibility or rigidity that characterizes the family, because they have a bearing on the type of counseling offered.

Another important consideration is the parents' ability to set limits and make schedules without creating too much stress. Social work practitioners are frequently faced with parents who describe their child as a living monster. Usually effective parenting would make the child very amenable to discipline. When a child is described as "impossible," especially by a family with emotional problems, the worker often discovers that the parents are actually unwilling for the toddler to relinquish the aggressive behavior because it satisfies the needs of some adults in the family. In such cases, the child may not give up the difficult behavior, and it is the interaction in the family that should be the target of therapeutic help.

In offering help with toilet training, social workers can call upon a wide range of methods, depending on the family's own child-rearing practices. Social workers see a variety of adult attitudes toward children's explorations of their bodies as well as toward their need for autonomy. Some parents may be harsh and severe in toilet training, imposing strict rules about all behavior that requires self-mastery and independence, including feeding, dressing, and general exploration. Other parents tend to be tolerant, flexible, and responsive to the child's needs. Some parents view "accidents" as intolerable and dirty; some are severe when a child breaks a plate or cup; some regard children's games in mud and sand as unhygienic. Social workers should remember all these factors when they deal with parents so as to offer help appropriately.

Social workers should be able to help parents respond meaningfully to behavioral cues from their infants. Accordingly, practitioners should have an understanding of the developmental changes that take place in infancy. They should also be aware of women's needs, as well as their expectations of themselves as mothers. Some may need more help than others to play the role of mothers, and some may need an understanding of the infant's growth and development.

Under any conditions, the practitioner needs to have a holistic understanding of the growth and development of an infant and the influence of racial, ethnic, and social-class factors on the parent–child relationship. Social workers should also be aware of the support systems that can be made available to parents and children.

Nine-month-old Jason was brought by his parents to a crisis intervention center for child abuse. The child's body showed large bruises as well as bone fractures. The mother was crying silently. The child was sent for emergency treatment and the parents were referred to a staff social worker.

The social worker discovered that child abuse knows no boundaries. The parents were well-educated members of the upper-middle class. The father was about to take his final exam in engineering; the mother had a degree in social sciences. The mother had wanted a child, and the father had gone along even though he was not anxious to become a parent. Jason was born with a delicate stomach and could not digest food easily. He cried for long hours because his immature digestive system caused him pain. The mother had wanted the baby so she would have someone to love her always, and she was not "rewarded" by this baby.

With his final exam a week off, the father became exasperated whenever Jason started to cry. The mother was already nervous because she did not envision that a parenting role would be so demanding. While the baby cried and her husband screamed, she felt unloved by both of them. Overcome by the mounting stress, both parents abused the child. If Jason had not had a delicate digestive system, his parents might not have responded to him in that manner. They were frightened and ashamed that they had done something wrong. The parents were referred to a support group for group counseling, where they would be helped to understand their own limitations as well as their misconceptions about the baby. They were genuinely regretful of their behavior, and the social worker gave them an emergency number to call in case they again became overwhelmed by stress.

Jim was a 1-year-old who had been placed with an agency on account of neglect by his family. The mother claimed that she loved her son but that the unusual circumstances of the preceding few months had caused her to neglect him. Her husband had been arrested for drug dealing and she was preoccupied with her livelihood. Several times, neighbors had found her son whining and crying because he had not eaten in a couple of days. At last the child was brought to the notice of the Social Services Bureau. In time, Jim was placed in a foster home. The available foster home could not offer Jim the sense of permanence that he required, and the social worker was not sure that any other home could. Meanwhile, the mother was overburdened with emotional turmoil, visits from the police, and lack of income. She was offered supportive services to help her deal with the loss of her husband and the circumstances of his arrest. The social worker tried to maintain as much contact as possible between Jim and his mother and continued to assess the mother's potential for offering Jim an environment in which he could grow up meaningfully without danger to his development.

Chapter Summary

The link between social and individual processes is important even during infancy. Development proceeds by the basic principles of movement from mass activity to specific activity, differentiation, and integration. Development of sensorimotor skills, postural control and locomotion, manual skills, and language, as well as physical habits such as feeding and sleep, are affected by the biological, psychological, and social environment of the child. With the supports available, the child responds to positive and negative environmental cues and copes with and adapts to stresses according to its potentials.

Erikson's theory of development emphasizes psychosocial and not psychosexual interaction. He believes that the developmental conflict of this early stage—autonomy versus doubt and shame—may be reworked and satisfactorily resolved later in life.

White emphasizes that all infants have an innate drive to be competent and efficacious. Eating, learning toilet habits, and playing are explorations of competence and efficiency.

Piaget's theory emphasizes assimilation and accommodation. Piaget classifies the child's cognitive development into four major periods, the first of which is the sensorimotor period (from birth to 2 years of age). It is subdivided into six stages: (1) the beginning of systematic use of natural reflexes, (2) primary circular reaction, (3) secondary circular reaction, (4) threshold of intelligent behavior, (5) tertiary circular reaction, and (6) the stage of schemata. During the sensorimotor period, infants acquire concepts that are connected with the use of familiar objects. The expression of their potentialities is seen in their play and their growing use of language.

In relation to critical environmental issues, attachment behavior was discussed. In a secure attachment, a child explores new things as well as new people. Infants first show anxiety about separation when they are about 9 months of age. It is part of the normal development of children as they learn to distinguish between familiar caregivers and strangers. Loss of attachment leads to serious consequences for the infant's personality development. A child who is not given the opportunity to develop a pattern of consistent responses with the primary caretaker will be unable to develop an attachment relationship.

Child-rearing practices vary from culture to culture. Caretakers' attitudes towards feeding and toilet training convey information to children about their ability to depend on themselves and the nature of their bodies. From the total sum of their social experiences, cognitive experiences, and growing cognitive skills, children develop attitudes about themselves.

As the number of working mothers increases, the need for daycare centers increases. Fathers are increasingly playing a role even during infancy.

Child abuse and neglect are problems that affect some infants and parents, and consequently concern social workers.

Institutionalized infants often suffer from maternal deprivation and an insufficiently stimulating environment.

Personality development begins when children start to distinguish themselves as separate individuals. Exploration begins when the child starts to feel secure. Self-assertiveness lays the foundation for meaningful personality development.

Social work practitioners must be aware of such factors as child-rearing practices, race, and ethnicity as they affect infants, their families, and their support systems. A holistic understanding of infancy provides a context for dealing with developmental issues.

References

Ainsworth, M. D. (1973). The development of mother–infant attachment. In B. M. Caldwell & H. N. Riccuito (Eds.), *Review of Child Development Research* (Vol. 3). Chicago: University of Chicago Press.

Ainsworth, M. D. S. (1963). Patterns of attachment behavior shown by the infant in interaction. In B. M. Foss (Ed.), *Determinants of infant behavior.* New York: Wiley.

Bates, J. (1977). The concept of difficult temperament. *Merrill-Palmer Quarterly, 26,* 211–226.

Benedict, H. (1975). The role of repetition in early language comprehension. Paper presented at the annual meeting of the Society for Research in Child Development, Denver.

Biehler, R. F. (1976). *Child development* (Introduction). Boston: Houghton Mifflin.

Boutlette, T. T. (1978). The Spanish-surnamed poor. In *Child welfare strategy* (Publication No. [OHDS] 78-30158). Washington, DC: U.S. Department of Health, Education and Welfare.

Bowlby, J. (1958). *Attachment* (Vol. 1). New York: Basic Books.

Bowlby, J. (1969). *Attachment and loss* (Vol. 1). New York: Basic Books.

Bowlby, J. (1980). *Loss* (Vol. 3). New York: Basic Books.

Braine, M. D. S. (1963). The ontogeny of English phrase structure: The first phase. *Language, 39,* 1–14.

Broussard, E., & Hartner, M. (1971). Further considerations regarding maternal perception of the first born. In J. Helmuth (Ed.), *Exceptional infant* (Vol. 2). New York: Brunner/Mazel.

Clarke-Stewart, K. A. (1978). And daddy makes three: The father's impact on mother and young child. *Child Development, 49,* 466–478.

Cochran, M., & Brassard, J. (1979). Child development and personal social networks. *Child Development, 50,* 601–616.

Cohen, L. J. (1974). The operational definition of human attachment. *Psychological Bulletin, 81,* 207–217.

Cohen, L. J., & Campos, J. J. (1974). Father, mother, and stranger as elicitors of attachment behaviors in infancy. *Developmental Psychology, 10,* 146–154.

Crnic, K. A., Greenberg, M., Ragazin, A., Robinson, W., & Basham, R. (1983). Effects of stress and social support on mothers and premature and full-term infants. *Child Development, 54,* 209–217.

Dennis, W. (1973). *Children of the creche.* New York: Appleton-Century-Crofts.

Devereux, E. C., Shouval, S., Bronfenbrenner, U., Rodgers, R. R., Veneki, K. V., Keely, S., & Kenson, E. (1974). Socialization practices of parents, teachers and peers in Israel: The kibbutz versus the city. *Child Development, 45.*

Dunn, J. E. (1976). Mother–infant relations: Continuities and discontinuities over the first 14 months. *Journal of Psychosomatic Research, 20,* 273–277.

Erikson, E. H. (1977). *Toys and reason.* New York: Norton.

Erikson, E. H. (1980). *Identity and the life cycle.* New York: Norton.

Flavell, J. (1963). *The developmental psychology of Piaget.* New York: Van Nostrand Reinhold.

Flavell, J. (1977). *Cognitive development.* Englewood Cliffs, NJ: Prentice-Hall.

Fox, R., Aslin, R. N., Shea, S. L., & Dumais, S. T. (1980). Stereopsis in human infants. *Science, 207,* 323–324.

Gesell, A. (1940). *The first five years of life: The pre-school years.* New York: Harper & Row.

Greenberg, M., Morris, I., & Lind, J. (1973). First mothers rooming-in with their newborns: Its impact on the mother. *American Journal of Orthopsychiatry, 43,* 783–788.

Henderson, S., Byrne, D., & Duncan-Jones, P. (1981). *Neuroses in the social environment.* New York: Academic Press.

Jersild, A. T., Telford, C. W., & Sawrey, J. M. (1975). *Child psychology.* Englewood Cliffs, NJ: Prentice-Hall.

Kagan, J. (1981). *The second year: The emergence of self-awareness.* Cambridge, MA: Harvard University Press.

Kagan, J., Kearsley, R. B., & Zalazo, P. R. (1978). *Infancy: Its place in human development.* Cambridge, MA: Harvard University Press.

Kalish, R., & Knudtson, F. W. (1976). Attachment vs. disengagement: A lifespan conceptualization. *Human Development, 19,* 171–181.

Kaluger, G., & Kaluger, M. F. (1979). *Human development.* St. Louis: C. V. Mosby.

Kelly, P. (1976). The relation of the infant's temperament and mother's psychopathology to interactions in early infancy. In K. Riegel & S. Meacham (Eds.), *The developing individual in a changing world* (Vol. 2). Chicago: Aldine-Atherton.

Kempe, C. H., Silverman, F. N., Steele, B. F., Droegenmueller, W., & Silver, H. K. (1962). The battered child syndrome. *Journal of the American Medical Association, 181,* 17–24.

Klaus, M. H., & Kennell, J. H. (1976). *Maternal–infant bonding.* St. Louis: C. V. Mosby.

Kotelchuck, M. (1972). The nature of the child's tie to his father. Paper presented at the annual meeting of the Society for Research in Child Development, Harvard University.

Lamb, M. E. (1977). A re-examination of the infant social world. *Human Development, 20,* 65–85.

Levine, L. (1983). Self-definition in two-year-old-boys. *Developmental Psychology, 19,* 544–549.

Lugo, J. O., & Hershey, G. L. (1979). *Human development.* New York: Macmillan.

Maccoby, E. E., & Masters, J. C. (1970). Attachment and dependency. In P. H. Mussen (Ed.), *Carmichael's manual of child psychology* (Vol. 2). New York: Wiley.

Miller, D. (1979). The Native American family: The urban way. In E. Corfman (Ed.) *Families today: A research sampler on families and children* (Vol. 1, pp. 79–815). Washington, DC: U.S. Dept. of Health, Education & Welfare.

Miller, D. R., & Swanson, G. E. (1966). *Inner conflict and defense.* New York: Schocken.

Nover, A., Shore, M. F., Timberlake, E. M., & Greenspan, S. I. (1984, April). Relationship of maternal perception and maternal behavior. *American Journal of Orthopsychiatry, 54,* 111–118.

Parke, R. (1974). Father–infant interaction. In M. H. Klaus, T. Leger, & M. A. Trause (Eds.), *Maternal attachment and mothering disorders: A round table.* Sausalito, CA: Johnston Systems Co.

Scanzoni, J. H. (1971). *The Black family in modern society.* Boston: Allyn & Bacon.

Specht, R., & Craig, G. (1982). *Human development.* Englewood Cliffs, NJ: Prentice-Hall.

Spitz, R. (1945). Hospitalization: An inquiry into the genesis of psychiatric conditions in early childhood. *Psychoanalytic Study of the Child, 1,* 53–74.

Spitz, R. (1946). Hospitalization: A follow-up. *Psychoanalytic Study of the Child, 2,* 113–117.

Steele, B. F., & Pollack, C. D. (1968). A psychological study of parents who abuse infants and small children. In R. C. Helfer & C. H. Kempe (Eds.), *The battered child.* Chicago: University of Chicago Press.

Tulkin, S., & Kagan, J. (1972). Mother–child interaction in the first year of life. *Child Development, 43,* 31–41.

Vander Zanden, J. W. (1977). *Human development.* New York: Knopf.

Weinraub, M., Brooks, J., & Lewis, M. (1977). The social network: A reconsideration of the concept of attachment. *Human Development, 20,* 31–47.

White, R. (1963). *The enterprise of living.* New York: Holt, Rinehart & Winston.

Yarrow, L. J. (1964). Separation from parents in early childhood. In M. C. Hoffman & L. W. Hoffman (Eds.), *Review of child development: Research* (Vol. 1). New York: Russell Sage Foundation.

4

Preschool Years

Physical Growth

New Skills

Cognitive Development

Language Development

The Psychosocial Environment

Moral Development

The Social Environment

Child-Rearing Practices and Patterns

Divorce

The Impact of Television

Implications for Social Work Practice

Chapter Summary

References

At 2 years of age, Frannie was becoming aware of herself as a person. She ran up and down and threw her toys around. She would tell her mother that she wanted to be taken out to the garden. Again and again she would say, "Frannie good girl, Frannie wants to go out." She would make up stories in which she was the most powerful person and say such things as "Frannie is *nice.*" This was the beginning of assertiveness and the development of self. By the time she reaches the age of 6, Frannie will have changed. She will be able to explain many of her feelings of loss and frustration and will be developing into a more thoughtful person.

Toward the end of infancy we find two distinctive features of development: the range of individual differences becomes more apparent, and the range of activities gradually shifts from those dominated by biological forces to those influenced by the forces of cognitive, social, and affective domains.

Physical Growth

Physical maturation follows a particular order. There are several aspects of physical development in the preschool child. Becoming aware of the concrete world around them, preschool children need to make solid contact with the outside world of people and objects, and they do many things to accomplish that goal. The tasks that the child has to perform at this stage are a continuation of the earlier developmental tasks.

Developmental tasks emphasize the maturational processes, or the unfolding of the child's natural potential for increased development of skills. The preschooler's developmental tasks have been classified by Kaluger and Kaluger (1979):

1. achieving integrated motor and perceptional control
2. completing control of the elimination of bodily wastes
3. achieving physiological stability
4. improving the ability to communicate and to comprehend what others say
5. achieving independence in self-care areas such as eating, dressing, and bathing
6. learning sex differences
7. forming simple concepts of social and physical reality and learning how to behave toward persons and things
8. learning to relate emotionally to parents, siblings, and other people
9. learning to distinguish between right and wrong and develop a conscience (to make value judgments).

Two-year-olds work at becoming competent. They can walk, run, and manipulate objects, but their coordination is still slow in improving. Compared to 4- or 5-year-olds, they are quite limited. Although they can push, pull, and hang by their hands, 2-year-old children have little enduring power.

They have to use both of their hands, arms, or legs for tasks that an older child would perform with one.

By the age of 3, the child is already likely to extend only one hand to receive one item and has begun to show a preference for either the right or left hand. Four-year-olds are able to vary the rhythm of their running, and many can skip rather awkwardly and execute a running jump. A child who is 4 can probably use a crayon to draw lines and circles, as well as simple faces.

New Skills

Preschool children learn physical-motor skills in everyday activities such as dressing themselves, drawing, skipping, and jumping. Kaluger and Kaluger (1979) report that Soviet preschool children are drilled in gymnastics and music, and they cite award-winning performances of 9-year-old gymnasts as evidence of the efficacy of this early training. American psychologists generally believe that young children learn best with a minimum of training and more free exploration. However, there is growing interest in the physical training given in other countries.

Developmental Tasks

There are also some developmental tasks that children learn at this age. One is self-control, which refers to children's ability to control their own impulses. Another is overt control, which refers to children's feelings that they can control events around them. Preschool children's responses are often vigorous and uncontrolled. They wish to have immediate gratification of their needs. Their temper tantrums are often expressions of extreme rage at the lack of gratification of some impulse. Although considerable attention has been paid to anger, there are other emotions that are equally difficult for the child to control, among them love, sadness, and fear.

Preschoolers seem to be particularly inept at modifying or interrupting an emotional response once it has begun. Although adults might succeed in distracting children and turning their attention to something else, toddlers often cannot do this for themselves.

As children grow older, they learn to control their impulses. In the later preschool stage, the child develops the ability to withstand delays in the gratification of impulses without experiencing the intense frustration characteristic of infancy. One factor enabling children to control frustration is the increased, though still rudimentary, sense of time, which involves some sense of the future. The control develops slowly as children come to understand that what they want, although not available to them at the moment, often is available after a brief delay. The knowledge that a need will eventually be met serves to reduce the intensity of the emotional response.

The development of symbolic imagination allows children to create imaginary situations in which problems that disturb them can be expressed and resolved. In fantasy play, children can control situations that far exceed their real-world capacities. In a make-believe world they can punish, forgive, harm and heal, fear and conquer fear, all within the boundaries of the imagination. They begin to learn to master their emotional needs.

Children also have high expectations of themselves. Many times, children's enthusiasm and confidence outstrip their real potential. They see a parent easily performing a task and would like to be able to do a similar task. Told by a parent that they may not try to do something, they become frustrated because they are certain that they will do a good job. They do not expect an unsuccessful outcome of their efforts, and denial of the opportunity discourages them. The best way to help a child is to offer assistance only as needed. As children engage in tasks that are beyond their capacity, they learn to assess their strengths and skills more realistically. By the end of their preschool years, children will be able to evaluate the requirements of a wide variety of tasks and judge whether they can accomplish them or not.

Physical Setting and Development

Physical surroundings affect a child's development. Some settings are more conducive than others to positive growth.

Shirley was born in the inner city. She was a single parent and had great difficulty managing on her limited finances. Frequently away from home to look for work, Shirley often left her toddler son Leonard in the apartment with her older daughter Clarissa, who was fourteen. The apartment was always disorderly, with clothing and food strewn everywhere. There was a constant bad odor. Clarissa attended school irregularly. She was more interested in getting her boyfriend to come home with her and having a good time with him than in taking care of her younger brother. When Leonard cried with hunger, Clarissa would hurriedly give him anything that was easily available just to shut him up. If he cried too much, she would beat him up, so Leonard learned not to disturb his sister. If he was hungry, he would whimper and cry softly as he did not know how to fend for himself in this disorganized atmosphere. Eventually his sister gave him something to eat. He was used to being beaten, so whenever his sister put out her hand he would shrink away in fear. He spent a lot of time watching TV and sucking his thumb. Seldom bathed, he had a strong body odor. His attitude toward people was one of suspicion. He would whimper and cry when he saw strangers and would shrink away if anyone tried to touch him, a result of the neglect and abuse in his environment.

Brought up in a middle-class neighborhood, Tony belonged to a close-knit family. Although Tony did not spend too much time with his father, he was comfortable around men, for his uncles, cousins, and grandfather lived nearby and visited each other often. Thus, he grew up as a member of a large family network. At a young age he felt secure and was friendly with everyone. He was verbal, sociable, and self-confident, having been nurtured by a large number of caring people.

Cognitive Development

There can be no cognitive development without sensory input. There can be no efficient perceptual development to provide the sensory input to the brain without a stable, balanced body position from which the senses can pick up stimuli with accuracy. There can be no stable frame of reference within which the perceptual constancy can take place without a sound motor structure on which perceptual systems can develop (Beck, 1976).

What happens internally when children learn? Something has to occur neurologically, because it is only by this means that any kind of cognitive consciousness can take place. The perceptual-motor processes must be adequately developed if children are to learn, read symbols, and understand abstract concepts. The more abstract, intricate, and complex the stimuli, the more the perceptual processes must be developed in order to perceive them and the more efficient perception must be in order to recognize differences and attach meanings to them. Developmental specialists and neurologists such as Gesell, Piaget, and Inhelder leave little doubt concerning the importance of combined perceptual and motor experiences in developing a neurological (mental) structure, organization, or pattern that can be responded to, retained, and recalled.

From a theoretical point of view, the basic neural system for learning consists of (1) a pattern of reflexes, including primitive motor, visual, auditory, vocal, and kinesthetic reflexes; (2) a motor response capability, including a postural weight-shift mechanism that provides symmetry and balance; (3) a memory endowment to retain and recall bits of information that have been learned; and (4) the ability to imitate certain behavior after a period of maturation (Kaluger & Kaluger, 1979).

Babies are bombarded with a lot of information from the world around them. To keep young children from overloading themselves, nature makes it possible for them to receive and perceive only the grossest stimuli and shut out the rest. As they become more capable of handling finer, more precise stimuli, they become more aware of them. Handling these stimuli and selecting those that are most significant for them are part of the perceptual process.

Piaget: The Preoperational Stage

During the sensorimotor period, infants show by their outward behavior and their interactions with the environment that their dominant mental activity involves overt actions. Very little internal intellectualization takes place until the close of the sensorimotor period. During the preoperational period there will be an increase in differentiating internalization of verbal and nonverbal symbols. The child is beginning to differentiate between verbal and nonverbal symbols, responds to them accordingly, and internalizes these perceptions into his or her personality. If a parent smiles at her 5-year-old son and tells him not to take the cookie from the plate, the child will take it anyway, because he is responding to her nonverbal communication, which says that it is all right to take the cookie. As children grow older, they differentiate between verbal and nonverbal communication as they observe it and also absorb it into their personalities. The child becomes able to make internal responses that represent objects or events even if those objects and events are not present.

The preoperational stage of cognitive development begins at approximately 2 years of age. There are several characteristics of cognitive function noted during this period that Piaget views as obstacles to logical thinking:

1. Egocentrism. The child is unable to imagine or realize that another person may be viewing the same problem or situation from another perspective or angle. The child believes, "Whatever I can see, everybody can see."
2. Centering. The child is centered on one detail of an event and cannot take into account other features that are also important. Thus, the child cannot see variations. Focusing on a single part, however salient, leads to illogical reasoning.
3. Irreversibility. The child is unable to change the direction of his or her thinking to return to its point of origin. For instance, a preoperational child taking a walk would be unable to retrace the route accurately.

Stages of preoperational thought.   The two substages of development in the preoperational period are called the *preconceptual stage,* or *period of symbolic thought,* and the *period of intuitive thought.* During the preconceptual stage, children begin to associate certain objects with other objects they represent. Children begin to participate in symbolic play. (Play and its importance in childhood will be presented in another section of this chapter.)

When a 4-year-old child is asked if he has a brother, the child replies affirmatively and mentions that his brother's name is John. If asked, "Does John have a brother?" the child would answer no. The child is unable to grasp the notion that having a brother necessarily involves being a brother or sister to someone else.

From about 4 to 7 years of age is the period of intuitive thought. During this period, children can think in a more complex fashion, and they can elaborate their concepts. Their egocentrism tends to be replaced by social behavior and social interaction.

Concept formation.   Children do not learn to internalize verbal images until the age of 2. After that age their language development provides them with words that represent objects and events in the environment. In the beginning stages, words do not have much meaning other than as labels—an answer to the question "What is it?" At a later stage they ask questions such as "Where does it go?" and "What makes it go?" Slowly, they begin to use words as mediators for reasoning. Concepts learned by children before the age of 5 have only surface meaning, with no depth of insight or relationship to other concepts (Kaluger & Kaluger, 1979).

Preschool children cannot cope with definite perceptions of various situations but can take into account only one idea or dimension at one time. Concepts such as time and numbers mean little to children. However, concepts of space and size develop more readily. When a child is mentally 3 years of age, he or she can select the largest as well as the smallest objects from a group of objects of varying sizes.

Classification, seriation, and conservation.   According to Piaget (Piaget & Inhelder, 1969), classification is the ability to sort stimuli such as colors, shapes, or sizes into categories according to their characteristics. From 2 to about 4 years of age, children learn to make figural designs. As children continue to grow, they perform quasiclassification, moving freely from one basis to another and mixing colors and shapes.

Seriation is the ability to arrange objects in sequence according to one or more relevant dimensions, such as increasing or decreasing size, weight, or volume. By age 4 or 5, children learn to pick up longer or smaller sticks. Seriation by weight is usually not attained until age 9 and seriation of volume not until age 12.

Conservation is the recognition that matter remains the same in quantitative characteristics—substance, weight, length, number, and volume or area—regardless of any changes in shape or position, so long as nothing has been added or taken away. For example, if we have a row of eight pennies, and move them farther apart in the row, we still have eight pennies. A 4- or 5-year-old may think that there are more in the row once it has been spread out. When a piece of clay is made into a ball then remolded into a log, the child may think that the log has more clay than the ball because it looks longer. According to Piaget, a child cannot conserve substance until age 6 to 7. The child learns the principle of conservation only when able to decenter perceptions, reverse operations, and attend to "transformations." ("Transformation" is Piaget's term for the ability to tell that one state or appearance has changed to another [Piaget & Inhelder, 1969].)

Language Development

Language development is one of the major accomplishments of childhood. By the time children are 2 years of age, they can use about 100 words. By the time they are $2\frac{1}{2}$, they can generally use twice that many. After $4\frac{1}{2}$ years of age, children acquire at least 50 words a month (Mussen, Conger, Kagan, & Geiwitz, 1979).

By 5 to 6 years of age, the child is proficient with speech and can use a wide variety of words. During this preschool period of life, a child asks a large number of questions about everything. Development of language is connected with a child's ability to think. Language makes it possible for children to put thoughts and feelings into words.

Children refrain from talking loudly unless they are talking to others and develop the art of covert speech while manipulating a toy or an object. The function of language begins to take on the purpose of communicating thoughts to other people.

Initially, children's vocabularies consist principally of nouns, although they use a few verbs and adjectives or adverbs. In the beginning of speech development, children hardly ever use pronouns, conjunctions, or prepositions. Much of their vocabulary is learned by hearing words in context. At this stage their grammar is anything but flawless; they may say "Bringed my toy," "I goed home," and so forth. But as their vocabulary increases, their grammar improves as well. Language is a social skill, and through it children learn to communicate complex feelings and motivations to others. They use language to solve problems and gather information. Slobin (1972) and his colleagues studied the acquisition of language in many countries and found that there are remarkably consistent patterns from culture to culture.

Language can be acquired through imitation, reinforcement, innate mental structure, and cognitive development. The first words children speak are acquired through hearing and then imitating. Reinforcement is the reaction to this imitative speech. Children are likely to repeat words that bring favorable responses such as smiles, hugs, and increased attention. All people are born with an innate mental structure for acquiring language, and this structure enables children to assimilate certain data before others. There is a close interrelationship between language and cognitive development.

The relationship between language and the transmission of cultural behavior from one generation to the next becomes important during the preschool period.

Language and Culture

Every culture determines what uses of speech are appropriate, just as it dictates pronunciation, syntax, and vocabulary. In many Asian cultures politeness is an important factor, and therefore children learn polite forms of expression at an early age. Learning correct use of language includes learning thousands of behavioral details, such as knowing what form of address to use, what tone of voice to adopt, and what is considered rude or polite.

Appropriate language usage is dependent on the social relationship between speaker and listener. People show their awareness of another person's status by their tone of voice, grammar, and mode of address. A domineering father will usually convey his expectations of obedience and respect from his children by his tone of voice and the use of command form rather than request. His children may respond by modulating their voices and using polite forms of address. Generally, children are quick to perceive degrees of status and to adapt their speech to conform to the requirements of a wide variety of social settings.

In 1979, Anderson studied how children between 4 and 7 years of age learn appropriate speech for a topic, listener, and situation. Anderson found that even the youngest children had a clear understanding of social context and power relationships, and they adjusted their vocabulary and speech accordingly. Four-year-olds expressed their understanding of social position by varying the pitch and loudness of their speech.

> Tina was 4 years of age and had a good relationship with her mother. However, she was afraid of her father, who had frightened her by disciplining her with his loud voice. Although Tina would laugh, scream, and shout in front of her mother, she became timid, shy, and polite when her father came home. She kept her voice low and played the quiet little girl, as was expected of her.

Status and role awareness are important aspects of language communication. The structure and content of language also reflect one's social class and ethnic identification. There is literature in the social sciences showing relationships between socioeconomic status and language style, although there also is considerable difference of opinion about the nature and implications of these relationships. Middle-class parents consciously use language to initiate questioning of cause and effect, whereas working-class parents tend to give commands that control behavior and to spend less time explaining rules and reasons to their children.

Hispanic cultures focus on people rather than abstractions and on familial values rather than the competitiveness and independent learning styles of individuals, and this focus is developed in part via language.

There is a distinction between a lower-class restricted language and a middle-class elaborated language. The middle-class language is more complex and offers children a wider choice of syntax to express themselves and greater opportunities to develop more flexible and creative speech patterns (Specht & Craig, 1982).

Labov (1970) cites the richness and complexity of Black English as evidence that nonstandard English is no less complicated in structure than middle-class English. Labov and other recent researchers view Black English as an ordered and syntactically consistent dialect rather than a collection of careless errors, and Labov addresses this issue in his theory of language deficiency (1970).

Language Disorders

Social workers need to be aware of language disorders in children, which lead to complications for them in the social world. In some children, the failure to learn normally is due to a disruption in the sensory system, as happens with deaf children, or in the conceptual system, as with a brain-damaged or mentally retarded child. Language problems could also arise in the child's affective and social development, as seen in childhood schizophrenia or autism (Bloom, 1980).

Children disrupt form, content, and use of language when they have a language disorder. Some children with behavioral disorders develop some ideas about the world (language content) and appropriate principles for interacting with other persons (language use) but are unable to learn words and structures that provide the forms of language. Some children may learn repetitive and mechanical ways of interaction but may not be able to represent regularities in language content in a meaningful way. Some children may learn linguistic forms to represent certain categories of content but will not be able to interact with other persons so as to learn the use of such content–form interactions. Some children may learn language in the same way as normal children do, but not as rapidly, and their language development may be arrested at some early stage (Bloom & Lahey, 1978).

A child who is 2 to 4 years of age and is learning a language slowly and with difficulty may also have trouble learning to read and write later in school. Thus, by the time the child is 7 to 8 years of age, he or she is seen as having a learning disability. Bloom mentions that it is not clear what happens to such children with language disorders through the life span. However, he adds (Bloom, 1980) that a language disorder is, by itself, a learning disability.

The Psychosocial Environment

Developmental issues in the preschool period include continued dependency and the growing need for autonomy, mastery, and competence. Erik Erikson (1963) points out that feelings of hope as well as competencies promote the feelings of autonomy essential to the development of greater independence. Preschool children also develop a sense of self-esteem. Growth during the preschool years takes place through the process of identification, the learning of sex roles, and a sense of conscience.

Erikson: Initiative versus Guilt

Erikson indicates that preschool children experience a developmental crisis as their decreasing dependency creates conflict in their lives—conflict between what is possible and what is permissible, as well as conflict between what is acceptable and what is unacceptable. As children develop their intellectual capacities, they also become aware of their powers, meaning the ability to make things happen. They become more and more aware that they can control their own bodies and consequently affect the physical environment. Their increased ability to be complex and creative is combined with new-found self-confidence and a well-established faith that parents watching from the background are ready to provide psychosocial supports. The preschool child is ready to explore the world with more vigor, incessant curiosity, and verbal eagerness.

During this stage, children are ready and eager to learn and work cooperatively with others to achieve their goals. At the same time, they begin to understand that other people have different motivations and perceptions. They learn from and are willing to accept the guidance of parents, teachers, and others. The child's energy is directed toward possible and meaningful goals, which permit the dreams of early childhood to be attached to the goals of a future active adult life.

The crisis of this stage is that children's newfound energies lead them to act in ways that will make them feel guilty. The child has a great sense of power, but it comes with an increasing awareness of required limitations on behavior. Violating those limitations produces guilt.

> Aaron was angry with his little sister and wanted to push her out of her crib, but he knew that if he did, his mother would punish him. He was angry with the baby for all the extra attention she was getting in the family, but he also understood that he had to control his impulse to hurt her because acting on it would bring him punishment.

Ethical behavior consists of more than avoiding punishments by behaving properly. It means understanding the needs of others as well as one's own.

Like Aaron, children face two important revelations in the preschool period: first, experiencing themselves as more powerful than ever, and second, beginning to realize that they must control their own behavior and that they will feel guilty if they fail to do so. As Erikson puts it, "The child indulges in fantasies of being a giant and a tiger but in his dreams he runs in terror for dear life."

If children handle the crisis of guilt well, they will function in ways that allow them to use their initiative constructively. They will find it pleasurable to use their own power and be able to cooperate and accept help from others. Erikson (1963) says:

> There is in every child at every stage a new miracle of vigorous unfolding, which constitutes a new hope and a new responsibility for all. Such is the sense and the pervading quality of initiative. The criteria for all these senses and qualities are the same. A crisis is more or less beset with fumbling and fear, and is resolved, in that the child suddenly seems to "grow together" both in his person and in his body. He appears "more himself," more loving, relaxed and brighter in his judgment, more activated and activating. He is in free possession of a surplus of energy which permits him to forget failures quickly and to approach what seems desirable (even if it also seems uncertain and even dangerous) with undiminished and more accurate direction.

For some children, however, matters do not work out so well; they may be unable to find a balance between initiative and guilt. Their own desires for control and mastery may come into conflict with either the wish for the acceptance and support of others or the dictates of conscience. The conflict may lead them to overcontrol themselves, and they may become resentful of their sense of inner control. Children who do not resolve such a crisis may grow into adults who have feelings of inadequacy.

School social workers sometimes see children who lack self-confidence and are not assertive with their classmates. Children whose parents do not encourage them in new activities or who frighten them when they wish to venture into new activities may become anxious and learn to deny, minimize, or even disguise their need for autonomy. This pattern occurs more often with young girls than young boys.

> Five-year-old Pam made the mistake of playing with the vacuum cleaner and accidentally turned it on. Frightened, she screamed and cried. Her mother came running to her rescue but also punished Pam for touching the vacuum cleaner. That scared Pam, and it was a long time before she would go near a vacuum cleaner again.

If parents constantly curb children's initiatives at this period through discouragement as well as punishment, they may induce anxiety in the child and prevent or slow down the child's development of autonomy.

Children with physical and mental handicaps have fewer opportunities than others to test their skills in interacting with the environment. However, actively employed disabled people are more visible than ever before and should provide meaningful role models for handicapped children in developing their own autonomy and initiative.

White: Developing Competence

White (1976) considers Erikson's formulation of the dynamics characterizing the preschool years in terms of the competence model. He believes that the child is brought nearer to his crisis by developments in three spheres of competence: locomotion, language, and imagination. (Discussion of White's theory uses masculine pronouns because White's theory has a male bias.)

Walking and running reach the point of being serviceable tools rather than difficult stunts. The child can walk and run freely, cover a large territory, and use his tricycle to get around wherever he wants to. He likes to race up and down the stairs or the gym. The development of these seemingly adult patterns makes it possible for children to compare themselves with grownups, yet they wonder about the differences in size. They also like to dress in adult clothes and imitate adult behavior.

As their language skills increase, children gain wider understanding of people's behavior and social exchange. Rhyme making attests to and produces a growing mastery of speech, and the child begins to understand such subtleties as the meanings of *could* and *might.*

Imagination is the third sphere of competence in which there is marked development during the fourth and fifth years. This is when the child can first maintain for a period of time the fantasy of an imaginary companion. Children can dramatize themselves, assuming various adult roles. They begin to have frightening dreams involving injury—for example, being carried away by wolves. As Erikson (1959) expresses it, "Both language and locomotion permit him to expand his imagination over so many things that he cannot avoid frightening himself with what he himself has dreamed and thought up."

The bearing of these developments on social competence is that the child reaches a stage of understanding his place in the family as well as in society. Children to some extent continue to experiment with crude social power, especially with their peers, whom they may hit, boss, or threaten in various ways. Children are learning the meaning of roles; they learn the culture's definition of sex roles, and they experiment with a variety of adult roles (White, 1976).

White indicates that the growth of competence leads to intrinsic emotional and interpersonal crisis. Though the child apparently has no interest in sex, there are other areas in which he develops competency (White, 1976). The child still would use locomotor, linguistic, and imaginative progress, would be interested in being like adults, and would make comparisons, for example, of size and height. He would be competitive and subject to defeats and humiliations. The child would be curious, ask endless questions and encounter rebuffs, have bad dreams, and have guilt feelings over imagined or real aggressive actions. He would learn about roles and understand relationships to other family members. All these factors arise inescapably from progress in the growth of competence and have important emotional consequences. In all these situations, there is a chance to maintain and strengthen a sense of initiative; in all of them there is also a chance that the environment will act so as to impose a burden of guilt (Mussen et al., 1979).

Moral Development

One of the important human abilities that people acquire as they grow is the ability to tell right from wrong. *Moral development, conscience,* and *ethics* are all terms that we use in discussing our efforts to deal fairly with others. Preschoolers, through training and experience, gradually learn what actions are considered acceptable by other people and which actions are viewed as unacceptable. The child learns that doing certain things could lead to punishment.

A study by Mussen et al. (1979) indicates that from the time children are 3 years old, they are aware that other people have feelings and that those feelings vary according to the situations in which people find themselves. The researchers note that children are better able to recognize happiness and fear in others than sadness or anger. The study found no difference between boys and girls in recognition of these emotions, but older children did reveal more empathetic capability than younger ones. As Piaget specified, egocentricity declines gradually toward the end of the preschool years.

A child's increasing social awareness accounts largely for the early manifestations of sympathy, conscience, and generosity during the preschool period. As children become more conscious of the needs and concerns of others, they begin to desire the satisfaction of meeting others' needs as well as their own. Preschool children's behavior shows a growing capacity for sharing and compassion. Generosity also was studied by Mussen et al. (1979), who found it linked to moral characteristics such as cooperation, altruism, lack of interpersonal aggression, and sympathy. These aspects of moral development in turn are closely related to the child's perception of the same-sex parent as being warm, affectionate, and nurturing.

Children develop a sense of social justice by the end of the preschool years. Kohlberg (1976) suggests that young children understand that returning a stolen toy is more meaningful than merely apologizing for having stolen it. They are able not only to make the distinction between right and wrong but to recognize that, to correct a wrong, it is not enough just to say "Sorry."

Many of Kohlberg's studies on moral development use Piaget's work as the starting point, but they do challenge Piaget's view of the preschooler as an egocentric being who behaves properly only in response to adult authority. Kohlberg found that preschoolers were well on their way to understanding and internalizing basic moral considerations (Lerner & Hultsch, 1983).

Theorists define morality in different ways. Current theoretical views of moral development take one of three approaches, stressing the role of nature (Freud's view), nurture (social learning theory), or interaction (interactional theories).

Psychoanalytic Theory

Freud views all stages of development as following an intrinsically determined, universal course. According to Freud, all people experience an oedipal conflict in their phallic stage. The successful resolution of this conflict will result in the formation of the structure of personality Freud termed the *superego,* which has two components: the ego-ideal and the conscience. The ego-ideal, as Freud viewed it, is the representation of the perfect or ideal man (the "father figure"). In modeling himself after his father, a young boy thus becomes a "person" in his society. The conscience represents the internalization in one's mental life of society's rules, laws, codes, ethics, and mores. By the time a child is 5 years of age, the development of his or her superego will be complete.

Freud himself was not fully satisfied with his development of the female superego (Bronfenbrenner, 1960). According to him, a girl desires her father incestuously but her mother stands in her way. The girl develops a fear that her mother would punish her through castration. But realizing that she has a clitoris which is inferior (according to Freud), she develops penis envy. Penis envy helps the girl to resolve her feelings and begin her identification with the mother. She develops a superego. However, Freud specified that as girls did not experience castration anxiety which is necessary for full superego development, the girl did not obtain full superego development. Thus Freud believed that girls were never as morally developed as boys (Freud, 1950).

Freud (1950) identifies a person as morally developed or not according to the consistency of the person's behavior with society's rules because internalization of those rules involves the formation of a conscience. Achievement of that consistency, termed *behavioral congruence,* is usually completed by the age of 5. It follows that if two people—say a 5-year-old and a 21-year-old—show an identical response in a moral situation, they are equally morally developed (Lerner & Hultsch, 1983).

Freud does not deal with the content of behavior as long as it conforms to the rules of society. Thus, different cultures can prescribe different types of rules. Freud indicates that no behavioral content is universally moral; rather, what is seen as moral behavior is defined in relative terms within a particular society.

Social Learning Theory

Social-learning theorists observe behavior as a response to stimulation. McCandless (1967) indicates that responses are linked to stimulation on the basis of reward or punishment and are related to a particular stimulus–response connection. According to social learning theory, the social environment determines which responses will be rewarded and which will be punished. Behavior develops accordingly: individuals learn to emit responses that lead to rewards and not to emit responses that lead to punishment. The social-learning theorists differ with respect to the details of how such learning takes place (Bandura & Walters, 1963). However, there is general consensus that development involves increasing coordination of behavior to social rules. The comparability of this position to Freud's is evident. Furthermore, a social-learning conception of behavioral development in general is virtually indistinguishable from that of moral development in particular. There is nothing qualitatively different between behavior labeled *moral* and behavior labeled *social* or *personal* or anything else. All behavior follows the principles of social learning, and thus all behavior involves the conformity of the individual's responses to society.

Interactional Theories

The interactional view of moral development, which began in the 1950s, not only rejects the focus on mere responses as an index of moral development but also stresses a universalistic view of moral development and thus rejects the idea of moral relativism (Lerner & Hultsch, 1983).

Piaget.   Piaget viewed children's morality as passing through two phases: heteronomous morality and autonomous morality. In heteronomous morality the child is objective in his or her moral judgment; an act is right or wrong in terms of its consequences. One who breaks a teacup would be judged by a child in this stage as morally culpable, whether or not breaking the cup was an accident. Moral realism in the child is based on the fact that the child views rules as being unchangeable, externally imposed requirements for behavior that are imposed by adults on the child, and require unyielding acceptance.

In the second phase, children become subjective and autonomous in their moral judgments. They take the intentions of the person into consideration while judging the moral rightness or wrongness of an act. One who breaks a teacup out of spite or anger would be judged morally wrong. But one who broke the cup out of clumsiness would not be morally culpable. Piaget believes the second type of judgment to be based on the child's moral reasoning. This view considers rules as the outcomes of agreements between people who are in a relation not of social constraint but rather of cooperation and autonomy.

Piaget's theory differs from that of the morally relativistic, response-centered approaches of psychoanalysis and social learning theories. It has stimulated considerable interest among developmental researchers because it offers a provocative framework for assessing changes in morality beyond the level of early childhood.

Kohlberg.   Lawrence Kohlberg's theory of moral development has its roots in Piaget's thinking. Kohlberg (1976) obtained evidence that Piaget's two-phase model was not sufficient to take into account all the types of change in moral reasoning through which people progress. Kohlberg thought it necessary to devise a theory involving several stages of moral reasoning in order to encompass all the qualitative changes he discerned.

Kohlberg's theory of moral reasoning, like Piaget's, is based on the notion that by focusing only on the response in a moral situation, one may ignore important distinctions in the moral reasoning of people at different points in the life span—reasoning differences that in fact may give different meaning to the same response at various developmental levels. Responses alone do not signify the underlying reasoning. An individual's response must be examined in light of how the person perceives the moral situation, what the meaning of the situation is to the person, and how the person's choice relates to that meaning; in other words, in terms of the cognitive and emotional processes involved in making the moral judgments (Turiel, 1969).

Kohlberg's theory was discussed in Chapter 1.

The Social Environment

Two-year-old children are egocentric. They take what others give them, they are possessive, and they believe that they are the center of the universe because they are treated as such by people close to them.

By the age of $2\frac{1}{2}$, children are usually comparing themselves with adults in the family, brothers and sisters, and a few children in the immediate neighborhood. The social world of preschoolers is their immediate neighborhood. Through these associates, children learn their limitations and develop into socialized persons. As they grow older, their increasing interest in playmates of their own age corresponds to a decrease in interest in adult associations. By age 3, they have become more mature in their play activity. Social play increases because they have gained in ability to control their body movements, to handle objects, and to talk.

Play

At 4 years of age, children are sufficiently mature, mentally and physically, to participate in play activities with others and are ready to learn social patterns. Attempts at playing with peers have their ups and downs during the preschool years. Limited attention span, fatigue, insecurity in a new situation, need for parental attention are a few of the potential problems in an extended play situation. The positive aspects are that this starts the beginning of a child-to-child relationship. Given the opportunity, 4-year-olds will spend about half of their playtime playing with others.

When children encounter frustrating experiences with one another, they will argue. On the whole, however, 4- and 5-year-olds are more outgoing and cooperative than otherwise. By the time they are 5, they are competing vigorously with other children.

Imaginative play reaches a peak when a child is 4 years old, but it is not unusual for a 5-year-old to have an imaginary playmate. Probably all imaginative life in children satisfies an inner need for companionship. Their imaginative play activity is also practical. Five-year-olds, both boys and girls, enter into home-centered dramatic play, making this age group ideal for trying out play therapy.

Uses of play. Much of the preschool child's time is spent in one form of play or another. Several viewpoints on preschool children consider play to be a serious and significant form of behavior. Just as the frolicking of young animals rehearses them in survival-oriented behavior, the play of boys and girls develops skills and maneuvers that prove useful in adapting to life. The dedicated inside-out theorist might maintain that children have play instincts which serve the biological purpose of honing children's beginning survival functionings. But an outside-in theorist would argue that play is one of the processes by which young children incorporate into themselves some of the opportunities and expectancies provided by society. (For instance, playing games with schoolmates and family.) Both ways, play is seen as significant and acceptable, because it has a functional value beyond itself. Kastenbaum (1978) calls it the play-as-practice view. Play for the child means fun, but sooner or later, play experiences will contribute to the child's adaptive, sociable behavior. Play is practice for later life.

Other theorists view play as a way of letting off excess energy—letting off steam. Indeed, there are no socially established pathways for the release of excess energy or excitement in early childhood, and young children certainly do run, leap, shout, and hurl themselves about when excited. According to this view, fun and pleasure are acceptable outcomes, but the essential purpose of play is to discharge excess energy.

The "letting off steam" theory has its limits, however. It does not explain why the child discharges tension in one way instead of another. Nor does it account for quiet play, which uses very little energy. Furthermore, the relationship it assumes between the child's play and his or her psychological world is rather mechanistic: inner or outer stimulation excites the child, who then discharges it pleasurably through vigorous play.

The psychoanalytical approach is one that views play as a means of learning skills and discharging excitation. Play for children is a sort of language in which they express thoughts and feelings naturally and spontaneously. Through play, children reveal their needs, fears, and triumphs, just as an articulate adult will verbalize them. This approach has practical implications. Play is a way of relating oneself to the outside world; the importance of play is not *that* children do it but *how* they do it—that is, repetitively.

Play situations often have value in the study and treatment of emotional problems in young children. An experienced social work practitioner "reads" the nature of the child's problem from play behavior. This technique is often used for research purposes as well, for it reveals aspects of children's thoughts, feelings, and social development apart from any particular emotional problem.

The psychoanalytical view indicates that play can also be work. Through *play-work*, a term coined by Robert Kastenbaum (1978), children learn to cope with new, challenging, and alarming situations. Because a range of problems and experiences have been identified as common to children, observers can begin with some clues to help them understand what is taking place in play.

> Four-year-old David felt displaced when his stepfather entered the family, and that feeling worsened with the birth of a baby sister. Formerly his mother's only child, David was overwhelmed and developed temper tantrums. He screamed and cried at night, wet his bed, and turned into a finicky eater. His parents were worried and took him to a child guidance clinic. The mother insisted that she had prepared David for the new stepfather and that both parents had prepared him for the birth of his sibling by simple, direct explanation of the birth process and what it might mean to him. Every time the mother looked at David, she said, "I told you everything, didn't I?" and he would nod his head obediently.
>
> Through the use of play, the social worker reached a better understanding of David's feelings. In playing house, David consistently beat the baby and called the older child "poor baby boy." The new father appeared as a peripheral person to whom David expressed subtle hostile feelings. He said that he and his mother had dinner and the father came late for dinner. At another point he mentioned that the father and the new baby went in a car and were killed.
>
> Observing David at play helped the worker to understand how intensely David felt about his stepfather, sister, and mother. This manifestation of the insecurity, anxiety, and stress that David felt in facing the competition surrounding him (and his mother) was a revelation. Play therapy helped to relieve the child's fears and anxieties. As time passed, the social worker, through use of play therapy and the help of David's parents, worked towards helping David to accept the new situation and reassured him that he was still a valued member of the household. As David's trust and self-confidence increased, his disruptive behavior began to diminish.

Play and thought.   Like other human activities, play reflects the level and type of thought that is at the disposal of its participants. A 4-year-old child throwing a ball is different from an 18-year-old quarterback releasing a pass.

Although both are playing ball, they differ not only in physical skills but also in their thoughts and strategies.

Different styles and types of play can be observed as young children progress from the sensorimotor stage to the representational stage. As they grow older, children are able to appreciate and enjoy having an effect on the world and on other people. Their play becomes more varied and idiosyncratic as they gain the ability to represent and symbolize. The world of "make believe" and "let's pretend" becomes available. The pretend games of the preoperational stage include people and animals as well as objects: "You be the bad guy and I will be the good guy," "You be the baby sitter and I will be the mommy coming home from work."

Parallel and cooperative play. At times, preschool children playing in the same place at the same time do not seem to be playing with each other. In this phenomenon known as *parallel play*, children may occasionally interact, reaching out for the same toy or imitating one another, but typically each child engages in solitary play while in a group.

Cooperative play, with its ups and downs, begins during the preschool years. Parents and other adults can either facilitate or impede cooperative play by their attitudes and the kind of instructions they provide. At times, children may have quarrels about which toy each child should play with. All the children may prefer a particular toy. Adults can help in solving such quarrels by insisting that children should take turns. Adults who are partial to one child's needs alone will hinder cooperative play among children. Using sound principles, such as everyone taking their turn, helps children understand the concept of sharing and how it applies to themselves. Cooperative play reflects children's growing capacity to accept and respond to ideas and actions that are not originally their own. It is the result of healthy self-esteem, as well as of normal maturation.

Fantasy. Fantasy play is a pleasant activity engaged in by children and adults alike. Through fantasy, children privately explore their ever-expanding social world (Singer, 1977). Often, fantasy is a reaction to real events and not a withdrawal from them.

Fantasy involves substitution of one object or situation for another. A little girl may alleviate her frustration at being unjustly punished by having her mommy doll apologize to her baby doll. Fantasy also involves imaginary companions. They may assume any form, human or animal, male or female, and have any type of relationship with and meaning to the child. They usually disappear when the child becomes more involved with real playmates.

Peer Relationships

The most significant advance that preschool children make in their relationships involves their peers: they establish one-to-one friendships. Three-year-olds may have various playmates, but at this early age their egocentricity prevents them from seeing much importance in the differences between them. Soon they develop preferences, seeing one playmate as passive, another as aggressive, and so forth. They pick out the child with whom they have the most fun as their special friend. The relationship may not yet be sustained or consistent because young preschoolers respond strongly to feelings that change from moment to moment.

Preschoolers choose friends whom they perceive as being similar to themselves. Children usually choose friends of the same sex and age as themselves. The establishment of personal friendships marks an important step in children's awareness of other people as distinct. In time, children begin to explore a new world of relationships, although the relationship with parents remains by far the most important as long as children continue to need parents' protection. For parent and child, there is an ongoing challenge to reach out for opportunities that lead to assertion, competency, and independence.

Child-Rearing Practices and Patterns

Parents influence their children through various styles of child-rearing practices, and children influence their parents in turn. Theorists assume that all parental action, intentional or not, plays a role in fashioning a child's expression of potential. Researchers have attempted to identify the aspects of parental behavior that are especially influential (Lerner & Hultsch, 1983).

Baumrind (1972) has identified clusters of parenting practices (that is, child-rearing and disciplinary behaviors) that may be seen in other independent studies, classifying them into three general types: authoritarian, permissive, and authoritative.

The authoritarian parent tries to shape, control, and evaluate the behavior and attitudes of the child, typically in accordance with a set of absolute standards. Parents of this sort value obedience to their authority and favor forceful, punitive measures to curb "self-will" whenever the child's behavior or beliefs conflict with those of the parent. The demand for obedience, a traditional parental value, is combined with an orientation to respect work and to maintain order and the accepted social structure. The authoritarian parent expects to be listened to and does not encourage verbal give and take. The child is expected to accept the word of the parent without question (Baumrind, 1972).

The permissive parent is nonpunishing, accepting, and affirming. The parent attempts to maintain a laissez-faire attitude toward the child's behaviors, desires, and impulses. This type of parent is a resource person for the child, someone whom the child can use for his own growth. The parent is the consultant who discusses the family policies with the child and offers the child rationales for family rules. This type of parent allows the child to govern his or her own behavior. Reasoning, not overt power, is used to control the child (Baumrind, 1972).

The authoritative parent attempts to direct the child's activities by the use of a rational, issue-oriented style. Through explanations and reasoning the parent tries to induce the desired behavior in the child. An authoritative parent encourages verbal give and take in order to share with the child the reasoning behind any particular policy or rule. This type of parent does exercise a firm control over the child, but not to the extent that the child is overburdened with restrictions. The child's interests, specific needs, and behavioral capacities are taken into consideration. Such parents see the rights and duties of parents and children as complementary, but they do keep their own parental and adult rights in mind, thus combining power with inducement.

Despite the classification, the lines dividing the three parenting styles are often unclear as parents attempt to find ways to do the best thing for the child as well as for themselves. All parents hope for the same end results of child rearing. Their expectations of children's behaviors include friendliness, cooperation, orientation toward achievement, and interpersonal dominance, which form a cluster of behaviors that describe a socially competent, responsible, and independent person. Baumrind mentions that extremely authoritarian or extremely permissive parenting has negative consequences for children. Each parenting style has its pros and cons. We will not debate them. It is sufficient for us to understand that there are different styles of parenting and that the style influences the child.

> Seven-year-old Peter had been a member of a single-parent household for three years. His mother, Ruth, had consistently taken a permissive approach to child rearing. Then Ruth decided to remarry. Her new husband, Jay, was familiar and comfortable with an authoritarian up-bringing. In his family, children had been punished if they questioned parents. When Ruth consulted Peter on what he needed to do for the weekend or planned things with him, Jay become uncomfortable and angry. He could not understand how she could confer with and talk to a little boy as if he were an adult. In time, Jay started to discipline Peter in his own way, causing Peter and Ruth a lot of pain and heartache. Peter began to act out, insulted his stepfather, and finally decided to run away from home. The second time he ran away, Ruth decided to see a social worker. After a number of sessions with the parents and Peter, the social worker concluded that Peter needed a more lenient kind of discipline. With help from the worker and through collaborative work, Jay and Ruth worked out an effective way of disciplining Peter on which they could both agree. Therapy appeared to work in this family because Ruth and Jay were committed to each other and sincere in their efforts to be good parents.

The Parenting Atmosphere

Sears (1970) found that both male and female children who had one warm and accepting parent had good self-esteem. A report by Rutter (1971) indicates that a good relationship with one parent may buffer a child from the potentially detrimental effects of a poor relationship with the other parent.

It is unfortunate that there have been so few studies on the effects of fathering on preschoolers. However, a few research studies do discuss the effects of mothering on preschool children. Jones, Rachel, and Smith (1980) found that maternal restrictiveness was associated with evasive problem-solving strategies in preschool children. Those children also had fewer negotiation and problem-solving strategies. Increased maternal nurturance was associated with children's increased reliance on authority.

Parents and extended family typically represent a necessary and ubiquitous part of the child's social world. Family relationships have to be understood in terms of socioeconomic factors as well as reciprocal socialization processes.

Parents and other chief caretakers are the first persons who should inculcate in the child the values and mores of their particular culture. In a homogeneous society, most people share the same culture, and children of that majority have little difficulty in dealing with the social environment. But in our multiethnic society there are many different cultural traditions and individual preferences. Some parents may inculcate in their children a culture that is different from the majority culture, and the children may have difficulty assimilating the majority culture. Many minorities have their own sociopolitical, ethical, and ethnic values. Children of the minority cultures learn their own group's values through the parents' approach to daily routines such as those involving food and clothing, their advocacy of a particular style of discipline and education, and their continued use of their native language.

Depending on child-rearing style, children may be brought up to be predominantly passive or aggressive, dependent or independent. The behavior that a child adopts is the result of the family's social, ethnic, and religious outlook.

Parenting Styles

Socialization processes include reward and punishment, modeling and identification (Lerner & Hultsch, 1983).

Reward and punishment.   Children who receive rewards for approved behavior are reinforced in constructive patterns. However, some children are so used to having every type of behavior rewarded that they expect a reward for everything they do and can become chronic whiners if not rewarded. They are motivated to repeat a behavior only by expectation of a reward.

The effects of punishment on children are difficult to see because the word *punishment* implies such a wide range of practices. Parental disapproval may take such forms as stern looks, isolating the child for a period of time in a locked or unlocked room, or mild or severe spanking, immediately or long after a misbehavior has occurred. All parental behavior has an effect on the child, and it can be either positive or negative. Within the normal range of thinking, however, the purpose of punishment is to help the child progress in the process of socialization and internalize the desired standards of behavior.

Extreme forms of punishment can extend into the realm of child abuse.

Child abusers today, as well as in olden times, view children as the property of their parents and deal with them accordingly. As Radbill (1974) notes, the Calvinists of the 16th century believed that children had an evil nature, and some of the early American colonies went so far as to enact a death penalty for youthful disobedience.

Modeling. Modeling, or imitation, is another manner by which socialization takes place. Children are capable of copying patterns down to the minutest detail. Parents will testify to children's imitation of a mother's or father's words or actions. Bandura (1977) indicates that the characteristics most likely to encourage imitation are power, nurturance, and perceived similarity. Children are more willing to imitate a powerful parent, one who controls resources, than a weak or passive one. Children are more willing to imitate a nurturing, rewarding model than a cold, punitive model. Finally, children are willing to imitate people to whom they recognize their own similarity; for example, a Black person may imitate another Black person, and a muscular child may imitate an athlete.

Identification. Identification is the process of internalizing and incorporating within oneself the values, attitudes, and behavior patterns of another person. By the processes of modeling and identification, individuals begin to form a sense of self in relation to others in their society (Sprecht & Craig, 1982).

Coping with Feelings

According to the way they are reared and socialized, children deal with their feelings in different ways. The strategic patterns that children develop for coping with emotions last them a lifetime.

> Carlos was a quiet, shy child of 6 who had come with his family from Puerto Rico. He impressed his new teacher by his cooperative and industrious behavior. He was always neatly dressed and never got into fights or arguments. One day he was playing by himself in a muddy place on the school grounds, apparently trying to draw something on the ground. Just then, the school cat majestically walked over his drawing and moved on toward a tree. Carlos became angry. He ran after the cat, picked it up, and dashed it with all his might against the tree.

Why was Carlos so provoked by the cat's behavior? Why is it that he appeared to be a model child but could not cope with his angry feelings? Perhaps his parental training had been extremely rigid, or the child had not been allowed to ventilate his own feelings.

There is a reciprocity to parent–child relationships. Changes in parenting depend in part on the changing nature of the child. For instance, as the child's cognitive skills develop, reasoning and delay of gratification become effective disciplinary strategies. Such efforts would be meaningless with a 3-month-old baby, but an older child becomes increasingly capable of controlling his or her own behavior. Parental control and development of a child's cognitive skills are methods of supporting the child's emerging competence.

A developmental approach to parenting increases the likelihood of highly valued outcomes for the child. In the developmental approach, changes that take place in the child are seen as systematic and organized. Also, from a scientific standpoint, the developmental approach illustrates the child's effect on his or her caregivers and thus the bidirectional nature of the parent–child relationship. Children's potentialities influence parents' behavior, which in turn influences subsequent child development.

Divorce

The divorce rate reached an all-time high in the 1970s and continues to climb. According to the National Center for Health Statistics in 1980, there are more than 1.15 million divorces every year, involving more than 2.3 million adults and more than 1.1 million children. About two out of every five divorcing couples have at least one child (Lerner & Hultsch, 1983). On an average, in every divorce involving children, there are at least two children under 18 years of age (Hetherington, 1979). The escalation in the divorce rate increases the number of children living with one parent.

Divorce can be a very difficult process for both parents and children. One of the troublesome areas of divorce is the custody of children. Although many fathers contest the awarding of custody to the mothers, the mothers still obtain custody more often. In regular custody cases, fathers obtain custody of the child only 10% of the time, whereas in 90% of cases, the mother obtains it. Thus the increasing number of one-parent households are more often female-headed than male-headed. There are efforts in some states toward offering both parents joint custody, though this is not popular.

Moreover, 75% of those who divorce remarry, and they do so relatively quickly. In fact, 50% of those who divorce have remarried within three years of the final decree. Thus, many children acquire stepparents during their childhood. Blended or reconstituted families do provide a different physical, emotional, and interpersonal context; children have to adjust to a new household in addition to experiencing normal maturation problems. In most but not all cases, the adjustment is fast and smooth. Besides other adjustments, such children have to deal with two sets of parents—two biological parents and the spouse of each—plus four sets of grandparents and even larger extended families.

What are the effects of divorce on children? Hetherington (1979) indicates that most children experience the transition from living in an intact family to living in one split by divorce as a painful event. Hetherington identifies the typical feelings a child must contend with during divorce as anger, fear, depression, guilt, and unhappiness. A year has to go by before the tensions of these children are reduced and more positive feelings begin to occur.

There are many indications that boys are more vulnerable to the adverse effects of divorce than girls are, but the reasons for this disparity are not clear

(Hetherington, 1979). The degree to which a child adjusts to a divorce situation depends on the child's level of social and cognitive development.

It doesn't take a divorce to disrupt children's functioning. One common finding is that children of maritally conflicted homes are likely to engage in aggressive and antisocial behavior (Gibson, 1969). Hetherington, Cox, and Cox (1979) were able to document that it is not divorce per se that affects children; rather, it is the quality of the marital and postdivorce relations between parents that has a direct influence on child development. When divorced parents maintain reasonably friendly relations, mothers who have custody of their preschoolers tend to be more involved with and supportive of their children than mothers engaged in continuing strife with their ex-husbands.

As students of social work, we need to understand the role that support systems such as informal networks and daycare facilities play in enhancing parental functioning. As people interested in child development, we should not overlook the immediate parental support system. The discussion of divorce has shown that the support that a marriage provides or fails to provide can make a sizeable difference in the way in which children develop in the family.

The Impact of Television

Television viewing has become a major force in the socialization of children in our society. Evidence of our increasingly greater exposure to television is the large proportion of households (97%) that own television sets. About 61% have a color television and 45% have two or more televisions.

Television watching is influenced by socioeconomic, intellectual, personality, and developmental variables. TV viewing starts when a child is 2 years of age, increases rapidly when a child is 7, and peaks when the child reaches adolescence (Schramm, Lyle, & Parker, 1961). Schramm, Lyle, and Parker found that upper-class children, children with higher IQs, and children of parents with higher education watch less TV than lower-class children, children with lower IQs, and children of parents with less education. A more recent study by Lyle and Hoffman (1972) yielded similar findings. Some personality characteristics appear to be of importance in television watching. It has been found that heavy viewing is related to interpersonal passivity. Schramm, Lyle, and Parker (1961) found that television viewing increases in times of personal stress or frustration.

According to Gerbner (1972), children's cartoons are the most violent fare on television. In addition, there are violent westerns, and some children watch adult programs containing a lot of violence. Some theorists argue that watching violent acts on television has a "purifying effect" on the audience: television stimulates violent fantasies but acts as a substitute for excessive aggression. Those children who are adversely affected by TV are those who have limited real-life models and who spend considerable time in front of the TV set. Often these children have emotional problems.

When 5-year-old Robert took a knife and stabbed his 3-month-old brother, he thought that he was playing a game. Robert spent a lot of his time watching TV. His mother was a single parent who had to work, so Robert was the part-time babysitter. One day while Robert was watching a fascinating show, his baby brother started to cry. Robert became angry, rushed to the kitchen, picked up a knife, and stabbed his brother "just like the Mighty Mouse in the TV shows."

How would you deal with this child? Could you call him a juvenile delinquent? No, but his life experiences were limited, and he did have some emotional problems and lack of caring by his mother, who had too much to do. Appropriate placement was arranged for him with the aid of a social worker and the cooperation of the mother, who needed help in dealing with him, particularly after her younger son died.

Television is not, of course, all bad. As research has shown, it does have the potential to teach children many forms of positive social behavior—adherence to social rules, attitudes of generosity, helpfulness, cooperation, and friendliness.

Carefully planned TV shows are able to portray themes such as cooperation, sympathetic attitude toward others, affection, and control of impulses. The most effective television models are those who resemble parents and teachers and who have the ability to demand certain behaviors.

In conclusion, it can be said that TV is a potent socializer that can influence children's behavior in either positive or negative ways. In light of the case study included, it can be said that a child who spends too much time in front of the TV set will grow up to be passive and imitative in comparison with children who spend time playing with their peers.

Implications for Social Work Practice

Individual differences in children's growth are compounded by family background, socioeconomic background, and ethnic and racial issues. When Johnny does well in kindergarten and Jim, who sits next to him, daydreams all the time, it may not mean that Jim is a failure or is stupid. Jim could be suffering from any of several impediments, such as learning disabilities or emotional problems, chronically or situationally. It is necessary that social workers treat each child as unique and give help accordingly.

Understanding and evaluating the important factors that influence children is a necessary aspect of the worker's assessment.

Five-year-old Tasha had difficulty in school. She had violent temper tantrums, got into trouble easily, and was always aggressive. The teacher was concerned and referred the child to the school social worker. To the worker's surprise, Tasha's younger brother, who was nearly 3 years of age and in the pre-kindergarten class, was cooperative, friendly, and obedient. It was a pleasure to be with him. The social worker was unable to understand this situation; she was concerned. When her efforts to change Tasha's behavior by counseling Tasha alone failed, she called Tasha's parents for a therapy session. Tasha's mother, Diana, came for therapy, and familial factors in Tasha's behavior were revealed. Tasha's younger brother was her stepbrother, and her mother as well as her stepfather treated the two differently. It appeared as if the mother wanted her daughter to misbehave; to Diana, this daughter resembled her former boyfriend, Tasha's father, who was an alcoholic. Once the feelings stemming from associating her daughter and former boyfriend were explored and dealt with, Diana could work with Tasha on their problems and relationship. Efforts included concrete help, such as structuring bedtime and playtime, as well as counseling from the social worker.

Although there were ups and downs, counseling helped; Tasha's self-esteem improved, in the classroom as well as at home. The social worker's taking into consideration the environmental and individual interactions of her clients allowed her to counsel them effectively.

Chapter Summary

The physical-motor activities of preschoolers lay the foundation for future cognitive and social-emotional development. Besides growing physically, in speed, coordination, and perception, the child grows in ability to learn. The process of learning a new activity involves readiness, motivation, and opportunity to focus on the activity, as well as feedback from the activity.

Preschool children are at the cognitive stage that Piaget calls *preoperational*. These children develop the capability for symbolic representation and can use words as well as images to represent both thoughts and experiences. Preoperational children are not logical thinkers; their cognitive processes are egocentric, concrete, and irreversible.

Language development is an important aspect of the preschool child's life. Language development is dependent upon the social relationships between the child and typical conversants. Language disorders cause children a number of problems. Social workers should be aware that language disorders in children can lead to complications for them in the social world.

In Erikson's thinking, preschoolers are in the stage of balancing initiative versus guilt. This is the period when their newfound energy helps children to understand themselves as powerful beings. Secondarily they begin to realize that they should control their behavior. Crisis in this period appears in the form of guilt, which arises when the child is not able to control his or her impulses.

In White's competence model, preschool children develop competence in three spheres: locomotion, language, and imagination. This is also the period when children are experimenting with a number of adult roles.

Moral development begins when a person develops a "conscience." The child learns that doing certain things could lead to punishment. An increasing social awareness appears in the early manifestations of sympathy, conscience, and generosity. This chapter briefly discusses moral development as viewed by Freud, social learning theorists, and interactional theorists.

An important aspect of children's lives is play, through which they learn to understand themselves and others. Cooperative play teaches the child to function as a member of society.

Baumrind identifies three types of parenting: authoritarian, permissive, and authoritative. Child-rearing practices teach children patterns of behavior through the use of rewards and punishments, modeling, and identification.

A factor that affects the upbringing of many children is divorce. The manner in which a divorce is handled can make a significant difference in the way children develop in a family.

Television plays an important role in socialization. Television watching is influenced by factors such as socioeconomic status and intelligence. There is considerable debate about programming that portrays violence. Some children may not have adequate models to counteract the influence of television, and some children may suffer by spending an excessive amount of time in front of the television.

References

Anderson, S. (1979, March). *Register variation in young children's role playing speech.* Paper presented at the Communicative Competence Language Use and Role-Playing Symposium, Society for Research and Child Development.

Bandura, A. (1977). *Social learning theory.* Englewood Cliffs, NJ: Prentice-Hall.

Bandura, A., & Walters, R. H. (1963). *Social learning and personality development.* New York: Holt, Rinehart & Winston.

Baumrind, D. (1972). Some thoughts about child rearing. In U. Bronfenbrenner (Ed.), *Influences on human development.* Hinsdale, IL: Dryden.

Beck, A. T. (1976). *Cognitive therapy and emotional disorders.* New York: International Universities Press.

Bloom, L. (1980). Language development and language disorders in children. In M. Bloom (Ed.), *Lifespan development.* New York: Macmillan.

Bloom, L., & Lahey, M. (1978). *Development and language disorders.* New York: Wiley.

Bronfenbrenner, U. (1960). Freudian theories of identification and other derivations. *Child Development, 31,* 15–40.

Erikson, E. H. (1959). Identity and the life cycle. *Psychological Issues, 1,* 1–71.

Erikson, E. H. (1963). *Childhood and society.* New York: Norton.

Freud, S. (1950). Some psychological consequences of the anatomical distinction between the sexes. In *Collected papers* (Vol. 5). London: Hogarth.

Gerbner, G. (1972). Violence in television drama: Trends and symbolic functions. In G. A. Comstock & E. A. Rubinstein (Eds.), *Television and social behavior* (Vol. 1). Washington, DC: U.S. Government Printing Office.

Gibson, H. (1969). Early delinquency in relation to broken homes. *Journal of Abnormal Psychology, 74,* 33–41.

Hetherington, E. M. (1979). Divorce: A child's perspective. *American Psychologist, 34,* 851–858.

Hetherington, E. M., Cox, M., & Cox, R. (1979). Stress and coping in divorce. A focus on women. In J. E. Gullahorn (Ed.), *Psychology and Women in Transition.* Washington, DC: Winston & Sons.

Jones, D. C., Rachel, A. U., & Smith, R. L. (1980). Maternal childrearing practices and social problem-solving strategies among preschoolers. *Developmental Psychology, 16,* 241–242.

Kaluger, G., & Kaluger, M. F. (1979). *Human development* (2nd ed.). St. Louis: C. V. Mosby.

Kastenbaum, R. (1978). *Humans developing.* Boston: Allyn & Bacon.

Kohlberg, L. (1976). Moral stages and moralization: The cognitive developmental approach. In T. Luckona (Ed.), *Moral development and behavior.* New York: Holt, Rinehart & Winston.

Labov, W. (1970). The logic of nonstandard English. In F. Williams (Ed.), *Language and poverty.* Chicago: Markham.

Lerner, R. M., & Hultsch, D. F. (1983). *Human development.* New York: McGraw-Hill.

Lyle, J., & Hoffman, H. (1972). Children's use of television and other media. In E. A. Rubinstein, G. A. Comstock, & J. P. Murray (Eds.), *Television and social behavior. Vol. 4: Television in day to day life: Patterns of use.* Washington, DC: U.S. Government Printing Office.

McCandless, B. R. (1967). *Children.* New York: Holt, Rinehart & Winston.

Mussen, P. H., Conger, J. J., Kagan, J., & Geiwitz, J. (1979). *Psychological development: A lifespan approach.* New York: Harper & Row.

Piaget, J., & Inhelder, B. (1969). *The psychology of the child.* New York: Basic Books.

Radbill, S. (1974). A history of child abuse and infanticide. In R. Helfer & C. Kempe (Eds.), *The battered child.* Chicago: University of Chicago Press.

Rutter, M. (1971). Parent–child separation: Psychological effects on children. *Journal of Child Psychology and Psychiatry, 12,* 233–260.

Schramm, W., Lyle, J., & Parker, B. (1961). *Television in the lives of our children.* Stanford, CA: Stanford University Press.

Sears, R. R. (1970). Relation of early socialization experience to self-concepts and gender role in middle childhood. *Child Development, 41,* 267–290.

Singer, J. L. (1977). Imagination and make-believe play in early childhood: Some educational implications. *Journal of Mental Imagery, 1,* 127–144.

Slobin, D. I. (1972, July). They learn in the same way all around the world. *Psychology Today,* pp. 71–74.

Specht, R., & Craig, G. J. (1982). *Human development.* Englewood Cliffs, NJ: Prentice-Hall.

Turiel, E. (1969). *Developmental approaches in the child's moral thinking.* In P. H. Mussen, J. Langer, & M. Covington (Eds.), *Trends and issues in developmental psychology.* New York: Holt, Rinehart & Winston.

White, R. W. (1976). *The enterprise of living* (2nd ed.). New York: Holt, Rinehart & Winston.

Middle Childhood

Physical Development
Cognitive Development
Moral Development
Socialization and the School Setting
The Psychosocial Environment
Parenting
Peer Influences on Personality
Learning Disabilities
Implications for Social Work Practice
Chapter Summary
References

Middle childhood is a period of stable physical growth lasting more or less from age 6 to age 12.

Physical Development

The child's rate of growth is slower now than it was during infancy and early childhood. The child continues to change along physical dimensions in a process called *stable growth*. During this period many of the basic measures of physiological functioning are completing their transition to adult levels. A careful analysis of the child's anatomy will show that there is a shift from infant/young-child status to adult status. Many children begin to look grown up. The head-to-body ratio closely resembles that of adults. Whereas in infancy the head of the child was quite large compared with the rest of the body, now the arms, legs, and long muscles are catching up. The circumference of the head has increased to about 90% of its final adult size. Physical coordination has improved and continues to improve. The child performs movements that are too sophisticated for preschoolers. The child shows a more secure sense of balance in activities such as jumping rope and climbing. Attempts to overreach present abilities bring fatigue and distraction, and the child is susceptible to falls.

By the time children are 6 years old, their permanent teeth have begun to erupt, affecting the contours of their faces. By the time the child is 13, most of the permanent teeth have appeared, except for the wisdom teeth.

The basic developmental pattern is the same for both sexes during early childhood. In middle childhood individual differences are more important than sex differences. However, the sexes differ in the use of their bodies. Boys tend to be taller and heavier and throw their entire bodies into actions, whereas girls tend to be more advanced in bone development, more flexible in the use of their muscles, and perhaps more adept at rhythmic movements (Kastenbaum, 1979).

Motor Development

Children's ability to adjust to changes proceeds from their observation of their own bodies, and the outcome of that perception is children's body images. Children take advantage of the greater strength and longer arm span they have, which contribute to a new sense of identity.

Children learn to make distinctions between left and right when they are about 6. However, they continue to have difficulty regarding their orientation in space, particularly with reference to other people and objects. When children are walking straight toward you, they may regard your right side as your left side because it aligns with their left.

When the ability to perceive spatial orientation develops accurately, it accompanies the ability to represent a situation verbally. The right–left concept thus appears to develop as an integral part of children's total comprehension of their other relationships to the world, not as a single or isolated phenomenon.

As young children mature, they gradually learn to orient themselves in space without having to take the momentary orientation of their bodies into account (Warper & Werner, 1957).

For children of this age it is difficult to observe other people's actions and perceive that others literally see things differently. Spatial egocentrism was tested by Piaget and Inhelder (1956) by asking young children to look at a miniature landscape of trees and mountains and report what a doll would see from various points of reference around the scene. Most of those who were 6 years old or younger believed that the doll's perception would be the same as theirs, no matter where the doll was standing. To a child at this age the body becomes a secure home base, but the developmental problem of recognizing others' bases or frames of references has not been solved.

From age 6, children improve in their muscular dexterity, increase their resistance to fatigue, and also have greater muscular strength. These factors make it possible for them to make increasingly fine use of their small muscles over longer periods of time, resulting in rapid improvement in their ability to control their bodies and manipulate objects. This ability in turn improves their agility and accuracy, as well as endurance. During this period children can jump and climb, throw and catch with ease. By the age of 9, the child's eye–hand coordination is very good. The child is ready to experiment with crafts and shop work (Newman & Newman, 1975).

Children's conceptions of human life show up in figure drawings and other forms of creative play. The child has different moods and purposes, and drawings represent them accordingly.

> Seven-year-old Joshua was angry with his father, who lived away from home for long periods of time. Without him, Joshua could not play some of the outdoor games he loved. When asked to make a drawing about his family, Joshua showed his anger with his father by representing a tree with a nest, and a mother bird in the nest with the small ones. The father bird was drawn flying away, bleeding, with a broken wing. As Joshua explained it, the father bird lived away from home most of the time and therefore was a "bad bird," so he was shot.

What types of body image do children develop? Researchers are not completely knowledgeable about these phenomena. The muscular type of physique appears to be the most popular, regardless of the actual body type of the child who makes the judgment (Lerner & Korn, 1972).

Children who have and do not have the most popular type of physique show important differences in the ways in which they view their bodies and how their total self-concept develops around their bodies. In their heightened sense of selfhood, schoolchildren are commonly interested in comparing their developmental status with that of other children as well as with adults.

> Ron, age 7, was undergoing treatment for defective growth glands. Very short and slight of build, he looked like a 4-year-old. He was self-conscious about his height. He was in the second grade and understood that he was the shortest boy in the class. He constantly measured himself

against his parents—particularly his mother, who was the shorter parent—and said, "I am up to here with you." Then he would add, "Next year, I will be up to there."

The child appreciates that physical growth continues—and there is more to come. In this significant sense, children are observers as well as participants in the developmental process.

Effect of Malnutrition on Physical and Mental Growth

Families with low incomes often survive on a substandard diet. Brock (1961) defines dietary subnutrition as an impairment of functional efficiency of bodies that can be remedied by better feeding. Subnutrition or malnutrition can produce populations of children who are stunted, disproportionate in their growth, and afflicted with a variety of anatomical, physiological, and behavioral abnormalities. In North America, despite its high level of industrialization, poverty continues to exist. Chronic subnutrition is often accompanied by dramatic manifestations of acute, severe, and even lethal effects.

A woman who was malnourished as a child experiences more problems in child bearing and may suffer intrauterine problems, as well as prenatal risk to the child. Her earlier malnourishment would also affect the functional adaptive capacity of the newborn child. Animal studies have been constructed to test the implications in this chain of associations (Chow, Blackwell, Hou, Anilane, Sherwin, & Chir, 1968). The findings show that second- and later-generation animals deriving from mothers who were nutritionally disadvantaged when young are themselves less well grown and behaviorally less competent than animals of the same strain derived from normal mothers.

Assuming that the primary criteria for normal intellectual development and for formal learning are the abilities to process sensory information and to integrate such information across sense systems, evidence shows that both severe acute malnutrition in infancy and chronic subnutrition from birth into the school years result in defective information. Malnutrition may interfere with the orderly development of experience and contribute to suboptimal intellectual functioning (Birch, 1972).

Severe malnutrition seldom occurs alone. It occurs in conjunction with low income, familial disorganization, poor housing, and a climate of apathy, despair, and ignorance.

A child protective services social worker was called to visit a family in which the mother, a single parent, was accused of neglecting her children. Pat visited the family in a run-down neighborhood. To her repeated knocks, the door was opened by a tiny boy who was merely skin and bones. It was dark inside, and as the social worker's eyes got accustomed to the darkness, she saw filth and piles and piles of dirty clothes, and even roaches and rats. There were four children in the house, all severely malnourished and all kept away from school. Pat was nauseated and shocked to see a child of about 1 catch a cockroach and eat it. Pat later found out that this child was 3 years of age. This was a case of complete neglect. Malnutrition had made the children quiet, dull, and totally submissive. The mother was a prostitute who stayed away from home for long hours and did not really care about her children.

Cognitive Development

Middle childhood is the period when children learn more about themselves and their environments.

Piaget called middle childhood the *period of concrete operations.* Children are bound by immediate physical reality but cannot transcend the here-and-now. Therefore they have difficulty dealing with the remote future and with hypothetical matters.

In the period of concrete operations, one test of cognitive development uses a set of sticks of varying lengths. Children mentally survey the sticks and then quickly place them in order, without any actual measurement. Earlier, in the preoperational period, children arrange sticks by size in their proper sequence by physically comparing each pair in succession. Children in the preoperational period are dominated by actual perceptions, and the task takes them several minutes to complete. However, children in the period of concrete operations finish the project in a matter of seconds because their actions are directed by internal mental or cognitive processes (Piaget, 1952).

Conservation Tasks

As concrete operational thought evolves, a liberation takes place in children's thought processes. Conservation problems are solved because of the unfreezing of rigid preoperational thought. The principle of conservation involves the recognition that the quantity of any substance or liquid remains the same despite changes in shape or position. Children in elementary schools come to recognize that pouring liquid from a short, wide container into a long, narrow container does not change the quantity of the liquid. They understand that the amount of liquid is conserved. This realization implies that they are capable of compensating in their minds for various external changes in objects. Thus, concrete operational thought entails reorganization of cognitive structure—a progressive amalgamation of expression and mental activity (Vander Zanden, 1978).

In concrete operations, children focus on transformations, such as the gradual shift in the height or width of the fluid in the container as it is poured by the experimenter. According to Piaget (1965), schoolchildren also attain reversibility of operations and understand that the initial state can be regained by pouring the liquid back into the original container.

Children acquire some conservation skills earlier and some later. Conservation of discrete quantities (numbers) occurs somewhat earlier than the conservation of substance. Conservation of weight (the heaviness of an object) occurs after the conservation of quantity (length and area) and is followed by conservation of volume (the space that is occupied by an object). Piaget calls this type of learning *sequential development:* that is, the acquisition of each skill is dependent on the mastery of earlier skills. Piaget uses the term *horizontal decalage* to indicate that repetition of behavior takes place within a single period of development, like the period of concrete operations. In middle childhood the child acquires conservation skills in steps. The child grasps the principle of conservation with reference to one task, such as the quantity of matter, but is still unable to understand a similar principle involved in another task, such as the notion of the conservation of weight. According to Piaget, children usually achieve the notion of the invariance of quantity a year or so before that of the invariance of weight.

Piaget (1950) shows that all children pass through the same stages of intellectual functioning between birth and adulthood, and to him everyone's intellectual development appears to move in the same sequence. Other psychologists have demonstrated that people differ in their ways of processing information. Each of us has a fairly consistent pattern of intellectual behavior, based on our own exposure to various environments. This pattern can be described as a person's personal style, which is the stable preference that people exhibit in organizing and categorizing their perceptions.

One difference in people's cognitive styles appears in their approaches to problem solving. Some individuals respond to a problem rapidly, without worrying about accuracy (impulsive behavior), whereas others who possess equal intelligence take considerably more time (reflective behavior) (Kagan, 1966).

Cindy and Karen, ages 10 and 11, had been given assignments by their mother before she went to work one Saturday morning. The apartment certainly looked chaotic. There were dirty dishes sitting in the sink as well as on the kitchen table, begging to be cleaned. Opening the windows to let the sunshine in, the girls also allowed some uninvited houseflies into their apartment. The temptation to go out and play in the street, with the sun warm on their backs, was too much to resist, so Cindy and Karen left their household chores undone and went out to play. In their hurry, they dropped their nighties right in the family-cum-living-cum-bedroom and left their beds unmade.

Their 17-year-old brother Steve, who worked in a fast food place, came home for an afternoon nap, having worked all night. He was irritated by the mess that he saw in the apartment and called out to his sisters, saying that he would complain about them to their mother. His loud, boisterous voice quickly brought the girls in. Cindy burst out crying and started to curse because she felt that her brother had treated them badly by yelling at them. Karen looked quietly at the mess in the rooms and started to clean, whispering that they had promised to clean up. Cindy's behavior was impulsive, whereas Karen's was reflective.

Another aspect of cognitive style is field independence and field dependence (Witkin, Dyk, Faterson, Goodenough, & Karp, 1962). In colloquial terms, some people tend to be "splitters" and others "lumpers." Field-independent people (splitters) analyze the elements of a scene, whereas field-dependent people (lumpers) tend to categorize a scene as a whole and to overlook the individual items that compose it.

Person Perception

The elementary school years are a period of rapid growth in knowledge of the social world and of requirements for social interaction. When we enter a social setting, we attempt to place people in a broad network of possible social relationships and assess such aspects of people's status as age, sex, and roles.

Children under 8 years of age describe people largely in terms of external, readily observable attributes. They categorize people in a simple, holistic, moralistic manner and employ vague, global descriptive terms such as "good," "bad," and "horrible."

Six-year-old Tommy complained to his mother that his classmate Paul was the "baddest" boy in his class. The reason was that Paul had given Tommy a candy but later changed his mind and took it back. Thus he was described in global terms by Tommy.

An 8-year-old child's vocabulary increases rapidly. The phrases become more specific and precise, and the child gains steadily in ability to recognize certain regularities or unchanging qualities in the inner dispositions or overt behaviors of other individuals. Younger children characterize a person entirely by the quality the person is displaying at the moment, so the same person may sometimes be "bad," sometimes "good," and sometimes "nice." As they grow older, children become capable of integrating various qualities into the idea of a whole person. A 14-year-old girl says of her friend, "Sometimes she gets angry, but that doesn't last long and soon she's her normal self" (Livesley & Bromley, 1973).

Sociocultural factors also influence person perception. In some cultures children are treated as adults when they reach 5 or 6 and are given adult roles to play. In the Koya tribe of India, girls become adults when they are 6 or so. They cook food, bring home firewood, and take care of their younger siblings. Koya girls learn at a very young age to cater to the needs of adult men as well as young boys, for the males are the hunters and go away from home for long periods of time in search of food.

Zena was a 10-year-old girl belonging to a lower-class Muslim family. At a young age, she learned to cook, take care of the house, and obey the commands of her brothers and her father because she was a girl. The family carefully followed the rules of their religion, which teaches that women are inferior to men and must learn to cater to boys and men and play a subservient role in the family.

Moral Development

People learn to live with their society's designations of what is right and what is wrong. All human enterprise requires rules. People also make the assumption that the rules will be followed. Each person's own welfare, as well as the existence of justice and equality, depends on people's acceptance of certain moral standards.

Moral development can be described as the process by which children adopt principles that are given to them and learn to evaluate behavior as right or wrong and govern their actions by those principles.

Psychologists have depicted moral development in many ways: as conformity to group norms, as increasing capacity for guilt, as the internal regulation of behavior in the absence of external sanctions, as behavior that is socially positive or helpful, and as the ability to reason about justice (Carroll & Rest, 1982).

Carroll and Rest identify the major psychological components involved in behaving morally. They propose that a fully developed morality exhibits the following features:

1. Recognition and sensitivity. An awareness that goes beyond the perception of ambiguity; the ability to recognize the presence of a moral problem in a given social situation and the capacity to be sensitive and recognize that someone's welfare is at stake.
2. Moral judgment. Determining what ideally ought to be done in a particular situation; also, being aware of what moral norms and moral ideals apply in a given situation.
3. Values and influences. Application of values and influences to take into account the good that a situation may activate for a person as well as the influence of external pressures.
4. Execution and implementation of moral action. Behaving in accordance with one's goals in spite of distractions, impediments, and incidental adjustments; organizing and sustaining behavior to realize one's goals.

According to Carroll and Rest, people can fail morally due to defects in any of the four processes:

1. being insensitive to the needs of others, and therefore not noticing that there is a moral problem; being confused about a social situation and unable to interpret what is happening
2. having simplistic and inadequate concepts of fairness and moral ideals
3. having moral ideas that are adequate but are compromised by the pressures of the situation (for example, threats from others, controversial opinions, or physical danger)
4. having insufficient energy to carry out the plan or becoming sidetracked by some diversion.

Eleven-year-old George was picked up in the classroom for drinking and disorderly behavior. Both his parents and his teacher were shocked because George normally kept within the range of acceptable behavior in school. He met with the school authorities, who advised his parents to take him to see the school counselor. When George had recovered from his alcoholic trance, he was ready to talk. He said that he had never taken a drink before, having been taught at home that it was improper to drink or take drugs. However, at school, some older boys got hold of him and forced him to drink alcohol. When he refused, they threatened to hurt him physically. George knew that he could not attend class drunk or misbehave in a classroom, but despite the moral values of his upbringing he did what was asked of him because of the pressures of the situation and the fear of physical danger.

The major contemporary theories of moral development were discussed in Chapter 4 with reference to the preschool years. Freudian theory views moral development in terms of the innate structure of the personality. Social learning theory represents it as a function of conditioning and modeling experiences. Interactional theories formulated by Piaget and Kohlberg place moral development within a cognitive context.

Psychoanalytic Theory

According to Freud, moral development is rooted in the emergence of the superego, a concept that is roughly equated to conscience. Children possess various inborn drives—basic sexual and aggressive instincts—known collectively as the *id*. Parents often thwart those drives in children in order to socialize them and to follow the standards of the larger society. Many times this frustration generates hostility in children toward their parents, but because revealing hostility would provoke withdrawal of parents' affection, children internalize the parental prohibitions.

How does internalization take place? To avoid guilt, self-punishment, and anxiety, children "become" their own parents through the mechanism of the superego. External punishment is transformed into self-punishment and external control into self-control. By incorporating the parental evaluation of their own behavior, children incorporate into themselves the moral standards of the wider society. Thus, according to Freud (1930), guilt feelings are turned toward oneself. Freud also argues that excessive guilt is the beginning of the foundation of many mental disorders. Most behavioral and social scientists do not accept the orthodox psychoanalytical theory, but the assumption that children identify with their parents remains a major tenet of much contemporary research and therapy.

Social Learning Theory

According to psychologists Albert Bandura, Walter Mischel, and others, children learn socialization behavior through imitative play. They acquire moral standards in much the same way they learn other behaviors. The psychologists insist that social behavior is dependent on situational contexts and not on one single aspect of the superego. Thus social-learning theorists believe that behavior is the result of modeling, especially when it is systematic and employs an appropriate system of rewards and punishments (Mischel & Mischel, 1976).

Studies have been carried out by social-learning theorists who are concerned with the effect of models on observers' resistance to temptations (Bandura, Ross, & Ross, 1961). In an experiment conducted by Walters, Leat, and Meizei (1963), children saw a person who either yields or does not yield to temptation. One group of boys watched a movie in which a child was punished by his mother for playing with some forbidden toys. A second group saw another version of the movie, in which the child was rewarded for the same behavior. A control group did not see any movie. The experimenter took each boy to another room and asked him not to play with the toys there. The study showed that the boys' responses depended on the model they had seen earlier. The boys who had observed the movie in which the boy had been punished showed the greatest reluctance to play with the toys. The boys who saw the movie in which the mother rewarded the boy for disobeying proceeded to disobey the experimenter themselves and played with the toys more often than did the boys in the other two groups. In short, observing the behavior of another person did seem to have a modeling effect on children's obedience or disobedience to social regulations (Ross, 1971; Rosenkoetter, 1973).

Interactional Theories

Piaget.   According to cognitive theory, morality, like intellect, develops in progressive age-related stages. Piaget's book *The Moral Judgment of the Child* (1932/1965) discusses the development of children's moral judgments.

On the basis of his interactional view, Piaget believes that moral development occurs as children act upon and modify the world they live in. In Piaget's two-stage theory of moral development, heteronomous morality arises on account of the unequal interaction between children and adults. Immersed in an authoritarian environment, young children occupy an inferior position and develop a conception of moral rules that is absolute, unchanging, and rigid. As children approach and enter adolescence, heteronomous morality gives way to autonomous morality, which arises out of interaction among peers. The relationship of equals, coupled with general intellectual growth and a weakening in the constraints of adult authority, creates a morality characterized by rationality, flexibility, and social consciousness. Through peer associations, young people develop a sense of justice, a concern for the rights of others, and a desire for reciprocity and equality in human relations. Piaget (1965) describes autonomous morality as egalitarian and democratic—a morality that is based on mutual respect and cooperation.

Piaget presents four dimensions that characterize the heteronomous stage:

1. Moral absolutism. Young children assume that rules are universal and accept rules as given and unquestionable.

Tim, age 5, is not allowed to eat candy except after dinner. When he sees his friend Brad eating candy before mealtime, he becomes upset and promises to tell on Brad. After all, if Tim is not allowed candy freely at home, Brad's family must have the same rules and regulations.

2. Belief in immutability. Children usually believe that rules are rigid and unalterable.

3. Belief in imminent justice by God acting in the world. Children think that misfortune is inflicted upon wrongdoers by nature or God.

> Eight-year-old Kathie had skipped breakfast and was thoroughly hungry before noontime. When she saw some candy in her friend Susie's bag while Susie was away, she took the candy and ate it. Then she was filled with remorse and guilt. While walking to the cafeteria, she fell down and bruised her knee, and she told herself, "This happened to me because I stole the candy."

4. Evaluation of moral responsibility in terms of its consequences. Children appraise an act by its results rather than by the intent of the actor.

Piaget's stages represent the *growth* of a sense of morality rather than the *existence* of moral behavior. According to Piaget (1965), children's moral sense develops from the interaction between developing thought structures and their widening social experiences. Eventually children reach the stage of moral relativism; they realize that rules are created and agreed upon by individuals and that the rules can be changed as the need arises.

In his study of game playing, Piaget observed that boys become increasingly fascinated with the legal elaboration of rules and the development of fair procedures for dealing with conflicts, a fascination that he notes is not found among girls (Piaget, 1968). Piaget observes that girls have a more "pragmatic" attitude toward rules, "regarding a rule as good as long as the game repaid it" (Piaget, 1968). Girls appear to be more tolerant in their attitudes toward rules, more willing to make exceptions, and more easily reconciled to innovations. A legal sense, which to Piaget is essential in moral development, "is far less developed in little girls than in boys." The bias in Piaget's thinking is that he equates male development with child development (Gilligan, 1982).

Kohlberg.   Kohlberg has extended Piaget's stages of moral realism and moral reasoning into five phases, calling them developmental types of value orientation, as described in Chapter 1.

Kohlberg and associates have elaborated the major points of Piaget's general approach (Colby, Gibbs, & Kohlberg, 1983; Kohlberg, 1969, 1971, 1976). Kohlberg's theory and research include a collection of theories and methods, all of which have in common these basic points (Carroll & Rest, 1982):

1. They focus on the underlying interpretive frameworks (global, unified systems of thinking) of a subject in perceiving social-moral situations and organizing judgments about what ought to be done.
2. They assume that these basic cognitive structures are not rules but schemas of social understanding developed by the person in interaction

with others. They are not developed by direct tuition, modeling, or reinforcement of socializing agents.

3. They hold that concepts of justice are a key to development in moral understanding. People learn to understand progressively more complicated and encompassing systems of reciprocal cooperation.
4. They propose that development takes place through the successive transformations of basic organizing principles; hence five stages instead of Piaget's two.

As specified earlier, those five stages are (adapted from Kohlberg, 1976):

Level 1: Preconventional
    Stage 1: Heteronomous morality
    Stage 2: Individualism, instrumental purpose, and exchange
Level 2: Conventional
    Stage 3: Mutual interpersonal expectations, interpersonal conformity and relationships
    Stage 4: Social systems and conscience
Level 3: Postconventional or principled
    Stage 5: Social contract or utility and individual rights.

Baumrind (1978) has criticized Kohlberg's theory because it ignores important cultural differences in the determination of what is moral. In Baumrind's view, moral development may depend less on cognitive processes than on values instilled during the process of socialization. Power and Reimer (1978) found other weaknesses in Kohlberg's theory. They determined that there is a difference between thinking about moral behavior and acting morally. Moral decisions are made at times of crisis, when people's behavior may not reflect their beliefs. Kohlberg reviewed his work (1978) and acknowledged these distinctions. In his modified thinking, Kohlberg specified that behavior should be studied partially in terms of the moral norms of the group to which people belong and partially in terms of people's internalized attitudes. Kohlberg also granted that the last level of moral development, principle orientation, may not apply to people of all cultures.

In some cultures, stealing is not a crime. Thrasher (1963) made a study of 1,313 gangs in Chicago. Gangs, like most other forms of people's lifestyles, have to be understood in their personal habitat. They spring up spontaneously and under favorable conditions as well as in a definite milieu. In Itschkie's Black Hand Society, which consisted of boys between the ages of 12 to 15 (adolescent age group), stealing offered the members of the gang the easiest way of getting the means to satisfy their wishes. When the boys in the gang wanted money and sport, their most common resort was the drunken man or the blind beggar. These unfortunate victims became a source of amusement as well as possibly providing large sums of money which they often had in their possession (Thrasher, 1963).

Today, modern organized crime culture has grown largely out of the fact that it has ceased to be sporadic and occasional but has become organized and continuous. The number of individuals and groups interested in the promulgation of illegal activities has become so great as to make the commission of crime safer, more effective, and more profitable (Thrasher, 1963). And, in North America where killing a person is a crime, the killing of people during wartime is accepted, and is conditioned by the crisis and political situation of a particular period.

Kohlberg's theory has generated a large number of research projects, which have confirmed some aspects of moral thinking but have neglected others. In a 20-year longitudinal study of 58 U.S. males who were 10, 13, and 16 years old at first testing, Kohlberg and his associates found that the boys progressed through the stages of moral development in sequence and none skipped a stage. Moreover, moral judgments correlated positively with the boy's age, education, IQ, and socioeconomic status (Colby, Kohlberg, Gibbs, & Lieberman, 1983). To some degree, cross-cultural studies confirm this sequencing of development.

The appropriateness of Kohlberg's definition of morality for women in U.S. society has also been questioned (Gilligan, 1982), an issue that will be discussed in later chapters.

Kohlberg's important theory has enriched our thinking about the manner in which moral development occurs, has furthered an understanding of the relationship between cognitive maturity and moral maturity, and has stimulated research and the elaboration of theory.

Socialization and the School Setting
The School Experience

Children in the 6 to 12 age group enter some kind of school setting and spend a significant amount of time interacting with a new and complex social institution. School systems vary in standards of achievement as well as in norms of behavior. Many schools in our country have school social workers whose role is to look into the problems that children may either encounter within the school system or bring with them from home.

Expectations.   When they enter a school situation, children have to meet a number of expectations. Separated from their parents or chief caregivers for a significant period of time, they learn to take care of themselves in small ways, such as making sure that they are neatly dressed before they start off on a long day. In school they learn to cooperate with others and develop an understanding of school rules and regulations.

> Ten-year-old Justin is an only child with two working parents. In the mornings, he is responsible for preparing himself for school. He bathes, brushes his teeth, and dresses. He eats the cereal that is left for him on the dining table, leaves the dirty dishes in the dishwasher, and makes sure he has his lunch money, then sets off for school.

School rules and regulations vary according to cultural values and educational philosophy. In the formal school setting that is typical of suburbia, the teacher spends a lot of time reviewing and enforcing certain codes of behavior: children should listen before they speak, line up for recesses, and get permission to go to the bathroom. It is fairly well accepted practice for a teacher to spend more time and energy in keeping order than in teaching the subject matter.

Eight-year-old Bill had been a student at a private school that encouraged "open classroom" behavior. Children were allowed to sit wherever they felt comfortable, could select their own work for the whole day, and could interact informally with the teacher and the other children in the classroom. By the unspoken rules of the classroom, each child worked independently and could ask questions but should avoid disturbing others. When his family moved to another town, Bill found himself in a public school whose standards did not reflect the sort of creativity he had experienced earlier. Discipline was strict, and Bill felt stifled by too many overt rules of behavior and the necessity of asking permission for "everything." He described his teacher as a "law and order" person who concentrated not on teaching the kids but on punishing disobedience and rewarding obedience of the rules.

Regardless of the type of school setting, children face a tremendous gap between what is acceptable at home and what any new school demands (Kozol, 1970; Holt, 1964; Read, 1971). Thus children internalize a whole range of new procedures. Children's ability to succeed in school depends on how the child deals with the transition from home to school. Successful adaptation depends upon factors such as how well the child can cope with dependency, autonomy, relationship to authority, and the need to control aggressive behavior and be in control of oneself.

Socialization.   School settings affect the social-emotional development of children. Concern with the effect of schooling is justified, for it is a fact of life for every child in the United States. Schools play an important role in the process of socializing children. In addition to the home, the school is the setting for development of self-esteem, self-image, identity, ego, and what one could operationally call a *sense of self.*

Because of changes brought about in the traditional American lifestyle by such forces as feminism and the employment of women outside the home, the nature of child care in the preschool years is changing. Consequently, many children who are entering the public school system at 5 or 6 years of age have already been exposed to some previous outside-the-home experience, such as nursery school or daycare, or early interventions, such as Head Start.

Relationships.   What is the impact on children of their relationships with teachers and schoolmates? Does schooling contribute to the development of social skills? Research in this area is plagued by difficulty because social relationships are both independent and dependent variables. However, in our discussion social relationships will be viewed as a dependent variable. Some of the research presented does not clearly reveal the cause–effect relationships. Among the independent variables discussed in this chapter are classroom practices and school-system environments.

In the public school system there are some specific practices that influence the child's relationships and development. The size of the class is one such variable. Intimate relationships in small groups promote maximal personality development; however, small class size also has some negative effects. Reisert (1971) reports that students in small classes tend to be more rude and discourteous, and students in large classes tend to share information with their peers more readily than those in small classes. The effect of class size on children's growth is complex. Although individual personality development is optimal in smaller classes, there is greater social development in larger classes. This research also considers relationships as an independent variable because it is relationships in small classes that promote personality development. Can it be that relationships in the classroom positively effect social development? An affirmative answer would suggest a circular function between social relationships and development, an idea that is supported theoretically but not empirically (Lerner & Busch-Rossnagel, 1981).

The School Environment

Variables that influence the child's social relationships and development are characteristic of an entire school rather than just a single classroom, and they reveal the philosophy of the school system. Variables include open-space (creative and democratic), closed-space (traditional) classrooms, racially integrated and bicultural approaches, and the socioeconomic-class orientation of the school setting. Hetherington (1971) suggests that most school teachers have a middle-class orientation, which often affects the personality development of lower-class children. Sometimes lower-class children have lower self-evaluations and low achievement motivation. These variables have, in turn, been associated with school failure and high dropout rates.

Being a member of a minority group poses a serious threat to a child's ego when the minority group is regarded unfavorably by others. Prejudices may show up, for example, when a child's parents invite some of the child's school friends to a birthday party but omit those who are members of a minority group. Minority children in the United States are sometimes faced with outright rejection, especially by parents of other children. That experience promotes feelings of inadequacy and insecurity. But a child who belongs to a high-prestige minority group develops positive rather than negative feelings toward the self (Jones, Garrison, & Morgan, 1985).

Busch-Rossnagel and Vance (1982) suggest that bicultural environments would help overcome the middle-class orientation of schools. Bicultural environments are defined as those in which two cultures are officially recognized in all aspects of school functioning and are an integral part of the setting (Goebes & Shore, 1978). Investigating the sense of self, Goebes and Shore compared girls in bicultural and monocultural schools and found that preadolescent Anglo and Latino girls in the bicultural environment had better self-images than the girls in the monocultural programs.

Traditional schools are designed for parallel activities, without students interacting with each other. This is called co-action. In contrast, interaction is seen as a sharing of activities.

Downing and Bothwell (1979) hypothesized that students in traditional schools would anticipate co-action with peers, whereas students in open-space schools would indicate (by their selection of seat) that they expect social interaction. These hypotheses have been supported by research. In addition, the rate of cooperation in a game situation was found to be higher for open-space students than for closed-spaced students. It is apparent that open-space schools enhance social development and thought and facilitate relationships (Busch-Rossnagel & Vance, 1982). It is quite possible, although not necessary, that teaching styles differ in the two school systems.

Moral Climate

One of the important functions of a publicly controlled school system is to teach the dominant values of the society to its students. Public schooling in the United States is associated by the middle class with American values, whereas private schooling or no schooling at all is seen as being inconsistent with American values (Bakan, 1971). The traditional approach to instilling morals has been termed *character education* or *conduct development*. However, nowhere in this country does school provide for careful, systematic, graded moral training. After seven decades, it is still true that there is no moral training per se in public schools. There is only what can be termed *incidental instruction* (Sneath & Hodges, 1914).

By character education and conduct development the students learn about and accept some of the responsibilities that they will have to face as adults. Because schools uphold middle-class values, some students from lower-class homes confront a conflict in learning the schools' values (Kay, 1975). Most upper- and middle-class children who attend public schools do not appear to have such conflicts.

Alice was a 7-year-old child of a lower-class family. Her parents worked for an upper-middle-class industrialist, employed in their home as a husband-and-wife team, and lived in the servants' quarters. Thus Alice had to attend a middle-class public school where neither the teacher nor her classmates understood her.

Alice was a victim of neglect at home. Her parents spent all their energy fighting each other. Physical abuse in the family was excessive. Alice frequently went to school hungry and sloppily dressed. Other children found her "coarse and difficult" and looked down on her, an attitude that was encouraged by the teacher, who was impatient with Alice's lack of self-discipline. The total lack of structure in Alice's family was reflected by Alice's classroom behavior: when she got tired, she tried to sleep, and when she got angry she cursed and screamed at the other children. In turn, the other children ridiculed her, thus perpetuating a negative cycle that affected Alice's already low self-esteem. Chances of

Alice attending a public school with lower-income children were nil. Irrespective of the school system, Alice had personal problems that had to be dealt with. The school social worker spent time counseling Alice and her parents—helping Alice to accept and adjust to her school.

Schooling has implications for the sense of morality that children develop. Kay (1975) found that when a teacher was authoritarian, children withdrew into submission, and in a laissez-faire atmosphere they became indifferent and irresponsible. Democratic situations had positive effects on the children; they developed responsibility and, with the dispersion of social power, adopted adult values. Kay concluded that children respond to the structure of the school situation.

In the typical school setting, children interact for the major part of the day with a number of classmates who are in their own age group and with whom they were originally unfamiliar. During loosely supervised recess and lunch periods, children learn to interact more closely with peers and build up a value system that helps them function meaningfully in the school setting.

Martin, the firstborn of four sons, was concerned that he was not well liked in his new school. One day, he brought in his pet frog and showed his unusual pet to his classmates during break time. Having something to show created an opportunity to initiate relationships with other boys. He told the boys that he had other pets, which he would bring to school shortly. This was Martin's way of gaining acceptance in a new school.

Special Problems in School

Like adults, children tend to be individualistic. A child's reactions to the school setting are affected by the complex interplay of intellectual, perceptual, physical, social, moral, and emotional factors.

Many kinds of problems may arise in a classroom. Sometimes a bright child is overlooked by a teacher because the child is restless or has poor motor coordination or poor writing ability. The child is not able to participate in a reading group because of emotional immaturity and disruptive behavior. Unless the problem is given attention, the child will be viewed simplistically as disruptive and may not get the kind of help that is appropriate for the root problem.

A child who does not speak English may enter a school in a small suburban town where children are exposed only to the English language and American ways of living.

Feda was a Lebanese child who had been uprooted from her home town and brought to New York City. There were no facilities for bilingual education, so Feda failed in school and was miserable. Her family was loving, but was unable to help her in her struggle to become bilingual. The school social worker put Feda and her family in touch with community resources that could help Feda to make the transition to a new language and culture.

In school settings, the social worker serves as a liaison between school and parent. The worker must attempt to become familiar with the family situation, including disparities between the family culture and the school culture. For instance, when a child from the Native American culture who has not been exposed to standard American values enters the American classroom, the teacher may be irritated because the child avoids eye contact or fails to respond to well-intentioned questions. A social worker who is familiar with the differences between the two cultures should be able to point out that the child is following traditional tribal customs in refraining from making eye contact. Native American children also have a way of dealing with unpleasant situations by withdrawing rather than by confronting them and may consider "normal" teacher–pupil interactions to be overly intrusive rather than helpful (Blanchard, 1979).

The Psychosocial Environment
Erikson: Industry versus Inferiority

According to Erikson, middle childhood is the period when children exhibit the belief, "I am what I learn." Children watch things and try to do them. Erikson's psychosocial theory suggests that a person's attitude toward work is established during the school years. As children develop their skills and acquire personal standards for evaluation, they evolve an initial assessment of whether or not they can make a contribution to the social community.

This period is characterized by the conflict of industry versus inferiority. Industry implies a willingness to perform meaningful work. During the middle childhood school years, many aspects of work are intrinsically motivating. Learning new skills brings children closer to the capacities of adults. Having skills also gives the child a feeling of independence and a sense of responsibility that increases self-worth. Children all over the world receive some type of systematic instruction during this period. In preliterate societies without schooling, children learn by what adults and others demonstrate in their ways of behavior (acclamation) rather than by educational/ formal tutoring. They learn the basic skills of the culture, such as handling utensils, tools, and weapons.

In our culture, the aim is to attain a sense of mastery. In addition to the self-motivating factors associated with competence, there are external sources of reinforcement that promote development of skills. Parents as well as teachers encourage children to become better at what they do, offering material rewards and additional privileges. Peers also encourage each other to develop certain skills. Some social organizations, such as scouting camps, add to the acquisition of skills.

In middle childhood, the child is encouraged to gain independence. If not guided or prodded too often by the parent, the child develops a sense of initiative. If children do not move away and are tied to the parents for directives, then their chances of becoming industrious are diminished. Such children do not feel a sense of initiative but a sense of shame.

Don was a bright 8-year-old, an only child overprotected by his mother. He loved to play ball and was very good at it. One day his friends called him to play ball, and he went without his mother's permission. In the course of the game, he fell and hurt himself. At that point, although he had enjoyed the freedom of playing ball and the initiative that went with it, he was filled with remorse and guilt because his mother had warned him that he should not play games without her permission. He felt that he should stay close to his mother and do only what she wanted him to do.

The quality Erikson pairs with industry in this stage's characteristic conflict is inferiority. When do children generate a sense of inferiority? Feelings of inadequacy and lack of worth come from two sources: the self and the social environment. Reward structures are so attuned to mastery that children who do not develop competency have heightened feelings of inferiority. Individual differences in children necessarily result in differences in aptitude, preferences, and capacity for learning specific skills. Children usually experience some inadequacy in some specific skill area. Success in one area can compensate for failure in another, minimizing the effect of individual areas of inadequacy on the resolution of the psychosocial conflict.

The environment provides different types of reinforcement for different types of success. Our culture values a six-year-old's reading a book more highly than playing with some mechanical toys. Participating in team sports and winning is valued more highly than watching a TV show and enjoying it with the family. Thus the social environment does play a part in providing social comparisons. Not only in school settings but also at home, children are confronted with statements that amount to, "You are not as good as so-and-so." Children are often compared, graded, grouped, and publicly criticized on the basis of how their efforts compare with another person's or group's. The intrinsic motive of engaging in a task for the pleasure of the challenge conflicts with messages that engender feelings of self-consciousness, competitiveness, and doubt.

The social environment stimulates feelings of inferiority by placing negative value on all kinds of failures. Thus failure is viewed as one form of embarassment. Doubt and guilt are intimately connected with feelings of inferiority. A few failures can generate strong negative feelings, and a child could avoid engaging in new tasks in order to avoid failure: "I can play tennis, but I am not as good as Joe, so I don't think I will try to play at all."

As the child grows older, he or she learns that work, effort, and perseverance will bring him rewards of competence, mastery, and approval.

Zack, age 11, lived in the ghetto. His family did not value schooling. His mother, a single parent, was unable to support the ten-member family. Zack took off from school often, and his mother did not question him. He stole food and picked pockets to bring home things that the family urgently needed. His stealing was overlooked—or rather, subtly encouraged—for it satisfied the needs of the family. In school, Zack was below average and had difficulty even in spelling simple words; however, family approval of his competency in stealing helped him to persevere. Although a child who did not do well in school would normally develop negative feelings, Zack earned rewards of approval by engaging in new tasks that appeared helpful to his family, irrespective of the fact that they were considered antisocial.

Among the points on which Erikson's theory has been criticized is his presentation of human behavior solely from the point of view of a male child. According to Erikson, it is in middle childhood that children learn to deal with industry versus inferiority, and demonstration of competence becomes critical for the child's developing self-esteem. However, Erikson is talking only about the male child. For the female child Erikson indicates that the sequence is a bit different (1968). This difference will be discussed further under the topic of sex-role development.

Sex-Role Development

Influence of parents.   Differential treatment of boys and girls begins on the day they are born. Rubin, Provenzano, and Luria (1974) interviewed fathers and mothers of 15 boys and 15 girls within 24 hours after the infants' birth. Parents rated their children on an 18-item bipolar adjective scale and were asked to describe their child to the investigator as they would to a close friend or relative. In reality, these male and female infants did not differ in average length, weight, or Apgar scores, yet the parents perceived them differently and labeled them accordingly. Both mothers and fathers labeled their daughters weaker, smaller, prettier, less attentive, more awkward, and more delicate. Sons were seen as firmer, larger featured, better coordinated, more alert, and hardier. There was only one measure on which the parents differed: fathers rated daughters more cuddly than sons, whereas mothers found their sons more cuddly than daughters.

Researchers report that when children are being socialized, working-class parents are less permissive toward children's expression of sexuality than middle-class parents, but there are no differences in parental responses to childhood sexuality according to the child's sex (Newson & Newson, 1968; Sears, Rau, & Alpert, 1965). Many sex-differentiated behaviors associated with achievement have been found, particularly in the attitudes of fathers. Mothers stressed competent task performance for both sexes, but fathers of girls were less concerned with performance and more concerned with interpersonal interactions with their daughters (Block, Block, & Harrington, 1974). In addition, it was found that fathers were more likely to reinforce inappropriate dependency behavior from daughters and task-oriented behavior from sons (Cantor, Wood, & Gelford, 1977; Hetherington, 1978). The importance of career, occupational success, and achievement is stressed more for boys than for girls, particularly by fathers (Block, 1978; Hoffman, 1975).

As these studies emphasize, sex roles are attained through socialization, as well as by imitation of the same-sex parent, other adults, and peers.

The notion that nurturance assists in sex-role learning has led some theorists to postulate that boys have more difficulty learning appropriate sex-role behavior than girls (Lynn, 1959). Because the mother is usually the chief caretaker and also the chief nurturer, boys have to form their initial attachment to her; later, the boy may have to shift his identification from his mother to his father in order to develop masculine behaviors. Girls, on the other hand, may continue identification with their initial model; hence the acquisition of sex-typed behavior for girls is thought to be simpler, more consistent, and capable of consolidation at earlier stages. Lynn suggested that anxiety and conflict arise in the boy when he must give up his attachment to his mother, shift, and develop an identification with a man to whom he has little direct or continuous exposure. The girl is able to observe her mother, chief caretaker, or female schoolteacher throughout the day and thereby maintains continuous contact with the adult members of her sex.

Absence of fathers from home has been found to have either temporary or permanent effects on boys (Drake & McDougall, 1977; Hetherington & Deur, 1971). Such sex-role problems were most apparent in preadolescence. They were more severe when the absence occurred before the child was 5 years old (Biller & Bahm, 1971).

A father's absence may also affect the nature of relationship between a single mother and her son. In a longitudinal study of both parents and children in single-parent homes, Hetherington, Cox, and Cox (1979) found that many single mothers treated their sons in an overprotective manner characterized by apprehension concerning adventuresome behaviors. If the single mother did not exhibit those overprotective qualities and she encouraged masculine exploratory behaviors, the son had fewer problems in sex-role development.

Influence of school.   School is another important area in which children learn sex-role behaviors. There are two viewpoints on sex roles and schoolchildren: that schools actually teach sex roles and that schools liberate the child from sex roles at home (Parsons, 1959).

The structure of most schools reflects the sex differentiations of the larger society, with its male-dominated patterns. It was found that elementary school teachers are predominantly women (87%), whereas the principals of schools are predominantly men (85%) (Kazalunaz, 1978).

In their review, Saario, Jackson, & Tittle (1973) conclude that teachers have well-entrenched sex-role expectations and that the idealized student is one who is conforming, dependent, and orderly. This role expectation conflicts with the traditional male sex role. Guttentag and Bray (1976) suggest that teachers hold different expectations for boys and girls, though perhaps not consciously. Pottker and Fishel (1977) indicate that sexism in schools is subtle and may not be perceived by educators, although the educators tend to categorize sex-typed behaviors for disciplinary purposes. Joffe (1977) argues that there is a considerable amount of sex stereotyping by teachers themselves, even in schools that stress nonsexist approaches.

Classroom practices also can be evaluated for sexism in the materials chosen. A number of studies show that books used in schools have sex-stereotyped contents. When the Princeton Chapter of the National Organization for Women (NOW) attempted to find books that portray men and women as equal in ability and aspirations, they found no such representations in 2760 stories in 134 books published by 12 companies (Kazalunaz, 1978).

Classroom experiences are also different for boys and girls. Research suggests that differential treatment in elementary schools leads to different types of achievement. A study by Leinhardt, Seewald, and Engel (1979) reveals that these differences in achievement could be due to differences in instruction. Observations made of second-graders showed that boys were better achievers in math, whereas girls tended to perform better in reading.

Sex-differentiated treatment also leads girls to become more acquiescent, conforming, and dependent, while boys become self-motivated and independent (Guttentag & Bray, 1976; Pottker & Fishel, 1977). Chodorow indicates that sex differences in early childhood appeared during the middle childhood years when children's games were studied (Chodorow, 1974). Children's games are considered by George Herbert Mead (1934) and Jean Piaget (1932/1965) to be important for the social development of children during the school years. In games children take the role of the other and come to view themselves through another person's eyes. They also learn to respect rules and understand the ways rules can be made and changed.

Influence of peers. Considering the peer group to be the agent of socialization during the elementary school years, Lever (1976) set out to discover whether there are sex differences in games that children play. She studied 181 White, middle-class fifth-graders ages 10 and 11. She watched the children as they played at school during recess and in physical education class, and she kept an account of how they spent their out-of-school time. Lever found that boys played more outdoor games than girls and played more often in heterogeneous groups. They played a larger number of competitive games, and their games lasted longer than girls' games because they required a higher level of skill and were less boring. Boys also tended to resolve disputes more effectively than girls. "During the course of the game, boys were seen quarrelling all the time, but not once was a game terminated because of a quarrel and no game was interrupted for more than seven minutes. In the most serious arguments, the final decision was always to 'repeat the game,' followed by a chorus of 'cheater's proof.'" It appeared that boys enjoyed the legal debates as much as the game itself, and even marginal players of lesser size and skill participated equally in these recurrent squabbles. In contrast, disputes among girls seemed to end the game.

Lever extends and corroborates the observations of Piaget that boys but not girls are fascinated with the legal aspects of games. The bias in the argument is based on our socialization, which until recently channeled boys' and girls' play energies into different acceptable games (this still continues in many homes).

Piaget argues that children learn respect for rules and thus prepare for moral development by playing rule-bound games; Kohlberg (1969) adds that these lessons are most effectively learned by taking the opportunities that dispute resolution affords for role taking. There are fewer moral lessons in boys' games than in girls' games. Traditional girls' games, such as jump rope and hopscotch, are turn-taking games in which the competition is not direct, since one person's success does not necessarily imply another's failure. Thus disputes are less likely to occur. In fact, most girls whom Lever interviewed mentioned that when a quarrel broke out, they ended their games. Rather than elaborating a system of rules for dealing with disputes, girls subordinated the continuation of the game to the continuation of relationships.

Lever draws her conclusions from games that children play. Boys learn the independence and the organizational skills that are necessary for coordinating the activities of large and diverse groups of people. Boys learn both to play with their enemies and to compete with their friends by participating in socially approved competitive situations. Thus they learn to deal with competition in a relatively forthright manner—in accordance with the rules of the game.

In contrast, girls choose to play in smaller and intimate groups, many times in the best-friend dyad and in private places. This type of play replicates the social pattern of primary human relationships in that its organization is more cooperative. Thus, as specified by Mead (1934), girls' play points less toward learning to deal with a large group of people and less toward the abstraction of human relationships. Rather, it fosters the development of empathy and sensitivity that are necessary to deal with one single person and points toward knowing the other as different from the self (Gilligan, 1982).

Effect on behavior. Some sex-role stereotypes are crystallized into well-defined expectations that exert pressure on the members of a particular group to display behaviors, attitudes, and traits consistent with their membership in the group. Sex-role stereotypes and sex-role standards result in judgments of boys and girls as suited for different roles. A child whose sex role has become more definite and similar to that of an adult of the same sex can be said to have developed a sex-role identification. A man who is a homemaker-husband and is nurturant and a woman who is completely career oriented are examples of sex-role preference.

Sex-typed behavior is behavior in which a person has integrated the traits, patterns, and attitudes appropriate to his or her biological sex. Sex typing is the process that takes place when a person internalizes a sex-role standard and becomes sex typed; therefore, this term is used synonymously with sex-role identification.

White: Competence

While utilizing his competency model, White (1960) comments that children reach a point of no longer being satisfied with just play and make-believe. In line with their interest in becoming adults, children need to feel useful and be able to make things and deal with things that have significance in the adult world. Erikson makes this need central for the humanly significant objective world; Sullivan (1953) makes it central for the social world. Once the problems of emotional development are exposed, practitioners begin to make connections with the findings of workers outside the psychoanalytical tradition who have observed the building of competence in great detail.

According to White, there is a definite pattern to the growth of social competence. In the age range from 6 to 9, children find out how to get along with others in the sense of competing, compromising, protecting themselves from hurt, and learning the rules of the game. They do this partly because they have been thrown in with others at school and partly because children afford each other opportunities to do something interesting in the environment. During this period, however, children's needs for dependency, security, and affection still find their satisfaction almost entirely within the family circle. Only a few assertive members of the juvenile society would find a sense of security in this world. As time passes, problems begin to emerge in the family and these include a desire for a special and favored position in the family, jealousy among siblings, or between a parent and child, guilt, and demands for affection from parents and others. All or some of these factors will characterize the child's emotional life at home.

> Joseph was the youngest of six children. The only son in the family, he was overprotected by his parents and shown favoritism. Joe nearly always got what he wanted. He had a special bed, more toys, and more clothes, and his mother catered to him all the time. His sisters were treated differently because they were girls. His immediate older sisters were envious of him. Joe, at 7, wished to get along better with them, but his need for love and attention as the favorite child in the family dominated other needs. In spite of the guilt he felt when his sisters accused him of being the center of attention, Joe found his sense of security in the family and was not entirely comfortable about his place with his friends and the outside world.

When a child is about 9 years of age, social competence and understanding advance to the point that the world of contemporaries begins to compete with the family circle. Membership in peer groups starts to have emotional appeal; what is known as the "we feeling" and friendships begin to supply some of the affective responses hitherto obtainable only within one's own family. As Helene Deutsch (1944) has revealed, these alliances serve the purpose of creating an alternative to the family world and thus open the way for a new growth of independence. White points out considerable potential for crisis along this route. One's sense of competence is challenged in many ways. The pursuit of mastery in school work and other adult tasks can build firm self-esteem and social approval but can also produce a deep sense of frustration and inferiority. Outcomes of competition on the playground yield either tremendous self-confidence or painful feelings of inadequacy. Attempts to participate in group, gang, and team activities can confer the rewards of membership or the punishment of rejection and ridicule. Young people seek friendships that can open avenues for warm, cherishing feelings or can lead to rebuffs and withdrawal into self.

Do these crises have any lasting importance for the development of personality? Freud has not attached much importance to crisis that occurs when a child is 9 years of age; a period of relative sexual calmness between the turbulent preschool years with their Oedipus and Electra complexes, and the storminess of adolescence. However, Sullivan (1953) identifies the juvenile period as the first developmental stage in which the limitations and pecularities of the home as a socializing influence begin to open for remedy. Even more influential, in his opinion, are preadolescent friendships, which under fortunate circumstances might rescue young people otherwise destined for emotional trouble or even mental breakdown.

White argues with Sullivan that the effects of the first five years of life can be substantially changed by developments that take place in middle childhood. In fact, a badly troubled first five years can lead to a relatively healthy outcome if the period after age 5 in a child's life encourages a rich growth of the sense of competence in many directions.

When latency encourages initiative and a firm sense of competence, there are many events in juvenile society that confer self-confidence. A boy who becomes prominent in school life is likely to enjoy some fortunate friendships, as well as self-assured relationships with girls. As White humorously puts it, a youth could have one or more love relationships that could be spoiled by oedipal residues(!), but the young person will not be without alternative resources. In creating social relationships, young people have to deal with jealousy and other negative feelings. Again White's interpretation of development portrays the experience of the male sex as universal. He says that young men acquire a number of characteristics in latency that are available to them in middle childhood and offer them a wide range of confidence-building activities (White, 1960).

It is not surprising that White uses the male model as the universal model for understanding behavior, both male and female, for this practice has been acceptable in our society until recent times.

Parenting

Parents' behavior affects children's behavior in many different ways. First, parents serve as models. Most parents have specific expectations of what they want from their children and how they want their children to behave. Parents also control the rewards and punishments that children receive. Child-rearing practices thus affect socialization and development of personality.

Baumrind has described three types of parenting—authoritarian, permissive, and authoritative (Chapter 4)—but Becker (1964) developed an excellent model for examining all parenting. He notes that parental attitudes can be classified on dimensions of restrictiveness–permissiveness, warmth–hostility, and anxious emotional involvement–calm detachment. By describing the dimensions of parental behavior instead of specific acts, the Becker model encompasses not only examples of extreme behavior but also actions of the great majority of parents whose behavior is not excessive.

How do these dimensions interact? Compare two mothers who are both highly permissive and calm. One mother is a warm person, and the other is coldly hostile. The difference on a single dimension produces a critical difference in parenting styles.

Nelly's mother was very permissive. When Nelly spilled her milk on the floor, her mother realized that it was accidental and told Nelly that she understood it was a mistake. She helped Nelly to clean up the spill.

Johnny's mother was also very permissive. When Johnny spilled his milk on the floor, his mother was aware that it was a mistake. But she looked at her son coldly and asked him to clean it up.

Becker describes the calm, permissive, warm parent as democratic and the calm, permissive, hostile parent as neglectful.

A large number of research studies have shown the effects of restrictiveness and permissiveness. Usually restrictive parents have dependent, submissive, and compliant children. A few studies described permissiveness as creating a noncontrolling, undemanding atmosphere and related it to active, outgoing, creative, and constructively aggressive behavior in children. Permissiveness does not necessarily produce independent children; when permissiveness is accompanied by hostility, children tend to become non-compliant and aggressive.

It is necessary that social workers understand these different modalities of child rearing and parenting in order to assess the strengths and weaknesses of any particular family constellation.

Effects of Child's Behavior

Not only do parents affect the behavior of their children but children have an effect on how parents deal with them. There is no shortage of studies that document such so-called child effects. Parke and Sawin (1975) found that the punitiveness of parents has a direct effect on the child's response to discipline. The defiant child, for example, is likely to elicit from his or her caregivers increasingly severe punishment strategies. This pattern implies that the authoritarian parent described earlier may find justification for the authoritarian style in the child's behavior.

The reciprocity of cause and effect in the parent–child relationship is constant, so it is difficult for any analysis to determine who is primarily responsible for a caregiver's behavior. Keller and Bell (1979) reveal a promising technique that experimentally shows children's effects on adults' caregiving strategies. (However, it is necessary to comment that methodologies that break down these dynamic interactions remain relatively undeveloped at this time.) Keller and Bell trained three 9-year-old girls to act as research confederates. The girls were trained to act either high or low in person orientation. Unaware that these children had been trained, 24 female college students participated in four 5-minute periods with one of the children. In all four periods, the adults were instructed to encourage the child to do something for another child (such as sew a pillow for a handicapped child), although the materials used differed from period to period. Showing high person orientation, the child paid attention to the adult's face and answered promptly; showing low person orientation, the child looked primarily at the toys and craft materials and delayed answering the adult. These experimental variations in the child's behavior affected the adults' attempts at socializing the child.

Another effect of children on parental behavior relates to their sex. In a study of mothers' attitudes toward their fifth-graders, the sons were treated with more assertion of power and withdrawal of love and less inducement than the daughters (Zussman, 1978). Similarly, Noller (1978) found that parent–daughter dyads show higher levels of overall interactions and affectionate exchange than do father–son dyads.

The age of the child has an influence on the quality of the mother's verbal interaction with him or her. Mothers of 3-year-olds had to give more complex explanations than mothers of 2-year-olds (Reichle, Longhurst, & Stepanich, 1976). The age of the child has been found to play a part in the behavior of both parents toward their children (Pakizegi, 1978). As the child grows older, the status of the child's physical maturation, rather than age or reasoning abilities, has been found to be an important element in influencing patterns of verbal interactions within a family (Steinberg & Hill, 1978).

Consideration of the child in the family has led us to recognize the fact that the child's effects extend to the marital relationship as well. Family sociologists have been interested in such influences, particularly in how the age of children—especially of the oldest child in the family—affects the quality of marital satisfaction (Lerner & Hultsch, 1983).

David was the oldest in a family of four children and the only son. At 12 he had started to take drugs. He was disorganized and stayed away from home for long periods of time. In despair, his parents went to a therapist. Each parent blamed the other. The wife felt that her husband had not done a good job of bringing up her male child because he was not a good role model. This accusation made her husband angry, and he retorted that she had favored the daughters and had only pressured David to perform and be good at everything. Their ongoing squabbles increased and affected not only their relationship with their children but also their relationship with each other. The therapist helped the parents to understand their own conflicts. The father drank heavily and the mother, along with the rest of the family, used David as the family scapegoat. The therapist helped the parents to deal with their own issues and to deal with David, who did not have a meaningful role model. The therapist and the rest of the family, through counseling, worked hard at removing David from the role of the family burden bearer, which included dealing with his current drug problems.

Limitations on Parental Power

If adults are so powerful, why is is that they do not have the kind of influence they would like to have on children? Maccoby (1979) indicates that as children grow older their parents have less physical control over them. When parents and children engage in long-term dialogue, it often leads to an agreement based on shared goals. Families that do not have shared goals have to negotiate constantly, from appropriate bedtimes to where to go for vacations. If one or both parents or the child dominate the atmosphere constantly, it makes negotiation impossible. Middle-childhood aged children may try to avoid excessive domination by staying away from home as long as possible. Extreme domination from parents would weaken the socialization process between middle childhood and adolescence and also make it difficult for children to make the transition from family life to independence as they grow older.

Another problem appears in the values reflected by child-rearing practices. Young parents are themselves still developing, and their values do not remain static. What the parent expects of the child is modified by the child's behavior (Fagot, 1982).

Changing cultural trends in raising children, as well as pressures from families and friends, may change a parent's expectations. As parents become more mature and their values continue to develop, the resulting behavior may influence children as much as or more than the methods used in early childhood.

Because parental patterns evolve, the child has to deal with complex peer relationships as well as adult influences. Since the child too is changing rapidly, as a result of his or her own cognitive development, the child's and adults' attitudes and behaviors are not always well matched. Such complexities make it understandable that people turn away from socialization research in despair.

In some families, parental power becomes deviant due to problems that one or both parents have and could affect a child brutally. One such continuing problem that has increasingly come to light in recent years is incest.

Eight-year-old Martha was constantly preoccupied and timid in class. She had turned from a lively, high-achieving child into a quiet and frightened person. She would no longer talk to her classmates, and had been failing consistently in all her exams. The teacher was aware that Martha's mother had recently remarried and that Martha was making many adjustments to having a new father in the family. Concerned that Martha's grades were not improving, the teacher spoke with Martha about her school work, pointing out how her performance had changed. Martha burst out crying but would not divulge any information.

The teacher sent Martha to see the school social worker. In that setting, Martha slowly but steadily revealed her painful story. Her new stepfather took her with him everywhere because he "loved his little new daughter," and in the process an incestuous relationship had developed between them. Martha was scared to tell because her stepfather told her that it would break her mother's heart and Martha would be responsible for causing her mother unnecessary pain; moreover, he said, her mother would never believe it. With much time and energy, the social worker intervened and placed Martha in a different setting until the stepfather had moved out of the family home.

An incestuous situation throws all child-rearing practices into disarray. The practitioner must work with a child who has to play not only a child's role but also that of a lover to a distorted adult. The practitioner has to hold onto whatever positives are present in the family's child-rearing practices and use them to work with the child.

Current Problems

Bronfenbrenner (1970) indicates that U.S. society is increasingly segregated by age, with children spending more time away from home, even if peer contacts are not always satisfying. Lasch (1977) found that contemporary parents have less capacity to influence children than did their predecessors; in other words, parents have difficulty transmitting their adult values to children against the values of the peer culture. The loss of parental authority is related to many factors, among them the family's loss of its traditional functions. Traditional values are weakened by processes of assimilation and acculturation.

> Twelve-year-old Felipe came to the United States from Mexico with his parents. School values undercut his home values, which were traditional and authoritarian. Felipe mingled with American children, learned to speak English, and adopted the American culture and way of life. The dramatic differences he saw between school and home values frightened him, but at home he constantly challenged his parents' authority. He talked to them about his American friends and the beautiful things they had. He wanted more freedom, more money, and more of everything. That upset his parents, who were angry with themselves for not understanding the culture. They disliked the new culture that was being imposed on them; it had already turned their son into a TV buff and a gum chewer. They lost patience with Felipe's constant demands for brand-name clothes.
>
> When Felipe refused to listen to his parents and stayed away from home one night, his parents went to see the school social worker. Short-term therapy helped them to understand their son's need to cope with the new culture and be accepted into it. Counseling focused on helping the parents understand their role in the new culture and at the same time opened new ways of creating understanding between Felipe and themselves.

Peer Influences on Personality

Children develop their own culture, and preadolescents (10 to 12 years of age) often have their own customs, rules, games, beliefs, and values. They follow a number of rituals that reflect adult social conventions and in many ways are more demanding and selective than adults. They have rigid rules about what games to play. Children at this age develop private clubs and make lifelong pledges to one another.

There are many different kinds of peer groups, including school, neighborhood cliques, scout troops, sports teams, and gangs. Representing one behavioral extreme, a gang may be oriented toward evading the rules and regulations of school and larger adult-dominated societies. Even nondelinquents often compare their parents with other children's parents when they find themselves in conflict with parental expectations, arguing, "The other kids are doing this, so why can't I?" At the other extreme, the expectations of peer groups may coincide with the rules of the adult groups, as is often true of scout organizations and religious youth groups.

Peer groups serve important functions. They provide children with an arena in which to exercise their independence of adult controls. Children receive support from their peer groups and thereby gain the courage and confidence they need to weaken their emotional bonds to their parents. By creating peer standards of behavior and appealing to these standards, the peer culture operates as a pressure group, as we saw in Felipe's case. Peer groups attempt to offer children a new road toward self-determination (Ausubel & Sullivan, 1970). The peer group extracts from its members important concessions with respect to bedtime hours, dress codes, and types of social activities they can perform.

Peer groups also perform the important function of giving children experiences in relationships of equality with others, unlike the adult world, in which children occupy subordinate positions while adults direct, guide, and control their activities. Dealing with peers calls for sociability, competition, self-assertion, and mutual understanding.

The peer group is the only social institution in which the child can acquire a position that is not marginal. Members have status, roles to play, and a "we feeling." Membership in a group, however big or small, furnishes children with security, companionship, acceptance, and a general sense of well-being. It helps children avoid boredom and loneliness during unstructured hours.

In peer groups, children transmit culture and gain informal knowledge about superstitions, folklore, fads, riddles, and secret codes of behavior. Peer groups also offer their members information as well as misinformation on many subjects. Early interest in sex could begin here.

Peer relationships are a necessary aspect of children's development because they help them to learn about and become part of the adult world. Older children have complex social lives, being involved in networks of both adults and peers.

Erika told her friends that she could play in the street with them for a short while, but that as soon as her "mama called her" she would have to return home, because "supper would be ready." While playing in the street, 7-year-old Erika was enthusiastic, followed all the rules, and basically had a good time. At home she followed the family's hierarchical system and obeyed the rules that her parents had negotiated with her as part of their lifestyle.

Same-Sex Peer Groups

Young boys and girls play together on school playgrounds during recess. However, by the third grade schoolchildren have divided themselves into two sexual camps: girls are friendly with girls and boys are friendly with boys. This separation into same-sex groups tends to peak at about the fifth grade, and much of the interaction between boys and girls at the fifth-grade level takes the form of bantering, teasing, name-calling, and frequently displays of open hostility. This "us against them" view of the opposite sex serves to emphasize differences between the sexes. Thus, this period functions as a protective phase in life during which children can fashion a coherent sex-based identity (Kerckhoff, 1972).

Social Acceptance and Rejection

Many peer relationships take on enduring and stable characteristics. In these properties they resemble a group, which can be described as an assemblage of two or more people who share a feeling of unity and are bound together in relatively stable patterns of social interaction. Group members normally have a sense of oneness, an assumption that their own inner experiences and emotional reactions are shared by other members. This like-mindedness gives each individual member the feeling of being not merely *in* the group but *of* the group.

> Bill, Arthur, and James are good friends. Although they have a larger group of friends in the neighborhood, they are especially close. All three of them are 8, and all like to play soccer and watch the same shows on TV. They are also members of a club that they created. They share their secrets, ideas, and dreams. They are loyal to each other and follow certain patterns of behavior. When Bill forgot to bring his lunch money to school one day, Arthur and James shared their midday meal with him. They visit each other in their homes and have good feelings for each other. Being together makes the three friends feel comfortable and well liked.

A group's awareness is experienced through shared values, which are the criteria that people use in deciding the relative merit and desirability of things (that is, other people, objects, events, ideas, acts, and feelings). Elementary schoolchildren's peer groups are no exception. The children arrange themselves in ranked hierarchies with respect to a variety of qualities. Even first-graders have notions of one another's relative popularity or status. Children differ in the extent to which their peers desire to be associated with them.

Physical Attractiveness and Body Build

Researchers have identified a number of qualities that children in late childhood find attractive in their peers. Among the most important are physical attractiveness and popularity. Children begin to acquire cultural definitions of these qualities at about age 6, and they are well set by the age of 8 (Walster, Aronson, Abrahams, & Rotterman, 1966; Byrne, Ervin, & Lamberth, 1970).

Children believe these physical characteristics to be highly individualistic. Children shift from the thought processes characteristic of the preoperational period to those of the period of concrete operations, and as they reach 11 to 12 years of age, they come to judge physical attractiveness in terms of features and body build, similiar to the manner in which adults judge physical attractiveness (Staffieri, 1967).

> Sam was a slightly built, puny boy. He dressed sloppily and was timid and shy in class. His classmates learned to ignore him because he was "no fun" and was constantly preoccupied with things that took place outside the classroom. He was viewed as different and ignored by his peers. Ignoring someone like Sam is very much what an adult might do in the workplace. If a person is sloppily dressed, is timid, and does marginal work that barely enables him to hold onto his job, he is not of much consequence to others (Staffieri, 1967, 1972).

Self-Esteem

Interacting with adults and peers, the child is provided with clues to their appraisals of his or her desirability, worth, or success. Constant interactions with others teach the child what is acceptable and what is not acceptable behavior. On the basis of responses they receive, children learn to understand who they are and how valued they can be. Their self-conceptions in turn influence and guide their behaviors. If children are accepted, approved of, and respected for what they are, they have a good chance of acquiring attitudes of self-esteem and self-acceptance. But if significant people in their lives belittle, blame, and reject them, they are likely to develop unfavorable self-attitudes.

> Michael was well loved and cared for at home. There was sufficient structure in his family to enable him to feel comfortable and to give him opportunities to respect and love his parents. When he was with friends, he respected their rights as well. One day, however, when things did not go well at his "clubhouse," he went home early. To his mother's questioning, he replied that no one could deal with Phil as the club leader because he always ordered the other boys around. Michael concluded, "that's not a good club where we cannot think for ourselves and be nice to each other."

Racial Awareness and Prejudice

An important aspect of children's peer experiences involves relations with members of racial and ethnic groups other than their own.

Williams and his associates (Williams & Stabler, 1973; Williams & Morland, 1976), summing up other research over a 15-year period, argue that the tradition of calling racial groups *"White"* and *"Black"* serves to link the good and bad associations of the color names to the respective racial groups. He feels that their research confirms this interpretation. A general preference for light over darkness may generalize to the colors white and black, and the preference may in turn be reinforced by various cultural and linguistic connotations associated with the words *white* and *black*. This in turn, affects racial awareness in children.

In a number of experiments, Williams employed a picture-story technique. Every child had an opportunity to choose between light-skinned (White) and dark-skinned (Black) figures. For instance, he showed a picture of two boys walking and said, "Here are two little boys. One of them is a kind little boy, and once he saw a kitten fall into a lake and he picked the kitten up to save it from drowning. Which do you think is the kind little boy?" (Williams & Stabler, 1973). Williams found that children who rate the color white highest on a color-meaning test also tend to rate the White figures more highly on the picture-story test.

These experiments suggest that a pro-White bias exists among all pre-schoolers, irrespective of whether they are Black or White. Moreover, there is a tendency for this bias to be present in the early school years. Among the White children, pro-White bias increases to the second-grade level and then declines. Black children usually maintain a moderate degree of pro-White bias throughout the early school years, with no appreciable shift in the first four grades.

Williams and Morland found that Black preschoolers show a definite White racial preference in choice of playmates. However, Black children usually shift to a Black racial preference when they enter an integrated public school situation. Hence it appears from the research of Williams and Morland (1976) that Black youngsters of early elementary school age have a Black racial preference in playmates, although they remain somewhat pro-White in the mental connotations that the colors black and white hold for them. Much of the research undertaken by Williams and Morland predated the full impact of the Black Power movement, with its emphasis on Black standards of beauty and Black cultural heritage.

A study was done by Rosenberg and Simmons (1972) using a random sample of 2,625 Baltimore school children in 1968, in order to test self-esteem. Their data revealed that Black children do not have lower self-esteem than Whites. In the Baltimore study, Black children who performed well in school and those children from higher social classes had higher self-esteem.

Bloom (1971) places three cautions about studies of self-esteem: (1) the Baltimore study data suggests that no assumptions about self-esteem can be made based on race; (2) factors like school performance, social class, and reference groups appear to be more important than race in explaining self-image, and finally, (3) the researcher's point of view affects the definition as well as the importance of including self-satisfaction, pride and self-respect in the study. All these assumptions may be justified, but it should be remembered that they are being made in all such research (Schaefer, 1979).

Learning Disabilities

Some children in later childhood do face critical problems. A boy or girl who begins as a slow learner may face several types of hazard depending both on the underlying basis for the difficulty and on how school and family respond. A slow learner—a child who does not have severe brain damage but who does have some impairments—may react differently from what teachers and others expect when introduced to the classroom for the first time.

Minimal Brain Damage

Educators, physicians, and child clinical psychologists have been paying increased attention to learning disabilities that are associated with relatively mild or specific neurological problems known as *minimal brain damage* (MBD).

What is MBD, seen through the eyes of a typical elementary school teacher? The child thus afflicted cannot concentrate on a discussion or activity as well as other children of his or her age group. The child is also easily distracted. Most children squirm and are restless, but this child is particularly restless, continuously moving—swinging feet, tapping fingers, and so forth. This hyperactivity is one of the most frequent indications of MBD. Among the number of other problems that may characterize a person with MBD are difficulty in fine visual discrimination; physical coordination that is not congruent with the supporting thought, as when a child cannot lift a glass to drink water without spills, or tumbles and falls down when intending to stand straight; problems with fine auditory discrimination; and a degree of memory impairment. MBD does not necessarily indicate a fundamental intellectual deficit. There are a number of specialized problems that interfere with learning, such as imperception of spatial relations and depth and some specific problems in the retention of information.

How do parents react to having an impaired child? Do they deny the problem, or do they overreact and conclude that the child is hopeless? Do parents become so absorbed in their own pain that they forget that they have a child who needs their help? Or do they believe that the child will grow out of it? The parents' attitudes strongly affect the manner in which the child is offered help, as well as treated.

Hazards in Coping with Learning Disabilities

Some learning disabilities are erroneously attributed to organic problems; in reality, a child may have a learning problem because his or her feelings and mind are absorbed elsewhere. The "elsewhere" could be anywhere—for instance, the child has a new brother or sister and must face the challenges of playing a new role, or the child may be ahead of the class and mentally engrossed in more advanced problems.

Debbie was quiet and shy in school. She was constantly distracted and did not even follow the simple addition that was being taught in the math class. The teachers assumed that Debbie was a slow learner, but in reality Debbie was preoccupied with guilt and her family's rejection. Six months earlier she had pushed her little brother into a pond, and he had nearly drowned. Part of his brain had been damaged, and at the time the family had directed anger and blame at Debbie. In the intervening months, the home situation had become more relaxed, but her brother was still receiving a lot of attention on account of his condition, and Debbie still experienced blame and rejection. Thus Debbie's inability to concentrate and participate in the classroom came from her inability to deal with her emotional situation.

Ten-year-old Kevin was tired of the same English and math lessons being discussed in the classroom, so he brought his book on lasers with him to class. He would constantly lift his desk, push his head in, and read his laser book. He would write and send out funny messages to his classmates that made them laugh. His teacher became very upset with him, and considered Kevin to be easily distracted and uncontrollable. He was referred to the school social worker based on the teacher's assumption that he was learning disabled. However, through the efforts of the social worker, Kevin was given an IQ test which showed him to be of above average intelligence and his overt distraction in the classroom to be the result of untold boredom.

Hyperactive children can be misdiagnosed as having disciplinary problems when their impaired coordination and short attention span cause them difficulties in learning.

Jonathan, who was very mischievous, was constantly punished in the classroom. His teacher had trouble tolerating him. There were 30 students in the class, and she assumed that Jon was merely seeking extra attention. She worked out a plan whereby Jon had to sit in a corner every morning as soon as class started to impress upon him that he had to "behave himself." This turned out to be the most difficult ordeal for Jon, for he could not control himself. He began to distract other children more overtly and was labeled the "troublemaker." Eventually he ended up with the school social worker, who with patience and understanding sought to check out Jon's problems. Tests proved him to be a hyperactive child. Medical efforts were made to reduce the hyperactivity. To make matters easier for Jon at school, his regular class schedule was changed so that he would spend more time away from the regular classroom and be allowed to perform more extracurricular activities.

Such understanding help is not always available to children with learning disabilities, and many children are damaged because of failure to recognize their problems early in life.

Labeling and Special Classes

Sometimes children are placed in special classes because of labels such as "mentally retarded," "emotionally disturbed," and "hyperactive." The anti-labeling movement indicates that labeling attaches a stigma to the children who are so labeled. Opponents of labeling consider the practice injurious to children's self-esteem and argue that special classes limit the growth of potential. Although specialized small-group instruction could offer some benefits, opponents of labeling feel that the losses often offset the gains. Besides, necessary special education could be offered within a wide range of settings from a regular classroom to special settings for handicapped children (Cromwell, 1975).

The Education for All Children Act in 1975 gave a legislative mandate to extend public education to all children in the least restrictive setting (Specht & Craig, 1982).

Rosenthal and Jacobson (1968) have cited evidence of the prejudicial effects of labeling on teachers' expectations of individual potential (Fleming & Anttonen, 1971). Labels affect what children feel about themselves; for instance, the "class clown" lives up to his or her image, and so does the "poor achiever" and the "difficult" child.

> Shirley, who was hyperactive, had been labeled the class clown, and she lived up to her role—saying and doing "funny" things to keep the class entertained. At times, her antics would get her into trouble, but that result only served the same purpose. Because she was the clown, she had to perform constantly to live up to her image.

A child's poor performance on an IQ test shows that the child would have difficulty in being successful at academics without special help. However, the test cannot explain to what degree cognitive, emotional, or physical factors are responsible for observed symptoms (Mercer, 1975).

Currently there are three approaches to remedial help: drug treatment, educational management, and psychotherapy (Specht & Craig, 1982).

Children are sometimes given drugs to calm them down. However, drugs have been overused, and that fact raises serious doubts about the ethics of recommending drugs for children when diagnosis may be inadequate and information about possible side effects is sketchy (Specht & Craig, 1982).

Educational management can take place both at home and at school. Through nurturing, love, and emotional support, children are given constructive structuring. A cooperative coordination can be established between parents and teachers. Structuring the child's life helps by reducing distractions, making expectations more explicit, and also reducing confusion. Such programs have had some degree of success.

Psychotherapy becomes a likely mode of treatment when emotional problems are suspected, once the possibility of an organically based problem is ruled out. The child receives counseling, and many times the family as well, to assist both parents and children in improving their understanding of each other. Better understanding leads, it is hoped, to more meaningful nurturing.

Behavior Modification

There are many controversial issues and unanswered questions in the area of learning disabilities. Further research could help us better understand the processes of normal child development. However, application of the techniques of behavior management offer the possibility of controlling and changing behavioral symptoms without having to find out the specific causes.

Behavior modification techniques are used in schools as well as in residential institutions to bring about change in behavior. Programs of behavior modification use praise, attention, tokens, and other positive, as well as negative, reinforcers to elicit a desired type of behavior. For example, a social worker in a residential setting for disturbed children may decide to give attention to those requests that are made in a reasonable and responsible manner but to ignore temper tantrums and outbursts (Specht & Craig, 1982).

A number of techniques have been developed for increasing the effectiveness of both positive and negative reinforcers of behavior. The techniques have been used extensively in schools, as well as in residential institutions, and with children as well as adults having special behavior problems.

Followers of the learning-theory school have focused on the stimulus–response connection, which they interpret as the basic unit of human behavior. According to the philosophy behind this theory, people simply react and respond to environmental influences and are shaped by the automatic process of associating stimulus (behavior) and response (consequences). Learning theorists do not pay much attention to internal mental processes because those cannot be objectively described. However, they do believe that people can give accurate descriptions of their subjective thoughts and feelings.

Dollard and Miller (1950) say that learning theory, in its simplest form, is the study of the circumstances under which a response and a cue stimulus become connected. After the learning has been completed, response and cue are bound together in such a way that the appearance of the cue evokes the response. Learning takes place on the basis of some definite psychological principles; the connection between the cue and the response can be strengthened only under certain conditions. The learner must be driven to make the response and be rewarded for having responded in the presence of the cue. To express this in ordinary terms, one must want something, notice something, do something, and get something. Other terms for these elements are *drive*, *cue*, *response*, and *reward*. Each has been carefully explored in the learning process. Learning theory has become a body of firmly knit principles that are useful in dealing with human behavior.

Some techniques that are frequently used in dealing with behavior problems are classical conditioning and desensitization. People may have an automatic response to a stimulus or a voluntary one; the terms *respondent* and *operant* are used to describe these two types of behavior.

The process of classical conditioning brings a response under the control of a previously neutral stimulus. The experiments of Ivan Pavlov are among the best examples; Pavlov, noting that dogs salivate when offered food, began to strike a tuning fork every time food was offered to a dog. He repeatedly paired the neutral stimulus with the food, and soon the sound of the fork alone was enough to make the dog salivate, even when no food was in sight. Thus the fork became a conditioned stimulus, eliciting the same response from the dog as the food had produced.

There are common phobias, such as fear of darkness and fear of closed places, that can treated by the use of counterconditioning techniques such as relaxation training and desensitization. These techniques help clients develop a new relaxation response to replace an old anxiety response. Instead of analyzing the reasons for their anxiety, clients are conditioned to learn new, competing responses, while old responses are destroyed by withdrawing reinforcements.

One of the disadvantages of behavior-modification theory is precisely that techniques are applied without diagnosis of the underlying causes. Some social workers consider the use of the techniques to be a limiting process unless it is accompanied by a nurturing and stable relationship between the adults and the child who is being treated. (For more information on learning theory, see Dollard & Miller, 1950.)

Anthony, age 7, was the only son of Louise, a single parent. They were on welfare. Louise had been divorced from her husband for six years and had cohabited for two years with a man who was violent with her son. During that period, Louise had been lenient with Anthony. However, after her live-in boyfriend left, her expectations of her son increased greatly. She was busy trying to find herself a "suitable job" and was away from home for long hours, but she expected Anthony to be the "man of the house." She expected him to take care of the apartment, clean up, cook, and do all the housework, in addition to performing well at school.

At school, Anthony acted out. He could not concentrate, was sleepy, and got into all types of trouble, from stealing things to provoking fights with other children. Anthony was also disruptive in class and constantly talked out of turn.

One day, in anger, he attempted to choke a child and was sent to see the school social worker. The social worker evaluated Anthony's behavior and asked his mother to participate in therapy as well. Louise was nervous that she might be blamed for Anthony's problems until she understood that the worker was helping her to strengthen herself in order to aid her son in coping with his problems. Louise then became more accepting of the worker, a change that helped in the therapeutic process. Through counseling, Louise realized that she not only had been overly demanding of her son, but had also changed her style from being lenient to demanding in her expectations. She wanted him to be "all in one"—a perfect student as well as the man of the house. Her expectations had served only to arouse Anthony's anxiety because he could not live up to them.

The social worker urged Louise to enroll in a parenting skills class and also helped her to understand the feelings of inferiority her son was facing. Meanwhile, Anthony was given an opportunity to ventilate some of the interpersonal problems confronting him in school. Parent and child were made aware of the disparity between their home atmosphere and the school atmosphere. Testing by a medical doctor revealed that Anthony had no organic problems and that he had an IQ of 105. He could do better in class if he were not so impatient in frustrating situations.

Counseling Anthony and his mother, the social worker recognized that Anthony would benefit from a highly structured classroom with a warm, understanding teacher who used behavior modification as a technique of reward and punishment. The social worker was able to place Anthony in such a class. The teacher gave Anthony small tasks in which he could succeed. His minor disruptions were usually overlooked; otherwise he was given "time out" until he could return to the task at hand. Anthony knew that the teacher cared about him.

Besides attending this special school, Anthony and his mother went to a Family Service Agency for help with their roles and their relationships with one another.

Implications for Social Work Practice

Social workers need to be aware that, during middle childhood, home and school play an important part in the child's life. The child is developing a sex-role identity, cultivating peer relationships, and learning the norms of the family as well as of society. During this period the child attempts to gain competency in verbal and manual skills. Achievement of skills makes the child feel competent, whereas ridicule and a lack of caring from chief caregivers make the child feel inferior and unwanted.

There are various areas in which problems could arise, depending on the child and the environment in which the child is placed. Attending school, developing peer relationships, acquiring a functional sexual identity, gaining cognitive skills, and internalizing moral values are all tasks in which the child may encounter obstacles.

When children grow up enough to function fairly independently away from their families, they must reconcile their self-images with new and often unpleasant stereotypes they may encounter. Children who are the subjects of stereotypes become overwhelmed and anxious. Studies of Jewish (Radke, Trager, & Davis, 1949) and Black children (Goodman, 1952) reveal that ethnic awareness appears in these minority-group children earlier than it does in the general population.

Social workers need to be aware of multifaceted aspects of the child's life and his or her place at home. There are children with special needs—those who come from deprived homes and those who suffer from mental or physical problems and need special attention. The type of family the child comes from and the kind of child rearing the family practices are critical factors for a social worker to look for while attempting to help a child in the middle childhood years.

The child continues to be a part of a family, at least for a few more years, and help in this life stage may best be offered either individually or in conjunction with the family. The social worker also needs to be aware of the pressure that parents face to conform to society's expectations and to produce an average child who looks, apparently feels, and certainly behaves in accordance with norms. Many parents experience severe shock when a child does not meet their preconceived expectations of a child whose physical and intellectual growth follows a relatively predictable pattern. Social work practitioners need to develop an awareness of parents' expectations, as well as helping them deal with their children's existing reality in a supportive fashion.

Chapter Summary

A child passes through a number of changes during middle childhood. The child's horizon expands to include the school world. Physical development appears to be fairly balanced between stability and continued growth. The ages 6 to 12 are a period of new self-awareness and responsibility. Children settle down, develop new skills, and are increasingly motivated to gain approval from family and from friends and other peers.

Children improve their dexterity. Malnutrition during this period has an effect on physical and mental growth. Children's perception of other people moves from global, vague terms, such as "good," "bad," and "horrible" to more specific descriptions in terms of a person's immediate behavior, without losing the perspective of how the person normally behaves.

When moral development takes place, children adopt principles and evaluate behavior as right and wrong. They conform to group norms and develop an increasing capacity for guilt.

In psychoanalytic thinking there are aggressive sexual instincts called the *id* that must be dealt with through parental discipline to help internalize socially acceptable behavior. At some point this internalization becomes the *superego*.

Social-learning theorists hypothesize that behavior is the result of modeling and an appropriate system of rewards and punishments. Piaget and Kohlberg indicate that moral development occurs when children act upon and modify the world they live in. They move from moral absolutism to moral relativism.

Schools have an effect on the socialization of the child. In the school setting the child develops a sense of self-esteem and ego identity. The traditional way to instill values is through character education and conduct development. These teachings become a part of children's moral development.

Special problems may arise in school settings due to physical factors, such as poor health and poverty, or due to emotional causes.

Erik Erikson calls this period one of industry versus inferiority. Children learn skills that bring them closer to their capacities as adults. When they do not learn such skills they feel inferior.

Sex-role development starts the day a child is born. Sex roles are attained through socialization by imitating parents and other adults and imitating peers of the same sex. Sex-role development also takes place in the classroom. The structure of most schools reflects the sex differentiations of the larger society, with its male-dominated patterns.

In keeping with his competency model, White comments that besides requiring play and make-believe, children need to feel useful. Competency develops both at home and at school as children learn the rules of the game—how to get along with others and how to compete, compromise, and protect themselves from hurt.

Becker classifies parenting on dimensions of restrictiveness–permissiveness, warmth–hostility, and anxious emotional involvement–calm detachment. Maccoby has expanded Becker's model of parenting styles to include not only the effects of parental behavior on children but also children's effects on their parents. The power of any child-rearing practice is limited.

Peers have influences on each other's personality. Peer groups develop their own cultures and often their own customs, rules, games, values, and beliefs. Peer groups perform an important function in giving children experiences in relationships in which they are on an equal footing. A child's sense of social acceptance or rejection is played out in the school setting and depends greatly on the acceptance or rejection received there. Physical attractiveness begins to play a role and affects children's self-esteem. Children develop race awareness, which comes earlier to minority children than to those of the majority population.

There are many critical problems that children face at this age level. Some children are slow learners. The reasons for this difficulty can vary. One reason may be minimal brain damage, characterized by the child's being easily distracted and by difficulties in physical coordination. Another cause of learning disabilities is emotional problems. If the underlying problem is not recognized early in life, the child may not receive constructive help.

Many children with learning disabilities attend special classes. There are both pros and cons in use of these classes. Labeling children has advantages for getting correct treatment, but there are disadvantages as well—labeled children can be stigmatized and overlooked.

Learning disabilities are handled by three different methods: drug treatment, educational management (involving structuring of the child's life), and psychotherapy. Behavior modification techniques include the use of praise, tokens, and other positive and also negative reinforcers. Further research is required to deal with learning disabilities and determine how they can best be handled.

References

Ausubel, D. P., & Sullivan, E. V. (1970). *Theory and problems of child development* (2nd ed.). New York: Grune & Stratton.

Bakan, D. (1971). Adolescence in America: From idea to social fact. *Daedalus, 4,* 979–995.

Bandura, A., Ross, D., & Ross, S. (1961). Transmission of aggression through imitation of aggressive models. *Journal of Abnormal Psychology, 63,* 575–582.

Bandura, A., Ross, D., & Ross, S. (1963). Imitation of film mediated aggressive models. *Journal of Abnormal Psychology, 66,* 3–11.

Baumrind, D. (1978). A dialectical materialist perspective on knowing reality. *New Directions for Child Development, 2.*

Becker, W. C. (1964). Consequences of different kinds of parental discipline. In M. C. Hoffman (Ed.), *Review of child developmental research* (Vol. 1). New York: Russell Sage Foundation.

Bem S. L. (1974). The measurement of psychological androgyny. *Journal of Counseling Psychology, 42,* 155–172.

Bem, S. L. (1975). Sex-role adaptability: One consequence of psychological androgyny. *Journal of Personality and Social Psychology, 31,* 634–643.

Biller, H. B., & Bahm, R. M. (1971). Father absence, perceived maternal behavior and masculinity of self-concept among junior high school boys. *Developmental Psychology, 4,* 178–181.

Birch, H. G. (1972). Malnutrition, learning and intelligence. *American Journal of Public Health, 62,* 773–784.

Blanchard, E. (1979). Social work practice with American Indians. A report from the Seattle School of Social Work, University of Washington, 1979.

Block, J. H. (1978). Another look at sex differentiation in the socialization behaviors of mothers and fathers. In F. Wenmark & J. Sherman (Eds.), *Psychology of women: Future direction of research.* New York: Psychological Dimensions.

Block, J. H. (1979, September). *Socialization influences on personality development in males and females.* Paper presented to the American Psychological Association, New York, September 1–5.

Block, J. H., Block, J., & Harrington, D. M. (1974). The relationship of parental teaching strategies and ego-resilience in pre-school children. Paper presented at the meeting of the Western Psychological Association, San Francisco.

Bloom, L. (1971). *The social psychology of race relations.* Cambridge, Mass.: Schenkman.

Blos, P. (1967). The second individuation process of adolescence. In A. Freud (Ed.), *The psychoanalytic study of the child* (Vol. 22). New York: International University Press.

Brock, J. (1961). *Recent advances in human nutrition.* London: Churchill.

Bronfenbrenner, U. (1970). *Two worlds of childhood: U.S. and U.S.S.R.* New York: Russell Sage.

Busch-Rossnagel, N. A., & Vance, A. K. (1982). The impact of schools on social and emotional development in education. In B. A. Wolman, G. Stricker, et al. (Eds.), *Handbook of developmental psychology.* Englewood Cliffs, NJ: Prentice-Hall.

Byrne, D., Ervin, C. H., & Lamberth, J. (1970). Continuity between the experimental study of attraction and real-life computer dating. *Journal of Personality and Social Psychology, 16,* 157–165.

Cantor, N. L., Wood, D., & Gelford, D. (1977). Effects of responsiveness and sex of children on adult males' behavior. *Child Development, 48,* 1426–1430.

Carroll, J. L., & Rest, J. R. (1982). Moral development. In B. B. Wolman, G. Stricker, et al., *Handbook of developmental psychology.* Englewood Cliffs, NJ: Prentice-Hall.

Chodorow, N. (1974). Family structure and feminine personality. In M. Z. Rosaldo & L. Lamphere (Eds.), *Women, Culture and Society.* Stanford, CA: Stanford University Press.

Chow, B. F., Blackwell, B., Hou, T. Y., Anilane, J. K., Sherwin, R. W., & Chir, B. (1968). Maternal nutrition and metabolism of the offspring: Studies of rats and man. *American Journal of Public Health, 58,* 668–677.

Colby, A., Gibbs, J., & Kohlberg, L. (1983). *Standard form for scoring manual.* Cambridge, MA: Center for Moral Education.

Colby, A., Kolhberg, L., Gibbs, J., & Lieberman, M. A. (1983). Longitudinal study of moral development. Presentation at the Center for Advanced Study in the Behavioral Sciences Institute on Morality and Moral Development, 1979.

Cromwell, R. (1975). Criteria for classification systems. In N. Hobbs (Ed.), *Issues in classification of children.* San Francisco: Jossey-Bass.

Deutsch, H. (1944). *The psychology of women* (Vol. 1). New York: Grune & Stratton.

Dollard, J., & Miller, N. E. (1950). *Personality and Psychotherapy: An analysis in terms of learning, thinking, and culture.* New York: McGraw-Hill.

Downing, L. L., & Bothwell, K. H. (1979). Open-space schools: Anticipation of peer interaction and development of cooperative independence. *Journal of Educational Psychology, 71,* 478–484.

Drake, C. T., & McDougall, D. (1977). Effects of the absence of a father and other male models on the development of boys' sex roles. *Developmental Psychology, 13,* 537–538.

Erikson, E. H. (1968). *Identity, youth and crisis.* New York: Norton.

Fagot, B. I. (1982). Adults as socializing agents. In T. M. Field, A. Huston, H. C. Quay, L. Troll, & G. E. Finley (Eds.), *Review of human development.* New York: Wiley.

Flavell, J. H. (1963). *The developmental psychology of Jean Piaget.* Princeton, NJ: Van Nostrand.

Fleming, W. S., & Anttonen, R. G. (1971). Teacher expectancy as related to academic and personal growth of primary age children. *Monographs of Society for Research in Child Development, 36,* 5, Serial No. 145.

Freud, S. (1930). *Civilization and its discontents.* London: Hogarth.

Gilligan, C. (1982). *In a different voice.* Cambridge, MA: Harvard University Press.

Goebes, D. D., & Shore, M. F. (1978). Some effects of bicultural and monocultural school environments on personality development. *American Journal of Orthopsychiatry, 48,* 407–498.

Goodman, M. E. (1952). *Race awareness in young children.* Cambridge, Mass.: Addison-Wesley.

Guttentag, M. & Bray, H. (1976). *Undoing sex stereotypes.* New York: McGraw-Hill.

Hetherington, E. M. (1971). Personality development. In L. C. Deighton (Ed.), *The encyclopedia of education* (Vol. 7). New York: Macmillan.

Hetherington, E. M. (1978). Mothers' and fathers' responses to appropriate and inappropriate dependency in sons and daughters. Unpublished manuscript.

Hetherington, E. M., & Deur, J. (1971). The effects of father absence on child development. *Young Children, 26,* 223–248.

Hetherington, E. M., Cox, M., & Cox, R. (1979). Family interaction and the social, emotional and cognitive development of children following divorce. In V. Vaughn & T. B. Brezelton (Eds.), *The Family: Setting Priorities.* New York: HBJ Legal and Professional Publications.

Hoffman, L. W. (1975). The value of children to parents and the decrease in family size. *Proceedings of the American Psychological Society, 119,* 430–438.

Holt, J. (1964). *How children fail.* New York: Dell.

Joffe, C. (1977). Sex role socialization and the nursery school: As the twig is bent. In J. Pottker & A. Fishel (Eds.), *Sex bias in the schools.* Cranbury, NJ: Associated Press.

Jones, F. R., Garrison, K. C., & Morgan, R. F. (1985). *Psychology of human development.* New York: Harper & Row.

Kagan, J. (1966). Reflection–impulsivity: The generality and dynamics of conceptual tempo. *Journal of Abnormal Psychology, 71,* 17–24.

Kastenbaum, R. (1979). *Humans developing.* Boston, MA, Sydney, & Toronto: Allyn & Bacon.

Kay, W. (1975). *Moral education: A sociological study of the influence of society, home and school.* Hamden, CT: Linnet Books.

Kazalunaz, J. R. (1978). Sexism in education. *Clearing House, 51,* 388–391.

Keller, B. B., & Bell, R. Q. (1979). Child effects on adults' methods of eliciting altruistic behavior. *Child Development, 50,* 1004–1009.

Kerckhoff, A. C. (1972). *Socialization and social class.* Englewood Cliffs, NJ: Prentice-Hall.

Kohlberg, L. (1969). Stage and sequence: The developmental approach to socialization. In D. A. Goslin (Ed.), *Handbook of socialization theory and research.* Chicago: Rand McNally.

Kohlberg, L. (1971). From is to ought: How to commit the naturalistic fallacy and get away with it in the study of moral development. In T. Mischel (Ed.), *Cognitive development and epistemology.* New York: Academic Press.

Kohlberg, L. (1976). Moral stages and moralization. In T. Luckona (Ed.), *Moral development and behavior.* New York: Holt, Rinehart & Winston.

Kohlberg, L. (1978). Revisions in theory and practice of moral development. *Dimensions for Child Development, 2,* 83–88.

Kozol, J. (1970). *Death at an early age.* New York: Bantam Books.

Lasch, C. (1977). *Haven in a heartless world.* New York: Basic Books.

Lee, P. C., & Gropper, N. B. (1974). Sex-role, culture and educational practice. *Harvard University Review, 42,* 369–410.

Leinhardt, G., Seewald, A. M., & Engel, M. (1979). Learning what's taught: Sex differences in instruction. *Journal of Educational Psychology, 71*(4), 432–439.

Lerner, R. M., & Busch-Rossnagel, N. A. (Eds.). (1981). *Individuals as producers of their development.* New York: Academic Press.

Lerner, R. M., & Hultsch, D. F. (1983). *Human development.* New York: McGraw-Hill.

Lerner, R. M., & Korn, S. J. (1972). The development of body-build stereotypes in males. *Child Development, 43,* 908–920.

Lever, J. (1976). Sex differences in the games children play. *Problems, 23,* 478–487.

Livesley, W. J., & Bromley, D. B. (1973). *Person perception in childhood and adolescence.* New York: Wiley.

Lynn, D. B. (1959). A note on sex differences in the development of masculine and feminine identification. *Psychological Review, 66,* 126–135.

Maccoby, E. E. (1979, March). *Parent–child interaction.* Paper presented at the biennial meeting of the Society for Research in Child Development.

Mead, G. H. (1934). *Mind, self and society.* Chicago: University of Chicago Press.

Mercer, J. R. (1975). Psychological assessment of the rights of children. In N. Hobbs (Ed.), *Issues in the classification of children.* San Francisco: Jossey-Bass.

Mischel, W., & Mischel, H. N. (1976). A cognitive social-learning approach to morality and self-regulation. In T. Luckona (Ed.), *Moral development and behavior: Theory, research and social issues.* New York: Holt, Rinehart & Winston.

Newman, B. M., & Newman, P. R. (1975). *Development through life.* Chicago, IL: Dorsey Press.

Newson, J., & Newson, E. (1968). *Four years old in an urban community.* Hammondsworth, England: Pelican Books.

Noller, P. (1978). Sex differences in the socialization of affectionate expression. *Developmental Psychology, 14,* 317–319.

Pakizegi, B. (1978). The interaction of mothers and fathers with their sons. *Child Development, 49,* 479–482.

Papalia, D. E., & Olds, S. W. (1986). *Human development*. New York: McGraw-Hill.

Parke, R. D., & Sawin, D. (1975, April). Infant characteristics and behavior as elicitors of maternal and paternal responsibilities in the newborn period. Paper presented at the biennial meeting of the Society for Research in Child Development, Denver.

Parsons, R. (1959). The school class as a social system: Some of its functions in American society. *Harvard Educational Review, 29*(4), 300–301.

Piaget, J. (1950). *The psychology of intelligence*. New York: Harcourt Brace.

Piaget, J. (1952). *The child's conception of numbers*. New York: Humanities Press.

Piaget, J. (1965). *The moral judgment of the child*. New York: Free Press.

Piaget, J. (1965). *The child's conception of numbers*. New York: Norton.

Piaget, J. (1968). *Six psychological studies*. New York: Viking Press.

Piaget, J., & Inhelder, B. (1956). *The child's conception of space*. London: Routledge & Kegan Paul.

Pottker, J., & Fishel, A. (Eds.). (1977). *Sex bias in the schools*. Cranbury, NJ: Associated University Press.

Power, C., & Reimer, J. (1978). Moral atmosphere: An educational bridge between judgment and action. *New Directions for Child Development, 2*.

Racial problems in Norfolk. (1986, March 10). *Virginian Pilot*, p. 1.

Radke, M. J., Trager, H. G., & Davis, H. (1949). Social perceptions and attitudes of children. *Genetic Psychology Monographs, 40*, 327–447.

Read, K. H. (1971). *The nursery school: A human relationships laboratory* (5th ed). Philadelphia: Saunders.

Reichle, J. E., Longhurst, T. M., & Stepanich, L. (1976). Verbal interaction in mother–child dyads. *Developmental Psychology, 12*, 273–277.

Reisert, J. E. (1971). Class Size. In L. C. Deighton (Ed.), *The encyclopedia of education* (Vol. 2). New York: Macmillan.

Rosenberg, M., & Simmons, R. G. (1972). *Black and white self-esteem: The urban school child*. Washington, DC: American Sociological Association.

Rosenkoetter, L. I. (1973). Resistance to temptation: Inhibitory and disinhibitory effects of models. *Developmental Psychology, 8*, 80–84.

Rosenthal, F., & Jacobson, L. (1968). *Pygmalion in the classroom: Teacher expectation and pupil's intellectual development*. New York: Harper & Row.

Ross, S. A. (1971). A test of generality of the effects of deviant preschool models. *Developmental Psychology, 4*, 262–267.

Rubin, J. Z., Provenzano, F. J., & Luria, Z. (1974). The eye of the beholder: Parents' view on sex of the newborn. *American Journal of Orthopsychiatry, 43*, 720–731.

Saario, T. N., Jackson, C. N., & Tittle, C. K. (1973). Sex role stereotyping in the public schools. *Harvard Educational Review, 43*, 386–416.

Schaefer, R. T. (1979). Racial and ethnic groups. Boston & Toronto: Little, Brown.

Sears, R. R., Rau, L., & Alpert, R. (1965). *Identification and child rearing*. Stanford, CA: Stanford University Press.

Sneath, E. H., & Hodges, G. (1914). *Moral training in the school and home*. New York: Macmillan.

Specht, R., & Craig, G. J. (1982). *Human development*. Englewood Cliffs, NJ: Prentice-Hall.

Staffieri, J. R. (1967). A study of social stereotypes of body image in children. *Journal of Personality and Social Psychology, 7*, 101–104.

Staffieri, J. R. (1972). Body build and behavioral expectancies in young females. *Developmental Psychology, 6*, 125–127.

Stein, A. H. (1967). Imitation of resistance to temptation. *Child Development, 38*, 157–169.

Steinberg, L. D., & Hill, J. P. (1978). Patterns of family interaction as a function of age, the onset of puberty and formal thinking. *Developmental Psychology, 14,* 683–684.

Sullivan, H. S. (1953). *The interpersonal theory of psychiatry.* New York: Norton.

Thrasher, F. M. (1963). *The gang.* Chicago, London: University of Chicago Press.

Vander Zanden, J. W. (1978). *Human development.* New York: Knopf.

Walster, E., Aronson, V., Abrahams, D., & Rotterman, L. (1966). Importance of physical attractiveness in dating behavior. *Journal of Personality and Social Psychology, 4,* 508–516.

Walters, R. H., Leat, M., & Meizei, L. (1963). Inhibition and disinhibition of responses through empathetic learning. *Canadian Journal of Psychology, 17,* 235–243.

Warper, S., & Werner, H. (1957). *Perceptions development.* Worcester, MA: Clark University Press.

White, R. W. (1960). Competence in the psychological stages of development. In M. R. Jones (Ed.), *Nebraska Symposium on Motivation.* Lincoln: University of Nebraska Press.

Williams, J. E., & Morland, J. K. (1976). *Race, color and the young child.* Chapel Hill, NC: University of North Carolina Press.

Williams, J. E., & Stabler, J. R. (1973, July). "If white means good then black . . ." *Psychology Today,* pp. 51–54.

Witkin, H. A., Dyk, R. B., Faterson, H. F., Goodenough, D. R., & Karp, S. A. (1962). *Psychological differentiation.* New York: Wiley.

Zussman, J. V. (1978). Relationship of demographic factors to parental discipline techniques. *Developmental Psychology, 14,* 685–686.

6

Adolescence

Physical Changes
Cognitive Development
Value Systems
Identity
Competence
Family Relationships
Sex-Role Identity
Peer Relationships
Minority-Group Culture
Critical Issues
Implications for Social Work Practice
Chapter Summary
References

Adolescence, the period of transition from childhood to adulthood, is marked by several central changes. Some of the most important changes are physical, but significant changes take place in cognition as well. An adolescent is not just a person who has reached reproductive maturity or moved beyond the dependent role of a child; adolescence involves many changes—biological, social, cultural, and historical. Some processes in the young person may be adultlike, such as those of cognition, but at the same time the emotions may be childish. Therefore, to define adolescence one must look at the most frequently occurring characteristics of adolescence. When the emotional, sexual, intellectual, and physical processes of a person fall within the range typical of a child, that person is labeled a child; if the processes fall within the range typical of an adult, then the person is called an adult. Lerner and Hultsch (1983) define adolescence as a period within a person's life span when most of the person's processes are in a state of transition from what is considered typically childish to what is considered typically adultlike.

In this chapter we shall follow the physical and cognitive growth of the adolescent from ages 12 to 19 as well as deal with the adolescent's increasingly turbulent emotional life.

> Maria slammed the door of her room. Her mother did not understand her; she still thought Maria was a child. Maria said to herself, "Can't Mother see what everyone else does? I am a woman and can handle responsibilities. After all, I am 15 and definitely know more than Mother does." She added, "Mother has never been outside the house, so what does she know?" Moodily, she lay on her bed. Her fingers wandered to her body and face, and then she noticed an ugly pimple on her forehead. On close examination, she found a couple more. She was devastated. How could she go back to school for the party? *Everyone* would notice how ugly she was. Her day would be ruined. She looked desperately for any medicine that would quickly get rid of those ugly pimples, but found nothing that would help. Finally she got up and ran to her mother, with whom she had just had an argument about how grown up and adultlike she was. She begged her mother to give her a remedy so that she could get rid of her pimples, otherwise the school party would be ruined for her.

The typical adolescent is a combination of child and adult, with physical growing pains as well as the need to be separate and be his or her own person.

Adolescence can be classified into three stages. Early adolescence is characterized by the bodily changes of pubescence and some cognitive changes. Middle adolescence occurs as the person is seeking an independent identity and beginning to date. Late adolescence or youth (Keniston, 1975) is a period in which decisions are made about further schooling, careers, and future paths.

At puberty, the young person becomes able to procreate. But the young person has not yet achieved the psychosocial development necessary to function appropriately in an adult sexual relationship.

Twelve-year-old Pam was an early bloomer. She menstruated at age 10. Her mother had never married and was busy trying to survive financially, with four mouths to feed. Living in a ghetto is not easy. If you are pretty, you are exploited. That is how Pam became pregnant. She did not think it could happen to her. After all, as she put it, she "did it just once, and can you get pregnant the first time?" Thus Pam, who had years of physical and mental growth ahead of her, was victimized and caught in the lifestyle of poverty and exploitation. She was still in the pubescent period and not ready for pregnancy, physically or emotionally.

Physical Changes

An adolescent undergoes development at a rate equivalent to or similar to that of the first two years of life. Growth in adolescence brings about rapid development of the reproductive organs, as well as the appearance of secondary sex characteristics. These modifications are made possible through the precipitation of hormones that are the chemical products of the endocrine glands. Most of the changes that occur are sex-specific. In this period, when production of hormones increases (Tanner, 1971), target tissues in the body respond selectively to the hormones that are circulating in the bloodstream. For instance, there are selective responses to two sex hormones, estrogen and progesterone (Garrison, 1973).

The delicate balance of the endocrine gland secretions leads to normal growth and functioning. The pituitary gland, located at the base of the brain, produces various types of hormones, among the most important of which is the growth hormone somatotrophin (Garrison, 1973). The pituitary gland also produces the secondary hormones that stimulate and regulate the functioning of a number of other glands, including the sex glands. The testes and the ovaries, inactive until this period, perform two functions: they produce gametes (that is, sperm and eggs) and they secrete hormones that are vital for the development of the reproductive organs (Specht & Craig, 1982).

The rate of growth for both boys and girls varies. Some boys and girls complete their physiological growth at an earlier age than others. Thus it is common to see some boys in high school who look like adults and others who are short and not well built and who look very young. For most girls, the rate of growth reaches its peak at about age 12; for most boys, at about 14 (Tanner, 1971). However, different parts of the body develop at different rates. Often, adolescents look "funny," with long hands and legs that are disproportionate to the rest of the body. There is a sequence to development—the extremities (hands, feet, and head) reach adult size before the torso.

Following the period of rapid growth comes accumulation of fat, especially in girls, sometimes causing them embarassment.

Sexual Maturation

Besides overall change in body size and shape, the important change that takes place in adolescence is the maturation of the reproductive organs. In boys, there is increased growth of the testes and scrotum. As they develop, boys experience spurts in height and growth in size of the penis, concurrent with development of the seminal vesicles and the prostate gland. Between the times of testicular growth and penile development, pubic hair starts to appear. An increase in the number of both oil-producing glands (sebaceous glands) and sweat glands causes body odor and acne (Tanner, 1971).

In girls, the breasts start to enlarge, and there is simultaneous growth of the uterus and the vagina, along with enlargement of the clitoris. Menarche, which occurs after the period of rapid growth, is the most dramatic and symbolic indication of a girl's changing status. Traditional psychoanalytic thought focuses on the potential of menstruation for causing emotional distress but pays little attention to girls who readily accept this event as a symbolic entrance into the female sexual role (Melges & Hamburg, 1976). Nontraumatic acceptance will be discussed further in the context of other cultures.

In our discussion of conception and pregnancy (Chapter 2), we saw the role of chromosomes as determinants of sexual identity. Sexual-response biases are built into the prenatal nervous system, and predispositions are created by the hormonal system (Diamond, 1976). However, the majority of the sexual differences represent quantitative distinctions and not discrete categories (Beech, 1976). The major part of gender identity occurs after birth as other factors intervene from earliest childhood through adolescence and into adulthood (Kagan, 1976).

All adolescents have to make adjustments to their body image. Adolescents watch themselves with pain and pleasure as they undergo the process of change. They attempt to revise their self-image on the basis of comparison with others. Being unique in status, neither adults nor children, they have an increased need for conformity and are intolerant of deviations in body types, such as obesity (Specht & Craig, 1982). Representations of teenagers as slim, beautiful people without any pimples, braces, or unattractive proportions place a lot of pressure on young people, for acne and uneven growth are a part of growing up. Many adolescents are uncomfortable with their bodies. Whether they mature early or late, boys and girls encounter stressful problems connected with physical changes; such problems are normative expectations of the period (Ganter & Yeakel, 1980).

Many adolescents worry about their sexual competency; that is, if they can perform a sexual act that is satisfying to them and their partners. There may be conflict between their own intuitive interest in masturbation and the urge to share sexual experiences with others. Their family or religious teachings may say that either behavior is wrong and even harmful to their bodies. But in reality, masturbation is one form of meaningful experimentation with their bodies. In some extreme cases, adolescents are totally deprived of their right to experiment, and as adults such people often reject all human sexuality as wrong and associate tremendous guilt with sexuality. Other adolescents overemphasize sexual feelings and actions and measure their worth solely by them.

At 19, Andy had been dating heavily. When confronted by his mother, who was concerned because he had been neglecting his school work,

Andy could only answer that he was "sowing his wild oats, wildly."
After all, he would become a man like his father, and he had to "prove
his manliness." He had repeatedly heard his father emphasize that a man
has to prove himself sexually.

Cultural Attitudes

Adolescence is viewed differently in different cultures. In our culture, we
assume that adolescence will bring with it dramatic changes. As the changes
occur, children begin to define themselves in new ways, seeing themselves as
men and women. Failure to change at the expected time could be a source of
embarassment and despair.

Accompanying the physical changes are emotional changes that affect the
way adolescents feel about themselves. All changes take place within the
social context of the culture, with its particular expectations and values.

Fourteen-year-old Bernadette appeared to be lagging behind her
classmates in her physical growth. She was tiny and timid. The taller and
more developed girls in her class were interested in boys, and their
conversation revolved around their dating. Bernadette became more and
more introverted because she had not yet reached that stage in her life.
Being told that she was just a late bloomer did not take away any of the
sting from the jokes she heard about herself. She often heard "Aren't you
ever going to grow up?" That affected her personality as well as her
performance in class. At home Bernadette grew increasingly moody
because her parents did not understand her problems.

By itself, growing up is difficult, but it becomes more complicated when the
adolescent has to come to grips with the increasing demands made by the
world; that is, pivotal decisions about work, lifestyle, friends, religion, and
politics. No person passes through this phase without being affected deeply
by it. This is the traditional view that has been accepted by Freud and his
followers in the psychoanalytic movement (Freud, 1946). However, this
traditional view has been challenged by evidence from other cultures. One of
the first persons who viewed it differently was Margaret Mead (1928), who as
a young anthropologist in the 1920s visited the island of Samoa and made
a study of the people in the South Seas. Mead wished to know whether
the physical changes of puberty necessarily yield our Western portrait of
adolescence.

In the 1920s the people of Samoa lived in an idyllic, unsophisticated
culture, surrounded by coconut palms and mango trees. There was clear
sex-role differentiation. Women spent their time looking after their young
and planting and gathering food. Men fished and hunted, constructed
buildings, and farmed.

Samoan girls stayed close to their mothers and siblings when they were
young but participated in the communal dances and activities. By the time
they were 7 or so, girls and boys had formed voluntary groups with members
of their own sex, revealing strong antagonistic feelings toward members of

the opposite sex. This segregation is similar to the behavior of preadolescents in our culture, who form same-sex peer groups.

With the onset of puberty, Samoan young people entered the fabric of society. During this period boys and girls were given formal names and roles that they assumed in religious rituals. After puberty, girls and boys were involved in sexual relationships. Girls continued to participate in the group with their elders by playing the ceremonial roles, and later they assumed more of the daily tasks of sewing, gathering, and planting. Gradually girls and boys mastered the roles that would soon dominate their social lives—those of wife or husband and parent.

As Mead described it, the adolescent period in Samoa possessed a gradualness, a smoothness and naturalness that distinguished it sharply from the adolescent years in our society. Young girls, apparently aware of the roles they would play, assisted in adult activities and took responsibility for child care. Sex and love relationships were easily accepted and there were no feelings of shame, privacy, or guilt about sex or any other matters.

According to Mead, growing up in Samoa was less complicated than it is in our culture. On the basis of her study, she commented that Samoan children had it much easier; they were less stressed and less conflict ridden than their American peers. Mead concluded that the Samoan culture was characterized by an integrated set of activities and that our culture was increasingly characterized by specialization, diversity, and fragmentation. Of course, in the Samoan culture children also experienced problems, but they were not as complicated or diverse as those seen in our culture.

Cognitive Development

During the preschool and middle school years, children learn to solve problems involving length, quantity, and number, and they master crafts and sports. But as they reach adolescence, they develop mental powers of a qualitatively different kind. They learn to combine and recombine symbols, draw inferences, and develop their own belief systems in science, religion, and politics, as well as arts. They perform better at perceiving and feeling, verbal and non-verbal communications.

Adolescent thinking represents a new level of reasoning. The ability to deal with situations is far more complex than before. The adolescent can state a group of principles about any set of objects, explain what forces act on them and how their behavior is altered by them, and explore the relationships among those principles (Gardner, 1978).

As adolescents develop, they begin to think of the world in new ways. Their thoughts become more abstract and they generate hypotheses about events that they have never perceived. The development of complex conceptual skills has been called the *stage of formal operations* (Inhelder & Piaget, 1958; Piaget, 1972). By this period, adolescents' thoughts are governed more by logical principles rather than by their own perceptions.

Piaget: Formal Operations

Adolescents become able to manipulate more than two variables at the same time. For example, they may consider the relationships among speed, distance, and time in making a trip. Adolescents think about facts that may change in a few years; for instance, that their relationship to their parents may be much different in ten years' time. Adolescents can hypothesize about a logical sequence of events that might occur. They may be able to predict college and occupational options open to them, depending on how well they do in school. They also try to anticipate consequences of their actions. Adolescents understand that dropping out of school will restrict their career possibilities. An adolescent can detect the logical consistency or inconsistency in a set of statements (Kagan, 1973).

Adolescents are able to think in a relativistic manner of themselves and the world they live in. In this stage, young people are able to make a commitment to the culture in which they live. They understand that they are expected to behave in a particular manner because of the norms of their own community and culture. They understand that other communities or cultures have different norms governing the same behavior (Newman & Newman, 1975).

Salma, a young Muslim girl, had fled with her parents to the United States from the Middle East with the emergence of restrictive Muslim rule. In the orthodox culture in which she was brought up, girls did not date boys; rather, marriages were arranged for them. Any form of relationship with young men was frowned upon and, according to the rules in her small, traditional Middle Eastern home town, a girl could be stoned to death if she developed a relationship without marriage.

Salma started school in the United States. One young man in her class was interested in her and asked her for a date. She was terrified and ran home and cried, not at all sure if she should even return to school. It took the school social worker tremendous effort and energy to understand the cultural background of this new student. Salma was helped to understand the local culture, as well as the compliment that the young man had paid her by asking her out. At the same time, the young man was informed of the cultural differences between them and what they meant to their personal lives. This exchange eventually led Salma and her admirer to respect each other's cultures and their respective lifestyles.

It is easier for adolescents to accept members of other cultures once they have realized that all people are products of their cultures, with different rules and norms. In time, many new immigrants become acclimated to American ways and become part of the "melting pot" or "salad bowl" culture.

Piaget claims that the stage of formal operations is the highest level of thought that can be attained. Conceptual development in early adolescence usually results in a flexible, critical, and abstract view of the world. Adolescents develop greater awareness of themselves and others and better imagination and judgment.

Adolescents apply their newly developed ability to analyzing their own thought processes and obtaining insight into themselves and others. Because these thought processes are accompanied by changes, adolescents frequently assume that others are fascinated by them and their behaviors. They anticipate the reactions of others and assume that their own self-assessment is matched by the approval or criticism of others. Elkind (1975) indicates that they have an imaginary audience before whom they try out their own feelings and behavior. Adolescents may also overdifferentiate their feelings; that is, assume that their feelings are unique and that no one else can share their personal agony or rapture. This period of egocentrism recedes by the time adolescents are 14 or 15 years of age, at which time they replace their imaginary audiences with real ones. At that time, adolescents begin to see themselves from others' point of view and to incorporate a number of outside judgments as part of their own self-concept.

What is the general course of transition from concrete to formal operations? In tracing it, Neimark (1982) found that component operational skills may originate early in the period of concrete operations. At that level, the developing operational skills are supposedly isolated, whereas at the formal level they attain greater power and generality through coordination with other formal operational skills. All adolescents do not move to formal operations simultaneously. Based on lifestyles and experiences, there are individual differences.

We see individual activity develop from simple coordination of reflexes at the infant's sensory-motor level to the logical, systematic consideration of all hypothetical possibilities at the level of formal thought. Probably the most fascinating thing about reading Piaget is that he makes us aware of the rhythm inherent in the process of growth: the young child can deal with concrete objects; the schoolchild can deal with them in thought; and the adolescent is freed from the bonds of physical reality to soar into the realm of hypothetical possibilities. The process of attaining equilibrium is repeated at each stage of development. There is a search for newer and better adjustments, a striving to achieve a balance between past experience and present uncertainties. When equilibrium is attained in one area, the restless organism begins to explore another. This is the common characteristic of all living beings, as Piaget sees them. At every biological and intellectual level there is an urge toward adaptation, understanding, and mastery. Human beings are not passive, empty organisms reacting to stimuli. Rather, they are active explorers adjusting to the world as they find it and also modifying the world to meet their needs.

For all his emphasis on discrete stages, Piaget views development as continuous and consistent; each stage evolves out of the one before it and contributes to the following one. Of course, some children mature faster than others, and by adolescence, their development is becoming more holistic. The structures of thought in each level are more complex, richer, and more inclusive. Piaget's life was a ceaseless search for those underlying structures of the whole, which exemplify the organizing and integrating properties of cognitive development (Pulaski, 1971).

Criticism of Piaget's Theory

Piaget's theory is the definitive of thought on adolescent cognitive development. However, not every psychologist agrees with Piaget's formulation of this final cognitive stage. Some point out that not all adolescents or even adults can think in formal operational terms. A certain degree of intelligence seems to be necessary; cultural and socioeconomic factors, particularly at the educational level, also play a part in this development (Neimark, 1975). Furthermore, even adults, when facing unfamiliar problems, are apt to fall back on a much more concrete type of reasoning. Some psychologists have therefore suggested that formal operational thought be considered an extension of concrete operations rather than a stage in its own right. Piaget recognizes that this may be the case, but he emphasizes that elements of this last cognitive stage are essential for the study of advanced science and mathematics.

Another limitation to Piaget's formulation of higher-level cognitive skills is that it explains how adolescents are able to speculate, analyze their own thoughts, and form self-concepts, but it does not explain creative ability. Some creative adolescents exhibit capacities for unusual ways of thinking that are different from the cognitive modes commonly used by adolescents with high IQ scores. However, it is typical for educational institutions and society to reward the conventional model of functioning rather than the highly creative and divergent person. This oversight results in an unfortunate loss of a great deal of creative potential (Getzels & Jackson, 1959).

Value Systems

As adolescents begin to think and mature, they give increased attention to the selection of ideals and moral values. Development of moral values is part of the long developmental process that the child begins by learning not to tell lies or steal. External morality is created by the processes of identification, modeling, and rewards and punishments. In the growing-up process, the child internalizes this morality. However, when children become mature adults, they eventually reassess these principles and build their own coherent set of values.

The content of adolescent values can be measured in many different ways. Two different approaches of understanding adolescent values will be presented here. In the first approach it is possible to ask adolescents to rank-order a list of values according to their importance to themselves. A study done by Beech and Schoeppe (1974) used groups of fifth-, seventh-, ninth-, and eleventh-graders; the Rokeach Value Survey (Rokeach, 1968) was used to assess the instrumental and terminal values of the subjects. Instrumental (or means) values can be classified as cheerful, helpful, and obedient. Terminal (or end-state) values can be a world of beauty, true friendship, loving relationships, and so forth. By testing the subjects from fifth to twelfth grade, the authors were able to examine the extent to which values held in common by adolescents tend to remain stable or to change over the adolescent years. There was a great deal of similarity between ages and sexes. For example, world peace, freedom, honesty, and loving were given consistently high priority by both boys and girls in all grades, whereas values like salvation, logic, and imagination tended to have lower rankings. The concept of family security was given higher priority by younger children than by older children and equality and social recognition were seen as important values by older adolescents. Instrumental values, such as cheerfulness, helpfulness, and obedience tended to decline in importance by the eleventh grade.

In the second approach, a German translation of the Rokeach measure was used with 400 German high school students (Gunther, 1975). No age or sex differences were reported, but there were differences across religious affiliations and political persuasion. Significant differences among Catholic, Protestant, and agnostic adolescents occurred on five terminal and three instrumental values. Catholics gave higher ranking than Protestants, and higher still than agnostics, to such values as world peace and salvation. Agnostics gave a higher ranking to values such as an exciting life and pleasure. Both Catholic and agnostic groups gave higher ranking to social recognition than did Protestants. Three instrumental values also distinguished the groups. Helpfulness was rated as highest by Catholics, whereas Protestants ranked it lower and agnostics ranked it still lower. Being logical and being independent were valued highest by agnostics, followed by Protestants and then Catholics.

David Friesen (1968) studied the value orientations of 1000 adolescents in two large Canadian cities. Both sexes were adequately represented in the study, which included three levels of socioeconomic status. Within each of the status groups, three different ethnocultural backgrounds were represented. Friesen's major findings were consistent with what Offer and Offer (1975) and others have said: most of the value indicators were directly related to the ethnocultural background of the students involved in the study. The current popular line of reasoning that youth culture is separate and distinct from the parent culture gets very little support from these data. Another popular suggestion that communication between generations is breaking down and that the generation gap is all-pervasive is not supported by these findings. The fact that youth's aspirations, activities, and attitudes are related both to socioeconomic background and, independently, to ethnocultural background suggests that forces in society other than the youth culture continue to share significantly in the development of value structures in modern youth (Friesen, 1968). That there is a continuity of values between parent and adolescent appears to be a general finding for different ethnic, racial, and socio-economic groups.

As a child, Ruby was battered by her parents—usually by her stepfather—for any mistake she made, however minor. At 9, if she spilled her milk, her stepfather belted her for being careless. Her mother supported her husband in his policy of strict discipline with Ruby. As she grew older, the physical abuse continued. Ruby grew up both careful and rigid in her idea of what was acceptable and what was not acceptable. When Ruby was 16, she found herself a part-time job as a baby sitter, taking care of an 18-month-old boy. One day when she gave him milk to drink, he poured it on the ground, more in play than in mischief. Ruby lost her temper and beat him severely. The more he cried, the more angry she got. According to her, he was supposed to stop crying, but he did not. Eventually, when she had completed her battering, the child had a swollen eye, a split lip, and marks all over his body. When this case was investigated, Ruby's value system was exposed. Though not a positive set of standards by comparison with those of the general society, it was the set she had experienced in her family, and it aided her in setting up her own standards of behavior for this young child.

Kolhberg's Theory

Kohlberg believes that most children in our culture outgrow the first stages of moral development by the time they reach adolescence. At adolescence, they begin to conform to conventional roles. They have learned to avoid punishment, have become obedience oriented, and are ready to live by conventional moral stereotypes (Specht & Craig, 1982). As children become teenagers, the basis of their actions becomes their own consciences. Adolescents take up a social-contract, legalistic orientation wherein right action is defined in terms of general individual rights and standards that have been agreed upon by the whole society.

Adolescents, becoming aware that people hold different values and that those values are relative, emphasize procedures for reaching consensus among reasonable people. The law is viewed as a changeable set of principles that should yield to what people believe to be in the public good.

Adolescents also develop the universal-ethical-principle orientation: one chooses a course of action by drawing a conclusion from one's own ethical principles, which have been arrived at as a result of an appeal to comprehensiveness, universality, and consistency.

As Kohlberg sees it, moral principles do not at heart allow exceptions. They are universal principles of justice, reciprocity, and equality of human rights.

Criticism of Kohlberg's Theory

Kohlberg's scheme of moral development has gained impressive research support that has been used in many educational programs. It also has generated much controversy. Researchers who have studied with Kohlberg have had the tools and knowledge necessary to apply the numerous measures and dimensions that are involved in assessing moral stages. However, work that has not received Kohlberg's sanction has unclear status, and those who have been privileged to use his complicated scoring system are critical of the cult surrounding Kohlberg's group (Hogan, 1973; Kurtines & Greif, 1974; McGeorge, 1973).

Another line of criticism concerns Kohlberg's claims about the universality of the stages of moral development and their sequence. Elizabeth Simpson (1974) argues that the schema reflects a cultural bias.

Kohlberg's approach may indeed overvalue certain cultural behavior; it may also be insensitive to variations among cultures. For example, when a cultural group seems to lack a particular moral level, it may be that the methods of testing have simply been inappropriate to identify it in that group. The Western experimenter in other cultures is often viewed with curiosity or regarded as a strange person, and responses may consequently be affected. Or the group may have some way of dealing with the dilemma that the outsider would neither recognize nor understand. The moral stances of other cultural groups and societies might have different basic premises, ones that are so invisible to observers that existing scales simply do not reveal them. It is debatable whether Kohlberg has devised a culturally unbiased measure.

A major criticism of Kohlberg's work concerns the relation between moral judgment and moral behavior. Perhaps even more important is the question of how necessary it is to talk about moral dilemmas at all. Gilligan (1982) argues and has shown that how a person reasons is only marginally predictive of how a person behaves in a particular situation. How one acts is of more importance than how one construes actions or what rationalizations are given to support a given action. Thus, in the famous experiment by Milgram in which one individual was instructed to shock another, many observers consider as crucial not the reasoning involved but rather the decision either to apply or not to apply the shock. (The case is famous because so many subjects did shock other subjects.) In this case, simple reasoning should have been preferred over complex reasoning in favor of shocking; "It will hurt" should have been preferred to the more complex reasoning in favor of applying shock—that is, "I am helping the experimenter in the pursuit of scientific truth." Dramatizing the divorce between reasoning and action, when people were asked how they thought others would behave in such shock situations, subjects invariably predicted far less shocking than actually occurred (Milgram, 1974).

At a later point, in view of the criticisms, Kohlberg (1973, 1981) changed his thinking and agreed that reasoning and action are separate enterprises, and that there is therefore, good reason to disregard reason and to focus on actions and consequences.

Kohlberg insists that reasoning exists in all different stages, but critics view this assertion as a bit hollow. Often, people decide what they wish to do, and even if their motives are base they manage to concoct a reason that could justify their behavior. Besides reasoning, there are many other factors, such as motivation, habit, and emotional state, that contribute to our behavior, even in morally ambiguous situations.

How can we evaluate Kohlberg's theory? There is an impressive body of studies that document the basic developmental levels. There is a persuasive theoretical account of the sequences of stages and of the view that moral thought can be tied to other aspects of intellectual growth. The difficulties with Kohlberg's work arise from the manner in which scoring decisions are made and the problem of cross-cultural validity, as well as from the relative importance of moral judgments and moral actions.

Kohlberg's studies become more instructive when applied specifically to the world of adolescents. Reasoning about moral values is decidedly an artificial activity for young children. They do not do it on their own, and their judgments can be easily swayed (Arbuthnot, 1975). But as children grow older they can consider courses of moral behavior other than their own and make the necessary connection to their own behavior. Kohlberg's theory becomes more important when issues of value and belief become significant, and especially when there are strong competing beliefs at stake.

Another important criticism of Kohlberg is that his five stages of moral judgment are based on a study of 84 boys whose development Kohlberg followed for more than 20 years. Although Kohlberg claims universality for his stage sequence, some groups not included in his original sample rarely reach higher stages of development (Edwards, 1975; Holstein, 1976; Simpson, 1974). One such group is women, as we will discuss in Chapter 7.

Identity
Erikson's Theory

Erikson views each of the major stages of life in terms of a crisis. According to Erikson, adolescence is the stage of the identity crisis, which is considered to be the central crisis of all development.

Adolescence is the period when autonomy is dawning on young people. They begin to choose their own friends and pastimes and to build meaningful emotional ties away from the family. They create their own value systems, often influenced by the family to which they belong, and plan for the future, and these enterprises consume a great deal of adolescent time. In our culture adolescents strive for heightened self-awareness, autonomy, sexuality, and a way to forge an adequate relationship with the wider society while realizing various personal goals. Thus, as Erikson asserts, an identity evolves that combines past identifications, future aspirations, and cultural issues.

As adolescents grow older, they become preoccupied with efforts to define themselves and they take into account the bonds that have been built between themselves and others in the past, as well as the direction that they hope to be able to take in the future. Identity serves as an anchor point that allows people the essential experience of continuity in their social relationships. Erikson states (1980)

> [T]he young individual must learn to be most himself where he means the most to others—those others, to be sure, who have come to mean most to him. The term identity expresses such a mutual relation in that it connotes both a persistent sameness within oneself (self-sameness) and a persistent sharing of some kind of essential character with others.

There is a cultural component to identity formation, and Erikson posits a cultural component to self-identity. Every individual has personal goals and expectations, and Erikson believes that young people in this age level begin active pursuit of their goals. The personal identity of an adolescent reflects to some degree the value orientation of the culture to which that person belongs. Resolving the identity crisis is the final step in the internalization of cultural values.

As young people pass through the stage of later adolescence, they find that family, teachers, neighbors, friends, and ethnic groups hold certain expectations for the behavior of a person at this age. People may be expected to marry, serve the country, attend church, vote, and, of course, work. Expectations of this kind are different from cultural values, but they too are accommodated in the formation of the individual's identity.

In the process of identity formation, a person may make certain decisions as a result of the persistent demands of significant others. Identity foreclosure occurs when a person slips into a role through premature decisions about his or her identity, often in response to the demands of others. For example, an adolescent may decide to become a doctor or a lawyer because it is expected by the parents or grandparents. The young person does not question the decision but is firm in the commitment to carry it out to please others, without even identifying their personal goals and social expectations (Newman & Newman, 1975).

Some young people develop a negative self-image (Erikson, 1980). Phrases like "failure," "good for nothing," and "juvenile delinquent" are labels that validate the person's identity. Adopting them encourages the person to behave in ways that will strengthen that identity.

In describing the adolescent period, Erikson uses the masculine gender to represent all people. The reason for this is obvious: like Freud, Erikson does not pay much attention to female development. The author uses the masculine pronouns in the next two paragraphs to represent Erikson's style of presentation.

The foreclosed identity and the negative identity are both examples of a resolution of the identity crisis that falls short of the goal of a positive personal identity and yet provides the person with a concrete identity. However, worse problems arise for a young person whose identity resolution leads to role diffusion. The young person is unable to make a commitment to any single view of himself and is unable to integrate various roles he has to play. He is often confronted with opposing value systems and suffers a lack of confidence in his ability to make meaningful decisions. This condition of diffusion arouses anxiety, apathy, and hostility toward the existing roles because the person feels uncomfortable in all those different roles (Newman & Newman, 1975).

In evolving a personal identity a person may experience temporary periods of confusion and depression. The adolescent is likely to experience moments of self-preoccupation, isolation, and discouragement as the diverse pieces of his life fall together meaningfully into a reordered total picture. Thus even a positive role identification involves some degree of role confusion. The negative outcome of role diffusion suggests that the person is never able to formulate a satisfying identity that provides for the convergence of multiple identifications, aspirations, and roles. The person has persistent fears that he is losing hold of himself and his future.

Abandoned by his mentally ill mother when he was 2 years old, 17-year-old Gregory had lived in six different foster homes, and was labeled a no-good troublemaker. Some families were good to him but did not love him enough to keep him with them for a long period; others viewed him as a problem. In one foster home he was sexually abused by his foster brother. In each of those homes, Gregory had experienced different rules, regulations, and expectations of himself. At 17 he was a member of a group home but received very little direction about what to do with his life. He was a confused young man who had been in trouble with the law for stealing a car and shoplifting. Although he would have to leave the group home within a period of one year, he was undecided what he wished to do with his life. He was living up to his label of no-good troublemaker.

How do individuals develop positive or negative self-images? We will look at two people on the threshold of adolescence and attempt to follow their growth experiences in order to gain a better understanding of the identity crisis in adolescence.

When Jack was an infant he experienced the world as good, giving, supportive, and dependable. He was born in a lower-class Black family whose stable, loving relationships strengthened his sense of the world's goodness, which he internalized. The outcome for him was a sense of basic trust in self as well as world. By 2 years of age, Jack enjoyed a sense of autonomy. He gained increasing control over mind and body through a nontraumatic achievement of bowel control and successful attempts in exploring the environment and making decisions on his own. He was able to love as well as cooperate and thus move easily to the stage of development in which he attained a sense of initiative. Jack was well loved and felt comfortable in exploring his own potentialities. Later he entered the school system, where he was challenged with the new demands of learning and peer competitiveness. Because he had been prepared for a confident, meaningful life, Jack came out of the school system with the feeling "I will do it" and a sense of competence and industry.

Perry came from a lower-class Black family in which there were constant marital conflicts. As an infant, he cried and nobody catered to him; often he cried himself to sleep. A harsh hand hit him if he did not drink the milk that was slipped between his lips, whether he was ready for it or not. Constant experiences of frustration and deprivation led Perry to develop a feeling of mistrust. As he grew older he had difficulty meeting the standards of his parents. He did not gain bladder or bowel control for a long period of time. Exploring his environment proved to be stressful. Perry did not lay a basic foundation of self-confidence; instead of security, he developed an essential feeling of doubt and shame. All these negative factors created a barrier to establishing an adequate love-identity relationship with his parents; rather, guilt became a dominant feature of his life. At a young age Perry was preoccupied with rejection and pain in his immediate environment. This preoccupation put him at a disadvantage when he entered the school system. Although school surroundings made new opportunities available, Perry felt a sense of inferiority and told himself, "I cannot make it at school."

What is the possibility that Jack and Perry will experience adolescence in the same manner? Practically nil. They have different orientations toward the new challenges and opportunities available to them. Jack is entering the period of adolescence with positive experiences behind him, whereas Perry remains burdened with adaptive concerns that date back to difficulties in early childhood and infancy. However, the outside world will see them as two Black teenagers. Stereotypes of teenagers will be applied to both of them, and they will both be expected to perform and conform. When problems arise, it is possible that the period of adolescence itself will be blamed. In our culture we are more apt to recognize problems at adolescence than at earlier points in the life span and to make assumptions that the problems are new and peculiar to this stage. What truly happens is that the earlier problems just take on new dimensions. Some of the negative attention that adolescents get reflects the limited recognition of problems that many children bring with them into adolescence. A failure to notice these problems before says something about our own perceptions as well as our values.

The distinctive feature of adolescence is the necessity of developing a sense of identity. In time, a person has to add new components to that identity and thus develop a clear and integrated self-image. The task of integrating identity is complex, taking into account past, present and future selves. Moreover, the young person has to perform this task in the midst of many new developments, including physiological transformations. Every individual who enters this stage has to face the risky task of identity integration; some will falter and leave adolescence with a sense of identity confusion.

Erikson's scheme of development is basically male in orientation. He asserts that a woman puts aside her identity as she prepares to define herself through the man she will marry. Though Erikson maintains that identity should precede intimacy (which will be discussed in Chapter 7), he specifies that women achieve both at the same time.

Freud described male and female differences with the statement "biology is destiny." Psychologists have added to this idea the notion that "socialization is destiny." There are differences between the sexes in defining identity, and though there has been subtle acknowledgment of these differences, it is only in recent years that the female's quest for identity has been researched.

Criticism of Erikson's Theory

In her studies of women, Carol Gilligan (1982) concludes that women define themselves less in terms of achievement and more in terms of relationships with other people, while preserving their separate identity. They tend to achieve identity through cooperative effort rather than competition (Papalia & Olds, 1986).

Based on his study of women, Marcia (1979) concludes that they develop stability in terms of identity as society pressures women to carry on social roles. Marcia argues as Erikson's male-based pattern indicates, that women do not have to wait to develop intimacy, but they develop both, identity and intimacy, at the same time. Marcia concludes that differences in male and female patterns are also due to the different ways that parents treat boys and girls. As several studies have shown, different child-rearing practices are associated with different identity statuses (Marcia, 1980). There is sufficient research evidence that indicates intimate friendships are more important for girls than for boys while in grade school (Cooke, 1979).

Sherman (1971) asserts that adolescence is not a period of stress and storm for most girls, although it tends to be unhappier for girls than for boys. For girls, sources of unhappiness tend to be the vagaries of acceptance by the all-important peer group rather than biological factors, such as menarche. The picture is rather one of struggle to manage conflicting feelings toward the mother, engendered largely by dependence–independence conflicts. The intense same-sex peer friendships of this stage may be a way of working through the mother relationship, and sisters as well as girlfriends may become more important than fathers at this point in providing substitute relationships that help to wean the girl from the mother. Thus, for girls, intimacy is a way of establishing identity, and proceeds along with it.

The discrepancy between womanhood and adulthood is very evident in a study by Broverman, Vogel, Broverman, Clarkson, and Rosenkrantz (1972). The findings of this study reveal what is deemed necessary for adulthood—the ability to think autonomously, make clear decisions, and take responsible action—and show that these traits are associated with masculinity. Thus the stereotypes suggest a splitting of love and work that relegates expressive capacities to women while placing instrumental abilities in the masculine domain. Yet, looked at from a different point of view, these stereotypes reflect a conception of adulthood that is itself out of balance, favoring the separateness of the individual self over connection to others and leaning more toward an autonomous life of work than toward the interdependence of love and care (Gilligan, 1982).

Some men discover in midlife what women have known from the beginning: the importance of intimacy, relationships, and care. However, because this knowledge in women has been considered intuitive or instinctive—that is, a function of anatomy coupled with destiny—psychologists have neglected to describe its development. Gilligan goes on to say that her research shows women's moral development centering on the elaboration of that knowledge and thus delineating a critical difference between the sexes in psychological development. According to Gilligan, the subject matter of moral development not only provides the final illustration of the reiterative pattern in the observations and assessment of sex differences in the literature of human development but also indicates more particularly why the nature and significance of women's development has been so obscured and shrouded in mystery.

All these observations about sex differences reinforce the conclusion reached by David McClelland (McClelland & Power, 1975), who says that sex role turns out to be one of the most important determinants of differences in human behavior in studies done by psychologists, right from the beginnings of empirical research. But it is difficult to say "different" without saying "better" or "worse," for there is a tendency to construct a single scale of measurement. This scale has been generally derived from and standardized on the basis of interpretations of research data drawn predominantly or exclusively from studies of males. Psychologists "have tended to regard male behavior as the 'norm' and female behavior as some kind of deviation from that norm" (McClelland & Power, 1975, p. 81). If women do not conform to the standards of psychological expectation, the conclusion has generally been that something is wrong with women (Gilligan, 1982).

With the new light being brought into the field by thought-provoking studies of women's development, it is hoped that we resolve some of the issues of using man as an ideal model for all people and move toward using the male model as an ideal for men and the female model as an ideal for women. Then practitioners in therapeutic situations can offer help to clients according to their sex, using their knowledge of typical male and female roles.

Competence

Robert White (1960) regards adolescence as the final stage of development, one in which newly strengthened sexual impulses bring about the possibility of sexual intercourse. White agrees with Anna Freud that this period brings increased instinctual drives and so threatens established patterns of ego control. According to White, some kinds of behavior are well handled by a competence model but neglected by libido and interpersonal models. Because the adolescent is reaching adult size, strength, and mental development, his or her overall behavior lies in the realm of serious accomplishment—serious and important in terms of either the youth culture or the adult culture.

White equates the concept of competence with what Erikson calls a *sense of industry* in the latency period. White sees this quest for competency as continuing more seriously after puberty than Erikson's account implies. White adds that he works chiefly with late adolescents whose sexual problems and social relations have, for the most part, not overwhelmed them. They have plans for studies; they learn to become aware of their abilities and limitations; they struggle with materials to learn and skills to be acquired; they attempt to become aware of their occupational leanings and to make career plans, as well as expressing concerns about modern society and its future. Competency in different spheres of their lives is what adolescents are searching for.

Adolescents learn to do things: to drive cars, compete, set adult records for sports, occasionally break such records, become part of the football or soccer team, play in the band, and so forth. Some of them try their skills at writing, at scientific discoveries, at music and drama. Some adolescents with fewer opportunities or talents follow other pursuits (White, 1960). The important point is that all these possibilities belong to the realm of work. At the same time, adolescents are making gains or losses in ego strength. White indicates that in theorizing about this subject we should not exclude the possibility that such developments significantly affect what happens in the erotic and interpersonal realms.

White argues that to view competence as a simple and sovereign concept is not sufficient. A person who has developed wholly in competence but has no dimensions of passion, love, or friendliness would never qualify as mature. Competence is not necessary for experiences such as enjoying food, immersing oneself in a sexual relationship, loving children, cherishing friends, and being impressed by great works of art, nor should it be used to repress problems that arise from aggression and anxiety. The competence model should be used in conjunction with other models that do full justice to such experiences as hunger, sexuality, and aggression. It could frustrate one's desire for logical simplicity to suppose that several models are required to understand a problem. However, it can never be claimed that human nature was designed in the interests of logic (White, 1960).

Dan, age 17, was brought up by parents who stressed that to make it in life he had to perform extremely well in school, spend his free time in studies, and devote all his time to intellectual pursuits. Dan had been trained to think in that manner from the time he was a few years old. Thus at 17 he took great pleasure in matters that other teenagers considered to be lofty but boring. He would spend hours in the library studying volumes on how to pursue a particular intellectual task that fascinated him. However, he completely neglected matters of etiquette and social and emotional relationships. He did not care how he dressed and looked sloppy most of the time, and yes, as often happens, he wore thick spectacles. Dan was a loner who had not acquired the art of being friendly with others. He could hardly ever date a girl, being viewed as "peculiar" by his classmates once they were outside the classroom. Although Dan appeared to be competent in the single area of intellectual pursuits, to be a well-rounded personality Dan also needed to be able to make friends, deal with sexuality, and engage in human relationships.

White points out that adolescents have to acquire social competence. Young people at this age attempt to become members of groups. Membership in a peer group is useful. This meaningful group behavior depends on group norms, the cognition of group expectations, and taking turns in handling group responsibilities. Particularly in informal games, whose purpose is fun, the nature of norms and reciprocal roles becomes abundantly important.

Another contribution of peer relationships to social competence is the provision of varied information about the human environment. The youth culture, though not always noticeably tolerant, offers adolescents an opportunity to compare notes on mothers, fathers, siblings, and families that are different from their own and to discover differences in family values. Adolescents also share their knowledge about teachers, whose personal qualities are subject to zestful psychological analysis on the way to and from school. In these ways young people shed light on their own society, as well as contributing to each other's education by exchanging information about both leading groups and rival groups. Successful handling of this portion of the social curriculum should be conducive to a perception of the relativity of perspectives and to a widening awareness of the vagaries of human behavior (White, 1976). Participation in groups can lead to a sense of interpersonal competence.

However, total commitment to peer groups and social competency can lead to social enslavement, which may betray itself in painful loneliness and anxiety when not in the company of one's friends. The most serious problem is compulsive conformity to group sanctions. The young person's preferences, tastes, and opinions are sanctioned by the group, and the person takes no chances in giving offense or incurring disapproval. Complete conformity will take a heavy toll on individuality and make it difficult for a person to think of herself or himself as an autonomous agent. Belonging to two groups with different value systems can produce severe conflict.

Social enslavement is a product of anxiety. What young adolescent would dare to wear a skirt that is 3 inches too long or too short, risking embarassment and ridicule, even if a skirt of that length had been right two years ago and would be right again in another two years? That is conformity. From the peers' point of view, conformity would appear to be a good adaptation to the group, but at the same time it is a form of enslavement.

Social isolation follows an adolescent's failure to gain acceptance by a peer group and may affect the person's social growth. For an adolescent's attempts to fraternize to be met with indifference or rejection creates the most elementary frustration; anxiety and shame may add their negative tone to the feelings of inefficacy. This result may lead to withdrawal, which stems from a combination of hurt feelings and moral indignation. Those whose social experiences are not pleasant may turn out to be shy, retiring, housebound, and limited in interests to things they can do by themselves. Unfortunately such an individual does not develop skills in competition or compromise, does not experience the give and take of group membership, and remains a stranger to convivial good peership (White, 1976).

Family Relationships
Autonomy from Parents

Over the last few decades the relationships of parents to their children have changed considerably. Families have become smaller, with fewer children and fewer relatives. Adolescents have developed more independence from parents and a heightened intimacy with their peers.

This is a period of dual ambivalence (Stone & Church, 1979); parents and children both have mixed feelings about each other. Parents want the best for their children and want them to succeed in the outside world. At the same time, they have doubts about whether their children are pursuing the right courses. Often they try to control their children's destinies or find themselves envious of their children's greater opportunities and freedom. For their part, youths may feel grateful to be dependent on their parents. At the same time, they wish to show that they can make it on their own and feel resentful of parental control.

Some studies reveal that there is a meaningful orientation of adolescents to both parents and peers—depending upon the issue of concern. Chand, Crider, and Willets (1975) found agreement between parents and adolescents on issues related to religion and marriage but not on issues related to sex and drugs. Similarly, Kelly (1972) found high parent–adolescent similarity on moral issues but not on issues pertinent to style of dress, hair length, and hours of sleep. Many studies indicate that, although adolescents and parents have somewhat different attitudes about issues of contemporary social concern (such as war, drugs, and sexuality), most of the differences reflect contrast in attitude intensity rather than attitude direction (Lerner, Karson, Meisels, & Knapp, 1975; Lerner & Knapp, 1975; Lerner, Schroeder, Rewitzer, & Weinstock, 1972; Weinstock & Lerner, 1972).

With a large number of parents currently working, there is also a trend to push adolescents quickly and continuously into the company of their peers, and this tendency has some hazards. As White (1976) mentioned, social enslavement and social isolation alike are increased by anxiety. Ideally, young people should work their way gradually into peer interactions, moving at their own speed, following their own inclinations (which are influenced by the family), and giving their anxieties an opportunity to subside. Young people should have the scope, in other words, to develop their own strategies. If parental anxiety and impatience result in pushing a child into company for which the child is not ready—and, moreover, if that company is represented as being, like spinach, good for him or her—the chances of this young person's performing well socially and having a good experience are negligible. The most usual outcome of such an experience is an anxious deference, which is the first step to enslavement, or equally anxious inhibition and abasement, which make interactions feel like a bad bargain. Social participation and autonomous development can easily be spoiled by pressure.

Angela was a 17-year-old member of an upper-middle-class family. On account of her father's business, the family was required to move to the West Coast. Angela's mother was a socialite who did not have much time for her only daughter. She wanted Angela to enter her new school system and get on with her life by making new friends who would be acceptable to the mother's upper-class connections.

Angela's life had been different while they lived in the East. She had attended the same private school from the time she was a young child and had grown up with children who understood and cared about her. Angela had become closer to her friends and their parents as her own parents became more and more involved in their social activities.

In the new private school, Angela felt totally lost. The young people appeared to be snobbish. She attempted to make a habit of going home early. Her mother was intolerant of that strategy and immediately started calling up the parents of Angela's classmates. The mother found out which parents were the most snobbish and recommended that Angela get friendly with their children because they were the "right kind." Angela lost a lot of her own spontaneity, became overly anxious to please, and attempted to buy friendships to satisfy her mother, as well as to feel accepted in the school. Her efforts would probably lead to what White calls *social enslavement*. The attitude of Angela's mother affected the manner in which Angela would develop her relationships and her own sense of self.

A relaxed parental attitude aids young people in developing autonomy.

Identification

Many children and adolescents find themselves in more than one family during their socialization. About 1 out of 5 children under 18 years of age in the United States do not live with their two parents (U.S. Bureau of the Census, 1978). There is a substantial number of single-parent families, and many children and adolescents live in families having two adults but only one biological parent. These variations in family living come about as a result of the high rates of marital dissolution found in the United States. Divorce and remarriage are common, and about 2 out of every 5 recent marriages are expected to end in divorce (U.S. Bureau of the Census, 1976). Moreover, about one-third of the people involved in divorce eventually remarry, and those who remarry do so, on the average, within three years after their divorces. Thus, many children—about 45% of adolescents—can expect to live in a family setting without one of their natural parents for a period of time before they reach adulthood.

The adolescent faces the seemingly impossible task of relinquishing parental ties and childhood identifications in order to establish a separate identity outside the family while still maintaining the continuity of parental and family relationships. For the child to become an autonomous individual, major adjustments have to be made in the family (Anthony, 1967). As Freud specified, detachment from parental authority is one of the most significant but also one of the most painful, psychically sensitive achievements (Freud, 1938). Usually it is the process of disengagement that provides the setting for the so-called adolescent rebellion and generation gap. Youths are often portrayed in literature and movies as alienated and troubled, and this picture does seem to have validity.

There is general agreement across a number of studies that parent–child conflict should not be equated with what is called the *generation gap*. As has been noted, most research reveals a relative compatibility of views and values held by parents and adolescents (Douvan & Adelson, 1966).

Normally, strong parental identification is associated with good adjustment. For young women, however, strong identification with the mother is negatively related to autonomy, adjustment, and self-esteem, whereas identification with masculine traits is associated with high self-esteem (Baruch & Barnett, 1980). This by itself is a complicated matter, touching on changes in the social structure as well as inviting treatment of a vast literature in the area of sex-role stereotypes (Broverman et al., 1972). The important point for our purposes is that strong identification with one or both parents is normative for adolescence.

It is important to consider Erikson's conceptualization of negative-choice identity in adolescence. Underscoring the importance of identity formation in adolescence and parental identification, which are building blocks, Erikson describes the negative identity as one that is perversely based on all those identifications and roles that at critical stages of development have been presented as the most undesirable or dangerous.

The major changes in family structure in recent years have important implications for identification with parents. One change is the increased prevalence of single-parent families. It was found that sons of working mothers, more often than others, express disapproval of nonworking mothers (Hoffman, 1970).

Absence of fathers has been the focus of much recent research. When girls lose their fathers through death or divorce they experience anxiety with males. They also exhibit attention-seeking behavior with boys, and they exhibit earlier heterosexual behavior than do girls from intact families (Hetherington, 1972).

Mona was the mother of three daughters. Deserted by her husband when her youngest child was 3 years old, Mona struggled with a full-time job, a poor income, and three children to clothe and feed. She had no time for anything else, and she was unable to work through her anger at her husband. The children did not have a meaningful male role model. As the three girls grew into adolescence they were fascinated with boys, always dressing up for them and constantly seeking their company. Although they craved such companionship, their relationships with boys were usually short lived, consisting of premature sexual contact and rapid rejection, usually by the boy, with consequent emotional turmoil for the young girls. Their high anxiety about male relationships overwhelmed them. Before long, Mona had two pregnant teenagers on her hands, with adolescent fathers who were unwilling to accept responsibility. Part of the girls' problems arose from the fact that these girls grew up making their own rules because their mother was out of the house most of the time. A second factor was their lack of a male role model in the family.

Lack of a father also has a negative effect on the masculine identification process (Biller & Bahm, 1971). There is no escaping the reality that sweeping changes in societal norms, values, and practices have telling effects on the individual psyche.

Typically the adolescent is between the extremes of compliance and conformity, on the one side, and alienation or rejection of parents on the other. The separation process normally occurs within the context of an enduring parent–child relationship. Thus it is normally within this framework of an outgoing, sustaining parental relationship that we view the adolescent's inner turmoil, fluctuating self-esteem, problems, and conflict with parents. This brings us to a crucial issue on which viewpoints diverge: namely, that conflict (such as adolescent turmoil) is a necessary condition for growth. Conflict in adolescent–adult relationships is expected at certain points and ought not to be denied. There is a critical distinction between the idea of a generation gap, on the one hand, and of intergenerational conflict, on the other. It is often conflict that allows for continued development. To view the issue positively, as Blos (1967) indicates, intergenerational conflict is essential for the growth of the self and of civilization.

Sex-Role Identity

There are several developmental tasks of adolescence. Young people have to accept the notion of a changed and sexually developed body, master intellectual challenges, and integrate a set of moral values. Thus they form what is called an *ego identity*. In part, ego formation consists of achieving emotional separation from parents by gaining independence, learning satisfying sexual roles, creating friendships, and acquiring a group identity.

Many cultures practice initiation rites, ceremonies in which the society marks the passage of youth from childhood to adulthood. In some cultures the rites occur at the beginning of puberty. In one subculture of India, when a young girl comes of age she is set apart from the rest of her family for 13 days. Afterward she is given a ceremonial bath, in which at least three married women wash and clean her body. Later she is dressed in beautiful clothes, made to sit on a decorated chair covered with flowers, and perfumed. Parents of eligible young men are invited, with the hope that the ceremony will initiate a relationship that ends in an arranged marriage between this young girl and a young man. Puberty signals to the girl that she has become a woman, and everything that is done thereafter signals the same—that she is an adult and has to learn to take on the responsibilities of adulthood.

Rites, such as the first date, driving a car, or first stable job, achieve the important goal of signifying that a person has reached a decisive step in the ascent toward adulthood in our culture too. When there are no initiation ceremonies, the lack may entail certain costs and increase the possibility of a long and difficult adolescence.

What are the various ceremonies that are followed in our culture? In the major religions, ceremonies like the Christian first communion or the Jewish bar mitzvah (which could have its origin in earlier, culturally traditional initiation rites) mark the young person's entrance into the adult congregation. Some social organizations, too, such as fraternities and sororities, conduct ceremonies of initiation—pledging fraternities or hazing freshmen.

In an informal effort to find signals of their transition to maturity, young people observe any number of milestones—the first ejaculation, the start of menstruation, the first date, the first sexual union, the first automobile, graduation from school, and, finally, getting married (Gardner, 1978). Because only some of these milestones are directly related to sex-role identity, it can be said that growing up in North America involves more rituals than coming of age in primitive cultures. The significance attached to such milestones reveals that there is a felt need for marking the beginning of adulthood.

North America is a melting pot, or a salad bowl, and the initiation rites that mark the beginning of this special period are diverse. Ethnic background appears to have an effect on the way puberty and adolescence are treated.

Francis Hsu (1953) compared adolescents of Chinese–American homes with adolescents of Anglo–American homes. He found that American children of Anglo-Saxon background generally came from households where the tie with the parents is strong; where childhood is considered to be a special time; where children are not given punishments; and where parents are ambivalent about their offspring's leaving home. Because of this type of home setting, children feel the need to define themselves as different and separate from parents. Therefore, they develop strong individual goals and become oriented to a peer group, and they also become critical of the parental culture and societal values.

However, in the Chinese culture, youths are absorbed early into the adult world. There is less mystery—in fact, a total reality orientation—to childhood and development. Parents become less upset when children begin to leave home, and they reveal less need to hold onto them. Chinese youth are more likely to maintain ties with their parents and to honor features of their cultural traditions. The amount of stress felt by the Americans in adolescence was high, whereas the stress felt by Samoans in the 20s, as mentioned earlier in this chapter, was minimal, and the Chinese-Americans fell midway on such measures.

However, as we have seen, heard, and experienced, adolescence in the United States is difficult. In our society, youths of 16 or 17 are not equipped to participate as full adults. Many continue to live at home and may require special training, more education, or more time to choose a lifestyle. Consequently they feel a certain degree of frustration, uncertainty, and in many cases, unparalleled tension. Although adolescence may not be a period of stress and strain for all adolescents, it continues to be so for American youth. Because of its ups and downs in our culture, adolescence is the period that developmental psychologists and social workers study most frequently.

Views of adolescent stress and strain are mixed. Some observers emphasize adolescents' freedom from their parents (Coleman, 1961; Musgrove, 1964), whereas others remark on their continuing dependence (Campbell, 1969; Kandel & Lesser, 1969). A number of opinions have been expressed about the turbulence of adolescence. The dominant view emphasizes the turbulence, whereas some authorities regard adolescence as free from stress and strain (Moore & Holtzman, 1965; Offer, 1969). Because experts disagree so strongly, generalizations are not reliable, particularly since they involve opinions about millions of adolescents.

Peer Relationships

During adolescence, relationships with peers assume great importance. From peers, adolescents pick up their own attitudes, values, and behavior patterns. From peers, adolescents receive signs of belonging and being successful. There are various phases in friendships.

Dexter Dunphy (1963) has studied the stages of group development during adolescence. As in Samoa, preadolescents in North America spend more time with members of the same sex. As adolescence approaches, these groups are attracted to the opposite sex. Later a third stage begins, when the two groups, girls and boys, unite in interactions such as dating; usually the individuals with the highest status in each clique are the first to date. In later stages of peer relations, the cliques become more and more heterosexual. Thus small clusters of dating couples come to replace the larger groups of early adolescence.

In Dunphy's view, this sequence of peer relationships appears to help adolescents in several ways. They help adolescents to break away from their parents; they lead to participation in healthy competition; and they promote heterosexual attachment. Peer relationships also lead to a high level of conformity, so that those who spurn common values are likely to be rejected. Dunphy indicates that peer groups are important, whether they occupy a major portion of one's existence or whether by the fact of exclusion they prove to be pivotal, many times having a depressing influence on a person's life.

Peer groups have also been studied from an ethological perspective. R. C. Williams (1975) found that when male children were left in a five-week camp their behavior appeared to change as they developed a hierarchical system among themselves. Some boys were regarded as leaders of the group, others as followers. Leaders had bunks close to their counselors, walked near the front in a file of hikers, and performed well in sports and on physical fitness measures. However, there was no correlation between leadership and physical maturity, intelligence, or creativity. The dominance hierarchy remained stable throughout the camping season. During the last days of the camp it was found that children who were pigeonholed as dominant actually did control interactions among peers, 92 times out of 100.

Typically, adolescents are conformists to their peers. Peers usually structure their own framework of acceptable behavior patterns. Thus close identification with peers is an important source of security. With peers, adolescents have opportunities to share their problems and experiences intimately and to find sympathy and understanding, as well as to learn to cooperate, give and take, and clarify their sex roles. Fischer and Bersani (1979) claim that youths are free to drift into crime when they have few or no bonds with peers and institutions that help to form high self-esteem.

Developmental psychologists agree that conformity is tremendous in early adolescence and diminishes in later adolescence (Jones, Garrison, & Morgan 1985). Male and female adolescents in groups of ages 13 to 14 and 18 to 21 were used in a study by Landsbaum and Willis (1971) to understand adolescent conformity. The researchers found that younger adolescents who were "low competency" subjects and who worked in pairs with "high competency" subjects displayed the most conformity behavior. Also, younger adolescents were more susceptible to the influence of peers than older adolescents. This pattern can be observed among junior high school students when nearly all members of the group follow and share a particular fad.

Lower-class peer groups usually serve important status functions for adolescents who are disadvantaged according to the criteria of such institutions of society as schools, churches, and businesses. For such teenagers, peer groups become important determiners of status; they stress achievement goals that are not easily attainable by the conventional norms and values of the larger society. For the lower-class youngster, the peer group is thus extremely important, and, as Sherif and Sherif (1964) point out, the greater the importance an individual places on a peer group, the more binding it is on them to participate in activities that are initiated by the group. Often, it is from this framework that negative peer-group developments, such as delinquency and street gangs, can begin.

> John and his friends were 14-year-olds who lived in a ghetto, where survival strategies have to be developed at a young age. They were without much supervision at home; most lived either with single parents or in two-parent families preoccupied with making a livelihood. John learned to cut classes so that he could sell drugs on the streets. The slightly older boys in his group, who recruited him into selling drugs, often used John as a cover-up when problems arose; with his tiny stature, he was easily mistaken for a young child and overlooked by normally suspicious adults. Initiation into taking drugs is not far away when a person sells drugs. Before long, John was totally out of the school system and was both user and seller. John became a drug vendor, gaining much-needed acceptance for himself, as well as the support of his wayward social group.

Even for normal adolescents, good emotional and social adjustment is connected to conformity with the peer group. There is some evidence that conformity to peer-group behavior is associated with feelings of inadequacy or insecurity because normal adolescents are growing physically, socially, and mentally and have a need to be accepted by their peers to deal with their new and different roles. Various subcultures have been identified in high schools and colleges. The high school groups can be subdivided, as Rice (1981) indicates, into three groups: (1) those organized for fun, (2) the academic, and (3) the delinquent. There are some factors that are typically part of the teenage culture. Slang gives special meaning to what adolescents say to one another. Clothes distinguish the manner in which adolescents view themselves. Automobiles and money add to the status of an adolescent. Adolescent subculture creates for its members identity and independence, as well as conformity.

Minority-Group Culture

After Blacks, the people of Hispanic origin—Puerto Ricans, Cubans, Mexicans, Central and South Americans—form the largest minority in our society. In most Spanish-speaking cultures the families are typically patriarchal and authoritarian. Puerto Rican and Mexican girls usually marry young, and there is a special concern for their virginity. Often they are closely guarded by their brothers and other family members. Marriage can be a form of escape for these girls from their strictly supervised home situations. But marriage is most often a transfer of authority: the husband assumes control and usually makes most of the decisions (Rice, 1981).

Many Puerto Rican youngsters who come with their parents to cities in the United States develop problems similar to those of their American counterparts as they assimilate the American culture and its values. The identity problem is complicated by the fact that they belong to a different background, and they are aware of their skin color. Often they develop a subculture with which they can closely identify.

Asians are coming to the United States in larger numbers than before. For adults, the cultural shock is significant, but they tend to adjust fairly well (Jones, Garrison, & Morgan, 1985). In many cases they have already learned to deal with the American way of life through radio and television. Younger people learn English quickly and adjust reasonably well to their school environments.

Critical Issues
Sexual Behavior

A number of problems arise during adolescence due to the fast pace of developmental changes.

Sexual urges manifest themselves first in boys even though girls enter puberty before boys do. Orgasm and arousal are initially self-oriented and explored through masturbation. For girls, initial heterosexual interests are directed toward companionship and holding hands as they look forward to developing emotional warmth. Boys are desirous of creating a relationship with a girl for the ultimate purpose of having sex. As Jones, Garrison, and Morgan (1985) put it, boys and men are intimate to obtain sex, whereas girls and women give sex to become intimate.

A summary of female teen sex based on two nationwide studies (Zelnick & Kantner, 1978) reveals certain patterns of sexual behavior:

1. At least 1 girl in 5 has engaged in some sexual activity by the age of 16.
2. By age 19, two-thirds have had sexual relationships.
3. More than 9 out of 10 have had sexual relations prior to marriage. One out of 10 girls becomes pregnant before age 17.
4. Eight out of 10 of them conceive prior to marriage.

Teenage Pregnancy

Teenage pregnancy is an important and fast-growing problem urgently requiring help. A teenager who becomes pregnant gets assistance either from both her parents, from one of her parents if hers is a single-family household, or through social welfare agencies. Some churches or other denominational groups offer help to teenagers. Many infants of teenagers are taken by adoption agencies, either because the teenage mother does not wish to bring up her child or because she has been persuaded by her parents or others not to bring up the child. However, when a teenager gets involved with a social service agency, the caseworker provides the help needed to make a decision. The worker provides teenagers with vocational and educational guidance as well as public financial assistance and birth-control information. If things do not work well for the teenager at her home, then the caseworker offers assistance in finding a temporary home until the baby is born.

Trisha was a 14-year-old Catholic girl who became pregnant the first time she had intercourse. Her parents were horrified. They did not wish to let her have an abortion because of their religion, but at the same time they did not want to be tied to the burden of explaining their daughter's absence from school, as well as her increased body size. After much contemplation they decided to send her away to a temporary home where she would be able to give birth to a child without much outside attention. The home was maintained privately by a few responsible people, who helped Trisha go through the pregnancy and accept the idea of giving the baby away. The young mother had to part with her child, even if she had learned to love the baby, for she had to abide by the decision she had reached with her parents.

Rosen (1980), who made a study of 432 pregnant teenagers under 18 years of age, found that 50% involved their mothers in pregnancy-resolution decision making. Many young unwed mothers who have to give away their babies for adoption are traumatized, and without the help and understanding attitude of people in the home, it could be practically impossible for them to go through this period of separating, which involves agony and pain as well as the guilt and responsibility associated with giving away a child.

For the pregnant teenage girl, most states offer educational facilities. Some schools, however, have policies that have not yet acknowledged local rulings in favor of such facilities, and some have yet to set times for termination of schooling during pregnancy. Edgar Allen Poe schools in Baltimore and similiar agencies in Azusa, California, Emory University in Atlanta, and the Young Mothers Educational Development program in Syracuse set up programs specifically to take care of young pregnant girls. These programs offer young parents a number of support groups, including medical and educational-vocational groups, and teach the teenagers about steady use of contraceptives if they are sexually active. There are programs that offer teenagers counseling and that help teenagers work on their self-esteem. A study by Strathe and Hash (1979) reveals that pregnant teenagers who have been offered a significant relationship during this difficult period do well in school achievements, as well as in terms of their own self-esteem.

Because only women get pregnant, we tend to think of pregnancy and its consequences for only the female; however, the male has feelings about it as well. Sexual relationships during adolescence have pitfalls as well as potential rewards for the males. Whether or not a pregnancy happens, sexual relationships can be troublesome for the male. If a pregnancy occurs, the male may have to pay for an abortion or enter a forced marriage; and at an emotional level he would have to deal with the role he has created for himself. Sometimes the young father may be emotionally involved with the young woman and may care about the baby but not be ready to support them emotionally or financially.

A boy who has intercourse with a girl could become a candidate for a paternity suit, not an easy situation for him. Some girls are afraid to admit to getting pregnant in willing intercourse and may claim that they were raped (MacDonald, 1973). The accusation has its own consequences; even if not followed through in court, it may leave a scar on the accused young man.

Many issues and problems arise out of adolescent sexuality because adolescents are dealing with a changing world and a changing self, which place tremendous pressure on them. An adolescent must integrate all inner and outer changes if he or she is to be adaptive.

Homosexuality

Homosexual contacts before the age of 15 appear to be more common among boys than among girls (Jones, Garrison, & Morgan, 1985). Sex play consisting of exhibitionism and voyeurism, as well as touching each other and mutual masturbation, often occurs in small groups between the ages of 8 and 13. This experimentation does not make a person a homosexual. About 10% of boys and 5% of girls engage in sexual relations with others of the same sex at least once during adolescence. "Bisexual" describes a person who could be aroused by either men or women; such a person may be mostly heterosexual and occasionally homosexual or the reverse. According to a study by Roesler and Diesler (1972), for young people to consider themselves homosexuals the following had to occur: (1) they experienced early homosexual play; (2) they sought homosexual partners in adolescence; (3) they overtly participated in the gay world. On an average, it takes people about four years of homosexual behavior to consider themselves homosexuals. Quite a few of them visit a therapist to find out about their sexual orientation. The reasons for a person's becoming a homosexual are not clearly known. There is some evidence of disturbed family relationships, social learning, prenatal endocrine factors, and, in some cases, living with homosexuals at a critical period in child development (U.S. Department of Health, Education and Welfare, 1978).

Numerous organizations cater to gays and lesbians, as well as to the parents of gay and lesbian people, and there are various types of churches for this community (Jones, Garrison, & Morgan, 1985).

Masturbation

Parents have great difficulty in talking to their children about masturbation. As it involves more stimulation than any other aspect of sexuality, it causes adults a great deal of anxiety (Roberts, Kline, & Gagnon, 1978). For many young people this is the first sexual practice they engage in; that is, physical satisfaction through sexual stimulation.

Attitudes toward masturbation have been changing. Recent research points out that young people are masturbating more than they used to and they are more willing to say so (Papalia & Olds, 1986). Findings from LoPiccolo and Lobilz (1972) and Barbach (1975) maintain that masturbation is healthy because it educates young people about their bodies, releases sexual pressure, and gives sexual pleasure without any emotional involvement with other people. Another benefit is that it helps young people to take good care of their bodies and also helps them to value themselves as individuals.

Juvenile Delinquency

Young people (between 16 and 18 years of age) are labeled delinquent for various reasons. Some of them violate criminal law by actions such as rape, theft, assault, and sometimes homicide. Based on state law, they are arrested and are punishable, after they have been found guilty. Some juveniles are called status offenders. Status offenses are actions that are illegal only because of the offender's status—typically age and sex. Status offenses include truancy and promiscuity.

The question of which adolescent is a delinquent can usually be answered by looking at arrest records of those who have broken the law. Arrest practices for teenagers vary considerably. Some communities "warn" an adolescent, whereas others "book" (arrest) them.

> Donald, a young man of 16, was arrested for running away from home and also for breaking into a mailbox. The police officer who dealt with him was extraordinary. After discussing the situation with a social worker, he placed the boy in seclusion in a jail cell for a night just to help him understand the stark realities of prison life. This cell, with only a commode in the corner and barely large enough to hold a tall man, had an effect on Donald. He was frightened of what he saw and vowed not get involved in such crimes again, not even "for the fun of it."

Many adolescents have at some time been involved in such illegal behaviors as shoplifting, drinking, and drug use. Whether or not they have been labeled delinquent depends on whether they were apprehended, as well as on their race and socioeconomic status.

Some delinquent acts are petty offenses; others are serious. The United States Department of Justice statistics reveal that, in 1977, people under 18 years of age represented 41.2% of all arrests; 9.7% of all those for homicides, 11.1% of those for negligent manslaughter, 16.3% for assault, 51.1% for burglary, 42.9% for larceny, and 53.0% for motor-vehicle theft (Federal

Bureau of Investigation, 1977). These data reveal that crime is more common in middle and late adolescence than during any other period of life (Specht & Craig, 1982).

Standards and laws applying to delinquency vary with different groups and in different states. The extent of delinquency has been underreported. Coupled with these problems in analysis of delinquency is assessing its incidence once it is defined, including, for example, some kinds of antisocial behavior, such as truancy and running away from home; uncontrollable behavior at home or school, such as the 70,000 assaults on teachers and $600 million worth of vandalism in one year cited by Tygart (1980); and drug use. Juvenile crime is evaluated more subjectively than adult crime.

Causes.   There are various causative factors for delinquent behavior. It is found in all socioeconomic classes, but it is the poor who are most often caught and punished. Ironically, the environment itself is a cause of delinquent behavior; delinquency breeds faster in high-density areas where there is high unemployment, overpopulation, deteriorating housing, and high crime rates.

In a study of families in Hong Kong, Mitchell and Rosa (1981) found minor marital unhappiness, feelings of lack of control over children, absence of privacy, and negative attitudes about entertaining neighbors or friends in high-density situations. In several studies, Short, Tennyson, and Howard (1963) found lower family morale and greater interpersonal irritation in densely populated situations. Thus, children who grow up in high-density areas spend more time outside their homes with friends because the home atmosphere is not congenial and children are encouraged to stay out. When young people from such homes "hang out" for long periods of time, they think up things to do that sometimes start as fun, like taking things from a store on a challenge or a dare, but end up being considered crimes.

Negative peer influence irrespective of socioeconomic status is another reason for delinquency. When peers experiment with drugs and alcohol, acts of vandalism often follow. The family also shares in the making of the delinquent. According to Lambert (1972), broken homes without proper structuring for teenagers and with intense family problems can lead to delinquency. Middle-class as well as upper-class families have their share of delinquents when the adults do not spend time with their children. Growing up in a family where little affection is shown, and where there is a high level of activity but little time for talking about the day-to-day problems that the adolescent faces, adds to the adolescent's problems.

When they must make a cultural change from one country to another or from one area to another, such as a move from a totally rural area to an urban setting, or when older family members do not understand cultural differences encountered by younger members, youths turn to peers for support and understanding as well as for protection. When the culture of the school system is overly strict, children's rebellion spills over into the world outside the school.

Other factors that lead to delinquency are biological; they include heredity, poor health, neurological impairment, and maturation. As Sheppard (1974) has shown, about 25% of delinquency is due to organic causes, such as endocrine problems, too little or too much insulin, hyperthyroidism, and other chemical imbalances; to poor health status, such as having chronic problems in sugar level, and being susceptible to allergies and injuries; or to neurological impairment. Pontius (1972) mentions that 15% to 20% of delinquents have neurophysiological dysfunction of the frontal lobe of the brain. There could be a link between the autonomic nervous system's responsiveness and criminality (Penner, 1982). Those youths who have not accepted their bodies and have low self-esteem have a greater chance of developing delinquent behavior.

Psychological factors contributing to adolescent delinquency include troubled home life, poor relations with parents, and personality difficulties with peers. Difficulty in acquiring social roles and lack of control over impulsive behavior also are involved with delinquency.

Prevention.   Many attempts have been made to affect the life of the delinquent through study programs, family therapy, foster homes, youth workers, various kinds of psychological assistance, and educational programs. Phillips, Phillips, Fixen, and Wolf (1973) found efforts successful in small group homes consisting of six to eight boys and two professional "parents" sharing their living quarters.

> It took 16-year-old Julio several months of therapy to understand that he could not go back to his home and live with his mother. She constantly changed the men in her life and had also set Julio against his own younger brother because she had difficulty in showing her love for both her sons at the same time. With the help of his social worker, Julio eventually understood how his home situation had frustrated and angered him and led him to commit petty crimes such as stealing and committing minor assaults on children who lived on his block. After he accepted the reasons for his relocation, he went to live in a group home, where he enjoyed independent living and at the same time learned to respect his professional superiors and deal meaningfully with responsibilities. The structure and the consistent discipline, caring, and therapy helped Julio to move away from delinquent ways and develop a more responsible attitude toward life.

Substance Abuse

Substance abuse is the misuse of a drug or other chemical, usually to alter the psychological or emotional state of the user. The two classifications of drug dependency are physical and psychological. Drugs of abuse are often grouped as narcotics, stimulants, depressants, inhalants, hallucinogens, and marijuana.

The magnitude of the drug-use problem among many teenagers has been staggering. Research by the National Institute on Drug Abuse (1982) showed that among youths in the age group of 12 to 17, about 14% were drug users; among the 18- to 25-year-olds, 39% to 53% were users. The National Institute on Drug Abuse (1982) revealed that 60% of high school seniors had used marijuana, and 90% had smoked cigarettes.

The National Commission on Marijuana and Drug Abuse (1973) listed patterns of drug use:

1. experimental, to satisfy curiosity
2. social-recreational, to share an experience
3. circumstantial-situational, to stay awake in order to complete a task (People who take stimulants such as caffeine or amphetamines often remain in the workplace and the social life of the community.)
4. compulsive, to obey a need (A person who takes a drug frequently for a long period of time in response to high-intensity needs is a drug addict and has great difficulty living without the drug.).

Despite the risk of addiction teens still use drugs heavily, and it was found that use of a drug over a period of time could turn any person into an addict (National Institute on Drug Abuse, 1982).

Smoking

Youths have a psychogenic need for novel experiences. Just like alcohol use, smoking experience has increased among adolescents, from 30.4% in 1963 to 41.3% in the 1980s. Information and attitudes toward smoking from a high school class graduating in 1978 (Johnston, Backman, & O'Malley, 1979) reveals that 28% smoked cigarettes daily, 75% smoked sometimes, and only 59% said that smoking one or more packs daily was harmful. Prevention takes place when peers influence each other to perceive the bad effects of smoking. However, as found by the U.S. Department of Health, Education and Welfare (1979), 95% of those who gave up smoking did so on their own. Often, adolescents start to smoke in order to impress peers, at times to be accepted by them, and also to act more grown-up.

Suicide

The incidence of suicide in the age group from 14 to 19 has quadrupled in the past two decades. Some authorities believe that preadolescents look to others for their love relationships and therefore are afraid to kill themselves, whereas older adolescents see the world as revolving around them. When things seem hopeless and they believe that there is no way out, some kill themselves. Statistics show that more boys than girls commit suicide. They do so most often in high school or in the first semester of college (Garrison & Garrison, 1975). The yearly toll of adolescent suicides exceeds 5000. Suicide has been found to be the leading cause of death in this age group. According to Cantor (1977), on college campuses it is second only to accidents as the leading cause of death.

Various causative factors contribute to suicide. Isolated young people who feel vulnerable to loss of love objects often come from disturbed backgrounds and are often depressed. They may not have meaningful parental figures with whom to identify. They often reveal poor impulse control stemming from immature personalities. They are more likely than others to be suggestible and may suffer from feelings of guilt or self-directed hostility. Any one of these factors or a combination of them can become components of suicide. A suicide attempt is an adolescent's cry for help or sympathy, or can be an attempt to manipulate others to rescue them; it is often an effort to try to adapt and not always an actual attempt to end his or her life.

Many young people attempt to commit suicide and do not succeed. Adolescents may use a suicide attempt to signal their troubles, much as they may use running away, rebellion, lying, or getting arrested. Young people who attempt suicides are obviously unhappy in their lives and wish to change them (Cantor, 1977). Their suicide attempts are ways of getting attention or obtaining help from friends or family. It is extremely important that parents make themselves available to young people who have made suicide attempts. Suicide-prevention hot lines also exist to assist people in suicidal crisis.

> Young Winter was very unhappy with her home life. Her mother had deserted the family when Winter was 7, and ever since, Winter had played mom to her younger brothers and sister. When she was 17, her father married a fairly young woman. Strife developed between Winter and her stepmother. Her father, who was not home often, readily took his new wife's side. Winter felt isolated, threatened, and unloved. She had been the center of attention as the "housework-responsible person." Suddenly things had changed dramatically; Winter felt that she was a "nobody." She could turn neither to her father, who would no longer listen to her, nor to her stepmother, who viewed Winter as her rival. To make matters worse, she failed in her exams at school. The report card became a point of contention between Winter and her stepmother, who ridiculed her performance.
>
> Winter had spent so much time at home with her younger siblings that she did not have any close friends at school. She gradually withdrew from interactions at home and became depressed. Nobody seemed to care; in fact, the stepmother was relieved that Winter was out of the way. Winter schemed to run away a few times, but reality struck her too hard: there was nowhere to go. Eventually, in despair, she attempted suicide. She took an overdose of sleeping pills, but was discovered in time.
>
> In family therapy, a number of issues that had divided this family were reconstructed. With empathetic help from the counselor, the family was able to get back together again and work on the issues that troubled them. Through understanding and support, Winter obtained the kind of nurturing she herself needed as a person. The case ended happily with the establishment of meaningful relationships among Winter, her father, her new mother, and the rest of the family.

Eating Disorders

Some adolescents put on weight as they enter their teens, and this change leads to a lifelong struggle to maintain a level of weight that is desirable for both health and beauty reasons. In many ways the effort reflects our society's stringent standards of female beauty, which exalt the ideal of slenderness above everything else.

Eating disorders among adolescents are receiving increasing attention. Two types of eating problems have recently gained popular notice: anorexia nervosa and bulimia. Both reflect individual pathologies as sufferers attempt to meet the standards of beauty through bizarre eating habits. And both of them affect adolescent girls and women.

Anorexia nervosa.   Someone suggests to an adolescent girl that she should lose weight—just a few pounds. The young woman loses the weight and continues to diet obsessively; she refuses to eat until she has lost at least 25% of her original body weight. Her behavior is characteristic of anorexia nervosa. If untreated, she may eventually die.

This disease affects the age group from 9 to 30 and older. The typical patient is a bright, well-behaved, appealing female in her teens or early twenties, well-educated and usually from a well-to-do family. She is preoccupied with food. She enjoys talking about it, cooking it, and urging others to eat it. But she herself does not eat (if she does, she then purges herself by vomiting or using laxatives, her disorder is called *bulimia*). The anorexic person has a distorted image of herself and considers herself beautiful when she is pathetically and gruesomely skeletal. Once the person starts to starve, other symptoms begin to appear. Menstruation stops, she grows thick, soft hair on her body, and her level of activity becomes intense.

What causes anorexia? There are various theories suggested by researchers. It may be a physical disorder, caused by a deficiency of a crucial brain chemical; a psychological disturbance related to depression or a fear of growing up; a sociological reaction to extreme societal pressures for slenderness; or the product of a seriously malfunctioning family. So far, no hypothesis has been conclusively supported, and research continues (Yager, 1982).

Bulimia.   A disorder closely related to anorexia is bulimia, which is becoming more common among teenagers and young women. A bulimic person indulges in binge eating; such a person could eat up to 5000 calories' worth of food in one sitting. This phase is followed by vomiting or use of laxatives in order to empty the stomach. Bulimics are often depressed and commonly suffer from such physical complications as hair loss, excessive tooth decay, and gastric irritation (Papalia & Olds, 1986). Some bulimics are also anorexic, whereas others maintain normal weight.

The syndrome is far from rare. Estimates are that at least 5% of the population is affected (Nagelberg, Hale, & Ware, 1983). In many recent surveys, half of the college women queried said that they sometimes binge and purge (Herzog, 1982). Bulimics have traditionally been secretive about their eating habits; however, recent reports indicate that more young women are openly admitting to this unhealthy method of weight control (Squire, 1983).

Dropping Out of School

Although the educational level of Americans continues to increase, only 85% complete high school. An equal proportion of boys and girls drop out of high school, mostly during the junior or senior year. All states have some form of compulsory attendance; the law requires school enrollment until the age of 16 or 17. Often, parents and the school are not able to force or convince a young person to attend school; thus a restless student drops out.

More than 800,000 adolescents dropped out during the school year 1975–1976. Most dropouts do not return to get their degrees, but a percentage do; about 3% graduated from high school by taking the high school equivalency examination and 1% graduated by attending night school or the day school part-time program (U.S. Bureau of the Census, 1977; 1978).

Spanish-speaking and Black people have low rates of high school completion. About two-thirds of Black students and about 55% of Spanish-speaking students finish high school. The completion rates for both males and females of these minority groups do not differ significantly (U.S. Bureau of the Census, 1978).

Adolescents may drop out of school because intellectual stimulation is little valued at home, or because they feel pressured by family to obtain work and provide support. A small percentage of parents may encourage their children to drop out because they do not see the value of education.

Nonacademic reasons for dropping out of school include depression and low self-esteem. Also, adolescents may get little help from home, get into trouble with teachers and administrators, show poor school attendance, and have behavior problems that are not tolerated in school.

The consequences of dropping out of school are difficult to assess. One type of evaluation is that dropouts do not do as well economically, generally speaking, as those who continue. High school dropouts can expect lifetime earnings of about $575,000 on the average, based on 1980 dollars. High school graduates earn substantially more, about $855,000 lifetime average. Those who earn a college degree may expect earnings of about $1,120,000, according to the U.S. Bureau of the Census (1977). Money is only one criterion, however. There is also more unemployment among dropouts. The employed hold blue-collar jobs that require minimal skills. Thus one's educational level determines one's employment opportunities.

Numerous other factors are related to lower educational level, although they cannot be directly connected with incomplete high school education. People with less education are often products of a lifestyle that includes poverty, early marriage, high rates of marital disruption, high mortality rates, and early death (U.S. Bureau of the Census, 1977; Spanier & Glick, 1980).

David was a 24-year-old man who had married when he was 17, had fathered four children, and was now unemployed. He loved his wife, he said, but regretted that he had married so young. All he could do was minimal-skills blue-collar jobs, which did not pay enough for his family to make ends meet. David felt that if he had received encouragement from his parents he would have stayed in school and studied. However, the importance of education was overlooked in his family, and that was the reason why David had dropped out of school.

Following his arrest for hitting a man in a street brawl, David was sent to see a social worker. He mentioned that he was normally easygoing but that the tension over money in his family had made him edgy and that was the reason for his sudden outburst. He informed the caseworker that he wished to go back to school under any circumstances, for he realized that education would help him progress in his skills, get a better job, and move ahead in life. With the social worker's help, David decided to enroll in a night school so that he could get his high school diploma.

David was lucky because at 24 he recognized the value of the diploma. Some people are 40 or more before they realize their situation. In most cases they feel it is too late to change the situation because they have already created a place for themselves in their jobs, family, and friends.

Implications for Social Work Practice

Attainment of physical maturity has a number of implications for adolescents. The acceleration of physical growth marks the end of childhood. The consequences of young people's biological maturation include changes in their feelings about themselves.

Most young adolescents, irrespective of their bodies, feel uncomfortable about themselves. They experience stressful problems associated with physical changes for a number of reasons, which include a great deal of uncertainty about becoming sexually competent. Their intuitive interest in masturbation and in sharing sexual experiences with others conflicts with their awareness of the persistent normative expectations that these activities are wrong and even harmful to their bodies.

Social work practitioners need to be aware of the sexual conflicts of adolescents and offer them information about their own bodies. Guilt is dysfunctional and does not make young people feel at home with their own bodies. Adolescents who are deprived of the opportunity to experiment with their own bodies may reject all human sexuality as bad and wrong. Others may overemphasize sexual feelings and actions and measure themselves only in this dimension. Social work practitioners should be able to identify sexual issues presented by adolescents and counsel them accordingly.

Adolescence is defined by an inner striving for identity and a desire to experiment with a number of adult roles, let go of childhood dependency, and take more responsibility for oneself and for others.

Young people usually have opportunities for choosing between a purely social self-definition and an individual self-definition. Society believes that adolescence provides some ambiguous images to young people in this life phase, and it is likely that a large number of adolescents actually have a psychosocial adolescence. Almost all young people struggle through adolescence, but it is usually the lower-income adolescents and adolescents belonging to minority groups who most lack opportunities to engage in the struggle for an identity of their own and to fulfill their potential.

Social workers need to have an awareness of cultural, ethnic, and racial differences as well as a concern for the difficulties of the human struggle. Social work practitioners need to understand the critical issues affecting the self-development of people in this age group and be sensitive while offering them help.

Although there is a tendency to lump all adolescents together as "teenagers," it is important to understand that this group is not homogeneous. There are many differences among individual adolescents and among groups of adolescents. Available opportunities differ, as does their ability to learn the skills of adulthood. There are no short cuts to adulthood. No young person can move from beginning sexual behavior to adult sexual behavior without trial and error, and no person can move from play to the working world of adulthood in a short period of time. There are no guarantees that meaningful work roles will be accessible to all adolescents.

Adolescents who thrive and develop good self-images are not the ones who come to the attention of the social worker. Rather, the adolescent who is confused about his or her role and sex identity, who has problems ranging from drugs or teenage pregnancy to suicide, or who suffers from low self-esteem is the one who needs the attention and counseling of a social worker.

Chapter Summary

Adolescence is the stage of transition between childhood and adulthood. It involves an extended period of education and dependency. Puberty and adolescence are dealt with differently in different cultures.

The biological changes of young people proceed at a rapid rate but on a variable timetable. Body growth and hormonal changes begin at an earlier age for some young people than for others. Sexual maturation has psychological as well as physiological effects, especially since adolescents place a high value on conformity in looks.

Cognitive development reaches the stage of formal operational thought, which involves the capacity to analyze one's own thoughts as well as to see oneself from the point of view of others. Not all young people develop this ability at the same time, nor do they use it consistently, but attainment of this complex stage of cognitive ability is necessary for the construction of an independent and logical system of values.

Kohlberg states that when children become adults they eventually reassess their principles and build their own coherent system of values. Kohlberg's theory has been criticized because it appears to generalize about people's moral development on the basis of an exclusively male perspective.

Erikson describes adolescence as a period when a number of factors converge to form a consistent ego identity. The search for identity may bring about growth rather than stress, depending on a number of internal and external factors. At times, there may be too many hurdles that affect a person's growth and this could lead to identity diffusion.

Carol Gilligan criticizes Erikson's theory from a female-adolescent perspective. Women define themselves through their relationships with others. For a female adolescent, intimacy goes along with identity, as the female comes to know herself through relationships with other people. This process is unlike men's development, in which identity precedes intimacy and generativity in the optimal cycle of human separation and attachment.

White equates the concept of competence to what Erikson calls the *sense of identity* in the latency period. Both competence in performance of work and competence in the social sphere become important.

Autonomy from parents is gained with a struggle. The smaller size of families—fewer children and fewer extended relations—has important implications for parents as well as children. Usually strong parental identification is associated with good adjustment.

Peer relationships become important at this period in life. Young people develop the attitudes, values, and behavior patterns of their friends.

Teenagers belonging to minority-group cultures often develop a subculture with which they closely identify. For some, belonging to a minority group increases role conflict. When reference groups differ in their behavioral expectations, teenagers who make new group affiliations may experience conflict between old and new loyalties. Such problems may be greater for ethnic and racial groups.

Sexual urges are manifested first by boys, even though girls enter puberty before boys do. There is sexual experimentation among adolescents; however, young adolescents still socialize in single-sex groups. The age at which adolescents become sexually active is related to factors such as education, biological maturation, psychological makeup, and family relationships.

Teenage pregnancy is becoming a familiar problem. Not only do the teenage mothers have problems but studies show that young unmarried males also have feelings about pregnancy.

Homosexual contacts take place for boys as well as girls at about the same time—before 15 years of age—and are more common among boys than girls.

Juvenile delinquency is another problem that has serious implications for adolescence. The crime rate is higher during middle and late adolescence than at any other period of life. There are many sociological as well as psychological theories about the causes of delinquency. Adolescents are brought to court for criminal offenses such as theft, rape, and assault. Truancy and promiscuity are also illegal because of the offender's minor status.

Substance abuse, too, accounts for a number of arrests of juveniles because the use of alcohol and drugs is as widespread as it is in adult society.

Smoking is increasingly a problem with teenagers. Adolescents are prevented from smoking when peers influence each other to perceive the bad effects of smoking.

Suicide in the 14-to-19 age group has quadrupled during the past 12 years. Isolation, vulnerability, and disturbed emotional backgrounds are often causes.

Eating disorders known as anorexia nervosa and bulimia are diseases that appear to affect young women from childhood to the 30s or older. Anorexia nervosa is characterized by refusing to eat food to the extent of starving oneself; bulimia is binge eating followed by vomiting or the taking of laxatives. The purpose of these habits is to maintain a low body weight. They are nutritionally unhealthy.

High school students may drop out because of little encouragement toward intellectual achievement at home. Some young people drop out because of poor self-esteem. These are often depressed people.

Social-work practitioners need to understand the overall, holistic development of adolescents, as well as to have an awareness of their specific needs, issues, and problems.

References

Anthony, E. J. (1967). Psychosomatic disorders. In A. M. Freedman & H. J. Kaplan (Eds.), *Comprehensive textbook on psychiatry*. Baltimore: Williams & Wilkins.

Arbuthnot, J. (1975). Modification of moral judgment through role playing. *Developmental Psychology, 11*, 319–324.

Barbach, L. G. (1975). *For yourself: The fulfillment of female sexuality*. Garden City, NJ: Doubleday.

Baruch, G. K., & Barnett, R. C. (1980). On the well-being of adult women. In L. A. Bond & J. C. Rosen (Eds.), *Competence and coping during adulthood*. Hanover, NH: University Press of New England.

Beech, F. A. (1976). Introduction. In F. A. Beech (Ed.), *Human sexuality in four perspectives*. Baltimore: Johns Hopkins University Press.

Beech, R. P., & Schoeppe, A. (1974). Development of value systems in adolescents. *Developmental Psychology, 23*, 10, 644–656.

Bettelheim, B. (1976). *The uses of enchantment*. New York: Knopf.

Biller, B., & Bahm, R. M. (1971). Father-absence, perceived maternal behavior and masculinity of self-concept among junior high school boys. *Developmental Psychology, 4*, 178–181.

Blos, P. (1967). The second individuation process of adolescence. In A. Freud (Ed.), *The psychoanalytic study of the child* (Vol. 22). New York: International University Press.

Broverman, I., Vogel, S., Broverman, D., Clarkson, F., & Rosenkrantz, P. (1972). Sex role stereotypes: A current appraisal. *Journal of Social Issues, 28*, 59–78.

Campbell, E. (1969). Adolescent socialization. In D. A. Goslin (Ed.), *Handbook of socialization theory and research*. Chicago: Rand McNally.

Cantor, P. (1977). Suicide and attempted suicide among students: Problem prediction and prevention. In P. Cantor (Ed.), *Understanding a child's world*. New York: McGraw-Hill.

Chand, I. P., Crider, D. M., & Willets, F. K. (1975). Parent–youth disagreement as perceived by youth: A longitudinal study. *Youth and Society, 6*, 365–375.

Christensen, H. T., & Gregg, O. (1970). Changing sex norms in America and Scandinavia. *Journal of Marriage and Family, 32*, 616–627.

Coleman, J. S. (1961). *The adolescent society*. New York: Free Press.

Cooke, S. (1979). A comparison of identity formation in preadolescent girls and boys. Unpublished master's thesis, Simon Fraser University, Canada.

Diamond, M. (1976). Human sexual development: Biological foundation of social development. In F. A. Beech (Ed.), *Human sexuality in four perspectives*. Baltimore: Johns Hopkins University Press.

Douvan, E., & Adelson, L. (1966). *The adolescent experience*. New York: Wiley.

Dunphy, D. C. (1963). The social structure of urban adolescent groups. *Sociometry, 26*, 230–246.

Edwards, C. P. (1975). Societal complexity and moral development: A Kenyan study. *Ethos, 3*, 505–527.

Elkind, D. (1975). Recent research on cognitive development in adolescence. In S. E. Dragastin & G. H. Elder, Sr. (Eds.), *Adolescence in the life cycle*. New York: Wiley.

Erikson, E. (1980). *Identity and the life cycle*. New York: W. W. Norton.

Federal Bureau of Investigation. (1977).

Fischer, B. J., & Bersani, C. A. (1979). Self-esteem and institutionalized delinquent offenders: The role of background characteristics. *Adolescence, 14*(52).

Freud, A. (1946). *The ego and the mechanisms of defense*. New York: International University Press.

Freud, S. (1938). Three contributions to the theory of sex. In A. A. Brill (Ed.), *The basic writings of Sigmund Freud*. New York: Random House.

Friesen, D. (1968). Academic-athletic-popularity syndrome in the Canadian high school society. *Adolescence, 3*, 39–52.

Ganter, G., & Yeakel, M. (1980). *Human behavior and the social environment*. New York: Columbia University Press.

Gardner, H. (1978). *Developmental psychology*. Boston: Little, Brown.

Garrison, K. C. (1973). Psychological development. In J. F. Adams (Ed.), *Understanding Adolescence* (2nd ed.). Boston: Allyn & Bacon.

Garrison, K. C., & Garrison, K. C., Jr. (1975). *The psychology of adolescence*. Englewood Cliffs, NJ: Prentice-Hall.

Getzels, J. W., & Jackson, P. W. (1959). The highly intelligent and highly creative adolescent: A summary of some research findings. In C. W. Taylor (Ed.), *The third (1959) University of Utah Research Conference on the identification of creative scientific talent*. Salt Lake City: University of Utah Press.

Gilligan, C. (1982). *In a different voice*. Cambridge, MA: Harvard University Press.

Gunther, H. (1975). Einversuch der Anwendung der Rokeach Value Scale in der Bestimmung von Verhaltungen deutscher Austauschschüler. *Psychologische Beitrage, 17*, 304–320.

Herzog, D. B. (1982). Bulimia: The secretive syndrome. *Psychosomatics, 23*(5), 481–487.

Hetherington, E. M. (1972). Effects of father-absence on personality development in adolescent daughters. *Developmental Psychology, 7*, 313–326.

Hoffman, M. L. (1970). Moral development. In P. H. Mussen (Ed.), *Carmichael's manual of child psychiatry* (Vol. 2). New York: Wiley.

Hogan, R. (1973). Moral conduct and moral character: A psychological perspective. *Psychological Bulletin, 79,* 217–232.

Holstein, C. (1976). Development of moral judgment: A longitudinal study of males and females. *Child Development, 47,* 51–61.

Hsu, F. L. K. (1953). *American and Chinese: Two ways of life.* New York: Abelard & Schuman.

Hunt, M. M. (1974). *Sexual behavior in the 1970s.* Chicago: Playboy Press.

Inhelder, B., & Piaget, J. (1958). *The growth of logical thinking from childhood to adolescence.* New York: Basic Books.

Johnston, L. D., Backman, J. G., & O'Malley, P. M. (1979). *Drugs and the class of 1978: Behavior, attitudes and trends.* Rockville, MD: National Institute on Drug Abuse.

Jones, F. R., Garrison, K. C., & Morgan, R. F. (1985). *The psychology of human development* (2nd ed.). New York: Harper & Row.

Kagan, J. (1973, July). The I.Q. puzzle: What are we measuring? *Inequality in Education, 17.*

Kagan, J. (1976). The psychology of sex differences. In F. A. Beech (Ed.), *Human sexuality in four perspectives.* Baltimore: Johns Hopkins University Press.

Kandel, D. B., & Lesser, G. S. (1969). Parental and peer influences on educational plans of adolescents. *American Sociological Review, 34,* 213–223.

Kelly, R. K. (1972). The premarital sexual revolution: Comments on research. *Family Coordinator, 21,* 334–336.

Keniston, K. (1975). Youth as a stage of life. In F. J. Havighurst & P. H. Dreyer (Eds.), *Youth: The 74th Yearbook of the NESSE.* Chicago: University of Chicago Press.

Kohlberg, L. (1958). The development of modes of thinking and choices in years 10 to 16. Unpublished doctoral dissertation, University of Chicago.

Kohlberg, L. (1973). Continuities and discontinuities in childhood and adult moral development revisited. In *Collected papers on moral development and moral education.* Cambridge, MA: Harvard University Moral Education Research Foundation.

Kohlberg, L. (1981). *The philosophy of moral development.* San Francisco: Harper & Row.

Kurtines, W., & Greif, E. B. (1974). The development of moral thought and a review of Kohlberg's approach. *Psychological Bulletin, 81,* 453–459.

Lambert, B. G. (1972). *Adolescence: Transition from childhood to maturity.* Pacific Grove, CA: Brooks/Cole.

Landsbaum, J. B., & Willis, R. H. (1971). Conformity in early and late adolescence. *Developmental Psychology, 4,* 334–337.

LeFrancois, G. R. (1981). *Adolescents.* Belmont, CA: Wadsworth.

Lerner, R. M. (1969). The development of stereotyped expectancies of body build–behavior relations. *Child Development, 40,* 137–141.

Lerner, R. M., & Hultsch, D. F. (1983). *Human development.* New York: McGraw-Hill.

Lerner, R. M., Karanick, S. A., & Meisels, M. (1975). One year stability of children's personal space schemata towards body build. *Journal of Genetic Psychology, 127,* 151–152.

Lerner, R. M., & Knapp, J. R. (1975). Actual and perceived intrafamilial attitudes of late adolescents and their parents. *Journal of Youth and Adolescence, 4,* 17–36.

Lerner, R. M., Schroeder, C., Rewitzer, M., & Weinstock, A. (1972). Attitudes of high school students and their parents towards contemporary issues. *Psychological Reports, 31,* 255–258.

Lerner, R. M., Karson, M., Meisels, M., & Knapp, J. R. (1975). Actual and perceived attitudes of late adolescents and their parents: The phenomenon of the generation gap. *Journal of Genetic Psychology, 126,* 195–207.

LoPiccolo, J., & Lobilz, C. (1972). The role of masturbation in the treatment of sexual dysfunction. *Archives of Sexual Behavior, 2,* 163–171.

MacDonald, A. P. (1973). College female drug users. *Adolescence, 8,* 189–196.

Marcia, J. E. (1979, June). Identity status in late adolescence: Description and some clinical implications. Address given at a symposium on identity development at Rijksuniversitat Groningen, The Netherlands.

Marcia, J. E. (1980). Identity in adolescence. In J. Adelson (Ed.), *Handbook of adolescent psychology.* New York: Wiley.

MacDonald, J. M. (1973). False accusations of rape. *Medical Aspects of Human Sexuality, 7,* 170–194.

McClelland, D. C., & Power, C. (1975). *The inner experience.* New York: Irvington.

McGeorge, C. (1973). Situational variation on level of moral judgement. Unpublished paper, University of Canterbury, New Zealand.

Mead, M. (1928). *Coming of age in Samoa.* New York: Morrow.

Melges, F. T., & Hamburg, D. A. (1976). Hormonal changes in women. In F. A. Beech (Ed.), *Human sexuality in four perspectives.* Baltimore: Johns Hopkins University Press.

Milgram, B. (1974). *Obedience to authority.* New York: Harper & Row.

Mitchell, S., & Rosa, P. (1981). Boyhood behavior problems as precursors of criminality: A follow-up study. *Journal of Child Psychology and Psychiatry, 22,* 19–33.

Moore, B. M., & Holtzman, W. H. (1965). *A study of youth and their families.* Austin: University of Texas Press.

Musgrove, F. (1964). *Youth and social order.* Bloomington, IN: Indiana University Press.

Nagelberg, D. B., Hale, S. L., & Ware, S. L. (1983). Prevalence of eating disorders in college women. Paper presented at the annual meeting of the American Psychological Association, Anaheim, CA.

National Commission on Marijuana and Drug Abuse. (1973). *Drugs in America: Problems in perspective* (second report). Rockville, MD: U.S. Government Printing Office.

National Institute on Drug Abuse. (1982). *Highlights from student drug use in America 1976–81.* Rockville, MD: U.S. Government Printing Office.

Neimark, E. D. (1975). Intellectual development during adolescence. In F. D. Horowitz (Ed.), *Review of child development* (Vol. 4). Chicago: University of Chicago Press.

Neimark, E. D. (1982). Adolescent thought: Transition to formal operations. In B. B. Wolman & G. Stricker (Eds.), *Handbook of developmental psychology.* Englewood Cliffs, NJ: Prentice-Hall.

Newman, B. M., & Newman, P. R. (1975). *Development through life.* Chicago, IL: Dorsey Press.

Offer, D. (1969). *The psychological world of the teenager.* New York: Basic Books.

Offer, D., & Offer, J. B. (1975). *From teenage to young manhood: A psychological study.* New York: Basic Books.

Papalia, D. E., & Olds, S. W. (1986). *Human Development.* New York: McGraw-Hill.

Penner, M. O. (1982). The role of selected health problems in the causation of juvenile delinquency. *Adolescence, 17*(66).

Phillips, E. L., Phillips, E. A., Fixen, D. L., & Wolf, M. M. (1973). Achievement place: Behavior shaping works of delinquents. *Psychology Today, 7,* 73–79.

Piaget, J. (1972). Intellectual evolution from adolescence to adulthood. *Human Development, 15,* 1–12.

Pontius, A. A. (1972). Neurological aspects in some types of delinquency, especially among juveniles. *Adolescence, 7,* 289–308.

Pulaski, M. A. S. (1971). *Understanding Piaget.* New York: Harper & Row.

Rice, R. P. (1981). *The adolescent* (3rd ed.). Boston: Allyn & Bacon.

Roberts, E. J., Kline, D., & Gagnon, J. (1978). *Family life and sexual learning: A study of the role of parents in the sexual learning of children.* New York: Project on Human Sexual Development, Population Education.

Roesler, T., & Deisler, R. (1972). Youthful male homosexuality. *Journal of the American Medical Association, 219*(8), 1018–1023.

Rokeach, M. (1968). Rokeach Value Survey. In M. Rokeach *Beliefs, attitudes and values.* San Francisco: Jossey-Bass.

Rosen, R. H. (1980). Adolescent pregnancy and decision-making: Are parents important? *Adolescence, 15*(57).

Sheppard, B. J. (1974). Making the case of behavior as an expression of physiological condition. In B. L. Krotoville (Ed.), *Youth in trouble.* San Rafael, CA: Academy Therapy Publication.

Sherif, M., & Sherif, C. W. (1964). *Reference groups.* New York: Harper & Row.

Sherman, J. A. (1971). Imitation and language development. In H. W. Reese (Ed.), *Advances in child development and behavior* (Vol. 6). New York: Academic Press.

Short, J. F., Tennyson, R. A., & Howard, K. I. (1963). Behavior dimensions of gang delinquency. *American Sociological Review, 28*, 411–428.

Simpson, E. L. (1974). Moral development. A case study of scientific cultural bias. *Human Development, 17*, 81–106.

Spanier, G. B., & Glick, P. C. (1980). The life cycle of American families: An expanded analysis. *Journal of Family History, 5*, 97–111.

Specht, R., & Craig, G. J. (1982). *Human development.* Englewood Cliffs, NJ: Prentice Hall.

Squire, S. (1983). *The slender balance.* New York: Putnam.

Stone, L. J., & Church, J. (1979). *Childhood and adolescence.* New York: Random House.

Strathe, M., & Hash, V. (1979). The effect of an alternative school on adolescent self-esteem. *Adolescence, 14*(56).

Tanner, J. M. (1971). Sequence, tempo and individual variation in the growth and development of boys and girls aged twelve to sixteen. *Daedalus, 100*, 907–930.

Tygart, C. E. (1980). Students' social structure and/or subcultures as factors in school crime: Toward a paradigm. *Adolescence, 15*(57).

U.S. Bureau of the Census. (1976, October). *Number, timing, and duration of marriages and divorces in the United States: June 1975.* (Current populations report, Series P-20, No. 297). Washington, DC: U.S. Government Printing Office.

U.S. Bureau of the Census. (1977, December). *Educational attainment in the United States, March 1977 and 1976.* (Current populations report, Series P-20, No. 314). Washington, DC: U.S. Government Printing Office.

U.S. Bureau of the Census. (1978, January). *Characteristics of American children and youth: 1976.* (Current populations report, Series P-23, No. 66). Washington, DC: U.S. Government Printing Office.

U.S. Department of Health, Education and Welfare. (1978). *Vital statistics of the United States, 1976.* Hyattsville, MD.: National Center for Health Statistics.

U.S. Department of Health, Education and Welfare. (1979). *Monthly vital statistics report: Advance report-mortality statistics.* Hyattsville, MD.: National Center for Health Statistics.

Weinstock, A., & Lerner, R. M. (1972). Attitudes of late adolescents and their parents toward contemporary issues. *Psychological Reports, 30*, 239–244.

White, R. W. (1960). Competence and the psychosexual stages. Papers presented at the Nebraska Symposium on Motivation, Nebraska University Press.

White, R. W. (1976). *The enterprise of living.* New York: Holt, Rinehart & Winston.

Williams, R. C. (1975, April). Lord of the flies: An ethological study of dominance ordering in a group of human adolescents. Paper presented at the Society of Research in Child Development, Denver.

Yager, J. (1982). Family issues in the pathogenesis of anorexia nervosa. *Psychosomatic Medicine, 44*(1), 43–60.

Zelnick, M., & Kantner, J. F. (1977). Sexual and contraceptive experience of young unmarried women in the U.S. *Family Planning Perspective, 9,* 55–71.

7

Early Adulthood

Changes in Adulthood

Psychosocial Environment

Cognitive Development

Erikson: Intimacy versus Isolation

Identity and Self

The Role of Work for the Adult

Household and Family Patterns

Sexuality and Intimacy

Parenthood

Implications for Social Work Practice

Chapter Summary

References

Amy and Ward, both in their early twenties, had just been married. Ward had graduated from college and had a degree in psychology. Amy had completed high school and worked while waiting to marry her high school sweetheart. Their marriage was a fulfillment of their dream. They moved into a small apartment of their own. They did not have much furniture, but they hoped to get some, and they saved all the money they could. Amy wanted to get a college degree eventually but felt that she would wait until Ward was further along in his career. Meanwhile she was also looking forward to starting a family in the near future. In their life there was a sense of purpose, a sense of futurity, as well as a feeling that everything would work out meaningfully—a sense of "I will make it."

Carol and her boyfriend Joseph got married when both were in their early twenties. They came from a lower socioeconomic background and did not have much money. After their marriage, they were invited to live with Carol's mother. Their living space was crowded and there was not much privacy. Joseph did not have a job but hoped to find one in the near future. In spite of all these limitations, Carol and Joseph were very happy. For them, their living arrangements were only temporary; they would move out of the house in a short while. Their love for each other, combined with their youth and sense of futurity, helped tide them over their everyday problems.

A sense of purpose and a sense of growth characterize young adulthood. Young adults possess a sense of directionality, of moving toward the future. This constellation of thoughts propels young people as they enter the prime time of their lives. For many, the self-imposed rule is, "I will make it, now."

It is not easy to define adulthood. Ganter and Yeakel (1980) describe it as the period between adolescence and old age. There is no sudden cutoff point of identity that defines the beginning of adulthood. The end of the teenage years is a rough marker; early adulthood usually begins in the early twenties and ends at approximately age 39. During this period there is less emphasis than before on physical maturation and less preoccupation with body image. Most individuals, depending on their childhood and adolescent experiences, become conforming adults who follow the rules and roles set up by society; they play a part that is socially acceptable in their culture.

The type of adulthood a person experiences is dependent on family culture and the immediate environment. Some young adults experiment with different lifestyles, and others simply do what is expected of them and engage in routine work. Some may be denied freedom of choice by the nature of political, social, and economic forces over which they have no control.

Changes in Adulthood

A person could be perceived to have reached adulthood by physical changes alone, but adulthood is defined in social as well as physical terms. Some individuals reach physical maturity and chronologically are adults but continue to feel like children among adults long after they have reached maximum physical growth and are well beyond their early twenties. Legal definitions use chronological age to mark the points when people can drink, drive, and join the armed forces. Normative behavior is, however, associated with economic independence, productivity, and caretaker roles, which are critical determinants of a kind of social timing within which it is presumed that people will fulfill their expectations (Ganter & Yeakel, 1980).

Adulthood is the period when social development in young people is transitional and intellectual development is essentially coming to a state of completion (Kaluger & Kaluger, 1974).

Psychosocial Environment

Young adults face a number of choices with respect to experiences and lifestyles. Young adults learn to tolerate some frustration and aggravation and learn to use logical reasoning and insight in making decisions. Up to the age of 30 it is common for men and women to be underdeveloped in some areas of behavior and judgment while showing considerable maturity in others. New experiences and new expectations bring with them a more even development on a more mature basis.

The social and economic roles of early adulthood are so familiar and clearly defined that young adults have no doubts as to what the expectations of society are. These expectations indicate developmental tasks:

1. select a mate
2. learn to live with a marriage partner and/or choose a career
3. start a family
4. rear children
5. manage a home
6. get started in an occupation
7. take on civic responsibilities
8. find a congenial social group

Successful achievement of these tasks leads to a better and more satisfying middle and late adulthood. Whether or not the young person is aware of the options, the choices made plant the seeds for the harvest in later years (Kaluger & Kaluger, 1974).

Cognitive Development

The process of cognitive development includes both the differentiation and integration of component skills and increasing knowledge of one's intellectual capacities.

Piaget

The differentiation and integration of component skills have been characterized by Piaget (1972) in terms of (1) a new group of symbolic transformations—formal operations—operating upon (2) abstract units as well as
propositions, organized into (3) a simple, flexible structure having the
properties of a mathematical system. The observable consequences of this
restructuring of thought is the appearance of hypothetico-deductive reasoning; that is, starting from any initial assumption, one could imagine and
explore its logical implications as a prelude to action. An additional character-
ization of formal operational thought invokes (4) different formal operational
schemes; that is, general conceptual frameworks for dealing with such
relations as proportion, correlations, equilibrium, and coordination of different frames of reference.

Arlin (1980) differentiates the formal operational thought of adolescence
from that of adulthood in terms of consolidation and application of schemes.
For the adolescent, the mastery of schemes is an intellectual goal; for adults
the schemes become means toward further advancement of understanding.
For example, the coordination of a frames-of-reference scheme underlies
appreciation of relativity. Relativity is an intricate concept; there are revolutionary advances in theories of physics and ethics that result from its
incorporation. This is true of concepts derived from such other schemes as
dynamic equilibrium and probabilistic (rather than strict) determinism, both
of which influence theoretical advances in physical, biological, and social
domains.

Arlin's description of the adult deals with the optimal capacity that may be
attained. Much earlier research and subsequent criticism of Piagetian theory
focused on mounting evidence (Neimark, 1982) that many individuals do not
operate on this hyperion plane. Partly as a result of such evidence, current
research has turned to identification of some of the additional factors that
moderate observed intellectual performance.

Piaget has observed that the highest stage of cognitive development occurs
in adolescence under typical or favorable conditions. He sees the development of formal operational thought continuing in early adulthood.

Kohlberg

According to Kohlberg (1973), developmental tasks continue to take place for
the following reasons:

1. Adolescents who are slow in cognitive development because of biological and cultural factors and are still at the concrete operational level
   at the age of 15 may develop formal operational thought in early
   adulthood.
2. There is a continuous horizontal decalage of formal operational thought
   in early adulthood that could be applied to more spheres and activities.
3. Related to this decalage there could be stabilization of formal thought

that could be equated with increased subordination or rejection of lower forms of thought for formal operational thought in adulthood.

Given that these three types of cognitive development occur in adulthood, the important question is whether any new cognitive stage could be found in adulthood. Since neurological maturation is apparently completed by adolescence, any new cognitive stage that can be formed in adulthood is based upon experience. The actual appearance of a cognitive stage in an individual may lag behind the requisite maturational change or may fail to occur because of experiential factors; the maturational stage is nonetheless an important, if not sufficient, condition for the existence of the new stage. This conclusion tallies with Piaget's view. Piaget does not rule out the possibility of a stage beyond formal operations, citing Gödel's proof that the impossibility of another form of logic cannot be proved by formal-operational logic.

If there is some new adulthood stage, it is not likely to appear in logical-cognitive tasks as such. This conclusion has two bases: (1) Piagetian cognitive growth is correlated with both the hereditary and the age-maturational factors found in general intelligence, and (2) logical stages by definition are normally experience-free. Experience appears to represent something of a hindrance to pure formal-logical thought, as evidenced by the fact that the greatest thinkers in mathematical and pure physical theory have commenced their work in late adolescence.

Adult Experiences in Moral Development

The literature of human development does not discuss moral stages per se in adulthood. It can be said that adult moral development has a cognitive structural component. However, moral changes are clearly a focal point for adult life in a way that cognitive changes are not. We don't need Erikson's studies of Luther and Gandhi to tell us that crises and turning points of adult identity are often moral in nature. Literature from Saint Paul to Tolstoy reveals the classic biographies and dramas of maturity to be the transformations of moral ideologies.

Erikson: Intimacy versus Isolation

According to Erikson, the major crisis of young adulthood is intimacy versus isolation. Erikson states that only after a reasonable sense of identity has been established can there be any real intimacy. Sexual intimacy, to Erikson, is only part of the real intimacy. Real intimacy would include sexual intimacy, and an ability to develop a true and mutual psychological intimacy with another person. Someone who is not sure of his identity would shy away from interpersonal intimacy, but as he becomes more sure of himself, he would seek intimacy in the form of friendship, combat, leadership, and love (Erikson, 1980). Erikson's formulation of the crisis in this period is based on observation of men. As we proceed, we will also discuss women's development.

The family is the appropriate context for sharing confidences and strong love, as well as revealing weaknesses and areas of dependency. However, the unique task for the young adult is to establish an intimate relationship with someone who is not a member of his or her own family. Losing and gaining love represent the greatest challenges in adulthood.

Intimacy is also the ability to experience an open, supportive, tender relationship with another person without losing one's own identity in the process of becoming closer. Stone (1973) describes intimacy as a relationship that supports the independent judgments of each member without stifling one another. Intimacy implies the ability to experience mutual empathy as well as mutual recognition of needs. One must give pleasure as well as receive pleasure within the intimate context.

According to Newman and Newman (1975), intimacy does not develop until a couple has been married for several years. Over that period of time the couple's relationship may be influenced by the early period of mutual adjustment, the birth of the first child, and the social expectations of the members of the extended family.

> Don and Mary came for therapy after they had been married for 6 months. Don had turned from a loving and caring husband to a quiet robot who would do what was asked of him by his wife but would not participate in any conversations. According to Mary, he changed from a very talkative and lively person into an unnaturally quiet person. Therapy revealed Mary to be a dependent person. She wanted her husband to take her everywhere and help her with chores outside the home, calling herself "inexperienced." Although Don had enjoyed Mary's dependency before marriage, now it appeared to bother him. He felt that his wife was too dependent and had no identity of her own, and therefore he found her to be a burden on him. Their relationship appeared to have started as a close one, but it was no longer so because both had to gain some adult perspective and, in the process, complete some developmental tasks, such as building a stronger sense of self or identity, and a mature sense of intimacy.

Male and Female Expectations

Men and women experience differences in socialization, and those differences lead to differential expectations of intimacy and to different problems in the establishment of intimacy. Boys are taught during childhood to restrain from overtly expressing their dependent feelings and to limit their emotionality. During late childhood and early adolescence, the emotional life of boys is guided by competitiveness and self-reliance. The male adolescent may withdraw from or resist expressing tenderness toward family members. His heterosexual relationships are often a way of expressing and demonstrating his virility to his friends. Although he may also express tenderness within those relationships, the male will usually resist any commitment until he has established confidence in his own independence. For the young man, the demand for intimacy may be difficult to meet, for he primarily resists intimate, interdependent relationships. However, the successful establishment of an interpersonal relationship offers a person an opportunity to express emotion in a safe and supportive environment (Newman & Newman, 1975).

Women's upbringing is different from men's. Women are usually well prepared for the emotional demands of intimacy. Women not only define themselves in a context of relationships but also evaluate themselves on their ability to care (Gilligan, 1982). A woman's place in the man's life cycle has been that of a nurturer, caretaker, helpmate, and weaver of those networks of relationships on which she relies as part of her place in life (Gilligan, 1982). However, there have been no major studies on female development in adulthood that have age-related sequences comparable to the ones reported for men by Vaillant (1977) and Levinson (Levinson, Darrow, Klien, Levinson, & McGee, 1978).

Why is it that researchers have not studied the female developmental sequence? It is because for many years the male pattern was considered to be the norm, and theorists tended to believe that if they described male development, then female development could be assumed to follow a similar course. Then, when women were shown not to grow as men do, their differences were unfortunately viewed as female deficiencies. Male researchers threw up their scientific hands in despair, not sure they would ever understand women. Female researchers, for their part, did not explore female psychology until recent times (Gilligan, 1982).

Some essential points of difference between men and women lie in their paths to identity. Men traditionally individuate by separating from their families of origin, becoming autonomous, and proceeding to pursue individual interests. Women, in contrast, tend to develop their identities not by breaking away from relationships with other people but by means of those attachments, as well as by accepting the responsibility that characterizes such ties (Gilligan, 1982; Baruch, Barnett, & Rivers, 1983; Chodorow, 1978).

One of the chief reasons for the differences is that women tend to be the ones who take care of babies and small children; daughters observe their mothers performing child-rearing tasks and identify with them. Their personalities become defined early in life in relation to other people, more than men's personalities do (Chodorow, 1978).

Another point of view highlights the importance of work in women's life, which is significantly different from its part in men's. Traditionally, women have defined themselves in the roles of mother, wife, and daughter, and not in career terms. Their outside-the-home work lives have been discontinuous because of child-rearing demands and societal expectations. In decades past, few women followed through on the career dreams of their early adulthoods, and even fewer had mentors that could help. However, this pattern is changing, in keeping with society's new expectations for women (Papalia & Olds, 1986).

Today's woman is finding out that there is a conflict between two sets of expectations. Although women are raised to think in terms of occupational fulfillment, they find out that they are still expected by society as well as their partners to take care of the tasks of homemaking and child rearing. Our present historical time is one of transition, and today's men and women are writing psychological as well as sociological history.

Gilligan mentions that, for today's women who have been encouraged successfully to fulfill themselves through work, an important element of personality is missing; that is, involvement with others. Gilligan continues that the line of development that is missing from current depictions of adulthood is a progression in relationships toward a maturity of interdependence (Gilligan, 1982).

Gilligan studied four 27-year-old women, all of whom were pursuing ambitious careers. When they were asked to describe themselves, none projected herself as a successful, achieving woman; all discussed themselves in terms of their relationships (as a mother, a wife, past lover, and adopted child), highlighting the concept of the fusion of identity and intimacy. Both career and relationships are important in adult development and theorists must see not only the need to achieve in one's work but also the need to nurture and to care for oneself and others as a vital task of adulthood.

Isolation

The negative side of the crisis of intimacy, according to Erikson, is self-absorption and isolation. The possibility of closeness with others seriously threatens the self-identity of some young people. They imagine intimacy to be a blurring of boundaries—their own and others'—and they have great difficulty in managing themselves in such relationships. People who experience isolation may erect barriers between themselves and others to keep their sense of self intact. Such a person develops a fragile sense of self from accumulated experiences of childhood, which fostered the development of a sense of personal identity that is rigid and brittle or else totally diffused. People who have a tenuous sense of self are so busy reminding themselves who they are—or so occupied in maintaining their identity or struggling to make sense out of diffusion—that they really cannot attain a sense of intimacy.

> Gregory, as we saw earlier, had lived in various foster homes as a child. He was taken care of reasonably well in some homes but was either overdisciplined or underdisciplined in others. To some extent he had also been abused, both mentally and physically. At 17 he was living in a group home and enjoying the lifestyle that it offered him. Later, he got a job in a gas station. He met a pretty girl who fell in love with him. Gregory cared for her in return, but only superficially; his own needs were paramount. Nothing that she could do for him was sufficient. His ability to take was tremendous, but he could not give in return. He was always afraid of being overwhelmed by her and would distance himself when she attempted to get psychologically close to him. The fear that he would lose his identity in this relationship forced Gregory to push her

away. His girlfriend was offended and sad but did not really understand that his inability to give or to care for her was not her fault. Gregory was afraid of losing his identity because he had never really structured his own ego. Thus at 24 he appeared to be floundering like an adolescent.

Identity and Self

All people who reach adulthood face developmental tasks. They have to select and prepare for an initial occupation, achieve socially responsible behavior, and develop concepts for competency in the moral, ethical, social, economic, and political aspects of life. Adults have to cultivate desirable personality traits, social and communications skills, and healthy attitudes in preparation for marriage and family life. Last, they have to acquire a set of values through the formation of identity and a concept of their place in society (Kaluger & Kaluger, 1974).

> Kevin, 24 years old and very good-looking, was still struggling with self-identity. He dated a number of women and had intense sexual relationships with at least 5 of them at different points in his life. For Kevin, there was never any kind of mutual, psychological intimacy, for he would drop a relationship as soon as his sexual partner wanted more serious involvement. Laughingly, he commented he liked sex, but had to know himself and his goals before he could make a serious commitment.

Self-Image

How do young people develop a self-image? Earlier, in adolescence, self-image was not much of a problem: adolescents either do what their parents want them to do or do the opposite. But in adulthood most are looking for a stable, balanced self-image, a reliable view of themselves that will remain more or less steady throughout life. Such an image comes out of the values of the community, family, and groups of contemporaries.

However, in today's society it is becoming difficult for young adults to find their own self-image. Often they appear to stand alone in an unstructured moral climate. There are no absolute guidelines and standards to contemplate or patterns to follow in leading their lives. The emphasis is on "doing your thing" without having a background of knowledge by which to judge what is desirable for them. Many young people have to proceed by trial and error and adopt those values with which they become comfortable.

The Role of Work for the Adult

In our society there is no meaningful alternative to work. Most adults work and that means the largest portion of our population. People define the characteristics of occupation, aside from pay, as enjoyment and exercise of skills (Garfinkel, 1982):

1. Work defines our position in society. When we meet or introduce ourselves to new people, the first thing they inquire, after learning our name, is, "What do you do?"
2. Work is the context in which we act out the major part of the human drama, in such areas as these:
   a. competition (for example, in a sales job)—finding out who performs better than others, who gets a pay raise for better performance, and so on
   b. territoriality—having one's name on the door, a corner room, a room with a window that overlooks a beautiful landscape
   c. bonding (the mentor relationship)—associating with people in order to achieve
   d. nurturing (the mentor relationship).
3. Work is the opportunity for doing, creating, and achieving. A craftsperson and a corporate executive have their interest in their work as commonalities. As Freud put it, work and love are important for meaningful achievements in life.

The issue of work has been ignored by a large number of developmental psychological theorists and human-factor engineers. Developmental psychology has until recently emphasized only the early part of life. Research and theory focus on the early years, with the assumption that human beings' "traits" and behaviors are formed and fixed by the time a person is 20 years of age. Unfortunately, work was not considered to be an important aspect of the study.

In his conceptualization of the developmental tasks of adulthood, Erikson (1980) has completely omitted work as a developmental issue. This omission has been corrected by Vaillant (1977) and by Levinson et al. (1978) in their longitudinal studies of healthy adult males. Vaillant suggests adding a period he calls *career consolidation* to the developmental sequence.

The concept of career consolidation is congruent with the challenges and developmental tasks of life. In adulthood the instrumental concerns of doing one's job—skillfully, successfully, and appropriately—are pervasive. One of Vaillant's subjects described his first 20 years of adulthood as the period of life in which he learned to get along with his wife and the next 10 as the years when he learned to do his job. Vaillant modifies Erikson's scheme by suggesting that after adolescents make some progress with identification, they begin to deal with intimacy and establish relationships with significant others. With the capacity for relationships established, the young adult attends to the task of work in the stage of career consolidation.

A developmental perspective of work is congruent with the concept of career. The orderliness of normative life events includes, but is not limited to, work activities, which have a strong impact on the quality of life of an individual.

Phil was a 24-year-old construction worker who worked in the inner city where an old school building was being renovated. He was always tired at the end of the day. At home, all he wanted was a good, heavy dinner, which he ate without a word. Then he played with his little daughters before they went to bed. Later, Phil spent time talking to his wife before he dozed off to sleep by ten o'clock. His wife understood his need to go to sleep early and did not feel offended when he dozed off while talking to her. He had to be up by five to leave for work in the morning. Phil's family was not wealthy by any standards—in fact, he made barely enough money to meet all his financial obligations. But he enjoyed his work. The family believed in making honest money, and that money came by the sweat of Phil's brow.

Hogan (1978) found that men who deviated from the normative order of first completing school, getting a job, and then marrying were more likely to become separated or divorced than men who conformed to the normative sequence.

If the developmental theorists are correct and each life stage contains its own agenda of tasks to be accomplished and issues to be resolved, then work must adapt over time to match the changing worker. The idea of *career* contains the movement that is necessary to convey the dynamic quality of the influence of work on the life of a person. The structure of career, its timing sequence and progress, as well as its content, contribute to the evolution of an adult. Sociology refers to *occupational socialization* as a process by which, over time, work experience fosters certain kinds of personal development. Lorence and Mortimer (in press) found that work autonomy that permits self-direction fosters work involvement. Even mental flexibility, a component of intelligence, can be stimulated or stifled by work (Kohn, 1973, 1976; Kohn & Schooler, 1978).

Marge worked as a cook in a school cafeteria. She spent all her time cooking and cleaning. When she got home, all she wanted to do was to go to sleep and get a good night's rest. Her lifestyle was dictated by her job.

Katie worked as a teacher in an elementary school. She lived in a poor neighborhood and had to go home early so the wayside drunks would not cause her trouble. However, her job did not end in school. She worked with emotionally disturbed children and hoped to publish a book about them. So when she reached home, her second job began. She went to work on her book about emotionally disturbed children and relived some of the earlier experiences of the day. Katie often worked until midnight before going to bed, although her work day began at eight in the morning. Her lifestyle was dictated by the kind of work she had chosen for herself.

The personal development engendered by work in turn becomes a factor in promoting the direction, order, and stability of career progress. In this fashion, the career trajectory influences the other facets of an individual's life, such as economics and family.

Erikson postulated that the developmental process in each stage depends on the successful resolution of the preceding stage. Thus, in order to be able to establish intimate relations, one must have a sense of identity. A person who has not moved beyond the stage of intimacy and has never resolved the issues of work or career consolidation will be unable in later adulthood to deal with the developmental task of that period. Developmental psychologists indicate that such a person would stagnate and would be unprepared for the generativity stage of life.

The Work Environment

The work environment can be conceptualized as a stimulus to which a person is exposed for a long time. Due to that prolonged exposure, the work environment can have a cumulative effect on adult development. Work exerts a multifaceted influence on us simply as a context. We review and judge one another within a particular setting and, to a surprising extent, the context determines what we see and consequently what we become.

This effect is illustrated by a study by Shinar (1978), who found that men and women are judged in different ways on such qualities as leadership and interpersonal adjustment, depending on the sex appropriateness or inappropriateness of their occupation. Evaluation of the worker is affected not only by the worker's performance but by who does the judging. Feedback from other people is a vital source of information from which workers learn their value. Growth and learning can take place when feedback is related to constructive advice. But when peers, supervisors, or subordinates respond to prejudged attributes instead of to the worker's actual performance, the result for the worker is confusion and anger. Responses that bear little relationship to the content and quality of one's work engender a feeling of helplessness and despair, which, if allowed to continue unabated, can ultimately contribute to depression. Thus the influence of work pervades our self-concept even below the level of consciousness.

Work is an occupation that involves values and attitudes. An occupation can be described as a complex social role as well as a set of behaviors and skills; incorporated in it are attitudes—what society expects of a person in that role. Lawyers, physicians, and insurance salespeople have differing social roles. Young men and women as graduate students in professional schools of law, business, social welfare, or medicine are learning customary attitudes and habits from their professors as well as the specific knowledge and technology of the profession.

The social climate varies from one workplace to another. The faculty members of most colleges and universities have informal, easy, and democratic relations among deans, department chairs, and teachers. This structure is different from, say, a hospital, where the physician has an authoritarian role in relation to other staff.

Career Development

Career development is an important aspect in a young person's life. Some individuals follow careers that they have planned for a long period of time (like engineering or medicine), carrying out decisions they have made with the help of parents or other older members of the family. Often, however, a career begins as just a job; later, when the individual becomes really interested in the field, the occupation takes on the color of a career.

It takes people time to select a job with which they are comfortable. Usually young people try a number of jobs in their early vocational life—a strategy that is common regardless of whether one later follows a professional career that requires university training. This has been called the *trial work period*. Many young people at this age are also newly married, and they may be adapting to a way of life in a new and different community. There could be some floundering and certainly some trial and error in the process, which could last for several years. Vocational guidance in high school or college can be helpful.

Miller and Form (1951) made a sociological analysis of career development through the life span. They found that the initial work period begins at about age 14 with a part-time job or summer work, usually in a marginal job, where a person requires minimal or non-specialized skills. The trial work period follows, with entry into the regular labor market occurring sometime between ages 16 and 25. Job changes continue until the worker reaches a stable period, which typically lasts from about 35 to 60. Usually a person retires in his or her sixties.

Career Patterns of Men

Taking work histories from a sample of men in Ohio, Miller and Form (1951) found four career patterns:

- conventional career pattern. Jobs follow the typical sequence from initial through trial and stable employment. This pattern is fairly typical of managerial, skilled, and clerical staff.
- stable career pattern. Workers remain in the type of work they entered directly from school or college. This is the pattern of most professions and some skilled, semiskilled, and clerical workers.
- unstable career pattern. The sequence of jobs is trial, stable period, trial. The worker may never reach career stability. This pattern is most frequently seen among semiskilled, clerical, and domestic workers.
- multiple-trial career pattern. Job changes are frequent, with no one type of job being dominant or prolonged. This pattern is most frequently seen in domestic, clerical, and semiskilled workers.

Miller and Form (1951) found that 73% of white-collar workers had stable patterns and only 29% of unskilled workers had stable histories. This is one of the classic studies on the career patterns of men. In the next chapter the career patterns of women will be presented.

Household and Family Patterns

A study by Carter and Glick (1976) indicates that 96% of the population or more marry at some time in their lives. Erikson indicates that the principal task as well as the goal of a young adult is the establishment of intimacy, as opposed to living alone. According to Rogers (1979), young women have a much easier task in establishing intimacy than their male counterparts.

Women's Role

On the basis of research by Carol Gilligan (1982), Dorothy Dinnerstein (1977), Luise Eichenbaum and Susie Orbach (1983), and Jean Baker Miller (1976), it has been established that women have the ability to create relationships. Psychological development starts at birth and occurs within the context of the relationship that the infant has with its caregiver. Thus, in the formation of women's psychology, the mother–daughter relationship is critical. Mothers and daughters share a gender identity and a social role, as well as social expectations. In mothering an infant, the woman is bringing up her daughter like herself, whereas she is working at making her son into a man. Mothers inevitably relate to their daughters and their sons differently. To a large extent, this difference is deliberate and is prescribed by common stereotyping; for instance, a son's sexual adventures are to be encouraged, whereas a daughter's sexual behavior is to be overtly restricted.

All mothers were daughters first, and nearly all mothers were brought up by mothers. Thus in most mothers' experience there is the memory, buried or active, of the struggles they had with their own mothers in the process of becoming a woman—of learning to curb their activities as required and to direct their interests in particular ways (Eichenbaum & Orbach, 1983).

Women's development, unlike men's, builds on a context of attachment and affiliation with others. Many women perceive the threat of disruption of affiliation not just as a loss of relationship but as something closer to a total loss of self. This type of structuring leads to depression in women when a significant person is lost.

Women throughout their lives are taught to be vehicles of the basic necessity of human communication. Men go a long way without recognizing that it is a necessity, whereas women are groomed from a young age for this role they have to play.

Women also learn at a young age that they should place their faith in other human beings, in the context of being a social being related to other human beings. Women learn early in life that they must rest primarily on this faith. They cannot depend on their own individual development based solely on achievement or power. An awareness of the female perspective enables people to appreciate the importance of both sexes and our connectedness with each other.

Marriage

For young people, dating eventually raises the possibility of marriage. Intimacy often leads to sexual activity and commitment. At its best, sexuality has the qualities of intimacy, trust, and devotion. Before a person's identity has been established, sexual union is usually dominated by physical urgings. Intimacy involves the possibility of being hurt or being rejected by one's love. Some men who struggle with their own identity will not take a chance. They can have multiple relationships without commitment. Men fall in love more easily than women, being more satisfied with their own qualities and believing in romantic love, and fall out of love more quickly as well (Hill,

Rubin, & Peplan, 1979). Women as a rule take more time, are more practical, and are more careful in choosing a spouse.

However, this pattern does not hold in all cultures. In the traditional Korean culture, parents arrange marriages for young men and women. After marriage, the son will continue to live with his parents, and the wife will become a part of the husband's household. Even after they have a child, the couple is still under the control of older adults in the family.

Marriage serves two purposes. In a traditional North American setting, it is a means to achieve certain individual or social needs. Marriage is entered into by legal contract and ritualized by ceremony, and it provides opportunity for progeny and independence from parents, as well as security. In North American culture, marriage typically signals that full adulthood has been legitimized with sexual monopoly and gratification and the opportunity for the couple to procreate.

The second purpose of marriage is that of a terminal event. Dreyer (1975) says that a large number of young people see it as a long-lasting event whereby they find new meaning in affirmation of personal identity, attain psychological intimacy, experience mutual pleasure, promote personal growth opportunities, and achieve transcendence and permanency. However, this promise does not always hold; when young adults marry for egocentric reasons and life does not fall into place, they instead experience disagreements, misunderstandings, and, in most cases, divorce.

The marriage rate continues to be high for adults, most of whom have been married at least once and tend to remarry after divorce (Cherlin, 1979). However, of the younger people in the study (between the ages of 22 and 26), only 70% were married. Some people see this rate as indicative of a new trend toward nonmarriage among a large segment of the young population.

Singleness

There are a number of alternatives to marriage, and one of them is singleness. One out of every four people remains single until the age of 35. Some people wish to keep their options open to find themselves new jobs, travel, and so forth without the responsibility of spouse or children. Some people do not marry because of their sexual orientation; that is, they are lesbian or homosexual.

> Ken was 27 years old, had never been married, and had no such intentions. He was a homosexual. He lived in a very conservative Catholic home with his parents, where his sexual preference would have been viewed as a crime if it were made public. The only way he learned to live his own life was to be deceptive. When Ken went out with men, he would tell his family that he was working late. Deception enabled him to maintain a lifestyle that he enjoyed but that he was forced to "keep in the closet" so it would not come into conflict with his family's value system.

Most women who plan to have children tend to marry before the age of 35, due to pressure from family. Pressure to have children before 35 is usually associated with the rising incidence of birth defects. However, in a new (though not particularly popular) trend, women have chosen to become mothers without marriage and have carried on their roles as single parents with careers. Besides taking care of the child or children, they spend their energies on economic independence.

In a study of Danish students, 95% of males as well as females reported premarital sexual experience (Stevens-Long, 1979). In the United States, by the age of 25, 75% of single women and 90% of men have had premarital sexual intercourse (Hunt, 1974). A study done in 1982 by Simenauer and Carroll showed that in a representative sample of singles from the ages of 20 to 55 (scientifically selected to reflect the demographic composition of the entire United States), approximately three-fourths of the men and nearly 90% of the women felt that it was difficult or impossible to be sexually involved with more than one person at a time.

Casual sex is typical among older single people and among recently divorced and separated people.

Stein (1976) interviewed 60 single men and women in the age group from 22 to 62 and listed a number of elements involved in their remaining single. The positive aspects were career opportunities, sexual availability, exciting life-style, plurality of roles, freedom, autonomy, and varieties of experiences. The negative aspects were poor communication, sexual frustration, fewer friends, less opportunity for travel, and less opportunity for new experiences. Some of these aspects tend to overlap, depending on one's age and the availability of companionship. Individual personality is the most strongly determinant variable in an assessment of characteristics of singleness (Jones, Garrison, & Morgan, 1985).

Living Together

Many young and older people believe in cohabitation. However, it is most common among young adults who have graduated from high school and are involved in careers. This practice is so widespread among college students that considerable research has been done on the subject. Macklin (1974) indicates that the number of college students who have cohabited varies from 10% to more than 30%, depending on factors that include the geography of the school's housing, parental regulations and their enforcement, the male–female student ratio, and the researchers' sampling methods and definition of cohabitation.

The reasons people decide to live together vary and include companionship, having a sexual relationship, aiding in self-understanding, and clarifying what they want in a marriage partner. Many people think that living together for two years or so has advantages that outweigh the problems. But living together is not without negative implications. In some states it can be a form of legal marriage. In some states, litigation over common-law marriage has increased. In Europe, little attention is paid to people's living together, whereas in the United States there is an implicit commitment. "Palimony"—that is, payment analogous to alimony based on what is acquired while living is shared—is getting more attention in the United States. The courts are ruling that, due to the impact of an eightfold increase in cohabitation among those under 25, members of couples who come to court may be required to define their obligations to each other, and one of the two may be required to support the other after they separate.

In the Macklin study, one-third of the respondents said that their parents did not know about their cohabitation, and some feared that their parents would find out about it. Nearly all cohabitors used some form of contraceptive.

> Sandy and Mike had been living together for four years. As time passed they became more and more dissatisfied with each other and eventually decided to separate. However, they had investments together, including the purchase of a house. Among the issues they negotiated were how much money they owed each other and how the profits from their house were to be divided.

Macklin (1974), in her comprehensive review of studies in this area, concludes that those who live together have a sexual life more comparable to that of married couples than to that of singles—that is, they tend to be committed to one person alone, with whom they share every aspect of their lives over a substantial time span. Among the strains that some experience in this type of relationship are the disapproval of relatives and a tendency for commitment to the relationship to be asymmetrical (women tend to be more committed). Compared with couples who have married, couples living together are less inclined to bring children into the world.

Communal Marriage

The basis of communal marriage is an agreement among three or more families to share living quarters, a division of work, social involvement, and sometimes sexual rights and responsibilities. There are economic advantages to such arrangements, and women who would otherwise be left alone with children are not left in isolation. Mutual support is one of the strong aspects of this type of relationship. However, jealousy can become a problem when there is sexual exchange. Most such groups do not survive for a long period of time; those couples who were married prior to group association usually survive the breakup of the group (Constantine & Constantine, 1977). In communal types of living there can be married couples with children and some singles. The usual situation does allow young singles, and for them the purpose of this arrangement is to have intimacy within a familylike unit. There are advantages as well as disadvantages to this type of arrangement (Jones, Garrison, & Morgan, 1985).

Berger and his associates (1974) found that such communes may be described as either creedal or noncreedal, with the former having a firm system of beliefs that guide relationships and expected behaviors. Berger specifies that noncreedal communes have an ideology based on countercultural values, such as open expression of feeling and affirmation of mystical rather than scientific values. Urban communes are easy to start; rural communes call for a more serious commitment from members and therefore have a more stable membership. Rural communes may have a shared economic enterprise, whereas urban groups vary in their economic arrangement. In some religious communes all members share all expenses, whereas in other communes, members merely share household expenses. Communes were more common in the 1970s; however only a few of them were successful, as most were unable to develop an enduring alternative lifestyle.

Extramarital Relationships

There have been a number of studies on extramarital relationships, but the problem with any such study is that statistics are insufficient to reveal the exact number of extramarital relationships in a given area. If at least one partner is married to somebody else, their responses may not be completely truthful. Also, because such relationships are a violation of the norm of marital exclusivity, people may not admit to them. Kinsey, Pomeroy, and Martin (1948), with their in-depth interviews, found that 50% of men in the 1940 sample and 25% of women had had at least one such experience. Several studies seem to indicate that men have not changed much and that women have closed the gap to a considerable degree (Bell & Peltz, 1974; Hunt, 1974; Levin, 1975; Tavris & Sadd, 1977; Wolman & Money, 1980).

Among the reasons for having an affair are resentment and dissatisfaction with one's own marriage itself (Edwards & Booth, 1976; Tavris & Sadd, 1977). Next in importance appears to be premarital sexual patterns; the more sexual partners one has before marriage, the more likely one is to be extramaritally active (Athanasiou & Sorkin, 1974; Bukstel, Roeder, Kilmann, Laughlin, & Sotile, 1978; Kinsey, Pomeroy, Martin, & Gebhard, 1953; Singh, Walton, & Williams, 1976). Another important issue is general traditionalism in personal attitude and lifestyle. For example, being romantic is related to fidelity among women (Glass & Wright, 1977), as is lack of interest in pornography and oral or anal sex (Bell, Turner, & Rosen, 1975).

The consequences of an extramarital relationship depend on the circumstances and attitude of the couple. At some life stages it is associated with higher rates of separation and divorce, but among older couples this effect disappears. Perhaps older women feel that the option of divorce is not real for them due to their economic dependency and poor opportunities for remarriage (Glass & Wright, 1977).

Men who leave a marital relationship do so most commonly in the first five years of marriage, whereas women who leave are more likely to do so after 15 to 20 years of marriage (Athanasiou, Shaver, & Tavris, 1970; Bell, Turner, & Rosen, 1975; Hunt, 1974; Kinsey et al., 1948; Kinsey et al., 1953; Levin, 1975). The male pattern may be tied to the pressures of pregnancy early in marriage and perhaps to the only gradual socialization of the man into a married perspective. For women it seems possible that elements of midlife crisis such as the empty-nest stage or menopause could play a part.

In spite of the stresses and strains of discovered infidelity, it stimulates many couples to improve their own relationships.

Homosexual Relationships

Homosexual relationships vary in their social context and personal meanings just as heterosexual relationships do. One study of men who engage in occasional homosexual relations (Dank, 1971) revealed that at least one-fourth of them were married heterosexually. In such cases, homosexual activities are confined to furtive encounters or clandestine affairs. Another substantial group appear as single heterosexuals in the world of employment as well as with some friends and acquaintances but escape into the "gay" world for other socializing and for sex. A third group chose to present themselves overtly as homosexuals (Broderick, 1982).

A study of homosexuals by Bell and Weinberg (1978) revealed five categories, which accounted for about 70% of a San Francisco sample. Some homosexuals lived as "closed-couple" pairs, adhering to such principles of heterosexual marriages as predictability and exclusivity. A relatively larger proportion of women and a smaller percentage of men belonged to this category. A larger percentage of men and a smaller percentage of women represented the second category, "open couple" relationships—they do not preclude other sexual partners, even though jealousy is a common problem. Bell and Weinberg labeled two other groups *functional* and *dysfunctional*. The functional homosexual has many sexual partners and few commitments, and the dysfunctional homosexual has few partners but is tortured by self-doubt and guilt. The final group is identified as asexual; the members are defined, for purposes of the study, by self-disclosure rather than by sexual lifestyle, since they are sexually less active.

In his review of the Bell and Weinberg study, Lief (1978) commented that the greatest difference between the lifestyle of the homosexual and the heterosexual is the level of promiscuity. Among White homosexual males, Lief found that 28% had 1000 partners or so; 15% had more than 500, and 17% had more than 250. Thus, it can be said that 60% reported more than 250 partners. Seventy percent reported that more than half of their sexual contacts were single encounters with strangers. As Lief sees it, this is a nonaffectionate, impersonal, shallow relationship, perhaps involving compulsive sex, and altogether different from most heterosexual relationships. The reason for this difference is not clear, despite speculation that it could be the result of a lack of the constraining influence of feminine attitudes toward sex. However, it was found that lesbians' numbers of sexual partners approximate those of heterosexual females (Lief, 1978).

Sexuality and Intimacy

All adults, whether single, married, or divorced, are to some extent involved in sexuality and sexual intimacy in reality or fantasy, and some have unresolved issues remaining. Adolescent sexuality is different from adult sexuality in the sense that sometimes it is confusing, embarrassing, and also overwhelming. Adults move away from merely physical sex to sexuality that is part of an enduring, satisfying emotional bond. Among some older adults, relationships may involve an emotional bond without too much physical sexuality.

Allen was a young adult who had been involved during his early twenties in a long-term relationship that ended because of personality clashes. Four years after that separation, he met a beautiful woman, and there was a strong attraction between them. In the process of developing their relationship, Allen mentioned that he had closed his heart to women because he had been hurt. By reflecting on his earlier relationship, he realized what he missed most was the emotional companionship and togetherness rather than sex. Allen explained to his new girlfriend what he wanted from the relationship. He described a satisfying, meaningful, emotional relationship as a piece of cake and the sexual aspect of the relationship as the icing on the cake. The icing in a relationship is good to have, he said, but it is very important for a couple to have good mutual understanding and a strong emotional bond that holds them together.

McCary (1978) suggests that there are several different components for intimacy. They include mutuality and choice. Two people usually choose each other because of mutual attraction. They exchange confidences, develop a sense of trust, and accept each other's vulnerabilities in a sharing way (McCary, 1978).

An enduring bond helps couples build up their relationship firmly and deal with other problems as they arise. When people are afraid to present themselves to each other due to fear of rejection, their intimacy is blocked, as couples deny their emotional feelings, like anger, and cover up their emotional needs. If ritual behavior was of importance in traditional courtship and dating patterns, this would discourage intimacy, as an honest exchange of feelings is blocked (McCary, 1978).

At 23, Gail wished to get married because all her friends from high school were already married. She had dated a number of men, but somehow those relationships did not seem to work out for her. Finally she met a man who could provide for her very well, so she started the dating game. She told him what he wanted to hear and agreed with all his dreams for the future, even though in reality she was aware that she would never agree to some of the things he was planning. She was willing to compromise her values and desires verbally so that she could end up in front of the altar with him. She hoped to change him to her way of thinking because, she told herself, after marriage he would have no choice but to listen to her as she would make him miserable otherwise. But what Gail forgot in the process was that the permanency of the marriage cannot be assured if they entered into it without any meaningful discussions of their joint dreams and hopes.

Heather was 27 years old and poor. She had slept with many different men; sex was her way of seeking love. At work she met a man who was attractive, well-to-do, and caring. Excited, she planned to marry him, and began to use all the games she knew to lure the man to her. She was willing to say and do anything to make him a part of her life. What Heather ignored was the fact that the relationship might not last long after marriage because the man knew nothing of her lifestyle or her likes and dislikes.

People often enter into the marriage contract without too much thought, and that can lead to early divorces.

Cultural Differences

Sexual behavior is highly dependent upon culture. For instance, where there are arranged marriages, as in orthodox Jewish culture, or in the Far East, where there is still cultural orthodoxy, a couple may not know each other well when they marry, but they participate in sex immediately after marriage because a legal bond has been created between them. This sudden intimacy would appear strange to a person in the North American culture, where two people are expected to know each other well before marriage. But people become acclimated to what is acceptable in their own cultures and tend to accept the lifestyles that are available to them without questioning.

It can be said, people from the Far East who have arranged marriages get married and then fall in love, whereas in the North American culture people fall in love and then get married.

Among the Samoans in the 1920s, sex was straightforward—when two people liked each other they participated in sexual activities.

According to Specht and Craig (1982), the farmers and fishermen who live on the island of Inis Beag in the North Atlantic receive very little sexual education. Nudity is not tolerated, and intercourse is performed very quickly without removal of clothing. There is little or no sex education or premarital sexual experience, and neither marital partner expects to derive much pleasure from sexual activity. Historically, men in this culture marry only after inheriting property, usually in their late 30s or 40s.

People in different cultures learn different sexual roles and are taught behaviors considered appropriate to those roles. In many cultures, men and women are expected to acquire distinctly different behavior patterns. In our culture there is more acceptance of various lifestyles as well as sexual behaviors.

Dimensions of Human Sexuality

Harvey Gochros (1977) identified five dimensions of human sexuality: sensuality, intimacy, reproduction, interpersonal influence, and sexual identity.

Sensuality in our culture is the mental enjoyment that an individual experiences with the release of sexual tension. Oftentimes sexual satisfaction is associated with a love relationship.

Intimacy is the interdependence and closeness between two people. People in our culture experience psychological closeness with only a few people, such as a spouse or other person with whom they have a sexual relationship.

At 25, Andrew, through inheritance, had become economically self-sufficient. He dated a number of girls because he claimed that he was a sensuous person. He quickly realized that the girls liked him for what he had, not for what he was. As time passed, he became more and more selective of his girlfriends. Eventually he began living with a girl with whom he developed both a sensuous and an intimate relationship.

Reproduction is another dimension of sexuality. Bearing children remains important to many couples. To procreate carries with it responsibilities, but also pleasures of seeing one's own child grow up. Historically, the desire for children has been a reason for sexual intercourse.

Interpersonal influence is the use of sexual activities for non-sexual purposes, such as gaining power and control over a partner. As Haley (1976) indicates, the power struggle between husband and wife partners is ever present. Young men's engaging in sexual activities in order to prove their adequacy exemplifies the use of sex for interpersonal influence. At the extreme, rapists utilize sexual attacks to express aggression or assert dominance.

Rita, a fairly assertive woman from a traditional middle-class home, met Frank at the office, where he was her boss. Frank's family was in a much lower socioeconomic class than Rita's, a disparity of which Frank was painfully aware. Rita and Frank married. He soon created rules and regulations about when she could see her parents and when she could invite them to their home. He threatened to beat her if she did not follow those rules. She did not believe that he would do such a "ghastly" thing and was surprised that when she "disobeyed" he beat her until she was black and blue. It was at a family counseling center that the couple were able to deal with Frank's feeling of inferiority about his family's status, his low self-esteem, and his need to control his wife.

Sexual identity is complex because it involves a person's biological gender, self-image, and sexual preference, or choice of love objects. For some people there is a physiological or psychological ambiguity about gender. For instance, transsexuals have anatomical features of one sex but clearly perceive themselves as belonging to the opposite sex. In a similar manner, hermaphrodites are people whose physical characteristics are neither entirely male nor entirely female.

Social work practitioners may see clients who appear to be clear about their gender identity but are confused about their sexual identity because of their attraction to a particular love object. They may see themselves as "straight" heterosexual, homosexual, or bisexual in orientation.

Pamela fell in love with a extremely good-looking man who appeared to care for her. But as time passed she found that he did not get closer to her physically. All he appeared to be interested in was her earlier sexual relationships with men. When she tried to confront him with his lack of physical interest in her, he teased and taunted her about being a "loose woman." Confused and emotionally involved almost beyond repair, Pamela began to see a therapist. She was amazed to find out that her boyfriend's sexual preference was for men and that he had entered a relationship with her in order to test himself out and find out whether he were still attracted to women. In the process, Pamela was terribly hurt, having been made to feel that she was not attractive and did not have much to offer him.

Sex Therapy

Couples who have sexual problems with either their spouses or their lovers need help. Various resources are available. William Masters (1970) found that about 75% of people seeking help with sexual problems are treated by professionals other than doctors. Social work practitioners also treat sexual dysfunctions. There are professional organizations which offer continuing education in human sexuality, so that social work practitioners can better understand and deal with sexual functioning (Specht & Craig, 1982).

Most problems that are brought to sexual counselors involve heterosexual adults—married couples and single individuals who are concerned about either their own or their partner's sexual adequacy.

Kim and her husband entered therapy because Kim was very unhappy in her sex life. She felt that her husband just got what he wanted and went to sleep. He really did not care whether he satisfied her needs. She had never had an orgasm. The therapist attempted to deal with the psychological blocks that her clients had, and also explained the importance of foreplay for women in sex.

One of the chief complaints brought to counselors is that women experience less physical gratification than men do (Hunt, 1974; McCary, 1978; Hite, 1976). Female dissatisfaction may be related to differences in the physiological and psychological patterns of men and women, with men climaxing before their partners have had sufficient stimulation to reach orgasm. Fortunately, there is a growing awareness of the importance of clitoral rather than vaginal orgasm in women and correspondingly less emphasis on simultaneous male and female orgasm (Gordon & Shankweiler, 1971).

Psychologically, it is important for women to express tender emotions along with sexual intimacy, whereas men have been taught not to express these emotions. Because of these substantial differences in male and female needs, couples who improve their communication can usually adapt more successfully to each other's needs.

After the publication of Masters and Johnson's *Human Sexual Inadequacy* (1970), there was tremendous optimism about and interest in short-term behavior techniques that were claimed effective in achieving erection, delaying ejaculation, and facilitating orgasm (Fischer & Gochros, 1975). However, Masters and Johnson's research has been criticized for being too methodical and for being flawed in failing to provide a sound theoretical base for sex therapists or to show cures for sexual dysfunction (Zilbergeld & Evans, 1980). The therapists' criticism highlights the fact that Masters and Johnson do not set behavioral criteria for defining successful treatment outcomes; they simply speak of having only a 20% failure rate. The extent of change achieved by the 80% is not discussed, and what is regarded as failure is also not discussed.

Zilbergeld and Evans (1980) also question how to measure success in treating a man's premature ejaculation when the criterion for success is the partner's subjective sense of satisfaction. Sex is such an intimate matter that when a partner's dissatisfaction stems from other than physiological causes, such as interpersonal conflicts and struggles for power, objective evaluation is not possible. What is needed is an integration of behavioral management with insights into relationships provided by psychodynamic theories. Symptoms may thus be relieved by short-term methods when the client is supplied with proper information and counseling. However, in most cases, the therapist must deal with the client's total pattern of relationships in order to be helpful.

Divorce and Remarriage

Bernard (1972) and others point out that marital relationships are often evaluated differently by the two people concerned. One cannot speak of a happy or unhappy marriage but only of how happy or unhappy each partner is.

> Sam and Cynthia had been married for fifteen years. They belonged to a lower socioeconomic level. Cynthia had been dependent on her husband from the time she was 17. At first her husband had viewed this as a "fun relationship." It had pleased him to have someone dependent on him when he was 25. As time passed, he got tired of having a completely dependent wife, and when he demanded that she do things by herself, he would be met with a burst of tears. She interpreted Sam's unexpected demands as a sign that he no longer liked her. Eventually the situation got more complicated, and Sam wanted to get out of the marriage. With counseling and the help of the extended family network, the marriage was dissolved.

Seen from the point of view of a therapist, Cynthia and Sam clearly viewed their marriage differently, and in divorce they also experienced different pain. Sam was the person who initiated the divorce. Cynthia went along with the divorce proceedings, but in the process she began to find her own strengths. The same principle applies to separation as well as divorce: a marital disruption is seldom symmetrical in its effect on the partners. Studies show that infidelity and other sexual problems are often contributing factors to marital breakup (Albrecht, 1979; Levinger, 1966).

> Drew and Tanya had been married for 15 years. It was a traditional marriage in which Tanya stayed home and took care of the babies. But when the children were older and less dependent physically, she found

herself a job. At first her husband was happy with the extra money, but as she started to climb the career ladder he became envious and insecure. Their bickering started in the morning and did not end even at bedtime. Eventually they got a divorce. Drew could not believe that Tanya would leave him. He had been completely dependent on her for doing all the housework. With divorce came the revelation that he had to learn to do housework on his own. Though painful, this was also the beginning of his growth as a whole person.

Divorce is not simple. It has social implications—it disrupts the lives of the couple and any children they may have brought into the world. There may be temporary feelings of anger and loss. Divorce may not necessarily reflect maladjustment in the marriage. Sometimes it is brought about by a crisis such as the injury or death of a child; in a state of depression (Wallerstein & Kelly, 1980), the partners start to blame each other, and before long the marriage is dissolved.

Aaron was an only son. When he was 15, he went fishing with his friends in spite of the family rule that he could not go to the river at that time of the year. The father was out of town on business when he received a call saying that his son had drowned.

The father could not forgive his wife; he saw her as the cause of their son's death. He blamed her because the son had not obeyed the family rule, and, in the father's perspective, it was his wife's duty to make sure that the rules were followed. She, in turn, blamed him because he had failed in the family as a parent figure and was not easily available to his son. She blamed his constant absence from home. Their anger and depression and the tremendous blame each leveled against the other ended their long marriage in divorce. The problems in the marriage arose immediately after the son's death; there had been no symptom of problems earlier.

Divorce would seem to be a welcome relief in a conflicted, intolerable marriage. However, there are many studies that reveal divorced people to be the unhappiest in our society. Divorce is affiliated with increased vulnerability to mental ailments (Bloom, Asher, & White, 1978), physical ailments (Renne, 1971), and suicide (Kitagawa & Hauser, 1973). Divorced people who dated were found to have fewer problems than those who did not. The large majority of divorced people appear to believe in the one-man–one-woman relationship and tend to marry again within a few months or a few years (Glick & Norton, 1977).

There is some evidence that remarried couples are not free from sexual problems or adjustments. The reemergence of marital problems in the second marriage is often due to each individual's belief that the problem is in the other partner and the consequent refusal to search themselves to find out what is wrong in their own ability to create relationships. In the absence of attempts at self-understanding, problems are apt to arise in new relationships as well. After a divorce, a person would probably have to remain single for a period of two to three years in order to understand the difficulties in his or her own personality and to develop emotional distance from the earlier relationship.

Another factor in the high divorce rate could be the increased number of women in the labor force and the increased acceptance of the view that unhappy marriages are to be terminated (Hannan et al., 1977).

Approximately two-thirds of divorced women remarry, and do so about six years after their divorce, on the average (Glick and Norton, 1977). Non-Whites as well as welfare recipients have low rates of remarriage (Wattenberg & Reinhardt, 1979). These demographic patterns suggest a growing acceptance of serial monogamy as a style of family life.

> Brenda was a 30-year-old woman who had been married at 18 and divorced at 22. She took charge of her life, studied, and found an extremely well-paying job. She met some good men in social situations and workplaces, but she viewed them strictly as people with whom she could have pleasure. She did not wish to get married. She had two consecutive relationships that she found gratifying, but she had made a decision that she was not ready for marriage at that point in her life.

In 1971, it was found that 24% of all marriages were the second or later marriage for at least one of the partners. By 1977 that number had risen to 32% (Price-Bonham & Balswick, 1980). Remarriages are more common among people who get divorced than among people who are widowed. Remarriage is more common among divorced Whites. Most people who remarry after divorce see their second marriage as distinctly different from their first marriage. They also report different expectations of marriage: more flexibility, more sharing of household work, and less willingness to remain unhappily married (Furstenberg, 1980). Most remarriages involve dependent children, and such reconstituted families have special adjustment problems, some of which reflect the lack of societal norms regulating contacts among various current and former extended-family members (Price-Bonham & Balswick, 1980).

> Eloise was a 30-year-old woman who remarried after having been divorced for three years. She had three sons, and as a single parent she had been more lenient than before in her upbringing of her children. The oldest, Jonathan, who was 12, would stay out for long periods of time, and Eloise did not question his behavior. He also helped the most in household chores and felt responsible for his younger brothers as well as his mother.
>
> When Eloise met her second husband, Terence, he was the custodial parent of two sons, Justin and Philip, ages 12 and 10. He was a loving father but strict. The boys had rules to follow and could not leave the house at will. For almost everything they did, the boys were required to get permission.
>
> When Eloise and Terence married, the children had a number of adjustment problems. Although both parents had 12-year-old sons,

Eloise's son Jonathan was more adultlike and more willing to take responsibilities, but he also wanted more freedom. Justin was more like a young child. This situation led to conflicts between Eloise and Terence, as well as between the stepbrothers. Therefore each parent had to reflect, compromise, and create new, joint rules and regulations for behavior.

Ethnic Variations

Whereas most research in the past has focused on middle-class White populations, there is a new bent of research to identify the various patterns of meeting needs for intimacy, companionship, and caring in other populations. The review of this new research by Staples and Mirande (1980) is summarized here.

Research on Black Americans has changed positively, reflecting a tendency to move away from the perspective of defining Black families as deviant and pathological and instead to see them in variant forms (for example, in terms of extended-family units and "fictive kin") that may be culturally equivalent to the modal White forms. Some of the critical findings are that a majority of adult Blacks are unmarried; the Black divorce rate has increased in the past decade; there has been a sharp increase in marriages between Black men and White women, and there is a high rate of dissolution of those interracial marriages.

Research on the Chicano family stresses machismo as being either a negative or positive factor in family life. This opinion has been revised recently. In Chicano families, marital roles seem to be predominantly egalitarian across educational levels, urban-rural residency, and region. Chicano families are characterized by high fertility, and most children under 18 live with both parents in intact families; about 60% of Chicano families are headed by a married couple. Relatively more families are intact and fewer people are divorced or widowed than in other ethnic groups.

Native Americans show great diversity in customs and languages, and they have generally been studied by White anthropologists who see them as cultural deviants posing a problem to society. Native Americans have high fertility rates. They have many children born out of wedlock. There are many female head-of-household families, unemployment is high and extended families form the basic family units.

Asian–Americans constitute less than 1% of the American population. Their cohort differences are marked because many of the oldest were immigrants in a previous historical era. Younger groups again include recent immigrants. Usually, compared to other North Americans, they have more conservative sexual values, lower fertility rates, fewer illegitimate births, and more obligatory kinship customs. Asian–Americans have found it more difficult to maintain the traditional "honorable" kinship status of elders, and this is reflected in intergenerational tensions.

Parenthood

One element of parenting is that it is cyclical. First an individual leaves her or his household—that is, her or his own family of origin (the family of orientation)—to establish an independent household. This step is usually followed by marriage, the second stage—a relationship with a new individual, developing a new family network. The third stage is the birth of the first child, and the beginning of parenting (the family of procreation). There are many milestones in marriage, including the birth of the first child, the departure of the last child from the family of origin, and the death of a spouse.

Families who are conflicted and face a number of constant problems could be classified as *dysfunctional* families, and those who have minimal problems are termed *functional* families. All families have structures. Some have extended-family structure and others have a nuclear family structure.

During the past 50 years there have been variations of the family life cycle. Not only are people living longer but the age level at which they first marry has risen drastically. There is also an increase in the number of women who wish to have their children after the age of 35 (Specht & Craig, 1982).

Tasks of Parenting

In all families there occur what are called *normal family crises*. A crisis can be described as a turning point or point of no return, such as marriage or an adult child's leaving home. If a crisis is handled meaningfully, it is assumed to lead the individual to some form of maturation or development. If conflicts are not handled well, then problems could arise in the family situation; weaker relationships or a state of weaker mental health may be the result (Rapaport, 1965).

The initial adjustment to parenthood is sometimes difficult. Previous lifestyle and routines may be disrupted, and both parents may find their freedoms curtailed. After the birth of the child, the parents have to learn different ways of behavior that help them to adjust.

At 4 months old, Ashley slept most of the day, but at nightfall she was up and crying for attention. Her parents were usually very tired and did not wish to stay awake. If they attempted to ignore Ashley, she started to cry and would not stop until she was picked up. So with great difficulty the parents reached a decision and a compromise. On workdays, when the father had to leave early and return late, the mother would get up at night to take care of the child's needs. But during the weekends, the father would attend to the child. Thus the parents' earlier behavior patterns were changed to suit the child, and with that change their lifestyle of partying and going out at night was altered considerably.

Rossi (1968) has divided parenthood into four stages:

1. The anticipatory period. Pregnancy leads the expectant parents to new roles. Couples face both domestic and external social adjustments as they prepare to become a family. Getting the home ready for a new baby involves obtaining necessities such as furniture, clothes, baby food, and diapers. Socially, the couple are no longer just husband and wife; their roles expand to include that of parent.

2. The honeymoon period. Parent–child attachment is formed. Although when the baby is new the parents are constantly fatigued, they also derive pleasure from their new roles as parents.

3. The plateau period. Parents assume roles of father and mother and learn to deal with family and community problems. Parenting includes socialization of the child and future family planning.

4. Termination. This final stage is usually reached when the last child leaves home to get a job, attend college, or get married. Termination can happen prematurely when a child leaves due to divorce or loss of child custody.

Some parents are able to cope with parenting very well. Other parents are unable to deal with one particular aspect of parenting, such as taking care of the newborn, but are perfectly capable of taking care of preschool and school-age children. If parents have difficulty, it is feasible to include other people in the parenting of the child, with responsibilities shared among extended families, support systems, and nursery and play groups.

A common form of family in North America is the nuclear family, consisting of a husband, wife, and children. Depending on the structure of the family, the rules, regulations, and ways of behavior vary. Minuchin and Fishman (1981) classify families into groups by "shape"—some of which are described below.

There is the pas de deux family, which has only two household members. They could be either a couple or a parent and a single child. This child, too, could be an adult. The two-person structure has the possibility of a lichenlike formation, in which the individuals become symbiotically dependent on each other. In such homes, individuals may be overly involved with each other.

There are also three-generation families, which are more typical of lower socioeconomic groups and lower-middle-income groups. In such multigenerational families, where there are grandparents and parents, parents and children, the question many times becomes, Who is parenting what child?

In so-called accordion families, one spouse leaves and enters the family as career dictates. For instance, in Navy families one spouse takes on additional responsibilities as a nurturer, executive, and guide of children when the other spouse is not living at home.

In fluctuating families, the family moves from place to place; the ability of members to belong to a particular place or identify a place as home is diminished. In a similar manner, in fluctuating families, an adult may move from one relationship to another, viewing no one relationship as meaningful.

From a systems perspective, the concept of family shape has some usefulness in understanding the structure and the responsibilities that families share.

Single-parent Families

The increased rate of divorce is one reason for a large number of families to have single parents. Other reasons are separation, death of a spouse, illness, and institutionalization.

There are about 11.3 million children in North America living in single-parent homes. One of the chief problems faced in such homes is task overload. If there is a high degree of organization and the family has appropriate support systems, then adequate task performance can be maintained. However, if the family has a low level of organization, there will be economic problems, high levels of anxiety, and a deterioration of task performance that parallels family disorganization.

One of the main functions of a family is to maintain social and family relationships and social networks. Usually, separated, single-parent women state that contacts with parents and siblings do not appear to improve their loneliness or depression. Women who are divorced tend to have fewer friends and belong to fewer organizations than those who are single parents after a spouse's death (Stack, 1972; Pearlin & Johnson, 1975; Spicer & Hampe, 1975). The social isolation faced by single parents tends to intensify the parent–child relationship in such a manner that the parent frequently complains of being trapped in a world of children. Because preschool children are less capable than adolescents of maintaining their own social contacts, socialization of parents tends to affect the functioning of young children more than the functioning of adolescents (Carter & McGoldrick, 1980).

Another important factor for single-parent families is that half of those headed by a female rely on welfare payments at least as a temporary source of income. (Such families receive welfare payments as a temporary source of income; U.S. Bureau of the Census, 1976). The incidence of female-headed families is three times higher for non-White- than for White-headed households (Ross & Sawhill, 1975), and this ratio is reflected in the high proportion of Black families among the very poor. Because social workers tend to see only groups who have serious problems, we often forget that two-thirds of urban Black families are headed by a man and woman living together (Scanzoni, 1971).

In 1975, approximately 84% of U.S. families were headed by couples, 13% were mother-headed, and 2.3% were father-headed. In mother-headed families, approximately 44% of the women were divorced or separated, 35% were widowed, 13% had never married, and 4% had husbands living in institutions or in other geographic areas.

All families have in common the need to establish an income, maintain a household, develop social and economic relationships in the neighborhood and at work, and relate to children in a way that makes them productive members of the society. The difference between an intact family and a single-parent family is seen in the types of relationships that are maintained in the family, both between parent and child and between spouses. Whatever caused the couple to break up has its own impact on the rest of the family. The length of separation, age of the child at the onset of separation, socioeconomic status, and birth order of children are also important factors (Hetherington, 1972).

Although intact families are similar in their performance of functions, the likelihood of diminished functioning in the single-parent family is increased by the added stress of modifying the family structure.

> Debra was a single parent living in the inner city of New York. Debra came from Atlanta with her parents when she was 15 years of age but was married by the time she was 17 and divorced by 20. She had one son, 8-year-old Lee. Her background was middle class. Single parenthood and economic responsibilities had reduced her status to a lower income bracket, and she found herself constantly overloaded with the task of being two parents to her child as well as holding onto her jobs as a cleaning woman, a part-time employee at a grocery store, and a part-time waitress. At times, when she came home tired, she would have loved to slip into a hot tub, but she had an active 8-year-old boy. Debra found that she had to spend more time with Lee. She realized that her life revolved around her child and she really did not have much of a support system. Her social life was practically nil. But she decided that when Lee grew up, she would have time for herself, so for the time being she could overlook some of her own basic needs.

Impact of the Child on Family Lifestyle

There are a number of effects that young children have on their parents. For instance, planning for children may result in change in residence (Davenport, 1965; Mead & Newton, 1967). Depending on the influences the parents would like the child to have, they may participate in organized religion or support other social institutions, such as schools. They may take their children to places they would not frequent by themselves (Harper, 1975).

There are economic strains as well as changes in work patterns when mothers stay home, leaving the labor force. In some families, when there is a need for two parents to work, available grandparents are called on for parenting and caregiving roles (Bell & Harper, 1977; Money & Ehrdhardt, 1972).

After the birth of the first child there are changes in the couple's marital relationship (Nye, Carlson, & Garrett, 1970; Ryder, Kafka, & Olson, 1971; Sears, Maccoby, & Levin, 1957). The presence of children affects the sexual practices of parents (Davenport, 1965; Ford & Beach, 1951; Mead, 1935/1950; Mead & Newton, 1967). In addition, there are changes in relationships with extended families. Ryder, Kafka, and Olson (1971) indicated that mothers have more contact with their own mothers as a result of having a child. Most new mothers also have more contact with other new mothers.

Parental patterns of consumption are affected by the presence of the offspring (Fimrite, 1970); for example, they may spend money on toys, diaper services, and formula.

Some adult values may change on account of the presence of the young. Kestenberg (1970) indicates that when parents do not conform they are confronted by their latency-age children with reminders of the culture's standards (Harper, 1975).

These examples are not exhaustive, but they do illustrate some of the effects of the young on the adult and the world of the adult. Taking care of children can influence the types of interaction and responsibilities that exist between parents and children and between adults within a family, and also impact interaction between adults outside the family (Bell & Harper, 1977).

Karen was married when she was 24 years old. Her husband Scott was loving and caring toward her. They started a family, and Karen was soon the mother of three children. Her life revolved around diapers and bottles and babies, and she slowly started to neglect herself. She put on weight and did not seem to care about her physical appearance. When Scott came home, Karen greeted him with a recital of all the problems she had had with the children. She gradually became more of a mother and less of a wife. Scott did not help her with the housework or with the children.

One day out of the blue Scott announced that he wanted to leave her. Karen was hurt and frightened because she did not have a job, although she had an undergraduate degree. In an attempt to hold onto her marriage, she went to a family agency for help. But when her husband was asked to participate, he abruptly left home and took a room in a hotel, saying that he did not wish to be involved in therapy. All Scott wanted was to be out of the marriage. With great pain Karen let go of him.

At the agency, the social worker helped Karen to deal with her own anxieties, as well as her children's, and to reassure the children that she would not disappear from their lives. A daycare program was found for the children while the social worker helped Karen to set limited goals for herself. As Karen accomplished each goal she found it easier to take the next step. Karen also joined a supportive social group for newly divorced women, where she learned to take on the new responsibility of being a single parent. With a part-time job, the future began to look hopeful for Karen, although she now felt that she had rushed into her first marriage and that she would wait a long time before marrying again.

James, a man in his midthirties, had found that his lifestyle as a religious born-again Christian did not fit well with other people's lifestyles. He did not wish to be married but wanted to adopt a young person. Knowing that private adoption agencies find older children with special problems hard to place and that some are accepting single people as parents, James felt that he had a good chance of becoming an adoptive parent. He asked for a particular child and waited a time before he was rejected as an adoptive parent by the private agency. He realized that the only route remaining was adoption through the state, and so he prepared for a long, tedious process. But James was a realistic person, was clear in his goals, and was willing to wait for his fondest dream of being a father to be realized. Meanwhile he underwent therapy to understand his basic needs and desires, as well as the urges toward of parenting that he experienced. He was religious minded and had made a decision not to marry, but he looked forward to participating in the emotional intimacy of raising a child.

Implications for Social Work Practice

Most young people do what society expects of them, and their self-assessments frequently depend on how well they perform their assigned roles. The role expectations of young adulthood are primarily those of marriage, parenting, occupation, and social value. These roles give people a feeling both of inner assuredness and of recognition from others who count in their lives. Our society provides an idealized family model that emphasizes romance in marriage and fairly inflexible distinctions between caretaker and provider roles with regard to parenting and child rearing that stress the marital partnership. For many young people, disenchantment and new identity conflicts arise when life goals are not shared. For some people, caring is associated with mutuality of regard and allowing for growth and change in the partnership arrangement (Ganter & Yeakel, 1980).

Young heterosexual couples may need the help of a social worker to resolve initial adjustment problems when they are newly married; they may need help in dealing with two sets of parents—natural parents as well as in-laws—and in acquiring skills for handling the home situation when a child is born.

Homosexual couples, too, present themselves for therapy, and there is a need to understand this lifestyle from an emotional aspect as well as a sociological one, so that the best kind of therapeutic help can be offered. Couples who adopt children are no longer purely heterosexual. There are homosexual couples, as well as single people, who would like to adopt. It is necessary that the social worker understand individuals' hopes and aspirations as well as their capacities, in order to help them formulate realistic yet exciting goals for themselves.

Some people can accept their limitations as well as their strengths more easily than others. Counselors should be sensitive to individuals' need for help to make the transition from an adolescent peer culture to the demands of work and varying lifestyles.

For a large number of young people, the issues of establishing autonomy and intimacy are not resolved during adolescence; they continue to be salient throughout the young-adult years. Social workers need to be aware of such unresolved conflicts.

Besides emotional situations, social workers are often presented problems such as lack of a job or a poor economic situation. Among people who often have difficulties in finding jobs are minorities, women, unskilled workers, and the handicapped. Their situations have a psychological as well as an economic effect; they influence people's aspirations and their perceptions of what is possible for them to achieve.

Chapter Summary

Human behavior and development takes a new turn in adulthood. In adults, growth no longer stems from physical development and the rapid acquisition of cognitive skills. Adult growth is defined to a large extent by social and cultural milestones, as young individuals terminate their dependent relationships with parents and assume responsibility for themselves and others.

Cognitively, there is continued development of formal operational thought during early adulthood.

Erikson's sixth psychosocial crisis is intimacy versus isolation. According to Erikson, to develop successfully, adults have to maintain their identities in order to develop close, intimate heterosexual relationships that lead to procreation. The alternative and negative outcome for this period is self-absorption and isolation.

Studies of adult women suggest that sex-related differences exist in paths of identity. Traditionally, males have defined themselves in terms of separation and autonomy, whereas females seem to achieve identity through relationships and attachment.

Work is an important element in young adulthood. Most adults feel that work is a major aspect of their identity. Some women view their careers in the same way men do, whereas others define themselves primarily in their familial roles. The proportion of women in the labor force has increased dramatically.

Preparation for work includes both formal and informal training. Early socialization, as well as cognitive and emotional development through the early years, sets the stage for later career choices. Career choice is a serious decision for young adults, some of whom may need assistance in developing effective strategies for making choices.

Being successful in work depends upon one's socialization, the ability to adapt to new challenges, and the relationship between the individual's skills and the demands of the labor market. Young people in the labor force have different needs. Some are caught in making a marginal livelihood. Others are concerned with doing work that gives them personal fulfillment. Men follow varying types of career patterns, as specified by Miller and Form. There are the conventional career pattern, the stable career pattern, the unstable career pattern, and the multiple-trial career pattern.

Family life cycles are set into motion by events such as marriage and parenthood. Some people choose singleness as an alternative to marriage. There are many young people cohabiting without marriage. Cohabitation is in many ways a maturing experience, although there are problems associated with it, particularly when young people are dealing with their parents.

A communal marriage is an agreement among three or more families to share living quarters and a division of labor, as well as a means of social involvement. It sometimes includes sexual rights and responsibilities as well as economic arrangements.

There have been a number of studies on extramarital relationships. The problem with studies of such relationships is that statistics cannot reveal the exact number in a given area because at least one partner is married to somebody else, and their responses may not be entirely accurate.

Homosexual relationships vary in context and personal meanings just as heterosexual relationships do. At least one-fourth of homosexual men were married heterosexually.

Another aspect of adult life is intimacy, which usually includes sexual intimacy. Sexual relationships are affected by both internal and external factors. Adults' sexuality includes more than simple gender identity. It includes sensuality, intimacy, reproductive behavior, interpersonal influences, and a sexual identity—that is, an orientation toward one sex (or both sexes) as love object.

Social workers are beginning to learn more about sexuality in order to meet the demand for sexual counseling. There is some question about early claims of high success rates with short-term treatment of sexual dysfunction.

The divorce rate is high in the United States. The high rate could be, in part, the result of the increase in number of women in the labor force and the increased acceptance of the view that unhappy marriages are to be terminated. Divorce entails a painful period of adjustment, even for the spouse who initiates it. Divorced people normally remarry after two to three years.

Parenting confers new social status on young adults, and it also makes unexpected new demands on them. Rossi classifies parenthood into four stages: the anticipatory period, the honeymoon period, the plateau period, and finally the termination period, when children start to leave home.

Besides the nuclear family, Minuchin and Fishman developed structures for familial groups and classified them as pas de deux families, three-generation families, accordion families, and fluctuating families.

There are more single parents today. The rise in single-parent households is due partly to increased rates of divorce and the desire of single women to have children. A large number of single parents have economic problems and so need economic as well as social supports.

Children affect their parents in a variety of ways. There are economic strains. There are changes in the marital relationships of couples. The presence of children affects the sexual practices, the consumption abilities, and the value systems of the parents.

References

Albrecht, S. L. (1979). Correlates of marital happiness among the remarried. *Journal of Marriage and the Family, 41,* 857–868.

Arlin, P. K. (1980, June). Adolescent and adult thought: A search for structures. Paper presented at meeting of the Piaget Society, Philadelphia.

Athanasiou, R., Shaver, P., & Tavris, C. (1970). Sex: A report to *Psychology Today* readers. *Psychology Today, 4,* 39–52.

Athanasiou, R., & Sorkin, R. (1974). Premarital sexual behavior and post marital adjustment. *Archives of Sexual Behavior, 3,* 207–225.

Baruch, G., Barnett, R., & Rivers, C. (1983). *Lifeprints.* New York: McGraw-Hill.

Bell, A. P., & Weinberg, M. S. (1978). *Homosexualities: A study of diversity among men and women.* New York: Simon & Schuster.

Bell, R. Q., & Harper, L. V. (1977). *Child effects on adults.* New York: Wiley.

Bell, R. R., & Peltz, O. (1974). Extramarital sex among women. *Medical Aspects of Human Sexuality, 8,* 10–31.

Bell, R. R., Turner, S., & Rosen, L. A. (1975). Multivariate analysis of female extramarital coitus. *Journal of Marriage and the Family, 37,* 375–384.

Berger, B., et al. (1974). Child rearing practices in the communal family. In A. Skolnick and J. H. Skolnick, *Intimacy, family and society.* Boston: Little, Brown.

Bernard, J. (1972). *The future of marriage.* New York: William Collins.

Bloom, B. L., Asher, S. J., & White, S. W. (1978). Marital disruptions as a stressor: A review and analysis. *Psychiatric Bulletin, 85,* 867–894.

Broderick, C. B. (1982). Adult sexual development. In B. B. Wolman & G. Stricker (Eds.), *Handbook of developmental psychology.* Englewood Cliffs, NJ: Prentice-Hall.

Bukstel, L. H., Roeder, G. D., Kilmann, R., Laughlin, J., & Sotile, W. M. (1978). Projected extramarital sexual involvement in community college students. *Journal of Marriage and the Family, 40,* 337–340.

Carter, E., & McGoldrick, M. (Eds.). (1980). *The family life cycle.* New York: Gardner Press.

Carter, H., & Glick, P. C. (1976). *Marriage and divorce: A social and economic study* (2nd ed.). Cambridge, MA: Harvard University Press.

Cherlin, A. (1979). At issue—cohabitation: How the French and Swedes do it. *Psychology Today, 13*(4).

Chodorow, N. (1978). *The reproduction of mothering.* Berkeley: University of California Press.

Constantine, L. L., & Constantine, J. M. (1977). Sexual aspects of group marriage. In F. W. Libby & R. N. Whitehurst (Eds.), *Marriage and alternatives: Explaining intimate relationships.* Glenview, IL: Scott, Foresman.

Dank, B. M. (1971). Becoming in the gay world. *Psychiatry, 34.*

Davenport, W. (1965). Sexual patterns and their regulation in a society of the Southwest Pacific. In F. A. Beach (Ed.), *Sex and Behavior.* New York: Wiley.

Dinnerstein, D. (1977). *The mermaid and the minotaur.* New York: Harper/Colophon.

Dreyer, P. H. (1975). Sex, sex roles and marriage among youth in the 1970s. In F. J. Havighurst & P. H. Dreyer (Eds.), *Youth: The 74th Yearbook of the National Society for the Study of Education* (Part I). Chicago: University of Chicago Press.

Eichenbaum, L., & Orbach, S. (1983). *Understanding women.* New York: Harper/Colophon.

Edwards, J. N., & Booth, A. (1976). Sexual behavior in and out of marriage: An assessment of correlates. *Journal of Marriage and the Family, 38,* 73–81.

Erikson, E. H. (1958). *Young man Luther.* New York: Norton.

Erikson, E. H. (1969). *Gandhi's truth.* New York: Norton.

Erikson, E. H. (1980). *Identity and the life cycle.* New York: Norton.

Fimrite, R. (1970, July 3). Dish night at the ball park. *San Francisco Chronicle,* p. 48.

Fischer, J., & Gochros, H. (1975). *Handbook of behavior therapy with sexual problems.* New York: Pergamon Press.

Ford, C. S., & Beach, F. (1951). *A pattern of sexual behavior.* New York: Harper & Row.

Furstenberg, F. (1980). Reflections on remarriage. *Journal of Family Issues,*

Gagnon, J. H. (1977). *Human sexualities.* Glenview, IL: Scott, Foresman.

Ganter, G., & Yeakel, M. (1980). *Human behavior and the social environment.* New York: Columbia University Press.

Garfinkel, R. (1982). By the sweat of your brow. In T. M. Field, A. Huston, H. C. Quay, L. Troll, & G. G. Finley (Eds.), *Review of Human Development.* New York: Wiley.

Gilligan, C. (1982). *In a different voice.* Cambridge, MA: Harvard University Press.

Glass, S. P., & Wright, T. R. (1977). The relationship of extramarital sex, length of marriage and sex difference to mental satisfaction and romanticism. Athanasiou's data reanalyzed. *Journal of Marriage and the Family, 39,* 691–703.

Glick, P. C., & Norton, A. (1977). Marrying, divorcing, living together in the U.S. today. *Population Bulletin, 32,* 5.

Gochros, H. L. (1977). Human sexuality. In *Encyclopedia of Social Work.* Washington, DC: National Association of Social Workers.

Gordon, M., & Shankweiler, P. J. (1971, August). Different equals less: Female sexuality in recent marriage manuals. *Journal of Marriage and the Family,* 459–465.

Haley, J. (1984). *Problem solving therapy: New strategies for effective family therapy.* New York: Harper & Row.

Hannan, M. T., et al. (1977, May). Income and marital events: Evidence from an income maintenance experiment. *American Journal of Sociology,* 1186–1210.

Harper, L. V. (1975). The scope of offspring effect: From caregiver to culture. *Psychological Bulletin, 82,* 784–801.

Hetherington, E. M. (1972). Effects of parental absence on personality development in adolescent daughters. *Developmental Psychology, 7,* 313–326.

Hill, C. T., Rubin, Z., & Peplan, L. A. (1979). Breakup before marriage: The end of 103 affairs. In G. Levinger & O. Moles (Eds.), *Divorce and separation: Context, causes and consequences.* New York: Basic Books.

Hite, S. (1976). *The Hite report.* New York: Macmillan.

Hogan, D. P. (1978). The variable order of events in the lifecourse. *American Sociological Review, 43,* 573–586.

Hunt, M. M. (1974). Sexual behavior in the 1970s. Chicago: Playboy Press.

Jacobs, R., & Vinick, B. (1979). *Re-engagement in later life: Re-employment and remarriage.* Stamford, CT: Greylock.

Jones, F. R., Garrison, K. C., & Morgan, R. F. (1985). *The psychology of human development.* New York: Harper & Row.

Kaluger, G., & Kaluger, M. F. (1974). *Human development.* St. Louis: C. V. Mosby.

Kestenberg, J. S. (1970). The effect on parents of the child's transition into and out of latency. In E. J. Anthony & T. Benedek (Eds.), *Parenthood.* Boston: Little, Brown.

Kinsey, A. C., Pomeroy, W. B., & Martin, C. (1948). *Sexual behavior in the human male.* Philadelphia: Saunders.

Kinsey, A. C., Pomeroy, W. B., Martin, C., & Gebhard, P. H. (1953). *Sexual behavior in the human female.* Philadelphia: Saunders.

Kitagawa, E. M., & Hauser, P. M. (1973). *Differential mortality in the US: A study in socio-economic epidemiology.* Cambridge, MA: Harvard University Press.

Kohlberg, L. (1973). Continuities in childhood and adult moral development revisited. In P. B. Baltes & K. W. Schaie (Eds.), *Lifespan developmental psychology*. New York: Academic Press.

Kohn, M. L. (1973). Occupational experience and psychological functioning: An assessment of reciprocal effects. *American Sociological Review, 38*, 97–118.

Kohn, M. L. (1976). Occupational structure and alienation. *American Journal of Sociology, 82*, 111–130.

Kohn, M. L., & Schooler, C. (1978). The reciprocal effects of the substantive complexity of work and intellectual flexibility: A longitudinal assessment. *American Journal of Sociology, 84*, 24–52.

Levin, R. J. (1975, October). The *Redbook* report on premarital and extramarital sex. *Redbook*.

Levin, R. J., & Levin, A. (1975, September). The *Redbook* report: A study of female sexuality. *Redbook*.

Levinger, G. (1966). Sources of marital dissatisfaction among applicants for divorce. *American Journal of Orthopsychiatry, 36*, 803–807.

Levinson, D. J., with Darrow, C. N., Klein, E. B., Levinson, M. H., & McGee, B. (1978). *The seasons of a man's life*. New York: Knopf.

Lief, H. I. (1978). *Homosexualities: A review*. SIECUC Report (No. 2), 1, 13–14.

Lorence, J., & Mortimer, J. T. (In press). *Work experience and work investment. The sociology of work and occupation*.

Macklin, E. D. (1974, November). Cohabitation in college: Going steady. *Psychology Today*, 53–59.

Masters, W. H. (1970, May 25). Repairing the conjugal bed. *Time*, 49ff.

Masters, W. H., & Johnson, V. E. (1970). *Human sexual inadequacy*. Boston: Little, Brown.

McCary, J. I. (1978). *Human sexuality* (3rd ed.). Princeton, NJ: Van Nostrand Reinhold.

Mead, M. (1950). *Sex and temperament in three primitive socieites*. New York: Mentor. (Originally published 1935).

Mead, M., & Newton, N. (1967). Cultural patterns of prenatal behavior. In S. A. Richardson & A. F. Guttmacher (Eds.), *Childbearing: The social and psychological aspects*. Baltimore, MD: Williams & Wilkins.

Miller, D. C., & Form, W. H. (1951). *Industrial sociology*. New York: Harper & Row.

Miller, J. B. (1976). *Toward a new psychology of women*. Boston: Beacon Press.

Minuchin, S., & Fishman, C. (1981). *Family therapy techniques*. Cambridge, MA: Harvard University Press.

Money, J., & Ehrdhardt, A. (1972). *Man and woman, boy and girl*. Baltimore, MD: Johns Hopkins University Press.

Neimark, E. D. (1982). Cognitive development in adulthood. In T. M. Field, A. Huston, H. C. Quay, L. Troll, & G. E. Finley (Eds.), *Review of human development*. New York: Wiley.

Newman, B. M., & Newman, P. R. (1975). *Development through life*. Chicago, IL: Dorsey Press.

Nye, I., Carlson, J., & Garrett, G. (1970). Family size, interaction, affect and stress. *Journal of Marriage and the Family, 32*, 216–226.

Papalia, D. E., & Olds, S. W. (1986). *Human development*. New York: McGraw-Hill.

Pearlin, L. I., & Johnson, J. S. (1975). *Marital status, lifestrains and depression*. Unpublished manuscript.

Piaget, J. (1972). Intellectual evolution from adolescence to adulthood. *Human Development, 15*, 1–12.

Price-Bonham, S., & Balswick, J. O. (1980). The noninstitution: Divorce, desertion and remarriage. *Journal of Marriage and the Family, 42*.

Rapaport, R. (1965). Normal crisis, family structure and mental health. In H. Parad (Ed.), *Crisis intervention*. New York: Family Service Association.

Renne, K. S. (1971). Health and marital experience in an urban population. *Journal of Marriage and the Family, 33,* 338–350.

Rogers, D. (1979). *The adult years*. Englewood Cliffs, NJ: Prentice-Hall.

Ross, H., & Sawhill, I. (1975). *Time of transition: The growth of families headed by women*. Washington, DC: The Urban Institute.

Rossi, A. S. (1968). Transition to parenthood. *Journal of Marriage and the Family, 30,* 26–39.

Ryder, R. G., Kafka, J. S., & Olson, D. H. (1971). Separating and joining influences in courtship and early marriage. *American Journal of Orthopsychiatry, 41,* 450–467.

Scanzoni, J. H. (1971). *The Black family in modern society*. Boston: Allyn & Bacon.

Sears, R. R., Maccoby, E. E., & Levin, H. (1957). *Patterns of child rearing*. Evanston, IL: Rows, Peterson.

Shinar, E. H. (1978). Person perception as a foundation of occupation and sex. *Sex Roles, 4,* 679–693.

Simenauer, J., & Carroll, D. (1982). *Singles: The new Americans*. New York: Simon & Schuster.

Singh, B. K., Walton, B. L., & Williams, J. S. (1976). Extramarital sexual permissiveness: Conditions and contingencies. *Journal of Marriage and the Family, 38,* 701–712.

Specht, R., & Craig, G. J. (1982). *Human development*. Englewood Cliffs, NJ: Prentice-Hall.

Spicer, J. W., & Hampe, G. D. (1975). Kinship interaction after divorce. *Journal of Marriage and the Family, 37,* 113–119.

Stack, F. B. (1972). Black kindreds: Parenthood and personal kindreds among urban Blacks. *Journal of Comparative Family Studies,* 194–206.

Staples, R., & Mirande, A. (1980). Racial and cultural variations among American families: A clinical review of literature on minority families. *Journal of Marriage and the Family, 42.*

Stein, P. J. (1976, September). Being single: Bucking the cultural imperative. Paper presented at the annual meeting of the American Sociological Association.

Stevens-Long, J. (1979). *Adult life*. Los Angeles: Mayfield.

Stone, W. F. (1973). Patterns of conformity in couples varying in intimacy. *Journal of Personality and Social Psychology, 27*(3), 413–419.

Tavris, C., & Sadd, S. J. (1977). *The* Redbook *report on female sexuality*. Englewood Cliffs, NJ: Prentice-Hall.

Treas, J., & Van Hilst, A. (1976). Marriage and remarriage rates among the older Americans. *The Gerontologist, 16.*

U.S. Bureau of the Census. (1976). *Money income of families and persons in the U.S. in 1976*. Washington, DC: U.S. Government Printing Office.

Vaillant, G. E. (1977). *Adaptation to life*. Boston: Little, Brown.

Wallerstein, J. S., & Kelly, J. B. (1980). *Surviving the breakup: How children and parents cope with divorce*. New York: Basic Books.

Wattenberg, E., & Reinhardt, H. (1979, November). Female-headed familes: Trends and implications. *Social Work, 24* (6).

Wolman, B. B., & Money, J. (Eds.). (1980). *Handbook of human sexuality*. Englewood Cliffs, NJ: Prentice-Hall.

Zilbergeld, B., & Evans, M. (1980, August). The inadequacy of Masters and Johnson. *Psychology Today,* 538.

8

Middle Adulthood

Character of the Middle Years

Physical Changes

Cognitive Processes

The Psychosocial Environment

Tasks of Middle Age

Changing Patterns of the Family

Career Adjustments

Implications for Social Work Practice

Chapter Summary

References

This chapter will focus on continuity and change between the ages of 40 and 65—the middle years. The viewpoints of psychologists, sociologists, and economists will be considered.

Middle age is a stage in the lifelong process of growth and development in which biological changes accompany aging and changes in social role. Old age is viewed either as a period of development or as a process of undoing or reversal of development. We enjoy the illusion that we know what is happening in childhood and adolescence, but in some ways we find middle age a difficult period to study. The in-between period does not lend itself so readily to the traditional ways of viewing human behavior and experience. Thus the middle-aged person remains something of a mystery to the developmental theorists. In many ways this period could be viewed as one of "holding on" during which the functional abilities that emerge proceed from the matured developmental process (Kastenbaum, 1979).

> Sheila was a middle-aged woman who had lived all her life in the inner city. She had been married twice and had lived with two men. In her early fifties, she was the mother of four grown children. All her children lived away from home. Sheila was a cleaning woman who earned her livelihood through some routine and some sporadic cleaning jobs. Although she had taken good care of her children, she was frustrated, for her children visited her only when they had to or when they needed some extra money. If she tried to be helpful and give advice, they protested. They were the young and upcoming generation, and they ignored her in order to seek their own power. But she tried hard not to relinquish her power and used her financial position (which was better than her children's) to exert some control over them. In her unique position in the family, she saw stress, aggravation, and harrassment as part of her life.

Middle adulthood is the period that represents the peak of a person's social integration. Although Sheila felt that her children took advantage of her in some ways, she was aware that she had to face important family and occupational responsibilities. To put it in another way, the middle-aged person is usually fully "engaged"—the person has obligations, expectations, and available opportunities to live up to (Cummings & Henry, 1961).

Character of the Middle Years

Definition of the middle years as from about 40 to 65 is approximate; the period can be longer or shorter for different people. Some are biologically slower; unlike those who realize that they are separate from young adults as well as from the elderly, some people appear to be forever young. This age group has often been called the "sandwich generation"; people in it have to meet major responsibilities and simultaneously develop new ways of responding both to grown children and to aging parents. People who are over 50 years of age are different from younger people. They have to learn to accept limitations, such as dietary restrictions, come to terms with what must be, and go on from that point. At age 50, the average person realizes that some of his or her dreams will not come true. For example, a person who always wanted to be rich may never become rich. People accept the lifestyle that they have adopted, can lead the kind of life that makes them happy, and can be satisfied with what they have done.

Juan was a 50-year-old man who had come to Los Angeles at the age of 12 with dreams of making it big in this country. However, he did not have the kind of education that he needed to make it on his own. As a young person he had been labeled as being incapable of doing mathematics, and that assessment demoralized him so much that he made no special effort to study the subject. His parents were fairly illiterate and did not push him to follow academic pursuits. After Juan graduated from high school, he found odd jobs to do until he became a superintendent of a large housing unit in a prestigious area of New York City. He held onto that job, married, and had three children. Meanwhile his aged parents, who also lived in New York City, became his dependents to some extent.

Juan found that he did not have time for following any of his own pursuits; he had to provide for his family as well as for his parents. To manage both, Juan took a second job as a cab driver during what would have been his leisure time. But there was only enough time to allow him just to get by financially. Over a period of time, his dreams of being a wealthy man dissolved. He was able to accept his role as a wage earner and the chief supporter of his family.

Married couples have learned to accept their partners as they are. Long ago they have given up the idea of changing the partner in their life. They accept the person along with his or her limitations. Positive attributes are praised and highlighted, whereas negative qualities are overlooked.

After 40, people also face some problems relating to death and mortality. They will probably begin to lose parents and old friends at this stage.

A person of 50 has no need to keep up with the Joneses. In fact, who cares about the Joneses? Middle-aged people are more worried about their own lives. They do what pleases them, and that is where they find their satisfaction.

People have developed some common sense and learned some valuable lessons from experience that typically have enabled them to get a better job than before. Some people now have their goals well within sight, others have reached their goals, and still others have attained what they had barely dreamed. Many, like Juan in the case study, have put early goals aside in favor of meeting the challenge immediately at hand.

By 40, people know that they are similar to each other. People realize that they do not know everything about life—nobody does—but when they need information, they know where to get it. People tend to become more reality oriented.

Middle adulthood usually involves upward and forward movement. This is the period when a person attempts to attain mastery over the external world and seek material gain. For one in middle adulthood, the characteristic thought is, "If I can maintain what I have already made, I will be happy in my life."

There are both psychological and social cues of having attained middle age. People realize that they have made certain basic decisions about career and family and that the future no longer holds limitless possibilities. Some people face this challenge confidently, whereas others feel a sense of crisis. Older women realize that their children are moving out of the family; others who have not married or had children realize that they may never have any children of their own. Women who have taken care of children and seen them grow up ask what they should do with the rest of their lives. That is why many older people, particularly women, reenter the labor force or go back to school to get a degree after a long hiatus: they are attempting to develop a sense of self.

Pat, at 48, found that she had a great deal of time on her hands. Her children had grown up, and she was by herself at home. There were no extra clothes to wash and no need to make cookies or bake cakes for her children. Though married, Pat felt alone. Her husband was involved in his job and intent on making it up the social and economic ladder. At last, she reached a decision. She made up her mind to take a part-time job. But she found it limiting—in fact, boring—to be a cashier in a supermarket. Pat had always been a creative person. Eventually, with a lot of fears and self-doubts, she decided instead to go back to school and study in a program that would make her feel self-fulfilled and also offer her opportunities to become an economically productive member of society. At last Pat got an opportunity to find her own interests and carry out the plans she made for herself.

Going to school changed her outlook on life. She found that there were interesting topics that she could share with her husband and that she could pursue her own interests in her immediate world. She also started to measure her success by her achievement in school.

Middle age is generally regarded as the period between completion of the traditional roles of child rearing and becoming established as a provider. It is the time when a couple starts to establish and maintain an adequate standard of living; when adults develop leisure time activities, adjust to the physiological changes of middle age, and adapt to aging parents. The most important challenge of this stage is to develop command of one's inner impulses, as well as competence in dealing with the responsibilities of the outer world. As Specht and Craig (1982) put it, this is when the middle-aged parents assume the power of the older generation and, more commonly, ensure the future of the younger generation. Middle age ensures more personal freedom, reduced economic strain, greater availability of leisure time, and fewer demands for material growth.

The developmental tasks of middle adulthood are both interpersonal and intrapersonal in nature. For many people, this is the first time they give weight to the comforts of life.

Physical Changes
Health

The body is functioning at its peak when a person is in middle adulthood. This characteristic distinguishes the middle adult from the older adult. Barring diseases, most people can withstand the physical rigors of the middle adult years. A few wrinkles appear in the face as the skin becomes dry and loses elasticity. There is a redistribution of fatty tissues and a limit to the expenditure of energy. Few middle-aged people can pursue career goals relentlessly and hope to fulfill all their social goals as well.

People place a lot of emphasis on physical fitness. Men are endlessly jogging, running, and working out in the gym. Women also tend to take care of themselves, but they place more attention on their mates than they did when they were younger.

The sense organs of middle-aged people change at an amazingly uniform rate. One of the most notable changes occurs in the eyes. Many people confront the shock of being middle aged when they find that they have to wear bifocal lenses. This change is the reason older people begin to hold their books or other reading material at arm's length. The condition usually develops when a person is 40 to 50 years of age.

There are internal changes as well—some physical decline and slowing down. Sensitivity to taste, smell, and pain decreases during this period. Other biological functions, such as reaction time and sensorimotor skills, may begin to slow. Motor skills may decline, but skills that have been learned and long practiced remain constant because of the many hours of experience (Ebersole, 1979). A skipper of a ship or a golf player will not experience any change in performance.

There is a slowing of the nervous system and a stiffening of the skeleton. The heart pumps blood with less force through the body, and the opening of the arteries is one-third less in middle age than it was in young adulthood. Lung capacity is reduced and thus lowers the potential for hard labor (Brody, 1979).

When people adjust themselves to a slower pace in life, they preserve their energies for special occasions. By exercising regularly, people can conserve and maximize strength in middle age (Timiras, 1972).

Climacteric

Sexual changes take place during this period. The term *climacteric* refers to the complex changes—that is, both physical and emotional—that accompany hormonal changes in midlife. In women it consists essentially of a gradual decline in ovarian functioning and the associated products (sex hormones and eggs) and the eventual cessation of menstruation (menopause). Women at this stage can also have shortened orgasms and a lessening of vaginal lubrication (Masters & Johnson, 1970). The age of menopause varies from the thirties to the sixties, with the median age being 50 years (McKinlay, Jefferys, & Thompson, 1972).

Menopause is not such a stressful period for women as has been thought, according to a research study done by Neugarten, Wood, Kraines, and Loomis (1963). When women who were 21 to 65 years of age were asked to respond to a checklist designed to measure attitudes toward menopause, some women reported concern about the resulting inability to reproduce. Anxiety related to the anticipation of menopause was greater than the anxiety reported as actually experienced. In this study, Neugarten et al. (1963) found no relationship between menopausal status and a variety of personality traits.

Some women do experience dizziness, palpitations, and "hot flashes" during menopause, and some feel depressed. However, Neugarten and her colleagues found that about 75% of the women in their study did not feel that menopause affected them in any important way. As with other changes, reactions to climacteric depend on extent of hormonal imbalance, individual personality makeup, cultural expectations, and degree of situational stress. Some women enjoy sex less because they are depressed; others enjoy it more because they do not have to worry about becoming pregnant. Similarly, Bart and Grossman (1978) found no relationship between menopausal status and self-evaluation in middle-aged women.

The experience of menopause is influenced by social class as well as cultural context. For example, menopause is seen as a turning point in cultures that emphasize the centrality of the child-bearing role for women (Datan, Maoz, Antonovsky, & Wijsenbeek, 1970). The bulk of evidence shows that menopause is not a particularly stressful period for most women in the United States (Lerner & Hultsch, 1983).

Considerable negative connotation nevertheless accrues to menopause (Newman & Newman, 1975). Young women associate it with all the negative connotations of growing old. This is because the younger woman is vested in her role as a mother and fearful of a potential end to her years of childbearing. The older woman, however, awaits the future of new roles and new freedoms.

Menopause is a significant symbolic event. For those successful in developing a sense of personal achievements, in personal life as well as in child rearing, menopause signifies not only the end of childbearing years but also the beginning of a period in which new energy is directed toward broader, community-oriented tasks.

Many women experience decreased production of estrogen and a temporary hormonal imbalance. Some doctors correct this condition by estrogen replacement therapy. The artificial supplementation of the female sex hormone reduces the potentially damaging side effects of menopause that have been identified, such as increased likelihood of uterine cancer.

There is not much information about the male climacteric. Many professionals have said that men also undergo changes in their middle years, but their changes are gradual and less dramatic. During the middle years, some men experience delayed erection and also reduced pressure in ejaculation. Middle-aged men experience a gradual decrease in the level of androgen, a male hormone, and a decrease in fertility and potency (Fried, 1967). Since "menopause" means the cessation of the menses, the use of that term to refer to men is incorrect. Males do, however, experience age-related changes in the reproductive system. For instance, there is a gradual decline in sperm production, although viable sperm is produced even by the oldest men. But unlike estrogen supply, androgen production declines over a long period of time. In spite of the gradualness of the reduction, men in the middle years have reported impotence and frequent urination. Some men and women experience similar symptoms in climacteric (Ruebsaat & Hull, 1975); some men, too, report a loss of self-confidence or become irritable, fatigued, and depressed. Whereas some symptoms are caused by changes in hormonal imbalance, others are caused by psychological stress, such as job pressure, boredom with a sex partner, family responsibilities, ill health, or the fear of ill health. Any or all of these changes may cause the individual to believe that he is losing his sexual abilities. However, there is no time in a man's life when he completely loses his sexual abilities as a result of aging itself.

Although a large number of individuals can enjoy full sex lives for many more years, there is a decline in overall sexual activity for most. Among people with sexual dysfunctions, obtaining a competent sex counselor is often difficult. Some sexual problems are treated by social workers, who do not belong to the medical profession but undergo specialized training to deal with such issues (Gochros, 1977).

Disease

As people grow older, their bodies age. Middle-aged people become aware of the effects of aging and their own mortality as they find out that their friends and older family members are dying. For Americans under the age of 34, the primary cause of death is accidents; within a few years, the leading cause of death is disease (U.S. Bureau of the Census, 1978b).

Cardiovascular diseases—heart disease, arteriosclerosis, and hypertension—are the causes of nearly 40% of all deaths in the United States. Throughout middle age, this threat is greater for men than it is for women. One-third of all deaths of men between the ages of 45 and 54 are caused by coronary arterial problems (Ebersole, 1979).

Cancer is the second major cause of death in the United States, and it too claims more lives of men than of women. Men are also more apt to get respiratory diseases in middle age. Diabetes occurs in increasing numbers of people and with increasing severity in middle age; however, it affects more women than men (U.S. Bureau of the Census, 1978a). Some diseases, such as arthritis, are not fatal but certainly trouble middle-aged people of both sexes.

There are interconnections among stress, personality, and genetic factors. Because men are more often the victims of heart disease, most studies of contributing factors have focused on men. Heart attacks are most common for women in executive positions. The number of women dying from breast cancer has diminished dramatically, whereas the number of women dying from respiratory disease has increased considerably.

In a study by Rosenman (1974), about 3400 men from ages 39 to 59 were examined and then reexamined at the end of two and a half and eight and a half years to determine how behavior habits affected the incidence of heart disease. At one extreme there were what researchers called *Type A personality* people, who were highly competitive, aggressive, impatient, and achievement oriented. Their muscles were tensed up and they were always functioning with a sense of urgency.

> Adrian, 47, was a busy executive of a large company. He was always attending company parties, working 14 hours per day, and flying around the country to expand his already large business. He would make a deal with anyone who could help his company get bigger and better than his competitors. He hardly had time for his family, and all his wife and children saw of him were his quick arrivals and departures. One day while traveling on a plane he had a sudden heart attack and died. Death at 47 of heart attack is not unusual for Type A personalities.

At the opposite extreme were men of Type B personality—patient, easygoing, and relaxed. In Rosenman's study, 10% of the subjects were defined as Type A or B personalities and the rest were somewhere in between. Among the men who developed coronary disease it was found that there were twice as many Type A who developed coronary disease as Type B men. The researchers found that the biochemistry of Type A personalities was similar to that of people who had a history of heart disease. In Type A men there were higher serum cholesterol levels and more accelerated blood coagulations than in Type B men. Such men also had more stress hormones in their blood during working hours. Type B men rarely developed coronary heart disease, irrespective of how much fatty food they ate, the number of cigarettes they smoked, or how little they exercised (Rosenman, 1974).

Cognitive Processes
Slowing Down

There is clear evidence that as people get older they slow down in performing speeded tasks (Welford, 1958, 1977). Speeded tasks are those in which errors would be unlikely if the individual had an unlimited amount of time to complete them. Usually they involve relatively simple responses such as pushing buttons or sorting items. The objective is to complete the task as quickly as possible.

Reaction time can measured in time that elapses between the appearance of a signal and the beginning of a responding movement. Reaction time (RT), which is part of the central nervous system's processing, involves perceptual and decision-making processes. For example, simple RT tasks involve only one signal and one response (such as pushing a button when a light goes on). Disjunctive RT tasks involve multiple signals and/or responses (such as pushing the right-hand button when the red light goes on and the left-hand button when the green light goes on, or pushing the button only when the red light goes on). Hodgkins (1962) examined simple RT performance (subject released a key when a signal light was lit) in more than 400 females of 6 to 84 years of age. Hodgkins found that mean speed increased with age until the late teens, remained constant until the middle twenties, and then declined steadily throughout the remainder of the age range. The degree of change in RT was 25% between the twenties and the sixties and 43% between the twenties and the seventies. The slowing down seen with age in simple RT tasks was magnified in the area of disjunctive RT tasks (Griew, 1958) and tasks requiring the subject to remember previous signals and responses (Kay, 1954). Slowing down was also seen in sorting tasks (Botwinick, Robbin, & Brinley, 1960).

As Lerner and Hultsch (1983) implied, the slowing of behavior appears with age in a wide range of tasks. Indeed, it appears to be a general characteristic of older adults. Younger adults may be fast or slow, depending on the characteristics of the task and situation—that is, for example, on familiarity and motivation. Older adults, however, seem to slow down generally (Birren, Riegel, & Morrison, 1962). This general slowing down does not appear to be primarily a function of peripheral nerve factors, such as sensory acuity (Botwinick, 1971), speed of peripheral nerve conduction (Birren & Botwinick, 1955), or speed of movement once a response is initiated (Botwinick & Thompson, 1966). It does appear to reflect a basic change in the way the central nervous system processes information (Birren, 1974).

Intellectual Functions

Early theorists surmised that intelligence reaches its peak when a person is between 18 and 25 years of age (Wechsler, 1958). However, this early descriptive work suffers from a number of methodological problems. Most of it was based on measures of intelligence that were developed within a strictly theoretical framework.

Later the question was reframed: does intelligence really decline with age? Although research has been extensive since Wechsler's study, we have witnessed an increase, not a decrease, in controversy over the timing, extent, and sources of intellectual change during adulthood. On the one hand, Baltes and Schaie (1974) have concluded that general intellectual decline in middle and old age is largely a myth. On the other hand, Botwinick (1977) has concluded that decline in intellectual abilities is clearly a part of the aging picture. The disagreements reflect differing sets of assumptions, which in turn reflect varying degrees of theoretical versus methodological approaches to the phenomenon. One solution is to discriminate types of intelligence and the ways in which they develop.

Certainly intelligence does change as people grow older. There are two types of intellectual ability commonly discerned. The first broad area of functioning, called *fluid intelligence*, appears mainly in the speed and effectiveness of neurological and physiological factors. This area includes such abilities as motor speed, induction, and memory. The term *fluid* refers to the fact that this type of intelligence can flow into various intellectual activities, including perception, recognition, and dealing cognitively with new information (Horn, 1970, Neugarten, 1977). Fluid intelligence seems to increase until late adolescence and then decline gradually (Knox, 1977, Neugarten, 1976). However, by the end of middle age it has declined only to the level that it occupied during the middle of adolescence, which is still high (Specht & Craig, 1982).

Crystallized intelligence can be described as the ability to process and record the kind of information that can be acquired through both formal and informal education. This includes verbal reasoning, vocabulary, comprehension, and aspects of spatial perception. Unlike fluid intelligence, crystallized intelligence increases over the life span, including through the middle years (Neugarten, 1976).

An increase in crystallized intelligence helps people in their forties and fifties compensate for any decline in fluid intelligence and thereby maintain their earlier overall level of intelligence. The exception is skills requiring various psychomotor processes, which do slow down in later years (Botwinick, 1977). (Declines in intellectual performance due to memory problems are more noticeable after middle age and will be discussed in Chapter 9.)

Knox (1977) and others use the term *cognitive style* to refer to a person's characteristic pattern of information processing. For instance, some people are characteristically reflective and deliberate, whereas others are impulsive. Some see the world in a clear black–white pattern, whereas others look at shades of gray. Some are tolerant of ambiguity, whereas others are intolerant. Is there is a difference in cognitive style as a person grows older? Does a person getting older—say a 50-year-old man—solve a problem the same way he did when he was 20 years of age?

Research seems to indicate that most cognitive patterns are developed in childhood and continue to be individualized in adulthood. They seem primarily to be part of the personality type and are also associated with early training and cultural lifestyle. Some people appear to shift toward analytic thinking sometime between childhood and adolescence, with the shift becoming more stable in early adulthood. Many aspects of cognitive style become rigid between middle age and old age (Knox, 1977).

The issue of cognitive style is particularly important in casework services, training programs, and formal and informal education for the middle aged. It is important to recognize that some middle-aged people may have difficulty in learning concepts, not because of a lack of intellectual ability but because of their inflexible cognitive styles. Being aware of this phenomenon may enable educators to help older students improve their intellectual performance (Knox, 1977). If educators understand a person's thought processes, they are better able to represent information in a way that is easily understood. This understanding is also of value in helping caseworkers assess the cognitive styles of their clients.

Miriam was 50 years of age and was returning to school after a lapse of nearly 30 years. In school, she appeared to perform very well in one class that made use of life experiences, but she failed miserably when she had to deal with new material that was statistically oriented. Her problem appeared to be not in the subject per se but in the cognitive style she had developed toward the subject while she was still in high school, where anything dealing with numbers was considered difficult. Her intellectual abilities in the area of mathematics had not been developed and, coupled with her attitude, that weakness created problems for her as she studied statistics.

The Psychosocial Environment
Erikson: Generativity versus Stagnation

Middle adulthood brings a new capacity for directing the course of action of one's own life and the lives of others. The adult now attempts to fulfill his or her long-term goals. From Erikson's perspective (Erikson, 1980), a middle-aged person grows by resolving the conflict of generativity versus stagnation; this growth can be understood as a response to pressure to improve life conditions for future generations.

Developmental factors in middle adulthood include mastering the ability to make decisions, planning for the future, and anticipating the needs of others, in order to make a meaningful impact on the future.

Generativity can be described as the capacity for contributing to the survival of any society. At some point, adult members of the society begin to feel an obligation to give their resources, skills, and creativity to the cause of improving the quality of life of the young. To some extent they are motivated by recognition of the inevitability of mortality. People cannot live forever, nor can they direct the overall course of events. It is common to notice people in this age group making contributions to society, on both personal and public levels, that will stand after their deaths. These contributions usually take the form of some personal, unique, creative expression of values and often reflect the wish to share what they have learned.

At a more practical level, generativity is expressed in the contribution of money, time, and/or skills to charitable groups. The skills of middle adulthood, as they give new direction to the efforts of growing institutions, thus become valued by the entire community.

At the other extreme of generativity is stagnation, which reflects a failure to meet the demands of the earlier stages of life. Stagnation usually implies a lack of psychological movement or growth. Adults who devote their energy and skills to the sole purpose of self-aggrandizement and personal satisfaction are likely to have difficulty looking beyond their own needs or experiencing satisfaction in taking care of others. Adults who are not capable of managing a household, raising children, or managing a career are likely to feel a psychological sense of stagnation at the end of middle age.

The experience of stagnation may differ for the narcissistic adult and the depressed adult. Narcissistic adults may expend their energy accumulating wealth and material possessions. They relate to others in terms of how others can serve them. This kind of person can exist quite happily until the physical and psychological consequences of aging begin to have their impact. At that point, their self-satisfaction can be undermined by anxieties related to death. Newman and Newman (1975) indicate that it is not uncommon for individuals of this type to undergo some form of religious "conversion" after a serious illness or emotional crisis that makes them acknowledge the limitations of a totally self-involved lifestyle.

Depressed people who do not make contributions to society may perceive themselves as being incapable of doing so on account of insufficient resources. These people usually have low self-esteem, are very doubtful about opportunities for improvement in the future, and are unwilling to invest any energy in conceptualizing future progress. Both the narcissistic and the depressed types fail to move beyond their own relatedness to themselves and cannot contribute to the future of the larger society.

> Isaac was a 50-year-old man who lived in the inner city. He was orphaned at a young age and had lived in the homes of many relatives. He was used to periodic changes in the rules and regulations of behavior. His self-esteem was always low because he never really learned to become part of any particular family. In middle age Isaac was still unmarried and very involved with his personal problems. He viewed life in terms of his own narrow personal needs. He expected everyone to cater to him, and that attitude prevented him from being successful in making friends or developing a career. He earned a comfortable enough livelihood, but he spent all his time hoarding money and living a meager life. Isaac appeared to be more of a stagnated individual than a productive, useful citizen who could think in broad terms.

True to the pattern of resolution of other psychological crises, a person cannot expect to have a sense of generativity until the end of the developmental phase. All the person's life experiences with home, family, and career management contribute to the needed sense of competence, which in turn helps the person pursue a course of action that will have direct impact on others. A person who is generative in his or her middle adulthood becomes aware of the ways in which society needs improvement and begins to generate creative ideas for resolving societal problems. Generative people begin to put into effect many of the creative solutions that they have conceptualized.

Men's Development

Vaillant (1977) headed the Grant study, a developmental project that began in 1938. A group of 268 male Harvard University students, chosen because they were healthy and self-reliant, were tested, interviewed, and followed for a number of years. The researchers found that the lives of their subjects were shaped not by isolated traumatic events, but by the quality of their sustained relationships with other people.

The researchers also looked at the adaptive functions of defense mechanisms. They found that repression and projection were meaningful adult coping styles. Coping capacities were classified as mature, immature, or neurotic. Vaillant found that mature and neurotic mechanisms were used by healthy men. However, those who used mature adaptive mechanisms were the most well-adjusted men.

Vaillant's findings coincide with Erikson's adult life scheme, but Vaillant terms this stage "Career Consolidation." It occurs between intimacy versus isolation and generality versus stagnation.

One subject of this research explains the typical pattern of these bright and achieving men:

"At 20 to 30, I think I learned how to get along with my wife. From 30 to 40, I learned how to be a success at my job. And at 40 to 50, I worried less about myself and more about my children" (Vaillant, 1977, 206).

Vaillant found that at age 20 these men were very much under parental dominance. In their twenties and sometimes in their thirties, these men spent time gaining autonomy and finding women to marry. By 25 to 35 years, these men worked hard at consolidating their careers and, by age 40, the career consolidation stage had ended. After this period, men may leave the compulsive, unreflective busy work and start to explore their inner selves (Vaillant, 1977).

In another study, Levinson, Darrow, Klein, Levinson, and McKee (1978) at Yale University conducted in-depth interviews of 40 men between the ages of 35 and 45. There were ten men in each of the following occupational groups: hourly workers in industry, academic biologists, business executives, and novelists. The purpose of the study was to show that the goal of an adult person is to build a *life structure*. The structure has both external and internal aspects to it. The external consists of participation in the sociocultural world of the individual, including his family, occupation, and other major external events. The internal consists of the individual's values, dreams, and emotional life. The researchers divided men's lives into two kinds of periods: stable periods, which generally last 6 to 8 years, and transitional periods, which last up to 5 years during which the men reappraise their lives and explore new possibilities.

There are 4 transitional periods leading to adulthood, and the first three are called novice stages. The first stage, *early adult transition*, usually occurs between the ages of 17 and 24 as a man moves from preadulthood to adulthood. During this time he leaves his parents' home and becomes financially and emotionally independent. The young man may go to college or into the armed forces, thereby entering an institution midway between childhood and full adult status.

Here is a typical (humorous) letter from a 19-year-old who has just entered college and needs financial help from his parents or even his sister. It was written on a torn cover of a book and mailed in an envelope made from a shopping bag to show how desperate he was:

Dear Mom, Dad, and Cathy:

This is a plea for help from your beloved son and beloved brother at Elon College. Due to unexpected expenses, I have run into some financial difficulty.

If you can find it within your heart to send me a few pennies it would be greatly appreciated.

I hope you *rich people* at home think of me when you sit down to a good meal. This letter is not meant to be a joke. *I am running kind of low on cash.*

I meant to ask you on Sunday but I forgot.

Just send me a little gift in the mail this week.
Your poor college student,
Steve.

The second stage is called *entering the adult world* (ages 22 to 28). The young man is now more in the adult world and less in his family of origin. It is at this time that he begins to build his first life structure. He may choose an occupation and become involved with women, which may lead to marriage. Two major features of this phase are the *dream* and the *mentor*. The young person may dream of becoming a well-known writer, which may motivate greater achievements. If this dream is not fulfilled, he may experience an emotional crisis later in his life. The second major feature of this period is the influence of a mentor, who may be 8 to 15 years older than the young man. The mentor offers guidance and inspiration both in career and personal matters.

The third stage is called the *age-30 transition* (28 to 30 years). The young man now reevaluates the commitments he made during the preceding decade and he now makes strong commitments for the first time. Some men slip into this stage with ease, whereas others experience developmental crises. Problems with marriage may arise and divorce may result; some change jobs or settle down after a period of uncertainty.

This is a crucial period. If a man has made sound choices, he will have built a strong foundation for his life structure. However, if he has made poor life decisions, he may have difficulty during the next stage.

Settling down is the fourth stage in middle adulthood, and it is during this period that a man builds his second adult life structure. By this time, he has set specific goals for himself, including establishing roots in family, occupation, and community. Now he attempts to become his own boss. At times he may be at odds with his wife, children, boss, and coworkers, and he may even discard his mentor. As identified by Levinson, the five different patterns occurring in this period are classified as sequences. A man may:

1. advance within a stable life structure,
2. experience serious failure or decline within a stable life structure,
3. start a new sequence in his life by trying a new life structure,
4. produce a change in life structure, or
5. remain in flux and experience an unstable life structure.

Women's Development

We deliberately present women's development as separate from men's. Although men and women complement each other and need each other, they are brought up to respond differently to situations and to life itself.

Horner (1972) found that there was something different about the anxiety women feel and show in reaching achievements. McClelland approached the concept of success from the point of view of "hope of success" and "fear of failure" at the same time. On the basis of her studies of women, Horner identified a third category, "fear of success." When women have a conflict between femininity and success, their dilemma has to be viewed differently from that of men. Sassen (1980) mentions that the conflicts that women face could be due to a heightened perception of their success as being bought at the price of someone else's failure. This perception suggests an underlying sense that something is rotten in the state when success is defined as being better than anyone else. Sassen reveals that Horner found success anxiety to be present in most women only when competition was directly connected with being successful at the expense of another person's failure.

Virginia Woolf (1929) observed that women's values are different from men's values. Women's deference to others is rooted in their social subordination as well as in the substance of their moral concern (Woolf). Being sensitive to others and assuming responsibility for taking care of others may lead women to voice opinions other than their own and to include in their judgments other points of view. Thus a woman's sense of morality is manifest in an apparent diffusion and confusion of judgment that is inseparable from her moral strength and her dominant concern with relationships as well as responsibilities (Gilligan, 1982).

When men describe themselves, their involvement with others is tied to a qualification of identity rather than to its realization. Whereas attachment is central to a woman's identity, for men individual achievement and great ideas or distinctive activity define the standard of self-assessment and success (Gilligan, 1982).

Theories put forth by Erikson (1968), Levinson (1977), and Vaillant (1977) have been the most influential theories pertaining to adult development. They have also been male oriented in their theoretical concepts and research examples. However, in recent years other researchers have begun studying the female experience of middle age and found it to be different in many ways from the role model of development (Barnett & Baruch, 1978, Baruch, Barnett, & Rivers, 1983, Rubin, 1979, Sheppard & Seidman, 1982).

Researchers Grace Baruch and Rosalind Barnett used questionnaires to study 298 women between the ages of 35 and 55, who had an average educational level of 2 years beyond high school, and an annual income range that averaged between $4500 and $50,000 (Barnett, 1985, Baruch, Barnett, & Rivers, 1983). The participants included: (1) employed women who had never married; (2) employed married women with children; (3) employed married women without children; (4) divorced women with children; (5) married homemakers with children; and (6) married homemakers without children.

In all, 60 women (about ten in each of the six groups) were individually interviewed. The purpose of the study was to learn about the pleasures, problems, and conflicts that these people found in their lives. This questionnaire was also administered to a random sample of 238 other women in the six categories mentioned above.

This research discovered that the two basic elements that determine the level of mental health experienced by these women are the degree of control that a woman had over her life, which the researchers called *mastery*, and the amount of *pleasure* the woman experienced from it. These criteria were not related to age, for the older women felt as good about themselves as younger women did. There was no evidence of a midlife crisis. There was no relationship between well-being of a woman and her marital status, having children, or whether she was pre- or post-menopausal. What emerged was evidence that the combination of a woman's work and her intimate relationships was of vital importance to her mental health.

Receiving pay for her work proved to be the most reliable predictor of mastery, while experiencing a positive relationship with her husband (including a good sex life), and children was the best predictor of pleasure. A challenging job with good pay that gave a woman an opportunity to use her talents, skills, and ability to make decisions added to the psychological well-being of a woman. The women who scored highest on both mastery and pleasure were employed married women with children and the lowest scores were from unemployed childless married women. The researchers concluded that the well-being of a woman is enhanced by taking on multiple roles, in spite of the stress that goes along with active involvement in several important aspects of life simultaneously. It was more stressful to be underinvolved, not having enough to do, with few personal and occupational demands. This study presented a positive view of women in their midlife transitions.

Tasks of Middle Age

Throughout their lives, people must accomplish certain developmental tasks in order to feel satisfied with their lives. Havighurst (1953) described the tasks of middle age in practical terms; that is, one needs to discharge adult civic and social responsibility and to establish and maintain an adequate standard of living. As mentioned earlier, the basic issue facing people at this time is generativity versus stagnation.

Peck, another theorist, has added some key concepts to Erikson's formulation and proposed a number of issues or conflicts that people face in middle age:

1. Valuing wisdom versus valuing physical powers. During this period there is a decrease in physical stamina and an increase in health problems that cause people to shift a good part of their energies into mental rather than physical activities.

2. Socializing versus sexualizing in human relationships. Many people have physical and social constraints imposed on them by divorce or widowhood that force them to redefine their relationships and emphasize companionship rather than sexual intimacy or competitiveness.

3. Emotional and mental flexibility versus rigidity. People make adjustments in middle age as families and friends move away and as new situations call for changed mental attitudes.

The rest of Peck's stages are more relevant to old age, but they begin in middle age:

1. Ego differentiation versus work-role preoccupation. Many people define themselves solely in terms of work roles, and those people tend to become disoriented when they begin to lose those roles through retirement, unemployment, or having children leave home.

2. Body transcendence (when a person's self is not wholly dependent on their sense of physical well-being) versus body preoccupation. Body transcendence is central to the individual's ability to avoid preoccupation with the increasing aches and pains that accompany aging.

3. Ego transcendence versus ego preoccupation. Ego transcendence means that people should not be mired in thoughts of death; rather, they learn to age successfully and transcend the prospect of their own extinction by becoming involved with the younger generation and accepting the fact that their legacy will outlive them (Specht & Craig, 1982).

Unlike Erikson's stages, each of which corresponds to a specific life phase, none of Peck's dimensions is completely confined to middle age or old age. The decisions made early in life act as building blocks to the solutions of middle age which in turn help to resolve some of the issues of old age.

Changing Patterns of the Family

In North American culture, relatively few families consist of three generations living together, with an additional aunt or an uncle. The nuclear family remains a constant, despite the rising divorce rate. The nuclear family, with two parents and children, plays a significant role in society by providing models for children. However, many functions that are associated with the family are taken over at least in part by a number of agencies. The functions of vocational guidance, recreation, religion, and social activities are carried on largely outside the family. In the present society, the major function of the family is to provide a basic facility for furnishing housing, food, and clothes; serving as an economic unit; inculcating values; and being a reference point for various governmental agencies in implementation of rules and regulations (Glick, 1975).

Jones, Garrison, and Morgan (1985) describe the role of middle-age people as including the tasks of emancipating teenage children and at the same time taking care of aging parents. (There is the additional problem of forwarding one's own interests.) Most people feel a need to take care of their parents, yet grandparents as well as grandchildren do not seem to want to live together. However, when people have limited economic circumstances and the health of older people is precarious, living together may be a necessity. There may well be advantages in such household arrangements, since some elderly grandparents have excellent rapport with young children and on occasion may look after their grandchildren. Some grandparents also contribute financial help to the family.

The manner in which older parents live depends on their socioeconomic status. Older persons with upper-class status usually retain their high status until their demise and frequently live alone, whereas older persons without adequate financial resources have to be dependent upon their children or on the state.

> Rachel was a 55-year-old woman who had been widowed for 20 years. Although she had had many opportunities to get married, she had avoided them and brought up her children single-handedly. After her children grew up she lived by herself and enjoyed the independence and quietness that life offered her. She was well-to-do and did not depend on her children for anything; in fact, she helped them out considerably. Rachel was an active member of a recreational club and headed many social and charitable organizations. She often contributed money to charitable causes.

Among middle-aged people, there is often considerable hostility between generations, only seldom involving money. Unresolved parent–child conflicts may surface when generations live together (Havighurst, 1972). Middle-aged people may start to help their older parents if either becomes chronically ill or one of them dies. At this point, the roles of parent and child reverse as middle-aged children assume all or part of the caretaking role from their parents. Adult children offer their parents economic assistance and transportation, as well as sharing holidays and travel, doing chores for them, and providing gifts for them. When parents have a disabling disease and cannot or will not live alone, then their children's intervention is imperative. Action on behalf of the parent could mean having a housekeeper in the parent's home, sending the parent away to a nursing home or to another relative's home, or bringing the parent into their own home. In caring for an ailing parent in one's own home, patience and fortitude are crucial.

> David and Toni were in their fifties. They had four adult children, two of whom were in college and required the assistance of their parents in pursuing their educational goals. Suddenly, Toni's 70-year-old father died of a heart attack and her mother was left alone without much economic support and no one to take care of her. She suffered from arthritis, which made it difficult for her to do anything useful in the household. So Toni, together with her husband, had to make the decision of whether it would be constructive to bring her mother into their household. David was agreeable but worried about having enough space for his children when they came home. They were both concerned about money and the need to make provisions for their children as well as providing special medical attention for Toni's mother. Eventually, after a long discussion, the couple decided to bring Toni's mother into their home. Although at times she was viewed as a burden, she contributed to the family in terms of emotional support both for her college-aged grandchildren and for her daughter and son-in-law.

When middle-aged adults bring their parents into a home where they have children of their own, the logistics of maintaining life as usual involve reestablishing rules of behavior to ensure everyone is treated with respect. Setting up such rules demands exceeding skill. If the relationship between the older parent and the adult child was good in the early years, then the child's expectations and feelings about the necessary adjustment will be realistic, making this task less awesome. In time it can become a rewarding experience. Some families may need to have counseling by family-service agencies to facilitate the transitional phase of relocation.

> Irene was in her fifties and lived with her second husband and their seven children. A few of the children were grown up and living away from home, but the rest were at home attending school and holding part-time jobs. Irene and her husband both had to work to meet all the household expenses. Irene's mother, who had been a single parent all her adult life, lived with them. It was a blessing to have her in the house; she took care of major household responsibilities and prepared a hot meal when the family came home for dinner. Moreover, the grand-mother received Social Security benefits, which she shared with the family. This type of living arrangement facilitates a meaningful livelihood for all members of the household.

Middle-Age Parenting Roles

According to Jones, Garrison, and Morgan (1985) there are two tasks that middle-aged parents have to perform: (1) they have to relate successfully to their children and help to emancipate them into the adult world, and (2) they have to adjust to the children's absence. The first of these tasks is difficult; parents have to let go of their children and allow them to become independent. Parents have to compromise, at least partially, on matters that involve their children's friends, styles of dress, vocational interests, and personal tastes. As children get older, the only manner by which parents can assist them is through discussion and examples that serve to inculcate values. When adult children have marital problems, many parents cannot stay out of their arguments, and their interference can complicate the situation. Keeping out of adult children's problems is difficult, particularly when they are serious—for example, the partner's drug abuse, multiple infidelity, or physical abuse.

The roles of middle-aged parents change according to the needs of their adult children. Some mothers reestablish closer bonds with their children through advice giving and taking a keen interest in the grandchildren. If there are problems between a daughter and her husband or a son and his wife, the mother may attempt to help ease the situation if she cares about her children. At times, though, interference from her as the mother-in-law may also create problems.

In middle age, Gutmann (1964) believes men become more passive and women become more protective and aggressive. Rosenberg and Farrell (1976) state that the mother's role in nurture and aggression is important to the family's emotional life. In time, "she pushes her husband from the stage and seems to draw strength from his decline" (p. 163). Men are less authoritarian during this period and men of lower class often abdicate any decision making about their children, leaving the field to their wives, particularly when the children have overtaken them in education. Many mothers of all classes serve as confidantes to their daughters.

> Vivian was 27. The more involved she became in her own family life, the more she seemed to need the help and support of her 53-year-old mother. Vivian had more in common with her mother than ever before and spent time talking to her mother about her children, her husband, and some of the money problems they seemed to have. She visited her mother frequently, helping her in household chores and sharing neighborly gossip.

Postparenthood

The postparenthood family is becoming more and more common in North America. This could be due to the trend toward smaller families with fewer children. Only recently have both parents lived long enough to see the marriage of their youngest child. On the average, men are about 54 and women about 51 when their children start to get married, and many middle-aged couples have completed their child-rearing roles before they reach 60 years of age. However, there is another new trend that may postpone postparenthood, as couples starting families later results in older parents.

The departure of children demands readjustment by both parents. Several areas of development are affected by these critical changes in roles. The relationship between husband and wife changes as the parental role diminishes. Each parent often undergoes an introspective evaluation of his or her performance as a parent. When children leave home during their parents' middle years, some women experience the "empty nest" syndrome, causing them to seek jobs or other activities. Finally, parents have to recognize that the energy and resources they formerly put into child rearing are available for other purposes, and so they search for new outlets.

If a couple has had a meaningful relationship, the quality of life usually improves when children leave home. If not, the change leads to deterioration in the relationship, which may result in a poor marriage maintained for economic and social purposes or may end in divorce. Improvement in the quality of life comes about as people have more time for themselves and as family resources that had been committed to educating and caring for children are used for travel, redecorating, clothes, and entertainment. For many grandparenting will soon begin. When they take care of grandchildren, adults feel a sense of continuity with future generations and the emotional satisfaction of feeling young again. Their pleasure depends to some extent on their degree of involvement and freedom to come and go as they please (Neugarten & Weinstein, 1964).

Grandparenting fills a void for many. On the basis of a number of studies,

Stevens-Long (1979) concludes that there is a high degree of satisfaction among women who have entered employment after their children were grown and who still have time for grandparenting. Their satisfaction and happiness with their employment depend on how they receive approval or disapproval from their spouses. However, many males are happy and willing to see their wives work because the money situation becomes more secure.

Intergenerational Adjustment

Middle-aged parents have to prepare themselves for the time when the children will leave home. Prior to that time, problems relating to the children's completion of education and embarking on careers frequently involve the parents to a high degree.

There are probably fewer differences now between young adults and their parents than there were in previous years because of better communication and the shift of focus of power in the family from authoritarian to democratic. Through their children, parents learn different ways of doing and thinking. As parents grow older they do stay current with their children's outside knowledge and contacts. A number of authorities say that the roles of parents who guide and of children who listen are essentially the same, and these roles cannot be altered without affecting society.

> Fifty-two-year-old Linda was happy that her daughter pursued higher education and became a nurse. Linda had yearned to work as a professional nurse, but because of family responsibilities she did not complete her education. However, her dreams came true when her daughter became a nurse, and that cemented the sense of belonging and mutuality that the mother and daughter had started to share.

Marriage in the Middle Years

The satisfaction that comes to marriage after the partners have reached their middle years has been judged by divorce statistics, questionnaires, and interview studies making use of case histories from psychologists and psychiatrists and taking the socioeconomic status of the subjects into account. Marriages are considered to be at their best in the beginning, when a general euphoria exists, and again many years later. However, as Blood and Wolfe (1960) observe, many marriages erode in time.

The role expectations that couples have of each other determine marital satisfaction. Udry (1971) found that the role expectations of the man and woman should become, more or less, equal over time if the marriage is to be satisfactory. But there are many forces precipitating role changes and expectations of marriage roles, among them (1) the Women's Movement, in its various forms, and colleges and universities that offer courses in women's careers and psychology, (2) discussion groups on awareness and self-confidence, and (3) available opportunities for women to pursue formerly male-dominated professions.

Some people think that for a marriage to be healthy and satisfactory, the couple should be equal partners. Rapoport and Rapoport (1975) believe that this principle is overrated. They contend that a marriage should be equitable rather than equal. They feel that people will change and shift at various points in their life, so that the domestic load will be shared in household chores, child care, and leadership in family affairs.

Wendy was 54 years old and had traveled widely with her husband. In her career as a journalist, she enjoyed writing, meeting people, and traveling around the world. She and her husband had four children. While her husband did most of the housework, Wendy was a good cook, and her meals were well appreciated in her family. In spite of her being a well-known journalist, what her children and husband looked to her for was the comfort she offered them both as a person and as a good cook.

Divorce and Aftermath

There are alternatives to traditional marriage. Among them are swinging marriages and group marriages, which are not popular alternatives to conventional marriage, to judge from the number of people involved in them. Obviously they are too fragile and hazardous to be considered by the traditional majority (Rogers, 1979). An increasing percentage of people are staying single longer, and there are also more people who are getting divorced and then remaining single. Greater permissiveness in sexual mores and the ability to establish emotional and financial independence allows many people freedom of lifestyle and freedom from responsibility for others. Most divorced men are between 35 and 44; a smaller number are in the 45-to-54 group. For women, the 45-to-54 group is first, followed by the 35-to-44 age group. Being divorced even at these late ages offers women and men many alternatives, although for the older woman, between the ages of 45 and 54, they are more difficult to find.

Factors in divorce.   A couple does not reach the point of divorce overnight, say Levinger and Moles (1979) in discussing the establishing of a marriage. Their model has two features: on the one hand, external support and internal attractions tend to keep the marriage together; on the other hand, external attractions work against the marriage. If the internal attractions are strong enough, then the marriage will be healthy. If the internal attractions are insufficient, then the marriage may stay together because of external supports, such as legal barriers, children, or career needs. When the external attraction to escape is stronger than the emotional tie, the marriage will be broken. If the impetus of these stimuli—the attraction of another man or woman, growth opportunities, and so on—continues, then divorce is inevitable.

No matter how desirable relief in the form of divorce may be, divorce rarely occurs without problems. The anticipated euphoria is outweighed by guilt, anguish, the legal matters as they affect others (especially children), and the necessity of making numerous adjustments. Many people, particularly women, when considering their future loneliness without the spouse, give up the idea of separating. Men may reflect on the fact that the wife has looked after their clothes, food, home life, and the like, and may give up the idea of divorce in sheer fright.

Hof and Dwyer (1982) have employed value analysis as a way of examining obstacles to divorce and explaining the current behavior of married couples as individuals. They have added to a cost-awareness analysis another important factor: perception of risks. This element is introduced into the marriage scenario to raise the issue of what might be lost in change—for example, security, status, children, and affection. The question adds an aspect to the contemplation of divorce that is frequently overlooked by couples.

Stress and divorce.   Holmes and Rahe (1976) examined stress in the lives of 5000 subjects from the United States, Canada, Europe, and Japan, and were able to rank life events according to stress. The highest value of a life event was 100 life-change units (LCUs), for a death of a spouse; the next-ranked events were divorce (73 LCUs) and separation (65 LCUs), and these were all higher than a jail term (63 LCUs). Sometimes people can avoid divorce by consulting a marriage counselor or minister who is trained to deal with their problems. According to Vedder (1965), many divorces might not have occurred if one partner of the couple had seen a counselor.

Widowhood

Because of men's shorter life expectancy, more women than men face the prospect of widowhood, although there is a trend toward equalization of rates. In 1978, the U.S. Bureau of the Census showed that twice as many middle-aged women live alone in the United States as middle-aged men. Widowhood is a difficult period for many women, particularly those who have never worked and have spent all their time taking care of others. These women have seen themselves primarily as wives and mothers and have not taken an occupational role. Such women typically suffer serious economic losses as well as loss of role. For people who have not developed hobbies, this is a particularly difficult time because they have extra time on their hands for mourning. It is at this stage that women face depression and loneliness. There are groups where they can both meet people and deal with their widowhood, but the pain is still always with them. Women who have worked and cultivated friendships find widowhood less lonesome than others, not in terms of their pain but in terms of their ability to meet and perhaps go out with other people. Having family and children around makes it easier for them, permitting them to reminisce about the dead person. Nevertheless, they find it difficult to adjust to the emotional, social, and economic disruptions caused by loss of a mate. Older women outnumber older men, so women have to make choices: do they wish to meet a man and get married once more, or will they resolve to live by themselves or with an adult child or enter a group-home situation where they can receive care? Economics becomes an important criterion in determining their lifestyles.

Bonnie was 52 when she lost her husband of more than 32 years. Her children were grown up and had left home some years before. Bonnie did not have a good relationship with her daughter, and therefore she had to depend for emotional support on her son, who lived in another state 900 miles away. She spent a lot of her time crying and contemplating her life.

Although she had had misunderstandings with her husband while he was alive, all that was forgotten. In her mind he had become a perfect human being, and she permitted nobody to discuss anything negative that had happened in the marriage. Bonnie started to live her life as if her husband were still alive. She would make the bed for two and set the table for two. She would not let anyone sit in his chair, saying that he would need it. Her friends became uncomfortable with her lifestyle. Her neighbors thought her actions were "spooky," and they reported her behavior and loneliness to an agency that dealt with bereavement.

Through the help of social workers who worked with groups of individuals who had similar problems, Bonnie learned to make a successful transition to her new role as a widow. However, Bonnie became unable to cope with her home situation by herself. She was very forgetful and would occasionally go to bed with the stove still lit or smoke in bed. Though chronologically young, she was eventually placed in a good nursing home for older people. Her removal from home was intended to prevent her from killing herself accidentally and to prevent damage either to her property or to her neighbors'.

Julia was 60 when her husband died; they had been married for more than 35 years and had three daughters. At the age of 50, Julia's husband had developed a cancer that slowly but steadily destroyed his body as well as his personality. Julia, too, lived in pain, for her children, tired of visiting a sick father, made their visits less and less frequent. Eventually, when she was drained physically and emotionally, her husband's end came, painfully and slowly. Julia was relieved that at last her ordeal was over. Although attractive and well-to-do, she kept away from men and told herself that once was enough. She had experienced marriage in her life; her reluctance to remarry was understandable.

During the past decade the number of people marrying in the older age group has increased substantially, but later-life remarriages have not changed much (Treas & Van Hilst, 1976). Older widowed women appear to be less likely to remarry than widowed men. In a recent intensive study of 24 remarried older couples, Jacobs and Vinick (1979) found that the men were more unhappy and lonely as widowers and thus more likely to remarry. Women in this study were more likely to express a negative opinion about remarriage, particularly if they had nursed their previous mate through a terminal illness.

Remarriage

Most divorced and widowed people remarry—4 out of 5, according to Glick (1975)—with the hope that the new marriage will be successful. Remarriages of divorced women are more apt to end in divorce than those of men. Many couples do avoid making the same mistakes that they have made before and avoid possible mismatches. The opportunities for men to marry are typically greater than those for women because men tend to marry younger women and women tend to marry older men. The pool of potential marriage partners gets larger for men, whereas for women it decreases because at every period of life more men than women die.

Singleness

In the United States, the number of unmarried people in the age group from 20 to 24 increased from 28% to 40% (Glick 1977). Glick feels that this increase was due to the postponement of marriage.

People choose to remain single for many reasons. Some take on responsibilities in their family of origin and, when they have completed their obligations, find they have lived a lifestyle with which they are comfortable, so they do not change. Other factors that contribute to singleness are the changes in sex-role expectations, particularly for women; the decreased emphasis on childbearing; and the presence of special facilities and services geared to singles, such as housing, newspapers and magazines, and entertainment spots. These factors could have contributed to the present popularity of the single lifestyle.

Campbell (1975) shows that single women of all ages are happier than married women because their responsibilities and problems are less. They also have fewer problems such as neurosis and depression than married women (Bernard, 1972). Gubrium (1975) found that singles who are middle-aged form a distinct group; their lifestyle is different from that of other middle-aged people. They are sometimes relatively isolated, but they are not seen as lonely. They see their singleness as an extension of their past (Lerner & Hultsch, 1983).

Career Adjustments

As middle-aged men reassess their lifestyles, some of them may regret the careers they have chosen. Rapidly shifting technology has made some jobs redundant or obsolete. Stress is placed on the entire family system when the wage earner becomes involuntarily unemployed. Affected employees may receive retraining to update their skills or assistance in making career changes. This also causes the family a certain degree of stress, but the availability of employment makes it easier on the family.

Values, careers, and attitudes interact. Normally people select jobs that suit their value system. For instance, a person who has a strong desire to help children would not choose a career in chemistry. Just as a person's value system affects choice of career, work molds the value system through social roles, environment, and atmosphere, as discussed in Chapter 7.

Usually the middle years are a period of career stability. It is during the middle years that most men and women reach their highest status and income in their careers. This applies to women if they have been employed all their lives. This is the period when a person who has made a successful choice and application of energy reaps the benefits of a productive career. But there are some interesting exceptions: some people in their middle years start over to fashion a different career for themselves.

A large number of people change their jobs because they are not physically suited for a particular type of work after a certain age. These people could be professional athletes, police officers, firefighters, or army officers whose work requires a level of physical skill and strength that they cannot sustain. Some of these people move into supervisory or executive positions, whereas others must find new career avenues.

Given a degree of success in this period, the career task is not so much to reach and maintain a peak of prestige and income as to achieve a flexible role—one that is interesting and productive, as well as financially satisfying.

Women and Careers

Our economy often demands two paychecks. More women than before have taken jobs, particularly in the 1970s and in the 1980s, with families having fewer children. The consensus is that the average number of children per woman in the United States during the remainder of this century will be slightly less than two (Havighurst & Levine, 1979).

The last 35 years have seen major changes in the work force. By 1975 there were 35 million women in the work force, amounting to about 40% of the total.

Despite the dramatic change in the proportion of women in the labor force, the picture drawn by Mueller in 1954 still holds true. Mueller describes the following categories of women in the labor force:

1. Stable homemaking career. The woman marries shortly after leaving high school or college and devotes herself to homemaking.

2. Conventional career pattern. The woman is employed for a relatively short time after completing her education and then marries and makes homemaking her career.

3. Stable working career. The career becomes the woman's way of life following preparation in college or a professional school.

4. Double-track career pattern. The woman goes to work after completing her education, then marries and continues with a double career of working and homemaking.

5. Interrupted career pattern. The woman follows the sequence of working, homemaking, working. (The latter stage may involve both.) The resumption of employment depends on the ages of the children and the interests and economic needs of the woman.

6. Uncertain career pattern. The woman alternates between working and homemaking. The amount of employment she takes depends on the economic needs of the family, her health, and the health of the family. This pattern is more common among lower-class women than among other groups.

Retirement and Second-Career Decisions

In their upper fifties or early sixties, people begin to think of retirement. Many find that a decline in their physical condition, due to accidents or the aging process, affects their job performance. A person who works on an assembly line may be hampered by failing eyesight. A person who has to lift heavy weights may become limited as the back muscles lose their elasticity. Some people simply desire to make a change, regardless of physical factors.

Today, flexible retirement offers various options. Some people want to change the nature of their jobs as they grow older. A reduction or increase in the number of workers in particular jobs also influences retirement options. The most desirable kind of retirement is one that maximizes the employment options of people after 50 years of age. Though the usual retirement age has been 65 years of age, encouragement to early or flexible retirement in some companies has opened many options for these people.

> Fifty-year-old Glenn opted for early retirement from his job as a policeman. His dream was to be a photographer, so he took a part-time job in a photo studio, where he did what he enjoyed most. He used his free time to take his own photos and develop them in his studio. He also began to participate in photo competitions. He was immensely happy with his work and felt fulfilled as a person.

Retirement is a fairly recent phenomenon. In the past, people worked at their jobs until they were overcome by ill health or their strength failed them. But today the situation is different. Studies of successful retirees show that people can maintain some involvement in their primary interest; for instance, an academician might continue to flourish through writing, research, and study.

As our population ages, older people have a growing need for jobs that are socially acceptable but are not really appropriate for younger people, who need to have stable jobs. Some programs have been funded by the federal government, among them the Comprehensive Employment and Training Act (CETA), the Older American Act, and the Action Agency. Other examples include Foster Grandparents, Senior Companions, and the Older American Community Service Employment Act, which provided about $42 million for use in the 1975 fiscal year. Those funds were reduced under the Reagan administration, which began in 1981.

There is also a growing need for recruitment in the staffing of senior centers and the provision of home-care services to assist older people in living independently in their own homes. Staff positions are usually full-time jobs, many of which could be second-career jobs for people past 50 years of age who have become interested in this kind of service.

Work and Environment

A middle-aged person has spent so much time on the job that it is difficult to view the developmental implications of work objectively unless it has remained constant over the decades. What is expected on the job today in terms of loyalty, hours spent on the job, decision making, exposure to hazards, and so forth, differs among people even in the same age group. One of the simplest illustrations of how life situations affect continued development in middle age is the matter of how much of a person's time is absorbed by work. Kastenbaum (1979) noted that an average person in 1870 started to work at about age 14 and worked until death at about the age of 61. This individual spent about 3120 hours on the job every year and accumulated about 146,640 hours in a 47-year work-life span (Miernyk, 1975). However, today it is estimated that the average person enters the work force at the age of 20 and retires at the age of 65. The number of hours each worker spends on the job each year has shrunk to about 2000, amounting to about 90,000 over the entire span. This total represents a reduction of nearly 40% in the number of hours a person spends at work.

Thus the working adult of today has more time free from on-the-job obligations than workers did a century ago. This gain in discretionary time means more opportunity to develop interests, skills, and a breadth of knowledge that was hard to come by for workers who were extensively bound to the work situation. Moreover, entering the work situation at a later age allows more time for education, both formal and informal, that could add to personality development.

The different meanings work has for different people become more distinct as people grow older. Workers who enjoy what they do become interested in learning and developing themselves in their particular areas. Some people learn to get the most out of their job situations, enriching themselves and developing specific personality traits they need to perform well. Other people grow stale and cease development early. There is much to be learned about the relationship between work and individual development through the middle years (Kastenbaum, 1979).

As the case illustrations show, people's lifestyles vary with their jobs.

Dominique, 49, worked as a telephone operator at a motel. She spent eight hours a day in front of the switchboard with a headset and answered telephone calls. People rarely saw her as a person with her own needs and wants; all they wanted from her was politeness. The job created a restrictive atmosphere for her; she was occupied with the telephone even when she needed to get herself a drink of water. Although Dominique called herself a happy-go-lucky person, she had little opportunity to show it because people took notice of her only as a telephone operator and nodded their heads if they wished to greet her. Her boss called her by her first name, whereas she had to call him by his last name and add a "mister" to it. Her role was very limited, allowing for no personal opinions, and she had no opportunities for personal growth. Her job was lonesome, although she realized that it was a necessity for the motel that employed her.

David, 49, was the executive director of a ready-mix concrete company. His day started at 7 A.M. when he started his rounds through the five concrete factories he owned. Following his morning rounds, David usually had breakfast with a client followed by office and board meetings. Late afternoons he spent in budgeting and planning as he had decided to open another new factory. He was constantly overwhelmed with all the stress he faced in the office. David saw his home as a place where he could feel peaceful, but he didn't spend much time there, and felt guilty that he was neglecting his family. Office pressures always seemed to be present and he accepted them as part of his lifestyle.

Barbara had been a cleaning woman from the time she was 20. At 50 she was a "regular" cleaning lady for a number of families. She enjoyed her job, but she was not comfortable with some of her customers. Some people treated her as if she did not exist; except for a hello and instructions about what needed to be done, they went about their business. Some of them expected to be addressed respectfully by their last names, though most called her by her first name. In other homes, she was invited to have a cup of coffee, and she appreciated being treated more like a person. She enjoyed listening to the conversations of the families, although she was never invited to participate. In spite of her limited interaction with the homeowners, Barbara enjoyed her job. She worked hard and cleaned each place as well as she could.

Anthony was a cab driver who had immigrated with his family from Puerto Rico. His job affected his lifestyle as much as the traffic affected his job. Anthony did not have much time for any type of recreation. He was always hustling his cab through the New York City traffic. The rush and the hassle got to him, but he had to get his job done, as well as compete for his fares. There was also the fear of robbery in the city, particularly in unsafe areas, and the possibility of running afoul of regulations in some way that could cost him his job. However, Anthony was grateful for his job, in spite of the dust, the sweat, and the agony of driving in a crowded city. He noticed two types of people who traveled in his cab—the talkers and the nontalkers. He enjoyed the stories that people told him and could even give advice to them based on his experiences with different types of people. He was comfortable with his job and relatively secure in it. His wife was a good woman who cooked for him and their four children. He was allowed to go home and lie down and sleep, and there was not much questioning about what he should or should not be doing at home. His home atmosphere was very comfortable and eased some of the tensions that he faced while working.

Sandy had worked all her life as a waitress. She liked her job and appreciated the tips that customers gave her. She had been at it for 25 years, and it showed. Some customers tipped her generously because they had known her for many years. Many still addressed her with remarks such as "Come on, girl" and "beautiful baby." But one day she overheard a young customer refer to her as "the old waitress." At first, Sandy felt insulted, and then she was scandalized because she thought of herself as being young and beautiful. The shock was real when she looked at herself in the mirror and saw a slightly older woman who had some gray hair and appeared to be in her fifties. Realizing that she was no longer as young as she was when she first entered her job, Sandy was momentarily depressed, especially in view of the value attached to youth in our culture. But after her initial depression, as well as anger at growing old, Sandy accepted her situation as inevitable. She thought of her family and felt grateful towards them. They were her only emotional support system through all her trials and tribulations and made her feel contented, proud, and comfortable.

Jake resigned his job as a "delivery boy" when he was 50 and took a job as a security officer in an apartment building. Both his job and the manner in which he was addressed were new to him. He was used to being treated as a young person, but now he felt that the people in the apartment building viewed him as an older person. Young girls would ask Jake to watch their pocketbooks and mothers would ask him to mind their babies while they ran some brief errand. At first that role puzzled him, but later on he accepted it. Eventually Jake realized that people's attitudes toward him were influenced by his age—and by his appearance, for he looked 60. The process of change was not painful for Jake; he enjoyed being treated differently, having resented the label "delivery boy" given to him even in his late forties.

Each of these six people have their personal lifestyle, growth, and development affected by their jobs or careers. Looking into the lives of these people shows that there is an overall relationship between life situations and the possibility of continued development from midlife onward. Each of these adults has undergone significant changes in his or her own personal development since the onset of adulthood and may continue to do so.

Implications for Social Work Practice

In offering therapy to middle-aged-people, social workers have to deal with many issues. One of the most important is the crisis that a breakdown in the health of a middle-aged person can precipitate in the family. When a middle-aged person is hospitalized, the person's family resources may have to be reassessed. The social worker may have to find resources to help the family survive the crisis.

Middle-aged people differ so widely in the resolution of their developmental issues that social workers are seldom able to make general recommendations, although they can often help a family keep its balance during transition. Some people make great efforts to prevent a decline in their physical strength, while others will surrender easily to the notion of being athletically "over the hill." Some widows and widowers reenter the competition for a new partner, whereas others (particularly women) substitute friendships primarily with members of their own sex. Activities for middle-aged people have to encompass their various adaptive styles.

Social workers may have to assist factory workers who have temporary disabilities connected with their jobs. The employees must rely on benefits from private disability plans, which do not always cover the costs of extensive rehabilitative services. Whenever long-term permanent services are needed, most people turn to federally funded programs of financial assistance for the permanently disabled.

In many ways, early retirement in middle age by subtle persuasion is made so attractive by employers that it appears better for the employees to leave their jobs and stay home. However, there is significant reduction in their monthly income and staying home often makes the person feel less useful. Few resources offer retraining of middle-aged workers who are no longer employed. Social workers retained by the government or private employers as members of interdisciplinary teams can participate in preventive education, diagnosis, referral for training, and counseling for the families of early retirees.

Middle-aged people, like others, can be classified as "simple" or "complex." A simple person tends to protect himself or herself from the environment, avoids stressful situations, and maintains a lifestyle that reveals neither many psychological resources nor many deficits. A complex person has a high share of resources as well as deficits and problems, has more motivation for growth, and seeks to expand his or her personality as well as range of functioning and life experience. Stressful experience contributes to an adventurous, stimulating life.

Most people are at neither extreme. A person's position on the simplicity–complexity continuum indicates the person's developmental status. The simple middle-aged person tends to be happier than the complex individual, who tends to achieve more and adapt better instead in early adulthood. Some complex people who have entertained high hopes and great expectations find themselves at a dead end.

Occupational dissatisfaction is an important factor with which middle-aged people may have to deal. Self-fulfillment through work is not always realistic. Social work practitioners should have knowledge to understand and deal with the stress levels of different lifestyles and offer help accordingly. Women appear to suffer more in this respect. Lowenthal, Thurnher, and Chiriboga

(1975) found that many middle-aged women experience a midlife developmental crisis. Many women become liberated from their energy-consuming parental roles. In middle age, they reevaluate themselves and look for ways to express their abilities. Some find themselves trapped; the alternatives are difficult either to find or to achieve. There are major obstacles to overcome to reach new or renewed life goals.

Lowenthal found that women who were high in competence and positive self-concepts were most apt to deal with occupational dissatisfaction meaningfully. However, the more complex and growth oriented a woman was, the greater the possibility for frustration. Complex and talented men were also stymied as they groped their way toward second careers and other forms of self-renewal. As women get older, the job market starts to shrink for them faster than it does for men. Thus they are burdened with two serious issues: ageism and sexism. Younger workers replace older workers in receiving promotions and climbing the social ladder. Such preferences are subtle, and so-called valid reasons are offered for overlooking the older person. Though talented older people move toward second careers/jobs, they are the last to be hired and the first to be fired, as most employers prefer to employ younger people, symptomatic of our society's negative attitude toward aging. Thus, sexism as well as ageism plays a role in wasting the potentials of mature men and women.

When a middle-aged person comes for therapy, it is necessary to know who the person is. Whether the individual views his or her life as being successful or unsuccessful depends upon what the person had defined as his or her own adult responsibilities and personal goals. Such issues could be explored with less stress if our society behaved as if it expected grownups to keep on growing. That awareness both among social workers and in the larger environment would make society a better place for adult development, and eventually create a safe and facilitating environment for child development as well.

There are more stresses, complications, and questions in middle age than in any other period of life, due mainly to people's responsibilities to two different generations: their children and their parents. Social workers, as understood in the values of social work, should have good self-awareness in order to help people to deal with their problems.

Chapter Summary

The middle years extend from 40 to 65 years of age. People vary in their responses to the biological, social, and psychological cues of midlife.

The middle-aged person is caught between two generations and has responsibilities to both.

Both sexes undergo physical and emotional changes that are related to hormonal shifts. These changes take place gradually in men; in women, menopause brings radical changes but does not necessarily cause great stress.

As people grow older, the main cause of death becomes diseases rather than accidents. Cancer, heart diseases, and arthritis are the chief diseases that afflict middle-aged people.

As people get older, they are likely to slow down in performing speeded tasks. Recent research developments have provided a better understanding of how intelligence changes as people grow older. Intelligence can be classified into two types: fluid intelligence, which declines after adolescence, and crystallized intelligence, which continues to increase with age. However, cognitive styles do become rigid with age.

Middle age is a period of reassessment. Erikson's seventh psychosocial crisis is that of generativity versus stagnation. The generative person is concerned with establishing and guiding the next generation, and one who fails to develop a sense of generativity suffers from stagnation, self-indulgence, and perhaps physical and psychological invalidism. Peck has expanded on Erikson's conceptualization and discusses the issues and conflicts that people face in middle age.

The life tasks of middle-aged people center on both taking over the responsibilities of the older generation and contributing to the future of the younger generation, as well as taking care of themselves. Some women look forward to release from child-rearing responsibilities, but others are affected negatively by the loss of this familiar function. Stresses in this period lead diversely to a feeling of being overwhelmed or of being confident of one's coping capacities.

Some of the stresses common to middle age arise from separation, divorce, and widowhood. Middle-aged couples divorce for a number of reasons. However, divorce does not happen suddenly. Either strong external supports or internal attraction between members of the couple could keep a marriage together; when these two factors do not suffice, external attractions can work against a marriage. Most divorced people do remarry. However, the opportunities for men to remarry are greater than for women.

The lifestyles of single people are distinctly different from those of other middle-aged people.

There are a number of career adjustments that a middle-aged person may have to make. Because of interaction among values, careers, and attitudes, normally people have by this time selected jobs that fit their lifestyle. Nevertheless it is not uncommon to see people making career changes as they grow older, despite problems involving retraining. Some individuals learn new career roles and obtain new jobs, but the potential of others is overlooked because the employer prefers younger persons as employees.

There are a large number of women in the labor force. Their career patterns may be classified as the stable homemaking career, conventional career, stable working career, double-track career, interrupted career, and uncertain career. Women form 40% of the labor force.

Retirement has taken many shapes. Flexible retirement helps middle-aged people to retire and find new jobs as well as lifestyles that enhance their potentials.

References

Baltes, P. B., & Schaie, K. W. (1974). Aging and IQ: The myth of the twilight years. *Psychology Today, 7*, 35–40.

Barnett R. C. (1985, March). We've come a long way—but where are we and what are the rewards? Presentation at conference, Women in Transition, New York University School of Continuing Education, Center for Career and Life Planning, New York.

Barnett, R. C., & Baruch, G. K. (1978). Women in middle years: A critique of research and theory. *Psychology of Women Quarterly, 3*, (2), 187–197.

Bart, P., & Grossman, M. (1978). Menopause. In M. Notman & C. Nadelson (Eds.), *The woman patient.* New York: Plenum.

Baruch, G., Barnett, R., & Rivers, C. (1983). *Lifeprints.* New York: McGraw-Hill.

Bernard, J. (1972). Sex-role learning in children and adolescents. Paper presented at the meeting of the American Association for the Advancement of Science, Washington, DC.

Birren, J. E. (1974). Transitions in gerontology—from lab to life: Psychophysiology and speed of response. *American Psychologist, 29*, 808–815.

Birren, J. E., & Botwinick, J. (1955). Age difference in finger and jaw and foot reaction time to auditory stimuli. *Journal of Gerontology, 10*, 429–432.

Birren, J. E., Riegel, K. F., & Morrison, D. F. (1962). Age difference in response speed as a function of controlled variations of stimulus conditions: Evidence of a general speed factor. *Gerontologia, 6*, 1–18.

Blood, R. O., & Wolfe, D. M. (1960). *Husbands and wives: The dynamics of married living.* New York: Free Press.

Botwinick, J. (1971). Sensory-set factors in age difference in reaction time. *Journal of Genetic Psychology, 119*, 241–249.

Botwinick, J. (1977). Intellectual abilities. In J. Birren & K. W. Schaie (Eds.), *Handbook of psychology of aging.* New York: Van Nostrand Reinhold.

Botwinick, J., Robbin, J. S., & Brinley, J. E. (1960). Age difference in card sorting performance in relation to task difficulty, task set and practice. *Journal of Experimental Psychology, 59*, 10–18.

Botwinick, J., & Thompson, L. W. (1966). Components of reaction time in relation to age and sex. *Journal of Genetic Psychology, 108*, 175–183.

Brody, J. (1979, June 6). Exercising to turn back the years. *The New York Times,* pp. C18–C19.

Campbell, A. (1975, May). The American way of mating. *Psychology Today,* 39–42.

Cummings, E., & Henry, W. E. (1961). *Growing old.* New York: Basic Books.

Datan, N., Maoz, B., Antonovsky, A., & Wijsenbeek, H. (1970). Climaterium in three cultural contexts. *Tropical and Geographical Medicine, 22*, 77–86.

Ebersole, P. (1979). The vital vehicle: The body. In I. M. Burnside, P. Ebersole, & H. E. Monea (Eds.), *Psychosocial caring throughout the lifespan.* New York: McGraw-Hill.

Erikson, E. H. (1968). *Identity: Youth and crisis.* New York: Norton.

Erikson, E. H. (1980). *Identity and the life cycle.* New York: Norton.

Fried, B. (1967). *The middle-age crisis.* New York: Harper & Row.

Gilligan, C. (1982). *In a different voice.* Cambridge, MA: Harvard University Press.

Glick, P. C. (1975). A demographer looks at American families. *Journal of Marriage and the Family, 37*, 15–36.

Glick, P. C. (1977). Updating the life cycle of the family. *Journal of Marriage and the Family, 39,* 5–15.

Gochros, H. C. (1977). Human sexuality. In *Encyclopedia of Social Work.* Washington, DC: National Association of Social Workers.

Griew, S. (1958). Uncertainty as a determinant of performance in relation to age. *Gerontologia, 2,* 284–290.

Gubrium, J. F. (1975). Being single in old age. *International Journal of Aging and Human Development, 6,* 29–41.

Gutmann, D. L. (1964). An exploration of ego configuration in middle and later life. In B. L. Neugarten and Associates (Eds.), *Personality in middle and later life.* New York: Atherton.

Havighurst, R. J. (1953). *Human development and education.* New York: Longman.

Havighurst, R. J. (1972). *Developmental tasks and education* (3rd ed.). New York: McKay.

Havighurst, J., & Levine, D. U. (1979). *Society and education* (5th ed.). Boston: Allyn & Bacon.

Hodgkins, J. (1962). Influence of age on the speed of reaction and movement in families. *Journal of Gerontology, 17,* 385–389.

Hof, L., & Dwyer, C. (1982, Spring). Overcoming ambivalence through value analysis. *American Journal of Family Therapy, 10,* (1), 17–26.

Holman, M. T. (1980). In W. H. Norman & T. J. Scaramelte (Eds.), *Midlife: Development of crucial issues.* New York: Brunner-Mazel.

Holmes, J., & Rahe, R. (1976). Age differences in fluid and crystallized intelligence. *Acta Psychologica, 26,* 82–91.

Horn, J. L. (1970). Organization of data on lifespan development of human abilities. In L. R. Goulet & P. B. Baltes (Eds.), *Lifespan developmental psychology: Research and theory.* New York: Academic Press.

Horner, S. M. (1972). Toward an understanding of achievement—related conflicts in women. *Journal of Social Issues, 28,* 157–175.

Jacobs, R., & Vinick, B. (1979). *Re-engagement in later life: Re-employment and remarriage.* Stamford, CT: Greylock.

Jones, R., Garrison, K. C., & Morgan, R. F. (1985). *The psychology of human development.* New York: Harper & Row.

Kastenbaum, R. (1979). *Human developing.* Boston: Allyn & Bacon.

Kay, H. (1954). The effects of position in a display upon problem solving. *Quarterly Journal of Experimental Psychology, 6,* 155–169.

Knox, A. (1977). *Adult development and learning: A handbook on individual growth and competence in the adult years for education and the helping professions.* San Francisco: Jossey-Bass.

Lerner, R. M., & Hultsch, D. F. (1983). *Human developmment.* New York: McGraw-Hill.

Levinger, G., & Moles, O. C. (Eds.). (1979). *Divorce and separation: Context, causes and consequences.* New York: Basic Books.

Levinson, D. (1977). The mid-life transition: A period in adult psychosocial development. *Psychiatry, 40,* 99–112.

Levinson, D., Darrow, C., Klein, E., Levinson, M., & McKee, B. (1978). *The seasons of a man's life.* New York: Ballantine.

Lowenthal, M. F., Thurnher, M., & Chiriboga, D. (1975). *Four stages of life: A comparative study of women and men facing transitions.* San Francisco: Jossey-Bass.

Masters, W. H., & Johnson, V. E. (1970). *Human sexual inadequacy.* Boston: Little, Brown.

McClelland, D. (1975). *Power: The inner experience.* New York: Irvington.

McKinlay, S. M., Jefferys, M., & Thompson, B. (1972). An investigation of age at menopause. *Journal of Biosocial Science, 4,* 161–173.

Miernyk, W. H. (1975). The changing life cycle of work. In N. Datan & L. Ginsberg (Eds.), *Lifespan developmental psychology in normative life crisis.* New York: Academic Press.

Mueller, K. H. (1954). *Educating women for a changing world.* Minneapolis: University of Minnesota Press.

Neugarten, B. L. (1976). The psychology of aging: An overview. APA Master Lectures. Washington, DC: American Psychological Association.

Neugarten, B. L. (1977). Personality and aging. In J. E. Birren & K. W. Schaie (Eds.), *Handbook of the psychology of aging.* New York: Van Nostrand Reinhold.

Neugarten, B., & Kraines, R. (1965). Menopausal symptoms of women in various ages. *Psychosomatic Medicine, 23,* 266–273.

Neugarten, B. L., & Weinstein, K. (1964). The changing American grandparent. *Journal of Marriage and the Family, 26,* 199–205.

Neugarten, B. L., Wood, V., Kraines, R., & Loomis, B. (1963). Women's attitudes toward menopause. *Human Development, 6,* 140–151.

Newman, B. M., & Newman, P. R. (1975). *Development through life.* Homewood, IL: Dorsey Press.

Papalia, D. E., & Olds, S. W. (1986). *Human development.* New York: McGraw-Hill.

Peck, R. C. (1968). Psychological development in the second half of life. In B. L. Neugarten (Ed.), *Middle age and aging.* Chicago, IL: Chicago University Press.

Rapoport, R., & Rapoport, R. N. (1975). *Leisure and family life cycle.* London: Routledge & Kegan Paul.

Rogers, D. (1979). *The adult years.* Englewood Cliffs, NJ: Prentice Hall.

Rosenberg, S. D., & Farrell, M. P. (1976). Identity and crisis in middle-aged men. *International Journal of Aging and Human Development, 2,* 153–170.

Rosenman, R. H. (1974). The role of behavioral patterns and neurogenic factors on the pathogenesis of coronory heart disease. In R. S. Eliot (Ed.), *Stress and the heart.* New York: Futura.

Rubin, L. B. (1979). *Women of a certain age.* New York: Harper-Colophon.

Ruebsaat, H. J., & Hull, R. (1975). *The male climacteric.* New York: Hawthorne Books.

Sassen, G. (1980). Success anxiety in women: A constructivist interpretation of its sources and significance. *Harvard Educational Review, 50,* 13–35.

Sheppard, S., & Seidman, S. (1982, March). Midlife women, the women's movement, and sexuality. Paper presented at 15th annual National Meeting of Sex Educators, Counselors, and Therapists, New York.

Specht, R., & Craig, G. T. (1982). *Human development.* Englewood Cliffs, NJ: Prentice-Hall.

Stevens-Long, J. (1979). *Adult life.* Palo Alto, CA: Mayfield.

Timiras, P. S. (1972). *Developmental physiology and aging.* New York: Macmillan.

Treas, J., & Van Hilst, A. (1976). Marriage and remarriage rates among older Americans. *The Gerontologist, 16,* 132–136.

U.S. Bureau of the Census. (1978a, March). *Households and families by type.* Washington, DC: U.S. Government Printing Office.

U.S. Bureau of the Census. (1978b). *Statistical abstract of the United States, 1978.* Washington, DC: U.S. Government Printing Office.

Udry, J. R. (1971). *The social context of marriage* (2nd ed.). Philadelphia: Lippincott.

Vaillant, G. E. (1977). *Adaptation to life.* Boston: Little, Brown.

Vedder, C. B. (1965). *The problems of the middle aged.* Springfield, IL: Charles C Thomas.

Wechsler, D. (1958). *The measurement and appraisal of adult intelligence* (4th ed.). Baltimore: Williams & Wilkins.

Welford, A. T. (1958). *Aging and human skill.* London: Oxford University Press.

Welford, A. T. (1977). Motor Performance. In J. E. Birren & K. W. Schaie (Eds.), Handbook of the psychology of aging. New York: Van Nostrand Reinhold.

Woolf, V. (1929). *A room of one's own.* New York: Harcourt Brace Jovanovich.

The Older Years

Models and Theories of Aging

Physical Aging and Disease

Personal Adaptation to Aging

Myths of Aging

Erikson: Integrity versus Despair

Cognitive Functioning

Social Aspects of Aging

Social Issues and Problems

Death

Implications for Social Work Practice

Chapter Summary

References

Seventy-nine-year-old Laila was thin and tiny. She sat in her old, creaky rocking chair, slowly rocking herself back and forth. In front of her was her 7-year-old grandson, who carried on a long monologue to which Laila responded with grunts and nods. Once in a while the child screamed, "Grandma, are you listening?" and Laila replied, "Yes, yes, what is it now, Tommy?" In a few minutes she had dozed off and was sound asleep.

Laila lived with her adult daughter and pitched in whenever and wherever she could. She enjoyed her grandchildren, most of whom were adults. Laila used to enjoy good health, but after two serious operations and a slow recovery, her energy level had diminished tremendously. Laila was well read and could participate in lively discussions on topics varying from politics to religion and sex, but her grandchildren did not pay much attention to her opinions because their mother did not seem to value them.

Attitudes toward aging have an effect on the adjustments that the elderly have to make. Schaie (1973) claims that negative attitudes could contribute to observed maladaptive behaviors among the aged and in some cases could lead to premature death. Negative views about aging, about life in general, and about oneself could result in an older person's unwillingness or inability to seek needed help. Negative attitudes of aging adults about themselves affect others who live in their environs, and those people may in turn feel free to respond negatively to old people or ignore them completely.

Attitudes affect the way people feel about themselves. If an elderly person is treated like a worthless person and is restricted in his or her behavior, the chances of this person's becoming an invalid, dependent and helpless, are high.

Tina and Diana were twin sisters in their midseventies who lived some distance apart. Tina had married when she was 18 and given birth to four children, of whom only two survived. Her husband had been her high school sweetheart. They were not wealthy, but they had a good life; they cared about each other and did everything to make each other happy. Tina stayed home, cooked, and cared for the children. Her sister Diana did not marry; she was a happy-go-lucky person who had her own job and enjoyed friendships and the freedom of being herself.

When Tina was 65, tragedy struck her family. Her husband died suddenly after a mild heart attack, leaving Tina devastated. She had never managed money and did not know how to take care of herself or her property. Her only son lived in another state. Her daughter Loretta, who lived close by, volunteered to take care of her. Loretta sold her mother's property and took her mother home. She set up a room for Tina upstairs, "away from noise and children," and let her live there. When Loretta's children wanted to talk to Grandma, she would tell them that they were tiring Grandma. Within a year and a half, Tina was no longer allowed to go downstairs because it was considered to be tiring for her. If the grandchildren wished to speak to her, they were politely told not to because "Grandma does not have the energy to listen." The grand-daughter who related this case mentioned that she felt that the grand-mother was longing to participate in the conversations and the family life that went on downstairs, but permission was never granted to come down and be a *person.*

Loretta would fuss over Tina's developing a cold when she came out of her room; she would fuss about allowing Tina to participate in conversations. Due to Loretta's attitude, Tina ironically became a virtual prisoner in her daughter's house. All that she was allowed to do was lie still in bed and not even get up except to go to the bathroom and go back to her room. The idea constantly put into her head was that she was an old person and therefore an ill person and needed this type of treatment.

Tina developed asthma and then had a heart attack. When she really became seriously ill, her twin sister Diana, who lived in another state, came to see her. Diana bounced up the steps two at a time to see her sister. She appeared to be young and was certainly energetic. At 67 years of age she had gone back to college to get an art degree, and she was proud of herself and her achievements. She was well liked by her friends and appeared to be overflowing with energy. Tina, after her heart attack, was pale, looked older than her years, was fragile, and had difficulty moving out of her bed.

How did these two sisters—twins, in fact—grow up to be so different? Diana never married, but she always worked and knew how to survive in the world. Tina had always been taken care of, so when her husband died, her daughter viewed her as a burden. Loretta made no bones about the time and energy she had to spend on her mother and called her an invalid even before she became one. The constant pressure that Tina should stay in her room and the family atmosphere that Loretta created spelled out the message that Grandma was weak and should not be bothered. That attitude eventually created Tina's ill health. Tina really had nothing to do but lie in bed, waiting to die. And why not? Life did not have anything to offer her. For her sister Diana, life was meaningful, and her attitude was reflected in her energy and the happiness she radiated.

Being old has different meanings for different adults. A culture that respects tradition treats growing old differently from one that discards old values and technologies in favor of anything considered "progressive." For example, an elderly person in traditional India would experience life differently from an older person in the United States. But the reverence and respect shown the elderly in rural India are disappearing in the cities, where the influence of the Euro-American culture is pervasive. The role and status of the elderly in a culture are affected by the role of cultural values in the family system.

Gopal was an elderly man in his eighties who lived in a rural area, where he owned land. He lived with his three married sons, their wives, and his grandchildren. His wife had been dead for a long time. All the household duties as well as work on the farms was taken care of by the sons and the daughters-in-law. Gopal got up early in the morning, had a heavy breakfast, and went for a long walk; he met the other villagers and chatted with them. At noon he came home, had his lunch, and took a nap. When family members had problems requiring solutions, Gopal was always sought out for his advice, and his word was respected and heeded by the rest of the family. Thus he carried a relatively high position in the family hierarchy.

Models and Theories of Aging

Aging is affected by two factors: the physical process of aging that is common to all human beings and the influence of cultural values.

Schaie's Three Models

Schaie (1973) proposes three models of the changes that take place in aging. Each has implications for research.

1. When individuals are pathology-free, or when they exhibit crystallized intelligence with little correlation between age-related pathology and performance, normal behavior can be assumed. Flavell (1970) also found this type of theoretical interpretation of cognitive changes in adulthood. He mentioned that biological variables do contribute significantly to cognitive maturation and growth in childhood. The result is that basic changes in level of thought do emerge in a fixed order, with a uniform directionality, and they are largely irreversible. In contrast, adulthood itself is the closest thing in experimenting with the change-making effects of experience. An assumption can be made that no biological changes in maturity are sufficient to impose strong constraints on cognitive growth. Flavell restricts his interpretation to such aspects of cognition as judgment, attitudes, and beliefs. It is not clear how late in the life span he would expect such an assumption to hold true.

2. An irreversible decrement in performance accompanies aging. This model is applicable to psychological processes but is based on relatively direct biological determination of performance. The model assumes that such behaviors are unaffected by immediate environmental inputs. This conceptualization of aging is known to many psychologists and social workers as the *medical model*. Investigators focus on behavioral manifestations of age that are correlated with either normal or pathological biological changes and assume such changes to be irremediable.

3. The model of decrement with compensation proposes that environmental inputs could partially compensate for biologically determined decrements. Such environmental inputs could consist of lifestyle changes and supports, such as improved nutrition and increased physical exercise. These changes are needed to enhance performance in specific problematic areas—for example, recent memory.

Schaie finds the third model to be the most practical for dealing with problems of aging. It is applicable to a broader range of behavior processes and ascribes a more optimistic and aggressive role to mental health professionals than the other models.

There is a professional need for a paradigm of change-oriented explanations in which behavior at all life-span points is viewed as some unspecified function of three classes of variables: (1) organismic or biological stimulus, (2) environmental response, and (3) behavioral factors.

In a theoretical metasystem, biological variables can be assumed to be causally related to some degree to behavior throughout the life span. In advanced age, as in early childhood, rapid physiological change does exert a relatively major impact on changes in cognition as well as in other behaviors.

Aging has been explained in terms of genetic theory, nongenetic cellular theory, and immunological theory.

Genetic Theory

According to genetic theory, aging takes place because the biological development of people is programmed by the genes, particularly the DNA molecules. In genetic terms, then, aging could be the result of inherited genes programmed to cause changes with age or the result of changes that occur in the DNA during aging.

Development among humans varies considerably in the life span, but there is evidence to show that aging effects are programmed in the genes. The programming operates irrespective of cultural and social differences, although there is variation in individual humans in rates of senescence and those with similar heredity show similarities in senescence. Both familial and environmental factors can alter the programming within a species (Schock, 1977).

The genetic theory of aging hypothesizes that the DNA makes errors in the process of synthesizing needed proteins or enzymes according to the genetic code it contains. The errors result in the manufacture of proteins and enzymes that are not up to the genetic specifications and therefore cannot function properly. The cumulative effect of these errors is the death of the cell and aging of the organism (Schock, 1977). This theory has some research support. However, more research is needed to pinpoint at what step errors occur in the process of synthesizing proteins and enzymes (Schock, 1977).

Nongenetic Cellular Theory

The nongenetic cellular theory is basically a set of theories that focus on the nongenetic factors that cause aging, and is based on a "wear and tear" theory that uses a mechanical analogy: the body, like a machine, eventually breaks down. The mechanical function performed by the valves of the heart supports this theory in that some forms of heart disease result from calcification of the valves.

The "waste product" theory indicates that the accumulated waste products in the body play an important role in the process of senescence. Various chemical wastes do collect in some tissues, but there is no evidence that wastes interfere with cell functioning in any important way.

The "cross-link" theory is much more promising. This theory indicates that over time, molecules in the body develop links either among their parts or with other molecules. These cross-links, which are very stable and accumulate over time, bring about chemical as well as physical changes that affect how the molecules function. Evidence for the cross-link theory comes from studies of collagen, a substance associated with the connective tissue. Research shows that cross-links result in the loss of elasticity in various tissues, including blood vessels and skin. Specific enzymes have been isolated that can break down cross-links in collagen. Other chemicals have been found to inhibit the rate at which cross-links are formed. However, none of this research can yet be applied to humans (Schock, 1977).

Immunological Theory

In an immune-system reaction, antibodies produced by one's immune system destroy cells—cells that have entered the body or mutant cells. The immune system recognizes minute deviations of such cells from like cells correctly produced by one's own body. However, over time the immune system loses its capability to recognize some deviations, and so loses its ability to destroy some foreign and mutant cells, which can harm the organism. In an autoimmune reaction, the immune system produces antibodies that destroy even normal cells produced by one's own body. With age, the number of autoimmune antibodies in the system increases, leading to such age-related diseases as rheumatoid arthritis and late-onset diabetes.

Physical Aging and Disease

What changes sturdy young people with taut skin into fragile elderly people is difficult to understand. Certainly, the physical effects attributed to aging do not develop at equal rates, even within one body. A person may be confined to a wheelchair or be totally blind, yet be more mentally alert than another individual who may look years younger.

Physical Decline

To see oneself growing older can be a shock, particularly if one wishes to avoid facing the fact of growing old. Our society encourages adults to look younger than they are and discourages or looks down on growing old. Its attitude of avoidance is apparent in the use of hair dyes and face lifts as a way of dealing with the physical symptoms of aging. Nevertheless, the elderly find that their skin has become less elastic, drier, and more wrinkled. Poor posture may be accentuated by shrinking muscles and the decrease in elasticity that follows calcification of ligaments and loss of space between vertebral discs. These skeletal and ligament changes in old people cause loss of stature and slump in posture (Tonna, 1977). Warts may appear on the face, trunk, and scalp, and some blood vessels break, producing black and blue marks. As muscle weight decreases with age, the structure and composition of the muscle cells are altered, and they accumulate more fat. The heart, a highly specialized muscle, suffers the same problem as other muscles.

As people grow older, their hearing becomes less efficient. Severe loss of hearing results in communication problems, which increase the social isolation of the elderly.

There are myths concerning the sexual functioning of the elderly. When older couples have been placed in institutions, each of the partners has often been assigned to single-sex living arrangements. Masters and Johnson (1966) helped to dispel some of the myths about the elderly in their study of human sexual response. Men and women who were sexually active throughout their lives were better able to maintain their sexual capacities than less sexually active people. After 60 years of age, men's sexual responses declined because of increased physical infirmities and mental factors such as fear of failure rather than because of the aging process itself. Fear of failure has been intensified by the cultural emphasis on intercourse as the proper form of sexual expression (Masters & Johnson, 1966).

The poor health of old age may be related to poor diet. The diminished physical activity typical of old age causes a slowdown in metabolism, and so the elderly require less food than younger adults. The diet of the elderly may include insufficient quantities of nutritious food for various reasons, such as inadequate income, depression or loneliness, or problems in obtaining transportation for grocery shopping.

> Anna, 82, had recently lost her husband. It was the biggest loss of her life; she had lived with him for more than 60 years. Her eating habits had been influenced by their joint lifestyle: Anna and her husband would eat whenever they were hungry and not on any specific schedule. After her husband's death, Anna became depressed. She ate sporadically and at infrequent intervals. While walking on the sidewalk of a busy street, she fainted. The hospital to which she was admitted for long-term care found that malnutrition was her biggest problem.

As people grow older they become aware of stiff joints, shortness of breath, and longer reaction time. As they focus on their limitations and decreasing agility, they become cautious about going down a staircase and feel vulnerable when crossing an intersection.

Aging can seem to occur suddenly. An illness or a serious fall can make a person feel that he or she has turned into an old person overnight. Recovery time in old age may be prolonged, and in fact the former energy level or muscle tone may not be regained. This sudden and drastic change could cause considerable confusion, stress, and frustration.

Many older people also suffer from chronic illness. As Hippocrates put it, old people have fewer diseases than younger people, but their diseases never seem to leave them. Chronic conditions account for many of the problems that the elderly face. The *Fact Book on Aging* (National Council on Aging, 1978) indicates that at least 85% of the problem conditions of the elderly are chronic, and most people over 65 years of age have at least one chronic condition. The most common conditions are vision and hearing impairments, arthritis and rheumatism, hypertension, and heart disease. Specht and Craig (1982) report that a smaller percentage of the chronically impaired are not limited in their activities. Some of the other chronic conditions common among the elderly are obesity, abdominal-cavity hernias, cataracts, varicose veins, hemorrhoids, and prostate disease. The elderly are susceptible to neurodegenerative diseases, EEG slowing, chromosome changes, and immune dysfunctions.

The health condition of the elderly is a fragile state—a balance so delicate that a minor illness can lead to major complications. For instance, taking aspirin for a headache can cause peptic ulcers to flare up. Physicians may advise caution in exercise, drug usage, and other matters if an elderly person is recovering from a serious illness.

Mental Impairment

Some of the mental problems that the elderly face are called organic disorders and are related to physical aspects of aging. These include temporary or permanent damage to the brain tissues, which causes impaired memory, poor judgment, intellectual decline, and disorientation. The impairment could be slight or serious enough to require hospitalization. Individuals who have the best coping abilities before they become disabled will be the best equipped to deal with the developmental tasks of disability and will be the most successful in dealing with organic impairment (Havighurst, 1953).

Cardiovascular and cerebrovascular diseases have a negative impact on cognition, but the extent of the effect differs widely and depends on the severity of the illness and the type of behavior examined. Studies that contrast patients having cardiovascular or cerebrovascular conditions with normal controls almost invariably report poorer performance for the patients on both verbal and nonverbal measures. By contrast, comparison of patients having hypertension with age-matched normals produces a more complex pattern of outcomes. Hypertension impairs speeded psychomotor performance more than it affects untimed tests of verbal abilities. Sometimes mild hypertension appears to enhance performance relative to that of normals and has been postulated to improve flow of blood to the brain. However, more severe hypertension ultimately lowers intellectual performance. Therefore it is unclear whether chronic use of antihypertension medications influences cognitive abilities in a systematic way (La Rue & Jarvik, 1982).

A small percentage of people are affected by serious organic disorders; a larger percentage of older people are affected by psychosis than those 35 and under. Sometimes, mental symptoms are caused by chronic brain syndrome—a gradual, irreversible deterioration of the brain cells—or by cerebral arteriosclerosis, which impairs the flow of blood to the brain.

With advancing age and its attendant physiological decline, factors like duration of disease and severity of symptoms, in combination with socio-economic factors and patterns of intellectual as well as physical stimulation, appear to account for the variance in observed disease–cognition relations more than any single factor. Dealing with old age, one could say in jest, but with an element of truth, that health + wealth = happiness, if happiness is viewed as the retention of those mental abilities that enable individuals to attain pleasure (La Rue & Jarvik, 1982).

Personal Adaptation to Aging

Havighurst says that the developmental tasks of the elderly vary with their lifestyles and personal histories. Sociologists have advanced many theories to describe the changes that take place in the elderly.

Disengagement Theory

In the 1960s, Elaine Cummings and William E. Henry (1961) formulated the disengagement theory, which assumes that aging is a progressive process of physical, psychological, and social withdrawal from the wider society. On the physical level, people slow their activity level and conserve their energy. At the psychological level, they withdraw their concern from the wider world and begin to focus on those aspects of life that immediately touch them, shifting attention from the outer world to the inner world of their own feelings, thoughts, and actions. At the social level, a mutual withdrawal is initiated that reduces the interaction between the aging and the other members of society. This is actually a process of double withdrawal; the elderly withdraw from younger people, who in turn, move away from the elderly. Cummings and Henry speak of the elderly as wanting to disengage, and, by doing so, reducing the number of roles they play and weakening or severing relationships.

In some sense, society encourages the disengagement of the elderly by transferring their functions to the young, both in work and in family responsibilities. Society thereby minimizes the problems that may be associated with increasing incompetence, illness, or death of the elderly.

The disengagement theory has been both thoroughly criticized and defended by large groups of people. A number of articles have questioned its meaningfulness. Cross-sectional studies have been used by both sides. Generational as well as age differences have been used either to support or protest this theory. On the whole, the bulk of evidence seems to weigh against its main tenets (Maddox, 1969; Palmore, 1975).

According to disengagement theory, the withdrawal of the elderly person is natural and even beneficial because the aging person's diminished life then can match his or her decreased physical and psychic energy. The person may maintain a sense of satisfaction but curtail social involvements and activities because he or she has less desire for them.

Activity Theory

A number of sociologists, including Havighurst and Neugarten (Vander Zanden, 1978), developed activity theory as an alternative to disengagement theory. The theory says that people will be more satisfied if they are involved in life and are active and resistive to the isolating effects of negative social attitudes. Older people will make better adjustments to retirement by finding productive substitutes for work and making new friends to fill the emotional gap.

Activity theorists indicate that the majority of older people maintain fairly stable levels of physical and social activity (Shanas, 1972; Neugarten, 1973; Palmore, 1975). The amount of engagement or disengagement that occurs depends upon past life patterns and socioeconomic forces, rather than on any inherent or inevitable process. Successful aging, then, is seen as requiring a substantial level of physical, mental, and social activity.

Role-Exit Theory

Sociologist Zena Smith Blau (1973) has formulated the role-exit theory. According to Blau, retirement and widowhood terminate participation by the elderly in the principal institutional structures of society—the job and the family. Therefore the opportunities for the elderly to remain socially useful are undermined. This loss of job and marital roles has a devastating effect, for these are core roles—the important points of adult identity.

Sociologist I. Rosen (1974) takes a similar position, saying that in the United States people are not effectively socialized into old age. The social norms as well as myths about the elderly describe them as old, weak, limited, and unworldly. Therefore the elderly have very little motivation to move into the societally ascribed role, which our culture does not value. Rosen concludes that this role excludes people from equal opportunities for participation and rewards in society.

Critics of the role-exit theorists say they exaggerate the social losses felt by most elderly people. Many elderly people indicate that their loss of work and parental roles is offset by increased freedom, as well as by opportunities to do things they always wanted to do but had little time for when they were younger.

Social-Exchange Theory

James J. Dowd and other sociologists have applied the social-exchange, or interaction, theory to the aging process. According to this theory, people enter into relationships because in doing so they derive rewards such as economic sustenance, recognition, a sense of security, love, or social approval. In the process of seeking such rewards they do incur costs, such as negative experiences, fatigue, or embarrassment. The costs may be high enough to cause them to abandon experiences that are also positive and pleasant, or they may abandon such experiences for the sake of pursuing a potentially more rewarding experience. Thus, in interaction theory, people are viewed as engaging in a sort of mental bookkeeping that involves a ledger of rewards, costs, and profits. By this view, a relationship tends to persist only as long as both parties profit from it (Blau, 1964; Homans, 1974).

Quite often, the elderly find themselves in a situation of increasing vulnerability because of their deteriorating bargaining position—emotional as well as economic. As they decline in power, the elderly retire with the hope that they will be well provided for through Social Security and Medicare.

Social-exchange theorists believe that the quality of the relationship between the elderly and society has been determined by the speed with which industrialization has taken place. Publications by Cowgill and Holmes (1972), Cowgill (1974), and Bengston, Cueller, and Ragan (1975) state that the position of the elderly in preindustrial societies was to accumulate knowledge and control through years of experience; the theorists believe that industrialization undermines the importance of traditional knowledge and control.

Consolidation Theory

Consolidation theory posits a consolidation of commitments by the elderly, as well as a redistribution of their energies so that they can cope with lost roles, activities, and capacities. With the disappearance of some of their active roles, older people may find it easier to redistribute their energies among their remaining active roles. Engagement in the remaining roles may be on par with preloss level, or there may be a reduction in the energy expended. Some people may not have enough activities to perform, and their remaining roles are not able to absorb the energy left by a specific role loss. Unless they find a substitute role, those people may be forced to disengage. Consolidation theory will not hold true when a person faces a major loss; even if plentiful, the remaining activities are inadequate to serve as the basis of life.

Ben and Charlotte, both in their eighties, were an extremely happy couple. They were financially independent and enjoyed good health. Their children visited them frequently, they participated actively in their community's affairs, and they occupied a prominent and significant position in their social group. One morning Ben woke up to find that Charlotte had quietly passed away in her sleep. This loss was devastating for Ben. Although there were many activities in which he could participate, the death of his wife made him withdraw from the social groups to which he belonged. Slowly and steadily, his pain was revealed in his disengagement from activities to which he had formerly devoted his energies. The loss of Charlotte did not bring about any consolidation in his life.

Myths of Aging

There are a number of myths about aging (Vander Zanden, 1978), and it is important to dispel them by presenting them as they are seen by people in our culture.

Myth 1: A large percentage of the elderly live in hospitals, nursing homes, and other such institutions. A very small percentage of the elderly live in institutions—less than 15% of the total population over the age of 65.

Myth 2: Many of the elderly are incapacitated and spend much of their time in bed because of illness. The percentage of the elderly who spend their time in bed is no larger than that of the rest of the population. About one-half to three-fifths function without any limitation; moreover, about two-thirds to three-quarters do not have to spend even a day sick in bed during the course of the year. One-third to two-fifths do not see a doctor from one year to the next.

Myth 3: All elderly people are always in poor health and develop infections easily. Although most elderly are assumed to be susceptible to illness, the National Council on Aging (1975) found that less than 20% considered health to be a serious problem. The number of self-reported illnesses, such as respiratory infections, injuries, and digestive disorders, is lower among the elderly than in any other group. However, chronic illnesses, such as heart conditions, diabetes, and varicose veins, increase steadily with advancing years.

Myth 4: Most people over 65 find themselves in serious financial circumstances. Sixty-two percent of the public assume that money is a major problem for people over 65, but only 15% of the elderly report that they do not have enough money on which to live. In fact, a number of decisions about the state and government are controlled by the money of the elderly. A larger number of younger people, those from 18 to 64, report that they do not have enough money for their livelihood (Harris Poll, 1975).

Myth 5: Most people over the age of 65 do not feel wanted or needed in society. Only a very small percentage of the elderly feel that they are unwanted in society. Either their financial power or available time makes them valuable assets to their children, grandchildren, and communities. A poll found that 54% of the general public felt that the elderly may feel unwanted, whereas only 7% of the elderly reported feeling unwanted.

Myth 6: Most elderly people are afraid of crime. About one-fourth of the elderly agree that crime is a serious problem for them, but a smaller percentage of younger people also fear crime. Thus, fear of crime is not a problem for the elderly alone. Degree of fear depends on the area people live in and the attitudes that they have developed through the years (Harris Poll, 1975).

Other myths as discussed by Saul (1974) include the *tranquility myth*, which states that old age is a time of relative peace and tranquility, a time when people can relax and enjoy the fruits of their labor. However, in reality there are a number of stresses that the elderly may face in their old age, including problems with health and finances, crime, loneliness, and isolation.

Another myth is called the *senility myth*, which states that all old people have deterioration of their mental powers. This is an imprecise label and robs older people of their dignity and worth. Finally, the myth of asexuality states that older people have no sexual needs or desires. As amply proven by Masters and Johnson's studies, this is not true (Saul, 1974).

There are other myths about the elderly, and some of the myths may contain more truth with respect to some minority groups or the poor than they do for the elderly population as a whole. However, in reality there is a large gap between the actual experiences of the elderly and the problems that are attributed to them by others.

Erikson: Integrity versus Despair

Erikson (1980) characterizes the period of transition to old age as a crisis of integrity versus despair. As a person's commitment to integrity increases, the ego strength of wisdom emerges.

During this period an individual begins to think in terms of life's coming to a close. According to Erikson, the integrity aspect of life now provides a person with both the knowledge and wisdom to understand his or her own life; it produces a balance between the decrease in potency and performance and allows one the opportunity to serve as an example to the upcoming generations.

People who have lived their lives carelessly may regret what they could have done but did not do. This recognition of lost opportunity affects the way they feel. Erikson calls this the despair stage of life. It represents a rejection rather than an acceptance of past life. Fear of death proceeds from the realization that there is insufficient time to make up for past mistakes.

> Norman was 72 years of age. He had been married once, when he was 18, but he played around with women and eventually his wife divorced him. He never again felt the necessity to get married. Norman continued as a happy-go-lucky person and took life as it came, but before he knew it he was an old man without too much to offer to others. He suffered a serious heart attack and then found that part of his body was paralyzed leaving him disabled. Norman had no one at home to take care of him, so he was admitted as an invalid to a home for the aged. When he met the social worker, he cried in despair and lamented that he wished he had spent his life more meaningfully when he was younger so that he would have someone to take care of him in his old age. Norman commented sadly that if he had his life to live all over again, he would have remained faithful to his wife and not have played around. He would have been a good parent to his children and shown better treatment to his sisters, who to him had always been "second-class citizens." While relating his life history, he cried constantly because he was miserable and unhappy.

Finally, in this stage, an individual may deny or fail to deal with the crisis at all.

There are questions about the adequacy of integrity as an organizing principle for development in later adulthood. Clayton (1975) notes that there are relatively few individuals who achieve a commitment to integrity and thus achieve wisdom in old age. Many individuals become fixated at an earlier point of development or a crisis point, particularly at a point of adolescent identity or other crisis, and do not move ahead. In old age a person becomes more intrapersonally than interpersonally oriented, reminiscing about past actions.

Having come to the end of Erikson's stages does not mean that we have come to the end of psychosocial crises, or that all people have resolved the integrity crisis. The older person who has achieved integrity in life is better able to deal with the facts of life, as well as to view life in an existential light. Integrity is not so much a matter of being honest or truthful as it is an integration of one's past history with one's present circumstances, yielding a feeling of contentment with the outcome.

An older person, to experience integrity, should incorporate into his or her self-image the lifelong sequence of conflict, failures, and disappointments as well as joy and happiness.

Despair arises in older individuals for many reasons. The person may have been treated negatively for a long time. Repeated comments about the person's incompetence, dependence, and old-fashioned ways eventually may lower one's sense of self-worth. The gradual deterioration of certain physical capacities, particularly loss of hearing, impaired vision, and limited motor ability, feeds frustration and discouragement.

All these factors could also lead to a sense of regret about life and about oneself. People wish in a nagging way that things could have been different. This attitude of despair about life makes it difficult to develop an attitude of calm resignation toward death. Either the individual seeks death as a way of ending a miserable existence or desperately fears death because there has been no compensation for past failures.

A sense of integrity is not based on physical achievements. There are people who are physically handicapped but have maintained a feeling of contentment throughout their lives and are satisfied with their lot in life. And there are individuals who have been fairly conflict free but who still view life with great dissatisfaction and unhappiness. In short, developing an attitude of integrity and not despair depends on the self-acceptance that comes through introspection.

Cognitive Functioning
Intelligence

There has been considerable controversy about the capability of older people to maintain their intellectual abilities. According to psychologists Horn and Donaldson (1976) and others, to declare that intellectual abilities diminish in old age or that the decline is inevitable or universal does a great disservice to the elderly. Their research reveals that there is a greater degree of elasticity in old age than has been traditionally accepted.

The effects of aging on intelligence have been overestimated, partly because of the results of cross-sectional studies. Those studies employ the snapshot approach, usually testing individuals of different ages and then comparing their performance. Longitudinal studies, in contrast, are more like case studies, retesting the same individuals over a period of years (Kagan & Moss, 1962; Thomas & Chess, 1977).

Psychologists Baltes and Schaie (1973) found that cross-sectional studies do not allow for generational differences in performance on intelligence tests. Increasing educational opportunities as well as social changes mean that larger numbers of Americans are performing at successively higher levels of functioning. Therefore, the measured intelligence of older adults keeps increasing. Individuals who were 50 in the 1960s had higher intellectual scores than those who were in their 50s in the 1950s.

There is an increasing awareness that optimal intellectual functioning in the later years is related to maintaining good health, physical activity, and intellectual interests throughout life. In many cases, reduced physical and mental activity is caused by emotional crisis and accompanying grief or depression or is brought about by pessimistic expectations of deterioration. Often physical exercising or meditation and exercise could successfully be used to awaken lines of thought that have lain dormant due to neglect or isolation.

Higher education may stimulate a desire to stay mentally alert and also impart skills that help the elderly to adjust to old age. There are many educated people who enjoy reading, analyzing, criticizing, and discussing throughout their lifetimes. One outstanding example of lifelong engagement is the great anthropologist Margaret Mead. In her late seventies she was still traveling, participating in discussions, teaching classes, and continuing to write. An extremely alert person, she let nothing escape her notice and she continually pointed out to students areas in anthropology that needed to be explored and studied.

There are also older people who are homebound. To cater to them, there are libraries that have outreach programs and that bring books and cassettes to the home. Neugarten (1976) found that the most influential factors in cognitive decline are not intrinsic to the aging process per se but to tangential problems that often are relievable, such as failing health, social isolation, and minimal formal education.

Baltes and Labouvie (1973) made a review of the literature and reached some noteworthy conclusions. They found that individual differences between the elderly are tremendous and therefore could badly erode the predictive value of age alone. Even more complicating, individual differences have differential impacts for various ability dimensions. In general it can be said that age changes are surprisingly small in comparison to generational (cohort) differences or to the change described as "terminal drop" that comes just before death. Further, age changes can be altered even after onset in old age. And, though biological aging undoubtedly influences intellectual functioning, there has been a tendency to underestimate or ignore the impact of the environments of many older people, which are not conducive to intellectual acquisition and maintenance. Botwinick (1970) concluded that, in terms of overall ability, education is extremely important in explaining individual differences.

Memory and New Learning

An increasing proportion of a population of older people will show some memory loss as their age advances. Memory is related to learning and intelligence. Remembering is part of the evidence of learning, and learning is part of the measurement of intelligence. If a person does not learn, then the person does not have anything to remember. If a person cannot remember, then there is no sign of having learned. Although we regard memory, learning, and intelligence as three separate processes we have not learned to evaluate them independently of one another.

> Seventy-year-old Theodore notices that his memory is starting to falter. He begins to forget days and dates. Slowly, the most familiar surroundings become strange to him, and he frequently becomes lost. As time passes, he becomes more and more confused, and it appears he can no longer recognize his own wife.

Theodore has Alzheimer's disease, a form of senile dementia affecting more than 1 million Americans, and killing nearly 100,000 Americans per year (Raeburn, 1984). Alzheimer's victims are usually irritable, restless, agitated, and suffer from impairments of judgment. In the final stages of Alzheimer's disease, there is progressive paralysis and breathing problems. Often, these breathing problems lead to pneumonia which becomes a frequent cause of death.

The brains of these victims show a destructive tangle of protein filaments in the cortex—the part of the brain responsible for intelligent functioning. Research indicates that there are biochemical causes for the disease and in about 15 percent of the cases, there is evidence of inherited disposition—passing from one generation to the next (Raeburn, 1984). One finding shows that victims of Down's syndrome, which is one form of mental retardation due to chromosome defect, may develop symptoms almost indistinguishable from Alzheimer's disease when they survive up into their 30s. This similiarity could be a clue to the causes of Alzheimer's disease. The exact causes of Alzheimer's disease are still unknown, but it is definitely a progressive disease, and placement in a nursing home is a necessity as the disease advances (Zastrow & Kirst-Ashman, 1987).

There are essentially four types of memory:

1. short-term memory—recall after very little delay, varying from 5 to 30 seconds
2. recent memory—recall of events after a brief period of time, from one hour to several days

3. old memory—recall of events that took place long in the past and have not been rehearsed or thought of since
4. remote memory—recall of events that took place long in the past but have been referred to frequently throughout the course of the lifetime.

Regardless of type, there are three stages of memory:

1. registration—the "recording" of learning or perceptions, analogous to the recording of sound on a tape recorder
2. retention—the ability to sustain registration over time
3. recall—the retrieval of material that has been registered and retained.

A failure in any of these stages could result in having no measurable memory (no recollection of events).

Bright people are less susceptible to memory loss with increasing age than their less intelligent counterparts. Again, there are some older people who escape memory loss completely. As a person becomes older, the ability to retain auditory information is better than the ability to retain visual information. People who exercise their memory power tend to maintain both remote and recent memory well into old age.

Memory loss among some older people could be due to some failure in the process of acquisition of new knowledge; among others, it could be related to retention of knowledge; and among still others, it could be related to the retrieval of knowledge. Older people tend to organize themselves less well and less completely than they did when they were younger (Hultsch, 1969, 1971, 1974; Denney, 1974).

After evaluating a number of studies, Craik (1977) summarized their findings and reported that memory loss is not a complete, all-or-nothing occurrence. Some of the elderly compensate for memory deficit better than others. Recall per se appears to be improved in the elderly if they are given more time for a task and supplied with careful instructions on how the material has to be organized in order for it to be learned. He found that performance improved with experience. Therefore it would be inappropriate to conclude that people over 65 cannot learn or make use of completely new material. Older people may not be as efficient as younger students in their speed of learning, but their past experiences and knowledge may well compensate for their lack of speed in learning.

Many colleges now cater to the needs of the elderly because there are more and more older college-educated people who wish to be retrained for other skills. Adult education does help the elderly to face the difficulties that confront retirees in our work-oriented society.

Social Aspects of Aging

Besides sexism and racism, our culture is guilty of ageism—a bias that may affect most of us as we grow older. Our society continues to value youth and beauty over any other capacity or ability. In the United States many people experience a reduction in wealth, influence, prestige, and political power as they age. They also cannot fail to see that being older disqualifies them from esteemed positions such as administrator, vice president of a company, and so forth. In our country the entry criteria for employment are health, age, sex, color, experience, and educational achievement. As long as old age is not viewed positively, elderly people will have more difficulty obtaining jobs than younger people.

Most couples are middle-aged when their children leave home, but some are in their old age. With the trend toward delayed marriage, it is becoming more common for parents to start getting the children ready to leave home rather than waiting for them to leave on their own. There are different attitudes about having the children leave home. Some women tend to look forward to launching their children, seeing it as an opportunity for greater freedom. Others are less eager, especially if motherhood has been the focal point of their lives and they have very few outside interests. The men's viewpoint has not yet been researched.

Though there has been discussion of the empty-nest stage and how it affects parents negatively, researchers have falsely attributed results to the empty-nest stage that are in fact caused by other factors. For instance, the absence of children may unmask an empty marriage, but it is the quality of the marriage that causes divorce rather than the empty-nest stage. There is no evidence to show that solid marital relationships are harmed by the departure of children. The stage is only a transition, and researchers will have to look at men and women both before and after the last child has left home in order to assess the effects on the marriage. Lifestyles and personal traits, too, influence responses to children's departure.

Eleanor was the mother of six children. Life with her alcoholic husband was difficult, but she devoted herself to taking care of her children and committed all her time to them. As long as her husband brought home part of his wages, she was satisfied. But soon the children were grown up and gone, and Eleanor found time on her hands and an empty house. Without her children her life was miserable; after all, her marriage had died when her husband's companion became the bottle. With the help of her sisters, to whom she was close, Eleanor planned frequent trips to interesting places. She contemplated divorce but did not have the courage to get out of the marriage. Thus, although she was married, in reality she led her own life. She looked forward to having her children visit her and taking trips with them.

Rosalind was 60 before her last child left home. Though initially sad, she was happy to have time to do the things she always wanted to do. Her husband and she began to behave like lovebirds, spending more time in bed, listening to music, and visiting the theater. Both Rosalind and her husband viewed this as a very happy aspect of their lives, for they finally found time for each other.

Lifestyles

When we observe people, we see not only their roles, relationships, group memberships, and environments but also how those elements are forged together by choices, by selective commitments of attention and energy, and by personal mannerisms, to make up a whole lifestyle. The values that are served by a person's lifestyle are determined in part by cultural and subcultural tradition and also in part by personal experience.

Growing old has the potential to alter life in many ways, affecting physical capacities, economic status, group memberships, activities, and environments. At the same time, aging brings with it a certain freedom from social restraints that can result in changes in way of life. Nearly all studies of lifestyles in later life are cross-sectional ones in which it is not possible to assess the impact of age on changes in lifestyle. All we can see from this type of study is what lifestyles predominate at various life stages.

In a study of people in their seventies, Maas and Kuypers (1974) found that just over 40% had lifestyles that centered around their families. Over 40% of the men led more solitary lifestyles revolving around hobbies and more cursory social contacts. The remainder of their lives was dominated by sporadic ill health and surface social contacts. Women in their seventies had a diverse lifestyle, owing largely to the facts that half of the women were no longer married and that a great percentage of the married women had a lifestyle that was job centered.

A study made of lifestyles of people over 65 years of age found that they followed basically six different types of lifestyle, characterized as familism, couplehood, world of work, living fully, living alone, and maintaining involvement. Familism implies that an older couple have children and other relatives to whom they are totally devoted. Couplehood means an older couple with no children, spending a lot of time with each other and other couples. Some elderly people were extremely work-oriented, others lived a full life working and recreating with and without friends. A small percentage lived alone and did not socialize much, and finally there were people who lived by themselves but were involved with other people. Following is a case of a couple living fully.

> Seventy-seven-year-old Will and seventy-four-year-old Candy had been married for 44 years. Their two adult children were married and had families of their own. Candy and Will started their day at 8 in the morning, after a leisurely breakfast. Then they drove to the shopping center or went to church activities. After a midafternoon nap, they both exercised on their stationary bicycles. In the evening, they visited their family, friends, or saw a movie. What is most important about this lifestyle is that they enjoyed each other's company and were very much in love with each other.

People perform many different types of activities, for varied reasons: one activity may be a source of personal identity or a source of legitimate interactions with other people; another may yield a sense of personal involvement with life—a way to get the vital juices flowing; yet another confers prestige or status. Activities may provide a source of new experience, service to others, a way to pass time, something to look forward to, a source of variety in life, an exercise of competence, peace and quiet or a means of escape, a sense of accomplishment, or just plain fun.

Retirement

Retirement is an institutional separation of people from their occupational positions with a continuation of income that is based on prior years of service. Although health could be a big factor, age is of primary consideration. About 80% of men and about 90% of women over age 65 do not have an occupational position. With larger and larger numbers of Americans living longer, retirement is becoming an important issue.

Changes.   When people leave their occupations, a number of changes occur in their lives, irrespective of whether they retired voluntarily or were forced to retire. Retirement spells fears and self-doubts for most Americans other than the well-to-do. Work is viewed as an important aspect of life; it provides people with their self-concept and self-esteem, as well as personal satisfaction, meaningful peer relationships, opportunities for creativity, and, in sum, enduring life satisfactions. Losing these experiences through retirement is seen as being demoralizing and a precursor of major problems in older age (Cummings & Henry, 1961; Miller, 1965; Back, 1969).

> Adam was 61 years of age and the manager of a big company. He had held his job for more than 30 years and thought of himself as being indispensable to the company. He was shocked when the company invited all senior staff to retire and offered a glamorous retirement plan. Adam was forced to choose the plan, but he was resentful that the company did not need him any more. He left the company feeling angry and unwanted, in spite of the fact that they acknowledged what he had done for the company and gave him a big farewell party.
>
> At home with time on his hands, he was scared and restless. He found his day to be aimless, and his immediate challenge became to give structure to the long, shapeless hours. He started having nightmares about his life; he would awaken in a sweat, having seen himself drowning or being dropped into a bottomless well. The fear of coping with a new life so suddenly thrust on him was almost too much for him to deal with. Though educated and well prepared for this type of life, he had to work consciously at scheduling his time, to find meaningful involvement in doing what would give him the most pleasure.
>
> It took Adam about six months to understand that he was no longer working for the company, that his time was his own, and that he could really do what he wanted with his time and his energy. Adam learned to understand and accept that he was responsible only to himself, his wife, and his adult children who were concerned about his welfare, as he

suddenly became very disorganized. Slowly and steadily Adam started to put time and effort into disciplining himself.

Traditionally, retirement has appeared to be a period in which people worried that they were unwanted by society or that they were no longer useful. However, nowadays there are people who work outside their homes even after they have retired. For some people, work is not the central feature in their lives, and very few workers find their primary social interests or relationships in the workplace. Research shows that what people miss most in retirement is money and that when people are assured an adequate income, they will retire early (Atchley, 1977; Shanas, 1972).

One meaningful way of dealing with retirement is to give people options. Some people would like to retire early and others would like to work longer. Some individuals may also want to start a new career, whereas others may prefer to withdraw from work obligations and spend time with family or by themselves.

Responses to retirement.   Among the factors other than economic status that affect the way of life for a retiree is the type of friends and colleagues a person has (Cox & Bhak, 1979). If a person's associates view retirement positively, then the person may retire without too much feeling of loss and make a successful adjustment.

A person's lifelong attitude toward work also affects feelings about retirement. Many people spend a lot of their time at their workplaces, and their self-esteem and sense of self-worth are bound up in their working roles. Retirement downgrades their roles. Disengaging from their work roles is particularly difficult for people who have not found satisfaction in hobbies and other activities.

The personality type of the individual also affects retirement. Lowenthal (1972) found that for a large percentage of people, their attitudes toward their jobs influence how they feel about retirement. There are four personality types of retiree: work-oriented, self-protective, autonomous, and receptive-nurturant people. A person who is extremely work-oriented would be depressed in facing retirement and may also have a fear of not being useful. The self-protective person sees retirement as a time of detachment and lack of responsibility for others. An autonomous person has usually selected a job from which he or she can determine when to retire. A person who can exercise that option is usually happy, but if retirement becomes mandatory then the person may experience depression and require reorientation. The receptive-nurturant individual is usually a woman who has developed intimacy and has a positive affect; her positive adjustment to retirement is dependent on the quality she perceives in her marital role and relationship. As long as she is satisfied with her marital status, she will view retirement as something meaningful for her.

A study by Reichard, Livson, and Petersen (1962) identified five personality types in terms of their adjustment to retirement:

1. well-adjusted people—the mature group who have no regrets about their past lives, accept their present circumstances realistically, and find genuine joy and pleasure in their retired lives
2. "rocking chair" people—those who welcome old age as a time when they are free to sit back and do nothing, and who find satisfaction in being passive rather than active
3. "armored" people—those who use activity as a way of fending off old age; who develop a highly satisfying lifestyle after retirement, a system that serves as a defense against anxieties about feeling old
4. poor adjusters—those who find little satisfaction in retirement and blame others for any failure that they face in their lives
5. "self-blamers"—those who blame themselves for everything that has not gone right in their lives.

Whether a person responds favorably to retirement or not is the result of many factors, including health, economic status, need for fulfillment, personal history, and attitude toward life. Retirement in its essence is not a breaking away from a lifestyle but merely a continuation of what has gone before. Whatever coping styles people have developed will stay with them when they grow old.

Reminiscing

Older people tend to reminisce about their past lives. Reminiscing can serve as an evaluation of how they have spent their lifetimes and the legacies they are leaving behind. Old age is the period when they finally confront the question of whether they have lived up to their expectations and have conformed to their earlier beliefs and values (Specht & Craig, 1982). A person who looks back on a meaningless life and realizes that there is insufficient time to make up for past mistakes may develop a fear of death. Some individuals may not deal with this crisis. Mostly, however, reminiscence is viewed as an activity that facilitates the feeling that life is complete.

Butler (1974) indicates that successful aging involves both a life-review process and also the shifting of focus from consideration of the future to enjoying the quality of life at present. Butler suggests counseling to help older people make use of this review process in order to relieve old guilts and resolve old conflicts.

Grandparenthood

The role of grandparent plays an important function in old age. During the 20th century we have seen a lengthening of the life cycle (Neugarten & Moore, 1968). Marriage, the birth and departure of children, and grandparenthood tend to occur later in life for people now than they did at the turn of the 20th century.

The grandparent role is not defined as clearly in today's society (Clavan, 1978; Kahana & Kahana, 1971; Robertson, 1976). Grandparents play varying roles. Some grandparents become babysitters to their grandchildren; other grandparents, who are well off but do not have time to spend with their children, lavish gifts on their grandchildren; distant grandparents, even if not well off, may lavish gifts in order to be remembered and show love in absence. Some grandparents make sporadic visits to see the grandchildren and merely play the role they have been assigned—that is, to be kind and caring and spoil them. Still other grandparents are economically dependent on their children and at times their grandchildren. Such older people may live in the homes of their adult children, and the attitude that the grandchildren develop toward them may be based upon the attitude that is encouraged by their own parents.

Some grandparents are happy in their roles. However, a significant number experience difficulty in accepting the roles ascribed to them. The style in which the grandparent role is enacted depends upon the lifestyle and philosophy of the grandparents.

In a study by Neugarten and Weinstein (1964), grandparenthood was judged to have five dominant themes, not all of them noted by all subjects:

1. a source of biological renewal and/or continuity, helping them feel rejuvenated and creating extensions of youth and self into the future
2. a source of emotional self-fulfillment, the development of the relationship between grandparent and grandchild evoking feelings of companionship and satisfaction that were sometimes missing from the earlier parent–child relationships
3. a source of vicarious achievement
4. the opportunity to be a resource person, offering financial aid as well as help based on their own life experiences
5. a feeling of remoteness and not really being well liked.

Neugarten and Weinstein (1964) also identified two styles of grandparental interaction with grandchildren.

1. Traditional, including:
   a. formal, in which the grandparents performed the prescribed roles;
   b. surrogate (found only for grandmothers), in which the grandmother actually took care of and responsibility for the grandchild while the parent worked;
   c. reservoir of family wisdom, in which the grandparents were a source of special skills and resources.
2. Informal, including:
   a. fun seeker style, characterized by informality and playfulness;
   b. distant-figure, in which the grandparents relate to the grandchild only on special occasions, such as birthdays or holidays.

Neugarten and Weinstein found that the traditional style was most prevalent among grandparents, with the relationship seen as fun for the grandchildren as well as the grandparents.

Grandparenting has a different meaning for women than for men. In a study by Robertson (1976), more than 80% of the grandmothers interviewed mentioned that they were excited, happy, and proud to be grandparents. Grandparents placed two types of emphasis on their relationships with their grandchildren. Some emphasized social orientation, more emphasized personal orientation, and still more emphasized both aspects. Grandparents were classed as having a social orientation if they answered "yes" to a question about whether their grandchildren should be honest and hardworking. Younger grandparents who emphasized social orientation were usually married and working. Older grandparents who placed an emphasis on personal orientation were usually widowed and unemployed. They paid more attention to their grandparenting role because they were also lonely and in need of companionship and fun. It was also seen that women had the greater amount of interaction with their grandchildren.

How do grandchildren view grandparenting, and how do they react to their grandparents? To some extent the attitude of the child is colored by the attitude of the child's parents toward their own older parents. Some grandchildren follow the attitudes of their own parents and some take the opposite attitude. Grandchildren in the 4- to 11-year-old age group tend to value their grandparents for egocentric reasons; that is, for what the grandparents give them in love, affection, food, and gifts. Robertson (1976) found that young adult grandchildren hold favorable attitudes toward grandparents; about 90% of this group of grandchildren mentioned that they did not find their grandparents boring or see them as being old fashioned or out of touch with their grandchildren, and about 70% of the teenagers mentioned that they did not feel that their grandparents were a bore.

Older adult grandchildren saw grandparents only in the role of people from whom they received gifts. About 59% saw the grandparents as providing financial aid. The ideal grandparent was seen as enjoying grandchildren as well as showing an interest in them. The most admired grandparents were those who were seen as gentle, helpful, and understanding, as well as industrious, talkative, and smart; or as a companion, mediator, and teacher. Low-ranking grandparents were characterized as lazy, childish, or both dependent and childish.

Religion

Older people's self-images as well as personalities are influenced by religious orientations. A higher proportion of elderly rather than younger adults say that a religious person is better prepared for old age.

Attitudes toward death are also influenced by religion. A sense of serenity and decreased fear of death are found among people who follow a conservative religious approach and view death as a portal to immortality. There are cultural efforts to deny death. Fear is associated most with what is left behind at death—the problems of survivors and responsibilities that have not been faced and dealt with. The greatest fear for the dying person is to leave behind friends and relatives. Nonreligious people facing death are less likely to have a reference group that can give them support and security.

Social Issues and Problems

Although research has long reported fairly close ties between adults and their aging parents, the phenomenon of adults' abuse of dependent elderly parents has only recently come to light. Just as child abuse and spouse abuse came to be viewed as major social problems in the 1960s and 1970s, mistreatment of elderly people is becoming an increasingly important social concern (Pedrick-Cornell & Gelles, 1982).

Abuse of elderly people can take many forms. It can be neglect—withholding of food, shelter, clothing, or medical attention—and it can also be psychological, in the form of tongue lashings or threats of violence and abandonment. At times it is actual violence: the beating, punching, or burning of old people who cannot take care of themselves.

Due to problems of definition and reporting (it is probably as much underreported as child and spouse abuse), estimates of the rate of elder abuse vary from one-half million to two-and-a-half million cases in the United States every year (Pedrick-Cornell & Gelles, 1982).

Typically, a person who is abused is infirm, very old, and a woman; the abuser is apt to be a middle-aged daughter who views the mother as the cause of overwhelming stress (Pedrick-Cornell & Gelles, 1982). There is no research evidence that such families have a history of family violence but the suspicion is that people who abuse their parents are those who were beaten when they themselves were children (Papalia & Olds, 1986).

Like child and spouse abuse, the problem of elder abuse has to be approached from the perspectives of both victim and abuser (Hooyman, Rathbone-McCuan, & Klingbeil, 1982). To protect the aged, procedures have to be developed to identify and report abuse, to take victims out of the house, and, if necessary and possible, to reduce the degree of isolation they feel, through contacts in the community, supportive legal and social work, and other services.

Social Institutions and the Elderly

Family. A great deal has been said about loss of status in old age, but the assertions are not grounded in research. McKain (1967) reported that attitudes of adult children had an effect on retirement marriages. He realized that some people were shocked to learn that their adult parents were planning to get married. In some cases the problem was related to the inheritance of property. A negative attitude on the part of the adult children prevented a large number of retirement marriages.

Despite talk about the rejected older person, there is considerable contact between older people and their adult children, even though the older person may live alone. According to a study by Shanas (1972), about three-fifths of older persons had seen a child of theirs on the same day they were interviewed or within the preceding week; there were few parents who had not seen their children in the previous year. It was found that adult children and their parents maintained meaningful kinship relationships. Small services were rendered reciprocally between parent and child; in some cases, parents offered more services than the adult children. Moreover, most parents were free of regular monetary dependence on their children.

Help between parent and children is also exchanged in kind. Reciprocity of help was seen in shopping, housework, babysitting, and home repairs. This form of kin assistance is an important characteristic of family role relations.

Although the postparental period is viewed as potentially traumatic, it is not so for most families. In spite of the picture painted, there is no gloomy empty-nest syndrome. In a survey of an urban, upper-middle-class neighborhood in Kansas City, 22 out of 49 older couples evaluated the postparental period as a "better" period than the preceding years. Fifteen said that it was as good as the preceding years, seven said that changes were not clear, and two said that it was "as bad" as the preceding phases.

Housing.   The immediate environment looms large in the lives of most older Americans. The living space of the elderly diminishes with age. Eventually older people cease to journey back and forth from work or to travel. As energy and health decline and financial resources shrink, the neighborhood grocery store and the nearby church may be the farthest points in an older person's travels. The living of the enfeebled and ill may be reduced to a home or an apartment and, ultimately, to a room, a bed, and four restricting walls. Thus the quality of housing becomes significant in the lives of the aged.

Since the 1950s, a new housing vocabulary has come into being and many of the spaces it describes are types of housing available to an aged population. Terms like *condominium, town house, cooperative, mobile home, retirement community, public housing, nursing home,* and *geriatic center* have become important for the elderly.

The housing needs of the elderly are similar to those of any other group of adults. Most older people wish to experience independent living. "Independent" implies that the type of housing they wish will enable them to be masters of their own households and to care for themselves; to be free to entertain friends and to perform roles to which they have grown accustomed.

Another aspect of life for the elderly that cannot be overlooked is that they are prone to accidents such as falls. Dwelling places should be carefully designed, constructed, and equipped to minimize injury. Climate also has an effect on older people. They become less tolerant of extreme changes in heating, cooling, and ventilation. Special attention should be given to lighting and also to noise control.

Most people have a sense of place—a feeling that they belong to a particular location and environment. Regardless of where older people live, they have a fundamental need to identify with a place—a dwelling, a neighborhood, a village or city, and a landscape. People who are forced to move have to develop a new sense of spatial identity.

A sense of relatedness is an important aspect of older people's lives, and the extent to which older people relate to and interact with other human beings is also affected by the design, size, and location of their dwellings. Like any other group of people, older people need to feel a sense of mastery over their environments; this may come about through gardening, decorating and furnishing the dwelling unit, displaying accessories, or otherwise making changes within a dwelling.

> Sharon was in her eighties. Her only daughter had died of cancer, and there was no one to take care of Sharon's medical needs. Because she was well-to-do, she was placed in a nursing home. All Sharon asked was that she be permitted to take her own furniture with her, but that is contrary to the policy of nursing homes. Denial of that request made Sharon feel alienated and gave her the feeling of being institutionalized.

It is increasingly understood that the elderly person, like any other individual, needs psychological stimulation and a variety of other stimuli. Ironically, as an older person's living space diminishes as a result of declining health, the loss of significant others, or a limited income, the person's major source of daily stimulation becomes that housing environment. With sensory decline, older people need more stimulation or their world becomes drab.

People need social stimulation as well. It is easy for two older people to be overinvolved with one another, and each other's constant company can lead to quarrels and misunderstandings. As husbands and wives retire it is common for them to be together all the time. There is a pressing need to make sure that they spend time apart. This separating should involve both auditory and visual barriers. In a real sense, houses are indispensable regulators of human interaction because they encourage both withdrawal and association. Doors, windows, walls, and closets do much more than enclose space and conceal; they serve the crucially important function of allowing privacy.

Insight into the housing and living-space problems of the elderly gives us a picture of the problems as well as the conditions encountered by the elderly. Type of housing as well as life style affects the aging person. Society should take steps to commit finances and technology to upgrade the services offered to the elderly.

Crime

Frail older adults do not go out after dark. The fears of the elderly are based on their recognition of their frailty and diminished ability to protect themselves from a potential attacker. The incidence of the most serious violent crimes—murder, rape, and assault—is quite low among the elderly; however, 25% of the elderly respondents to a survey identified the fear of crime as a serious problem among the elderly (National Institute on Aging, 1982; National Council on Aging, 1984).

The crimes that most threaten older people are fraud, vandalism, and purse snatching (National Institute on Aging, 1982). Con artists rob the elderly of their savings, sometimes leaving them virtually penniless. Because of the victims' fear of embarrassment, many of the crimes go unreported when the victims have other means of support.

Cross-Cultural Patterns of Aging

The experience of aging is affected by a person's culture. In some cultures aged persons are admired for their wisdom; in another culture they are left on an ice floe to die; in still others, they are simply ignored. Among the cross-cultural variables are typical lifestyle, level of health, medical care, diet, and exercise. Within the United States alone, cross-cultural factors vary considerably.

The plight of the Black elderly is a state of "double jeopardy"—that is, subject to discrimination based on both race and age. This description still holds true. Today it could also be applied to other groups, including Native Americans, Mexican–Americans, and Puerto Ricans.

All the problems that the elderly face are even more agonizing for the minority elderly. They tend to be poorer, experience more frequent illness, and be less likely to have their illnesses treated. They tend to be less well educated, have a history of unemployment, and live in poorer housing. They have shorter life expectancies. They have greater needs for social and medical services and they live in areas where such services are less accessible.

Another tragedy that is common among minority groups is the inability of workers to collect the Social Security and Medicare benefits they have earned; they die too young to qualify for them. Another disadvantage is that many minority-group workers hold jobs not covered by Social Security.

The experiences of aging are made more meaningful by the families to which they belong. The family structure creates for the elderly person a sense of mutual responsibility. For instance, among Hispanic families, the elderly are treated with respect. Grandparents play an important role in child rearing, as well as exerting considerable influence over family decisions. In recent years, with assimilation, this pattern is breaking down, and the relationships between generations are becoming more like those in the population in general. The extended-family pattern is still prevalent in this group, however, and the position of the elderly is still relatively high.

Black families protect their own through an extensive kinship network by which the generations help each other with financial aid, child care, advice, and other supports. This network usually supplements formal assistance from community and governmental agencies by providing extra help for needy family members (Mindel, 1983). However, Blacks still need help as 1970 statistics show that in every state twice as many Black aged need financial help as White aged. Blacks also tend to define themselves as old at a chronologically younger age than Whites (Lowy, 1979).

Hobart Jackson (1975) wrote that there are unfortunate implications of the latest emphasis on the development of programs as an alternative to institutionalization. He indicated the problem was not how to keep the older Black person out of an institution, but how to get him into a good one. All minorities constitute about 4 percent of the total nursing home population, with the Black aged constituting about 3 percent of that total.

Jackson proposed the development of a multi-purpose, multi-service geriatric center that would provide both institutional and non-institutional services, to be located in minority neighborhoods.

Lowy (1979) indicates that the average life expectancy for the Native American is 44 years of age. There is very little information about the aged Native American. The majority live on reservations, with very little income and very poor housing.

Many old people of various ethnic groups in the United States—especially people born in other countries—do not take advantage of many community and governmental services for which they are eligible. They see such services as a form of charity, which they are too proud to accept, and they are also unwilling to travel outside their own homes because they are uncomfortable in dealing with other groups whose ways they do not understand. The suicide rate for aged Asian Americans is three times higher than the national average, indicating that this population could greatly benefit from programs offered (Lowy, 1979).

The Rural Elderly

Most elderly people who live in rural areas are poor. About one-third of the men and even more of the women have an average annual income of less than $2,000. Only one-quarter of the elderly work after the age of 65. In non-metropolitan areas, about 60 percent of the elderly occupy substandard housing. The rural elderly have been self-sufficient in their youth and therefore are often ashamed to ask for or take advantage of services. There is a need to develop outreach programs for the elderly, including providing them with transportation (Manney, 1975).

Older Women

Another group that is particularly discriminated against is older women. As mentioned before, there are two prejudices operating against them, ageism and sexism. There are such stereotypes as the ever-ready mother-in-law stories, the unmarried aunts who are scorned as old maids, and the grandmother who outlives grandfather and becomes a family nuisance. There is low visibility of older women in our country and they are rarely viewed as viable, valuable human beings.

Seventy-year-old Winsome, a Jamaican, lived in the United States. She had three sons whom she struggled to educate while she worked as a maid. With great difficulty, her sons graduated from college, married, and struggled in their jobs to reach their idea of American middle class standards. Two of the married sons moved away. The youngest, who still lived close by, hardly visited his mother, who had had a stroke and was hard of hearing. She felt neglected by her son and often complained to him about her situation.

As a stroke patient, she came to the attention of the hospital social worker. Through interviews, the worker came to understand Winsome's plight, got her a hearing aid and visited her regularly. The social worker met Winsome's son while he was visiting his mother. The son apologetically told the social worker that he could not visit his mother on a day-to-day basis because there were demands in his life as well. He was working hard to reach the middle class standards his mother had set for him. He also felt that his mother was over-demanding. The social worker spent the rest of that interview trying to help the mother and son understand each other's perspectives and trying to improve communication between them. This eased the situation and greatly improved the mother-son relationship. The son promised to visit the mother on a more regular basis, and Winsome promised to try to understand her son's situation and not complain if he was unable to visit every day.

However there are two areas in which older women are not powerless to help themselves and their peers. Politically, older women are at an advantage. With a voting strength of many millions, about 90 percent of them are registered voters and vote regularly. They have the political strength to elect into office candidates who are sympathetic to their causes.

Although many older women are poor, some do have tremendous amounts of money. These women could use their resources to provide backing to women's movements, particularly to those who are attempting to solve the problems of their own age group (Butler & Lewis, 1973).

Death

The final stage of life is death.

Death can be defined as a process of transition that starts with dying and ends with being dead (Kalish, 1976). There are various ways of describing death. Dying is the period when the organism loses its viability. The term *dying* refers to a dying trajectory, which encompasses the speed with which a person dies and the rate of decline in functioning. The word *death* can also be defined as the point at which a person becomes physically dead. Often when we mention that a person has died at a certain time we are referring to the process by which a person has passed from being something to becoming something.

It has been possible to stimulate artificially both breathing and heartbeat; thus, there is currently a legal tangle over determining when a person is physically dead. Physical death can be described as a physical process at the end of which people are no longer feeling, thinking beings. Social death occurs when the dying person is no longer capable of hearing, seeing, and understanding what others are saying. Sometimes social death occurs before physical death.

The most frequent causes of death of the elderly are heart attack, strokes, cancer, influenza, and pneumonia. In contrast, the leading causes of death for people between 25 and 44 are accidents, heart diseases, cancer, suicide, and cirrhosis of the liver.

Contemplating death appears to occupy a large portion of the elderly person's life, particularly when the person is sick or bedridden with permanent physical disabilities. Although the inevitability of death does cross their minds, few people can really grasp the meaning of their own death or the idea of their own extinction, especially by natural causes (Kübler-Ross, 1969). People usually view their own deaths as being the result of an act of an outside force. It is impossible for them to visualize lying quietly in bed and allowing death to overtake them.

How people react to death or the dying depends on the manner in which they have been helped to cope with such situations, as well as on their previous patterns of coping and adaptation. Older people who live past their expected number of years may feel that they are living on borrowed time. Dealing with the deaths of their friends can help socialize older people toward acceptance of their own death.

Fear of death is also associated with the lack of religious belief. Those people who are religious do not fear death as much as those who are irreligious; and atheists do show more fear of death. Uncertain and sporadically religious people show the greatest fear of death.

To deny death is to believe that people continue to experience some form of life after their physical death. Physical death is undeniable, but mental death is deniable. Belief in an afterlife, belief in the existence of ghosts, spirits, angels, or demons, and belief in reincarnation are all ways of denying death and the ability to experience death. Denial can also mean that when physicians tell their patients that they are going to die, they realize that their message was not really heard (Kalish, 1976).

Dying

Dying can be quick or lingering. When a person is diagnosed as terminal, that individual is assigned the role of a dying person. Young people with terminal conditions are expected to fight death, to try to finish business, and to cram as much experience as possible into their remaining time. We expect younger people to be active and antagonistic about dying. All dying persons are apt to find that the role of the dying person means having less control over their own lives. At first the younger person fights to maintain control over his or her life, but slowly the person realizes that he or she does not have much control. This realization is particularly strong among older people, and they are allowed less time than the young for expressing anger and frustration about death.

Kübler-Ross's stages.   For a long time there was no literature on death and dying, but today there are books, magazines, and professional journals on the subject. The first person who made a detailed study of death and dying was Elisabeth Kübler-Ross. She focused on the short-term situation that follows a person's first recognition that death is an imminent possibility. For instance, when a person is overtaken by a fatal illness the person may realize that he or she is involved in a serious situation. Kübler-Ross identified five stages of death and dying: (1) denial, (2) anger, (3) bargaining, (4) depression, and ultimately, (5) acceptance.

Once the initial shock that death is inevitable wears off, people may try to deny the coming event. Later they are overcome with anger because they do not have any control over the situation. Next people start to bargain, thinking that maybe somehow they can prolong life. Eventually, hopelessness and depression may take hold, in one of two forms: reactive depression and preparatory depression. Reactive depression is a response to losses incurred so far—physical deterioration, depletion of financial resources, and the crumbling of one's hopes and dreams. Preparatory depression is grieving for oneself, just as elderly people, like others, may suffer anticipatory grief at the prospect of a spouse's death. It is very difficult for dying people to speak of their own grief. However, their expressions of sorrow may ease the way for their death and move them toward the final stage—acceptance of death, not only by themselves but to some degree by the rest of the family. When dying people are kept in the dark about their own impending death, they are deprived of participation in it and denied the opportunity of bringing any final, meaningful conclusion to their lives.

Surrounding circumstances. Many people die in health-care institutions, but most people prefer to die at home. A death at home imposes a heavier burden on the family, but most family members are glad when death at home is possible.

A consideration receiving increasing attention is when and how long a person should be allowed to live. An elderly patient may ask that no extraordinary measures are to be taken to prolong his or her life. Kalish (1976) reports that some patients make "living wills" spelling out their wishes. The dying person's participation in decisions about the where and when of death is important.

It is important that dying persons not be abandoned, humiliated, or lonely at the end of their lives. Encouraging as well as maintaining their intimate personal relationships with others is a critical aspect of the social care of elderly persons.

A person who undergoes a long dying trajectory may understand and resolve the issues of dying and allow the survivors actually to work through their grief reactions in advance. In some cases, the dying process is so slow that the final event brings more relief than grief (Kalish, 1976).

The "right to die" movement advocates the rights of terminally ill patients to decide when they want to die, despite the wishes of their doctors to prolong their lives. Proponents of this movement favor the use of euthanasia (mercy killing), withholding the use of life-sustaining procedures and equipment, and letting nature take its course. Voluntary euthanasia has become an increasingly controversial issue as science and technology develop more and more methods for sustaining life. The laws that govern the rights of terminally ill patients to terminate treatment are often unclear and vary from state to state (Shapiro, 1978).

Hospices.   Hospices are innovative means of organizing the efforts of health-service providers and families around the goals of minimizing the pain associated with terminal illnesses and allowing terminally ill people to die with dignity. The multidisciplinary hospice staff seeks to care not only for the dying but for their families as well.

The first well-known hospice, St. Christopher's, was started in 1967 in London, with the primary function of freeing the patient of pain and of any memory or fear of pain. Besides freedom from pain, the staff at St. Christopher's provides comfort and companionship to their patients. Families, including children, are free to visit at any time except for Mondays, when no visiting is permitted. Families are not made to feel guilty if they do not visit. However, family members are encouraged to help with patient care; patients often go back and forth between hospice and home. The median stay at the hospice is two to three weeks. Half of the patients return home to die with dignity. Interest in the hospice concept has grown rapidly.

In the United States, hospice care can be offered at home, in an institution, or in a hospital. There are approximately 1,100 hospice programs in the United States. These programs highlight family-oriented, warm, personal patient care. In this setting the medical and helping professions work together to ease the pain and treat the symptoms of patients, keep them comfortable and alert, as well as show interest and concern to the patient's family and help them deal with their loved one's impending death.

The difference between hospital and hospice care is the fact that the hospice team is able to spend more time with the patients and their families in helping them to cope with their situation (Kane, Wales, Bernstein, Leibowitz, & Kaplan, 1984).

Bereavement

Bereavement is the process of recovery from the death of another individual. The process of bereavement could finish quickly or it could take a long time. It was found that 48% of widows felt that they got over their husband's deaths very quickly, whereas about 20% felt that they had never gotten over it and did not expect to. Individual reactions took three forms: physical, emotional, and intellectual. Some common physical reactions to grief include shortness of breath, frequent sighing, tightness in the chest, feelings of emptiness in the abdomen, loss of energy, and stomach upset (Kalish, 1976). These reactions are particularly common in the period immediately following the death and generally diminish with time. The mortality rates of widowed people are higher than those of married people.

Emotional reactions to death include anger, guilt, depression, and anxiety, as well as preoccupation with thoughts of the deceased (Parkes, 1972). These responses diminish with time. A longitudinal study of widows and widowers shows that those who reacted to bereavement by becoming depressed were more likely than others to report disproportionately poor health a year later (Bornstein, 1973).

The intellectual aspect of bereavement consists of what Lopata (1973) calls the "purification" of the memory of the deceased. In this process the negative aspects of the person are stripped away, leaving behind an idealized, positive memory. Even women who had hated their husbands mentioned that they felt their husbands had been good people.

Glick, Weiss, and Parks (1974) found that men and women react somewhat differently to bereavement. In terms of reaction to loss, men feel that they have lost part of themselves, whereas women feel that they have been deserted and left to fend for themselves. Recently bereaved people are exempt from certain responsibilities. Family and friends help with cooking and caring for dependents. Older women find that their decisions are being made for them by their adult children. These social supports for the bereaved person are temporary. Usually people are expected to reengage in the social world as quickly as possible.

Widowhood.   Widowhood is usually seen as something that happens to women, but it happens to men as well.

The role of a widow in U.S. society is primarily a long-term role for older women. Young widows play the widow role for only a short time, and then they are considered single rather than widowed (Lopata, 1973). Widowhood is seen by society as something that would make younger people feel stigmatized. Older widows, even those who are only in their sixties, see their status as being different; the prevalence of widowhood in later life combined with low rates of remarriage can produce for older women a lower social position.

The role of the older widow is a vague one. Ties with the husband's family are usually drastically reduced. The position of older widow serves to label a woman as a member of a social category with certain important features: older widows are to keep the memories of their husbands alive; they are not supposed to be interested in men; they are supposed to do things with their children or with other widows.

Being an older widow changes the position and self-identity of a woman. For traditionally oriented women, the role of wife is central to life. Widowhood may therefore mean not only the loss of the person whom they can support but a changed concept of themselves as persons.

How these women cope with their identity crisis depends on whether their status is based on personal qualities type: role-invested people may take up jobs, or they may increase their investment in jobs they already have; people who are primarily acquirers may place their identity in things rather than in people. For these women, an adjustment in self-concept is required if widowhood brings a substantial change in acquisitional power. Unfortunately, many widows find that their quality of living changes markedly. Sometimes all three orientations may be present in the same person, and coping strategies may reflect all three changes in investment of energy.

Loneliness is an important aspect of the widow's life because of the absence of a significant relationship. Some of this loneliness could result from economic factors, too. Kunkel (1979) found low levels of loneliness in a small-town sample of widows; only a quarter felt lonely. But in urban areas a larger percentage of widows felt lonely. Both Atchley (1975) and Morgan

(1976) have pointed out that economic conditions are an important component to loneliness. Aloneness should not be confused with loneliness. Many widows quickly become accustomed to living alone, and more than half continue to live alone.

One of the most dreaded roles that an elderly person may have to play is that of dependent. The dependency role could be either physical or financial, and either way it is a very difficult position for most adults to accept. This is easy to understand. We have been taught that it is important to be independent and self-sufficient. Therefore, it is not surprising that older people are hostile to the idea of giving up their autonomy and becoming dependent on others. With dependency come changes in roles, especially for parents who have to depend upon their adult children. The elderly parents resent having to depend upon them; they become frustrated and angry by their reversal of positions and feel guilty that they are a burden to their children.

The experience of losing a spouse is different for men and women. Although statistics may change as more and more women get into the work force, by present averages women tend to outlive men. As Lopata (1975) indicates, for most women, widowhood spells disaster because they have been economically dependent on their husbands. Life without a spouse also means the loss of some friendships, because married couples tend to socialize more with other couples than with widowed women. The income of the Black widow was found to be far less than that of the White widow, but the ratios of widowed and married women were similar for Blacks and non-Blacks. Both groups of widows had lower incomes than married women.

Women's adjustment to widowhood also depends on the social background and the social roles that the women played before the deaths of their husbands. Those women who were highly involved in the role of wife, particularly those who were educated middle-class women, suffered the strongest disruption after the deaths of their husbands (Lopata, 1975). Other women, who lived in a more sex-segregated world, or who held jobs or were involved in their neighborhoods, did not find the deaths of their husbands as devastating.

Lopata (1975) classified widows into five groups:

1. the traditional widow, who spends time with her children, her grandchildren, and her siblings
2. the liberated widow, who has led a life that was multidimensional
3. the merry widow, who is socially active
4. the working widow, who focuses on her job
5. the "return-to-work" widow, who spends much time on her work but does not get much economic reward

This last classification of widow is called the *widow's widow;* she remains in this role and is unwilling to relinquish it through remarriage or devotion to grandparenting.

Normally both men and women find all aspects of their life affected: their psychosocial needs, their household roles, nutrition and health care, transportation, and education. Usually widowers are more lonely, have a lower morale, and are more dissatisfied with life than widows. Often they need help with household chores, they eat poorly, and they have strong negative images of themselves. Widowers are often more unwilling to talk about widowhood or death than widows are. Many do not want to have a confidante. However, widowers tend to remarry; they view the loss of a wife as devastating.

Remarriage.   Many people remarry in their old age. Remarriage constitutes a workable alternative for older widows and widowers; the number of remarriages has doubled during the past 20 years. In a study on older people who remarried, Vinick (1978) interviewed more than 60 people in order to determine how those individuals experienced the event of remarriage. Most widows as well as widowers chose to live alone for a period of time after the death of the spouse, but men tended to remarry rather quickly, whereas women tended to wait. Men were remarried within a year of their widowhood, but only three women were remarried three years after the deaths of their spouses. Most of those new couples had known each other for a long period of time; they had been the spouses of friends or were introduced by mutual friends after the deaths of their spouses.

The most significant reason for remarriage was the need for companionship. Men also mentioned that they had a desire to care, whereas women mentioned that they liked the personal qualities of their respective spouses. Vinick further noted that a large percentage of these couples were satisfied in their new marriages—80% of the women and 87% of the men. It was only when people married for external reasons that they found they were not happy; one woman admitted that she married her husband for financial security but found him to be autocratic and miserly. Older married people were found to have serenity in their marriages that was not present among young married people. In many ways, older marriages are different and also less stressful; they are free from the strains of early marriages in the sense that they are free from child rearing, ambition for higher status, and conflict with in-laws. Older people have learned that it does not pay to get into an argument, that one should contain one's feelings, and that it takes two to get into an argument. One of the chief difficulties of marriage for older women is that there are fewer available men. The life expectancy of men is less than that of women and therefore the number of potential male partners is drastically reduced.

At 70, Rebecca had spend her lifetime helping her husband carry on his business. They did not have any children. After 40 years of married life, her husband passed away. Rebecca had always been dependent on her husband, and after his death she became dependent upon her younger sister Margaret, who was financially very well off. Margaret looked down on her older sister and did not encourage her to do anything but vegetate. When Rebecca commented that she would like to remarry, Margaret responded that she would never be able to do it because she did not have the looks for it. Rebecca did not have the self-confidence to resist that type of criticism or act on her own initiative. Used to doing what her husband told her, she was dependent on other people's opinions. Her dilemma seemed to be, "I want to do something, but I don't know just what it is or how to go about doing it."

Harry retired at 65. His wife died a few months later. Harry was totally lost; he had depended on her for everything from cooking and cleaning to emotional support. She was the first person to whom her children turned when they needed help or advice. Her death altered Harry's life completely; he was devastated. He would lie in bed for hours, not knowing if it was day or night. In a short period of time he aged considerably, most of it as the result of mourning for his wife. His children visited him sporadically and decided to place him in an institution for the elderly because they did not know if he would survive by himself. They did not consider Harry's opinions because at that point they viewed him as a burden and felt he would be better off under institutional care. Harry protested mildly but soon decided to take his chances and become a resident in a nursing home.

Implications for Social Work Practice

According to social workers, human aging is developmental. From this perspective, there are losses and gains to be made at every point in life. An elderly person continues to grow as long as the gains outweigh the losses.

Older people need support systems to function independently. They need support groups in order to continue active participation in society. They need freedom of choice with regard to their degree of disengagement from activity, they need to integrate their life experience, and they need protection of their integrity as their lives come to an end (Ganter & Yeakel, 1980). Social workers should be aware of the social support systems with which people function; these include family, friendships, the community of neighbors, and professional, occupational, religious, and self-help networks.

Causes of intergenerational conflicts cannot be determined in general terms; such conflicts arise and are dealt with differently by different social groups. The expected patterns of behavior and cultural values of Asian–Americans and Puerto Ricans, for example, engender respectful behavior toward elders.

Eighty-year-old Srinath is a farmer. He lives in an extended family home in rural India. His sons, grandsons, and all their wives live in the same home. Srinath is revered and viewed as the head of the family. When any important decisions have to be made, Srinath's opinion is considered very valuable. His adult children obey and respect him.

Abuse of the elderly is becoming more obvious in our culture. Services for the abusers can reduce their stress and give them different options, to allow them to be caregivers instead of paingivers. Some of these services could be financial assistance, education, emotional support, and also caregiving help, so that the overstressed caregiver can take a day or weekend off, for their own revival.

In work with aged people, social workers make the bridge between the individual and the social reality. Their task is to redefine a set of expectations; to help older adults organize their lives in accordance with the older adult's expectations, as well as helping them make social contributions that complement new goals. The pressures on the aging to conform to the societal stereotypes of infirmity and uselessness make the task of orienting them toward productivity very difficult. The new goals entail recognition and support for the rights of the individuals to continue to grow, to free their life force, to integrate their own life experiences, and to liberate themselves from restraints so that they can be what they wish to be. Without this liberation, the aged can devalue themselves and fail to move ahead toward new accomplishments.

Chapter Summary

In our society the prevailing negative attitude toward the elderly colors old people's feelings toward themselves as well as society's manner of treating them.

There are various models of aging. Schaie proposes three models of change: one that applies when older people are pathology-free, one that describes an irreversible decrement to psychological processes, and one that describes decrement with compensation, in which environmental inputs compensate for biologically determined decrements.

The genetic theory of aging specifies that aging is affected by the genes. The nongenetic cellular theory proposes that the body is affected by wear and tear and functions accordingly. The cross-link theory indicates that chemical as well as physical changes affect how molecules function. These theories have not been tested by research with humans. The immunological theory holds that as age increases, the number of autoimmune antibodies increase, leading to age-related diseases such as rheumatoid arthritis and diabetes.

Physical aging is characterized by an increase in chronic diseases, such as arthritis, heart conditions, and high blood pressure.

Adaptations to aging have been presented in the disengagement, activity, role-exit, social-exchange, and consolidation theories of aging. Disengagement theory speaks of withdrawal from society. Activity theory says that participating in activities can lead to more successful aging. Role-exit theory states that as people get older, the number of roles they play diminishes. Social-exchange theory proposes that when people enter relationships they receive rewards such as a sense of security and nonrewards such as fatigue. Consolidation theory describes a consolidation of commitments as well as redistribution of energies so that people can cope with lost roles and have more energy for other activities.

A number of myths about aging and the elderly have been refuted by statistics.

The eighth and final stage of life in Erikson's theory is that of integrity versus despair. Aging people develop either an acceptance of their lives or a fear of impending death accompanying the realization that time is too short to correct past mistakes.

Age itself is not a good indicator for evaluating cognitive performance. Although there is a slowing of performance and some loss of memory, a person's overall cognitive functioning is most closely related to his or her education and previous levels of performance. People vary in their abilities to compensate for cognitive deficits.

The pattern of one's adjustment to old age is related to previous personality type and lifestyle. People react variously to retirement. Some look forward to retirement and, thereafter, a gradual further disengagement; others find continued involvement in some job or perhaps an unpaid occupation necessary. Whether a person reacts well or poorly to retirement depends on health, income, personal lifestyle, and whether the retirement is chosen or involuntary.

Successful aging involves both a life review and a coming to terms with one's life and the inevitability of death.

There is no one role for grandparents in the United States. Different styles of grandparenting have been identified.

Religion plays a role in the lives of many elderly people; self-images and personalities are influenced by religious orientations.

Many older people fear crime. Statistics show that their fear far exceeds their likelihood of being victimized by violent crime.

Aging differs in its effects on the elderly according to culture. In some cultures the aged are respected, and therefore they continue to be active as older adults; in some they are not respected, and older people tend to devalue themselves accordingly. All problems faced by old people in the United States are complicated by membership in minority groups.

The influence of one's living arrangements on the quality of one's life increases as one's mobility is reduced. The variety of alternative living arrangements for the elderly has increased in recent times. Type of housing affects the lifestyles of the aging.

The inevitability of death becomes apparent as people grow older. Kübler-Ross identifies five stages of dying: denial, anger, bargaining, hopelessness and depression, and acceptance.

There is an increasing concern for the psychosocial needs of the elderly ill. Terminally ill patients may want more control over their treatment and a lessened emphasis on prolongation of life. One major advance in care for the dying is the hospice movement beginning in our country, following the lead of Great Britain.

Bereavement is the process of recovery from the death of another individual. Loss of spouse is a major stress that affects the aged population. Grieving over loss is part of the adjustment process.

Given the different life expectancies of the sexes and the tendency of men to marry younger women, more women than men tend to be widowed. Although widowhood affects people differently, those who adjust best continue to lead active and engaged lives. Remarriage, particularly for companionship, tends to be a positive experience for the elderly.

References

Atchley, R. C. (1975). Dimensions of widowhood in later life. *The Gerontologist, 15.*

Atchley, R. C. (1977). *The social forces in later life* (2nd ed.). Belmont, CA: Wadsworth.

Back, K. W. (1969). The ambiguity of retirement. In E. W. Busse & E. Pfeiffer (Eds.), *Behavior and adaptation in late life.* Boston: Little, Brown.

Baltes, P. B., & Labouvie, G. V. (1973). Adult development of intellectual performance: Description, explanation and modification. In C. Eisdorfer & M. P. Lawton (Eds.), *The psychology of adult development and aging.* Washington, DC: American Psychological Association.

Baltes, P. B., & Schaie, K. W. (1973). *Lifespan developmental psychology.* New York: Academic Press.

Bengston, V. L., Cueller, J. B., & Ragan, P. K. (1975). Stratum contrasts and similarities in attitudes toward death. *Journal of Gerontology, 32,* 76–88.

Blau, P. M. (1964). *Exchange of power in social life.* New York: Wiley.

Blau, Z. S. (1973). *Old age in a changing society.* New York: New Viewpoints.

Bornstein, P. E. (1973). The depression of widowhood after thirteen months. *British Journal of Psychiatry, 122,* 561–566.

Botwinick, J. C. (1970). Learning in children and in older adults. In L. R. Goulet & P. B. Baltes (Eds.), *Life-span developmental psychology: Research and theory.* New York: Academic Press.

Butler, R. N. (1974). Successful aging. *Mental Hygiene, 58.*

Butler, R., & Lewis, M. (1973). *Aging and mental health.* St. Louis, MO: C. V. Mosby.

Clavan, S. (1978). The impact of social class and social trends on the role of the grandparents. *The Family Coordinator, 27.*

Clayton, R. R. (1975). *The family, marriage and social change.* Lexington, MA: D. C. Heath.

Cowgill, D. O. (1974). Aging and modernization: A revision of theory. In J. F. Gubrium (Ed.), *Late life.* Springfield, IL: Charles C Thomas.

Cowgill, D. O., & Holmes, L. D. (Eds). (1972). *Aging and modernization.* New York: Appleton-Century-Crofts.

Cox, H., & Bhak, A. (1979). Symbolic interaction and retirement: Adjustment—an empirical event. *International Journal of Aging and Human Development, 9, 3.*

Craik, F. (1977). Psychopathology and social pathology. In J. Birren & K. W. Schaie (Eds.), *Handbook of the psychology of aging.* New York: Van Nostrand Reinhold.

Cummings, E., & Henry, W. E. (1961). *Growing old: The process of disengagement.* New York: Basic Books.

Denney, N. W. (1974). Classification abilities in the elderly. *Journal of Gerontology, 29.*

Erikson, E. (1980). *Identity and the life cycle.* New York: Norton.

Flavell, J. H. (1970). Cognitive changes in adulthood. In L. R. Goulet & P. B. Baltes (Eds.), *Lifespan developmental psychology: Research and theory.* New York: Academic Press.

Ganter, G., & Yeakel, M. (1980). *Human behavior and the social environment.* New York: Columbia University Press.

Gardner, W. J. (1971). *A history of Jamaica from its discovery by Christopher Columbus to the year 1972.* London: Frank Cass.

Glick, I. O., Weiss, R. S., & Parks, C. M. (1974). *The first year of bereavement.* New York: Wiley.

Harris Poll & National Council on Aging. (1975). *The myths and realities of aging in America.* Washington, DC: National Council on Aging.

Havighurst, R. J. (1953). *Human development and education.* New York: Longman.

Homans, G. C. (1974). *Social behavior: Its elementary forms* (rev. ed.). New York: Harcourt Brace Jovanovich.

Hooyman, N. R., Rathbone-McCuan, E., & Klingbeil, K. (1982). Serving the vulnerable elderly. *The Urban and Social Change Review, 15* (2), 9–13.

Horn, J. L., & Donaldson, G. (1976). On the myth of intellectual decline in adulthood. *American Psychologist, 31,* 701–719.

Hultsch, D. F. (1969). Adult age differences in the organization of free recall. *Developmental Psychology, 1.*

Hultsch, D. F. (1971). Adult age differences in free classification and free recall. *Developmental Psychology, 4.*

Hultsch, D. F. (1974). Learning to learn in adulthood. *Journal of Gerontology, 29.*

Jackson, H. (1975, August). Crisis in our nursing homes. *Urban Health Journal.*

Kagan, J., & Moss, H. A. (1962). *Birth to maturity: A study in psychological development.* New York: Wiley.

Kahana, B., & Kahana, B. (1971). Theoretical and research perspectives on grandparenthood. *Aging and human development, 2.*

Kalish, R. A. (1976). Death and dying in a social context. In R. Binstock & E. Shanas (Eds.), *Handbook of aging and social sciences.* New York: Van Nostrand Reinhold.

Kane, R. I., Wales, J., Bernstein, L., Leibowitz, A., & Kaplan, S. (1984, April 21). A randomized controlled trial of hospice care. *Lancet,* 890–894.

Kübler-Ross, E. (1969). *On death and dying.* New York: Macmillan.

Kunkel, S. R. (1979). Sex differences in adjustment to widowhood. Unpublished master's thesis, University of Miami, Florida.

La Rue, A., & Jarvik, L. F. (1982). Old age and behavioral changes. In B. J. Wolman & G. Stricker (Eds.), *Handbook of developmental psychology.* Englewood Cliffs, NJ: Prentice-Hall.

Lopata, H. (1973). *Widowhood in an American city.* Cambridge, MA: Schenkman.

Lopata, H. Z. (1975). Widowhood: Societal factors in lifespan disruptions and alternatives. In N. Datan & L. H. Ginsberg (Eds.), *Lifespan developmental psychology: Normative life crisis.* New York: Academic Press.

Lowenthal, M. F. (1972). Some potentialities of a life-cycle approach to the study of retirement. In F. M. Carp (Ed.), *Retirement.* New York: Behavioral Publications.

Lowy, L. (1979). *Social work with the aging.* New York: Harper & Row.

Maas, H. S., & Kuypers, J. (1974). *From thirty to seventy.* San Francisco: Jossey-Bass.

Maddox, G. L. (1969). Disengagement theory: A critical evaluation. *The Gerontologist, 4,* 80–83.

Manney, Jr., J. (1975). *Aging in American society.* Detroit, MI: Wayne State University, Institute of Gerontology.

Masters, W. H., & Johnson, V. E. (1966). *Human sexual response.* Boston: Little, Brown.

McKain, W. C. (1967). Community roles and activities of older rural persons. In E. G. Youmans (Ed.), *Older rural Americans.* Lexington: University of Kentucky Press.

Miller, S. J. (1965). The social dilemma of the aging leisure participant. In A. M. Rose & W. A. Peterson (Eds.), *Older people and their social world.* Philadelphia: F. A. Davis.

Mindel, C. H. (1983). The elderly in minority families. In T. H. Brubaker (Ed.), *Family relationships in later life.* Beverly Hills, CA: Sage.

Morgan, L. A. (1976). A re-examination of widowhood and morale. *Journal of Gerontology, 31,* 6.

National Council on Aging. (1978). *Fact book on aging: A profile of America's older population.* Washington, DC: National Council on Aging.

National Institute on Aging. (1982). *Crime and the elderly.* Washington, D.C.: Government Printing Office.

National Institute on Aging. (1984). *Be sensible about salt.* Washington, D.C.: Government Printing Office.

Neugarten, B. L. (1973). Personality change in late life: A developmental perspective. In C. Eisdorfer & M. P. Lawton (Eds.), *The psychology of adult development and aging.* Washington, DC: American Psychological Association.

Neugarten, B. L. (1976). *The psychology of aging: An overview.* Presentation from APA Master Lectures. Washington, DC: American Psychological Association.

Neugarten, B. L., & Moore, J. W. (1968). The changing age-status system. In B. L. Neugarten (Ed.), *Middle age and aging.* Chicago: University of Chicago Press.

Neugarten, B. L., & Weinstein, K. K. (1964). The changing American grandparent. *Journal of Marriage and the Family, 26.*

Palmore, E. (1975). *The honorable elders.* Durham, NC: Duke University.

Papalia, D. E., & Olds, S. W. (1986). *Human development.* New York: McGraw-Hill.

Parkes, C. M. (1972). *Bereavement: Studies of grief in adult life.* New York: International University Press.

Pedrick-Cornell, C., & Gelles, R. J. (1982). Elder abuse: The status of current knowledge. *Family Relations, 31,* 457–465.

Raeburn, P. (1984, March 5). Alzheimer's disease of the aged. *Wisconsin State Journal,* p. 1.

Reichard, S., Livson, F., & Peterson, P. G. (1962). *Aging and personality: A study of eighty-seven older men.* New York: John Wiley.

Robertson, J. F. (1976). Significance of grandparents. Perceptions of young adult grandchildren. *The Gerontologist, 16,* 137–140.

Rosen, I. (1974). *Socialization to old age.* Berkeley: University of California Press.

Saul, Shura. (1974). *Aging: An album of people growing old.* New York: Wiley.

Schaie, K. W. (1973). Reflections on papers by Looft, Peterson and Sparks: Intervention towards an ageless society. *The Gerontologist, 13,* 31–36.

Schock, N. (1977). Biological theories of aging. In J. Birren & K. W. Schaie (Eds.), *Handbook of the psychology of aging.* New York: Van Nostrand Reinhold.

Shanas, E. (1972). Adjustment to retirement: Substitution or accommodation? In F. Carp (Ed.), *Retirement.* New York: Behavioral Publications.

Shapiro, M. (1978). Legal rights of the terminally ill. *Aging, 5* (3), 23–27.

Specht, R., & Craig, G. J. (1982). *Human development.* Englewood Cliffs, NJ: Prentice-Hall.

Thomas, A., & Chess, S. (1977). *Temperament and development.* New York: Brunner/Mazel.

Tonna, E. A. (1977). Aging of skeletal and dental systems and supporting tissue. In L. E. Finch & L. Hayflick (Eds.), *Handbook of the biology of aging.* New York: Van Nostrand Reinhold.

Vander Zanden, J. W. (1978). *Human development.* New York: Knopf.

Vinick, B. H. (1978). Remarriage in old age. *The Family Coordinator, 27.*

Zastrow, C., & Kirst-Ashman, K. (1987). *Understanding human behavior and the social environment.* Chicago: Nelson-Hall.

Index

Abortion, spontaneous, 42
Abuse of the elderly, 324, 336–37
Accommodation, development of, 83
Accordion families, 252
Action Agency, 289
Activity theory of aging, 309
Adolescence, 28–29, 179–218
  biological changes, 216
  issues in, 205–215
  and single parents, 253
Adulthood:
  body transcendence, 279
  concept of, Erikson's theory, 194
  defined, 225–26
Affiliative behaviors, 86
Age:
  and casual sex, 239
  child's, and parenting, 158
  segregation by, 160
Ageism, 316–317
Aging:
  adaptation to, 337
  adults, 30–31
  cross-cultural patterns of, 327–329
  cross-link theory of, 305, 337
  and kinship relations, 324–325
  myths of, 311–312
  negative attitudes, 301
  process, theories of, 303–305
Ainsworth, M. D., 78, 85, 86
Alzheimer's disease, 315
Ambron, S. R., 3, 42, 43, 44, 45, 47, 51,
  53, 56
Amniocentesis, 47
Anencephaly, 47
Anorexia nervosa, 213
Anoxia, 50–51
Atchley, R. C., 320, 333
Attachment:
  behavior in infancy, 86, 99–100
  development of, 85–90
  measure of, 86
  threats to, 90
Attitudes and work, 235

Authoritarian:
  child-rearing practices, 122
  parenting, 130
Authoritative:
  child-rearing practices, 122–123
  parenting, 130
Autonomous development, 256–257
  in adolescence, 199, 217
  and confidence, 80
  of morality, 117–118, 141
  and parental pressure, 198–199

Bahm, R. M., 152, 200
Baltes, P. B., 2, 7, 18, 19, 21, 271, 314
Bandura, Albert, 117, 125, 140, 141
Barnett, R. C., 200, 230, 277
Baruch, G. K., 200, 230, 277
Baumrind, D., 122, 143, 156
Becker, W. C., 156, 172
Behavior:
  beginnings of, 65
  biological variables and, 304
  defined, 2
  goals of, 16
  parental, and infants, 62
  patterns, 270
Behavioral congruence, defined, 116
Behavior modification, 172
  and learning disabilities, 168–170
Bell, R. Q., 157, 254, 255
Bengston, V. L., 6, 310
Bereavement, 332–336, 338
Bernard, J., 247, 287
Bertalanffy, L. von, 8, 9
Best, C. H., 51, 52
Bicultural environments, 146–147
Biller, H. B., 152, 200
Birch, H. G., 61, 135
Birth, 53–57
  natural childbirth, 57
Bisexual, defined, 207
Block, C. R., 54, 55
Bloom, L., 112, 164

Bonding, 59–60
  father to newborn, 87
Botwinick, J., 271, 272, 315
Bowlby, J., 85, 86, 89, 90
Brodzinsky, D. M., 3, 42, 43, 44, 45, 47, 51, 53, 56
Bronfenbrenner, U., 94, 116, 160
Broverman, D., 194, 200
Broverman, I., 194, 200
Bulimia, 213–214
Busch–Rossnagel, N. A., 146, 147

Cantor, P., 211, 212
Career development:
  adjustments in middle adulthood, 287–292
  consolidation stage, 233, 275
  patterns, 236, 288–289
  in young adulthood, 235–236
Carroll, J. L., 139, 142
Centering, in preschool development, 108
Ceremonies, marking maturity, 201
Change:
  as action on environment, 9
  in adulthood, 225–232
  and chronological age, 18–19
  developmental, 3
  inter– and intra–individual, 17–18
  kinds of, 6–7
  nonnormative life events, 3
  as result of external forces, 8
Charles, A., 54, 55
Chess, S., 25, 61, 314
Children:
  abuse of, 94–95
  behavior of, and parenting, 157
  child-care centers, 93–94
  view of grandparents, 323
Chodorow, N., 16, 230
Chromosomes, 44
  abnormalities of, 42–43, 45–46
  and sexual identity, 181
Chronic illness:
  and aging, 311, 337
Circular reactions, 83
Clarkson, F., 194, 200
Climateric:
  female, 268–269
  male, 267–268
Clinical studies, 22–23
Closed–space classrooms, 146–147
Cognitive development, 14
  in adolescence, 183–186, 216
  in infancy, 99
  in institutions, 95–96
  in middle childhood, 136–38
  periods of (Piaget), 83
  and person perception, 138
  preoperational stage (Piaget), 107–109
  and sensory input, 107
  and spacial orientation, 133
  in young adulthood, 226

Cognitive functioning:
  of the ego, 10
  in old age, 313–316
Cognitive learning:
  in infancy, 82–85
  in middle adulthood, 270–272
  and moral development, 118
Cohabitation, and legal commitment, 239–240
Cohen, L. J., 85, 86
Colby, A., 15, 142, 144
Communal marriage, 240–241
Competence:
  in adolescence, 195–197, 217
  defined, 12
  experimentation and development, 28
  infant pursuit of, 70, 81–82, 99
  in middle adulthood, 274
  model, 172, 196
  in middle childhood, 154–156
  in the preschool child, 114–115, 129
Comprehensive Employment and Training
    Act (CETA), 289
Concept formation, 108–109
Conception:
  diagnosis of, 40–41
  physiology of, 39–40
Concrete operations, period of, 136
Conflict:
  adolescent–adult, 201
  in adolescence, 194
  femininity vs. success, 276, 277
  in middle age, 278–279
  parent–child, 280
  women's roles, 230–31
Conformity, and anxiety, 197
Conger, J. J., 40, 42, 110, 115
Conservation:
  and cognitive development, 136–137
  concept development, 109
Consolidation theory of aging, 310
Control:
  and experiments, 24
  overt, in preschool years, 105–106
Cooperative play, 121, 130
Coping:
  with learning disabilities, 165–166
  men's styles, middle adulthood, 274–275
Cox, M., 127, 152
Cox, R., 127, 152
Craig, G. J., 44, 46, 48, 54, 57, 84, 111, 125, 167, 168, 180, 181, 188, 244, 246, 266, 272, 279, 307, 321
Creative potential, 186
Crime, fear of, 326
Crisis, 11–12
  midlife developmental, 293–294
  pregnancy as a, 37
  preschool, and guilt, 113
Cross-link theory of aging, 305, 337
Cross-sectional design, 25
  consistency with longitudinal studies, 26

Crystallized intelligence, 272
  and the older years, 303
Cultural:
  attitudes toward adolescence, 182–183
  bias and moral behavior, 189–190
  component to self–identity, 190–191
  differences in adolescence, 216
  differences in sexual behavior, 244
  factors in infants, 87–88
  trends in raising children, 159
Culture:
  and adolescence, 202
  and aging, 302–303, 327–329, 338
  and child-rearing practices, 100
  effect on infant socialization, 97
  and language, 76, 110–111
  and malnutrition, 135–136
  minority-group, 205
  and moral development, 143
  and pregnancy, management of, 38
  and school rules, 144
Cummings, Elaine, 264, 308, 319
Cystic fibrosis, 46

Danziger, S. K., 55, 56
Darling, R. B., 37, 46
Darrow, C. N., 230, 233, 275
Data:
  collection, 20, 24–26
  mapping of, 2
  raw data, defined, 2
Death, 63, 323, 329–336
Decrement model of aging, 303–304
Dennis, W., 22, 95
Deoxyribonucleic acid, 44
Dependency:
  defined, 85–86
  of the elderly, 334
Depression:
  in middle adulthood, 274
  and singleness, 287
  and widowhood, 285
Detachment, reaction to separation, 90
Development:
  and conflict resolution, 12
  defined, 3
  fetal, 43–44
  in middle adulthood, 274–278
  in middle age, 290, 293–294
  and physical setting, 106–107
  principles of infant, 70–77
  process of, 16
  reactive model of, 8
  stages of, 13–15
Developmental:
  abnormalities, 60, 62–66, 71
  factors in middle adulthood, 273
  sequence, female, 230
  tasks, 70–71, 104, 226, 227–228, 232, 266, 278–279, 308–310
Diabetes, 46

Diet (*see also* Malnutrition):
  and health in the aging, 306
Differentiation, 3–4, 71–72
  of component skills (Piaget), 227
Digestive disorders in infancy, 73
Dinnerstein, Dorothy, 16, 237
Disabilities:
  and development of initiative, 114
  language disorders, 111–112
Disease:
  in middle adulthood, 269–270
  and physical aging, 305–308
Disengagement:
  in adolescence, 199–201
  and retirement, 320
  theory of aging, 308–309
Divorce, 126–127, 130
  demographics of, 248–249
  in middle adulthood, 284–285
  and remarriage, 247–250
Dollard, J., 168, 169
Dominance hierarchy, 203
Domination:
  and middle childhood development, 159
Down's syndrome, 315
Dropping out of school, 214–215, 218
Drugs, 198, 210
  in the fetal environment, 51–52
  pain relieving, at childbirth, 56
Dying, stages of, 330–331, 338

Early adulthood, 225–258
Early childhood, and single parents, 253
Eating disorders in adolescence, 213–214, 218
Ebersole, P., 269, 267
Economic status and retirement, 320
Edgar Allen Poe Schools, 206
Education for All Children Act (1975), 167
Ego, 9–11
  adaptive function of, 10
  differentiation in adulthood, 279
  executive functions of, 11
  functions of, 32
  identity, 201, 217
  integrative functions of, 11
  object-relationship functions, 11
  as organizer, 85
  perceptive functions of, 10
  protective functions of, 10
  psychology, 10
  theorists, 11–16
  transcendence, 279
Egocentrism:
  in adolescence, 185
  and moral development, 115
  in preschool development, 108
  spatial, and growth patterns, 134
Embryonic period, 41–42
Emotional:
  bonds in young adulthood, 243
  reactions to grief, 332
  reactions to infancy, 76–77

Empty-nest stage, 317
Engrossment, 87
Environment:
 defined, 4
 of the dying, 331–332
 factors and birth defects, 63
 family, and pregnancy, 53–54
 fetal, 49–54
 and the older years, 303–304
 physical, 16
 preadaptation to, 10
 social, 16
 and work, 290–292
Erikson, Erik, 11–12, 32, 79, 193
 acculturation and developmental stages,
  78–81
 generativity vs. stagnation, 273–274
 identity in adolescence, 190–193
 initiative vs. guilt, 112–114
 integrity vs. despair, 312–313
 intimacy vs. isolation, 228–229, 231, 232,
  233, 234, 277
 on middle childhood, 149–151, 155, 171
Ethnic awareness:
 in adolescence, 216
 in minority-group children, 170
Experimental studies, field and laboratory, 23
Explanation, as a developmental task, 18
Exploration, as a human characteristic, 185
Extramarital relationships, 241

Failures, inadequacy, 150
Family:
 blended, 126
 decision making in Hispanic, 205
 demographics of, 253–254
 fluctuating, 252
 impact of children, 254–256
 and juvenile delinquency, 209
 kinship relations of the elderly, 324–325
 patterns in middle adulthood, 279–287
 patterns in young adulthood, 236–242
 reconstituted, 249
 relationships in adolescence, 197–201
 shapes of, 252
 single-parent, 253–254
Fathers:
 loss of, and adolescent development, 200
 relationships to infants, 93
Federal Bureau of Investigation, 208–209
Fishel, A., 152, 153
Fishman, C., 252, 258
Flavell, J. H., 82, 83, 85, 303
Flexibility, development of, 141
Fluid intelligence, 271–272
Foreclosure, identity, 191
Formal operations in adolescence, 184–185
Freud, S., 9, 116, 140, 156, 182, 191, 193
 views on middle childhood, 156

Ganter, G., 181, 225, 226, 256, 336
Gardner, H., 183, 202

Garrison, K. C., 146, 203, 205, 207, 211, 239,
 240, 279, 281
Geiwitz, J., 110, 115
Gender (*see also* Sex-role; Sexuality):
 and bereavement, 333
 bias in Erikson's work, 12, 151, 191
 bias in Kohlberg's work, 190
 bias in White's work, 114
 and child's reaction to divorce, 126–127
 and development of the superego, 116
 and effect on parenting, 158
 and Erikson's scheme of development,
  193–195
 and genetic defects, 46
 and grandparenting, 323
 identity, 181
 and legal sense (Piaget), 142
 and moral development, 15–16, 144
 and parental behavior, 62
 and peer groups, 162
 and physical development, 133
 and prematurity, 63
 and responses to widowhood, 335
 and self–esteem, 199–200
 and occupation, 235
 and play, 153
 and sex-roles, 152, 154
 and socialization in young adulthood, 229–
  231
 and suicide, 211
 and values of adolescence, 187
 womanhood vs. adulthood, 194
Generation gap, 199
Generativity vs. stagnation, 273–274, 278–
 279, 295
Genetic:
 counseling, 46–49
 defects, 45–46
 diagnosis of defects, 47–48
 factors and fetal development, 66
 theory of aging, 304, 337
Gesell, A., 81, 107–9
Gewitz, J. L., 40, 42
Gibbs, J., 142, 144
Gilligan, Carol, 15–16, 18, 32, 142, 144, 154,
 189, 193, 194, 195, 230, 237, 277
Glick, P. C., 214, 236, 248, 249, 279, 287
Gochros, Harvey L., 244, 246
Gormly, A. V., 3, 42, 51
Grandparenting, 321–323, 338
Greenberg, M., 87, 92
Grief:
 intellectual and physical reactions, 332
 on loss of infant, 63
Growth, intellectual, 14
Guilt and adolescence, 215
Guttentag, M., 152, 153

Hall, R. E., 52, 53
Harper, L. V., 254, 255
Havighurst, R. J., 29, 278, 280, 288, 307,
 309

Health (*see also* Disease):
  and juvenile delinquency, 210
  in middle adulthood, 267, 292–293, 294
Henry, W. E., 264, 319
Heredity:
  and birth defects, 63
  defined, 4
  and juvenile delinquency, 209
Heteronomous morality, 117–118
  dimensions of, 141–142
Heterosexual development, adolescent, 203–204
Hetherington, E. M., 41, 126, 127, 146, 152, 200, 254
Hierarchical integration, 3–4
Holistic principle of physical development, 71
Home delivery, 57
Homosexuality:
  and adolescent development, 207, 217
  in young adulthood, 242
Hope and development of independence, 112
Horizontal decalage, 137
Horn, J. L., 271, 313
Hospices, 332
Housing of the elderly, 325–326
Hultsch, D. F., 8, 21, 116, 117, 122, 124, 126, 158, 179, 268, 271, 287, 316
Human development, beginnings of, 65–66
Human Sexual Inadequacy (Masters and Johnson), 246
Human sexuality, 244–246
Hunt, M. M., 239, 241, 246

Identification:
  in adolescence, 199–201
  defined, 125
Identity:
  and adolescence, 190, 215
  negative-choice, 200
  sex-related differences, 257
  sex-role, 201–202
  types of (Gordon), 6
  women's, 193–195
Imagination, development, 114
Immunological theory of aging, 305, 337
Inadequacy:
  roots of, 113
  and the social environment, 150
Incest, 159–160
Individual differences:
  of newborns, 60–61
  and singleness, 239
Industry:
  in middle childhood, 149–151
  period of, 171
  sense of, 195
  vs. inferiority, 149–151
Infancy, 27, 70–100
  assimilation, 83
  attachment preferences, 86
  feeding schedule, 72–73
  sleep patterns, 73

Infertility, 40
Inhelder, B., 107, 109, 134, 183
Inheritance, mechanisms of, 44–45
Initiative vs. guilt, 112–114
Institutionalization:
  of children, 95–96
  in the older years, 327–328
Integrity vs. despair, 312–313, 338
Intellect as organizer, 85
Intellectual ability:
  crystallized intelligence, 272
  fluid intelligence, 271–272
  and malnutrition, 135
  in middle adulthood, 295
  of older people, 313–315
Intellectual reactions
    to grief, 332
Intelligence, *see* Intellectual ability
Intelligence tests, 314
Intelligent behavior, development of, 83–84
Intergenerational adjustment:
  conflicts and culture, 336
  in middle adulthood, 283
Inter–individual and intra-individual
    changes, 17–18
Interpersonal influence, 245
Intimacy, 256–257
  and sexuality, 242–244, 245
  vs. isolation, 228–229
  in young adulthood (Erikson), 228–229
Intuitive thought development, 108
In vitro fertilization, 41
Irreversibility development, 108
Isolation, 231

Jarvik, L. F., 307, 308
Johnson, V. E., 246, 267, 306
Jones, F. R., 146, 203, 205, 207, 239, 240
Jones, R., 279, 281
Justice:
  and moral development, 143
  and peer association, 141
Juvenile delinquency, 208–210, 217
  and high-density population, 209
  and neurological impairment, 210
  and peer influence, 209

Kagan, J., 40, 42, 76, 77, 93, 96, 110, 115, 137, 181, 184, 314
Kalish, R. A., 329, 331, 332
Kaluger, G., 73, 74, 75, 82, 104, 105, 107, 109, 226, 232
Kaluger, M. F., 73, 74, 75, 82, 104, 105, 107, 109, 226, 232
Kastenbaum, Robert, 119, 120, 133, 264, 290
Kay, W., 147, 148
Kazalunaz, J. R., 152, 153
Kennell, J. H., 59, 88, 89
Klaus, M. H., 59, 88, 89
Klien, E. B., 230, 233
Kohlberg, Lawrence, 14–15, 32, 116, 142, 154, 171, 188, 227–228

Kohlberg, Lawrence (*cont'd*)
  theory of moral development, 118, 142–144
  criticism of, 188–190

Labor force, and women, 288–289
Labouvie, E. W., 17, 18
Language, 75–76
  and concept formation, 108–109
  in middle childhood, 138
  in the preschool child, 109–112, 114, 129
  disorders, 111–112
  and prejudice, 164
  as a social skill, 110
La Rue, A., 307, 308
Latency and self–confidence, 156
Later childhood, 28
Learning (*see also* Cognitive learning):
  disabilities, 172
  in middle childhood, 165–172
Learning–theory school, 168
Lerner, R. M., 8, 21, 116, 117, 122, 124, 126,
    134, 146, 158, 179, 198, 268, 271, 287
Levinson, D., 230, 233, 275, 276, 277
Levinson, M., 230, 233, 275
Lewis, M., 62, 85, 329
Life:
  expectancy, 30, 328
  structure in adulthood, 275
  transitions and normative life events, 19
Life cycle, female, 15
Life–span perspective, 27–31
  defined, 16–17, 32
  organizing principles of, 32
Lifestyles:
  of the aging, 318–319
  impact on parenting styles, 58
Living together, *see* Cohabitation
Locomotion, development of, 114
Longitudinal research design, 25
  consistency with cross-sectional studies, 26
Lopata, H., 332, 333, 334
Loss of relationships, 237
Lowenthal, M. F., 293, 320
Lowy, L., 327, 328

McCary, J. I., 243, 246
Maccoby, E. E., 85, 158, 172, 254
McClelland, D., 195, 277
McGee, B., 230, 233
Macklin, E. D., 239, 240
Malnutrition, 135–136
Manual skills development, 74–75
Marriage:
  changing rate of, 238
  kinds of, 258
  in middle adulthood, 283–284
  in young adulthood, 237–238
Masters, W. H., 246, 267, 306
Mastery for women, 278
Masturbation, in adolescence, 208
Maturation, 4
  and infants, 74, 96

Maturation (*cont'd*)
  and juvenile delinquency, 210
  and family interactions, 158
Mead, Margaret, 64, 182–183, 254, 314
Mechanistic, paradigm, 8
Medical model of the older years, 303
Medicare, 310, 327
Memory:
  and new learning, 315–316
  stages of, 316
  types of, 315–316
Menopause, 268
Mental impairment in the elderly, 307–308
Meyering, S., 54, 55
Middle adulthood, 29–30, 264–295
Middle age, defined, 266
Middle childhood, 133–172
Midlife crisis for women, 278
Miller, Jean Baker, 16, 18, 237
Miller, N. E., 168, 169
Minimal brain damage (MBD), 165
Minuchin, S., 252, 258
Mischel, H. N., 141
Mischel, W., 8, 140, 141
Mistrust, by infants, 78
Model of aging, 303–304, 337
Modeling, 125
  and moral development, 140–141
  parental, 156
Money, J., 241, 254
Monotropy, 89
Moral development, 14–15, 171
  adult experiences in, 228
  in middle childhood, 139–144
  in the preschool child, 115–118, 129–130
  and sensitivity, 139
Morality:
  in schools, 147–148
  universality of principles, 188
  a woman's sense of, 276, 277
Moral Judgment of the Child (Piaget), 141
Moral relativism, 142
Morgan, R. F., 146, 203, 205, 207, 239, 240,
    279, 281
Morland, J. K., 163, 164
Mothering, 91–92
  multiple, 94
Motor development, 133–135
Mussen, P. H., 40, 42, 49, 110, 115
Mutuality in infancy, 89
Myogenic response, 43
Myths of aging, 311–312

Narcissistic individuals, 273–274
National Center for Education Statistics, 29
National Center for Health Statistics, 48, 60,
    126
National Council on Aging, 311
National Institute on Aging, 326
National Institute on Drug Abuse, 211
National Organization for Women (NOW),
    153

Natural experiments, 23
Naturalistic studies, 21–22
  correlation and conclusions, 24
Natural reflexes, 83
Neglect, 94–95
Neimark, E. D., 185, 186, 227
Neonate, 60–61
Nesselroade, J. R., 19, 21
Neugarten, B. L., 5, 30, 268, 271, 272, 282,
    309, 314, 321, 322
Neural system for learning, 107
Neurological impairment, 210
Newman, B. M., 134, 184, 191, 229, 230, 268,
    272
Newman, P. R., 134, 184, 191, 229, 230, 268,
    272
Nongenetic cellular theory of aging, 304–305,
    337
Normative history-graded influences, 19
Norms:
  continuity of, 6
  male behaviors as, 195
Norr, K. L., 54, 55
Norton, A., 248, 249
Nuclear family, 252

Object permanence concept, 84
Offer, D., 187, 202
Offer, J. B., 187, 202
Older American Act, 289
Older American Community Service
    Employment Act, 289
Older years, 301–339
Olds, S. W., 22, 24, 43, 194, 208, 213, 230,
    324
Open–space school, 146
Operational thought in adulthood, 227
Optimization:
  of cognitive development, 227
  as a life–span developmental task, 18
Orbach, Susie, 237
Organismic:
  paradigm, 8–9
  perspective, 13
  theory, 32
Overton, W. F., 8, 9

Palmore, E., 308, 309
Papalia, D. E., 22, 24, 43, 194, 208, 213, 230,
    324
Parallel activities:
  play, 121
  in schools, 147
Parenting (*see also* Grandparenting):
  developmental approach to, 126
  limitations on parental power, 158–160
  middle–age roles, 281–282
  in middle childhood years, 156–160
  parent-child relationships, 125–126
  in preschool years, 122–126
  reciprocity in, 125
  roles in development, 80–81, 91–93

Parenting (*cont'd*)
  stages of, 252
  styles of, 130
  tasks of, 251–253
  and young adulthood, 251
Parke, R., 41, 87, 157
Pas de deux family, 252
Peers:
  groups, 155, 204
  influences, 172
  and juvenile delinquency, 209
  in middle childhood, 160–164
  relationships with, and development, 29,
    121–122, 162–163, 196, 203–204
Perceptual:
  development, 75
  distortion, 92
Perinatology, 54
Permissiveness:
  effects of, in middle childhood, 157
  in parenting, 122, 130
Personal development and work, 234–235
Personality:
  development, 96, 100
  type and retirement, 320
Physical development:
  in adolescence, 180–186
  in infancy, 71–75
  in middle adulthood, 267–270, 294
  in middle childhood, 133–136
  in the preschool years, 104–105
  rates of, 72
Physical setting, and development, 106–107
Piaget, Jean, 13–14, 22, 32, 109
  and cognitive learning, 82–85
  criticism of work of, 186
  formal operations, 184–186, 227
  instructional theory of morality, 117–118,
    134, 136, 141, 153, 171, 183, 184–186, 227
  and moral development, 141–142
  preoperational stage, 107–109
  on young adulthood, 227
Play:
  games and social development, 153
  and moral development, 142
  in the preschool years, 108, 118–121, 130
  symbolic, 108
  and thought, 120–121
Pleasure, in middle adulthood, 278
Postparenthood, 282–283
Postural control, stages of, 74
Pottker, J., 152, 153
Power:
  and aging, 310
  limitations on parental, 158–160
Preconventional stage of development, 143
Pregnancy, 27, 37–66
  in vitro fertilization, 41
  surrogate motherhood, 41
  unwanted, 40
Prejudice, 163
Prematurity, 63

Preoperational stage (preschool), 107–109, 129
Preschool development, 27–28, 104–130
  classification concept, 109
Problem solving, personal styles of, 137
Proximodistal principle, 72
Psychoanalytic theory of moral development, 116–117, 140
Psychomotor processes in middle adulthood, 272
Psychosis in the aging, 307–308
Psychosocial development in infancy, 76–78, 99
Psychosocial environment:
  in middle adulthood, 273–278
  in middle childhood, 149–156
  needs of the aging, 338
  in the preschool years, 112–115
  in young adulthood, 226
Punishment, extremes in using, 124

Race:
  and defined delinquency, 208
  and development in adolescence, 216
  and the experience of aging, 327
  and prematurity, 63
  and self–esteem, 163–164
Radiation and environment, fetal, 52
Rationality:
  assumption about, 8
  development of, 141
Reaction time in middle adulthood, 270–271
Reality mastery, 10, 12
Reciprocity:
  and moral development, 141
  in socialization of infants, 79
Reese, H. W., 8, 9, 21
Rejection in middle childhood, 162
Relationships:
  parent–infant, 61–62
  peer, and physical attractiveness, 162–163
Reliability, 20–21
Religion, 338
  agreement between generations, 198
  and fear of death, 330
  in the older years, 323
  and values in adolescence, 187
Remarriage:
  for the elderly, 335–336, 339
  in middle adulthood, 287
Reminiscing:
  as adjustment, 321
  and aging, 31
Reproduction, 245
Research methods, 19–20, 21–23, 32
  clinical studies, 22
  cross–sectional design, 25
  ethical issues, 26–27
  experimental studies, 23
  longitudinal design, 25
  naturalistic, 21–22

Research methods (*cont'd*)
  sequential strategies, 26
  time–lag design, 26
  validity, 21
Rest, J. R., 139, 142
Restrictiveness, effects of, 157
Retirement, 319–321, 338
  defined, 319
  early, 293
  and second–career decisions, 289
Reversibility, concept of, 136
Reward, extremes in using, 124
Rh factor, 51
Rice, R. P., 204, 205
Right to die movement, 331
Ritualization of interactions, 79
Rivers, C., 230, 239, 277
Robertson, J. F., 322, 323
Rogers, D., 236, 284
Rokeach Value Survey, 186
Role diffusion, 191–192
Role-exit theory of aging, 309
Role learning, 5
  and identity, 6
  and status, by gender, 18
Rosenkrantz, P., 194, 200
Rosenman, R. H., 269, 270
Rossi, A. S., 252, 258
Rural elderly, 328

St. Chrisopher's hospice, 332
Sampling, 20
Sandwich generation, 29
Scanzoni, J. H., 97, 253
Schaie, K. W., 19, 25, 271, 301, 314
Schemata, development of, 84–85
Schock, N., 304, 305
School, 171
  class size effects, 146
  and creative potential, 186
  dropping out of, 214–215
  and juvenile delinquency, 209
  and sex-role learning, 152
  and socialization, 144–146
  special education, 167
Sears, R. R., 123, 254
Self–control, development of, 105
Self–esteem:
  in middle childhood, 163
  and parent–child relationships, 123–124
  of pregnant teenagers, 206–207
  and race, 164
Self–identity threats to, 231
Self–image, 191–193
  and integrity, 313
  in young adulthood, 232
Senior Companions, 289
Sensorimoter skills, in infancy, 73–74
Sensory input, 107
Sensuality, 244
Separation, 90–91
Sequential development, 137

Sequential strategies, 26
Seriation concept development, 109
Sex–role (*see also* Gender):
  development, 151–154, 171–172
  identity, 201–202
Sex therapy, 246–247
Sexual:
  behavior in adolescence, 198, 205–210,
    215, 217
  identity, 245–246
  maturation, 180–182
  relationships, kinds of, 258
Sexuality:
  dimensions of, 245–246
  and intimacy, 242–244
Shanas, E., 6, 309, 320
Shore, M. F., 92, 146
Sickle–cell anemia, 46
Simpson, Elizabeth L., 189, 190
Singleness:
  in middle adulthood, 287
  in young adulthood, 238–239
Single–parent families, 253–254
Smoking, 211, 218
Sociability, effect of daycare
  on, 94
Social:
  acceptance, with peers, 162
  aspects of aging, 316–323
  class and reactions to pregnancy, 37
  competence, development of, 196–197, 155
  consciousness, development of, 141
  development, defined, 5
  enslavement, example, 198–199
  environment, 59, 118–122
  institutions, and the elderly, 324
  integration in middle adulthood, 264
  interaction in infancy, 77
  issues and the elderly, 324–329
  justice, developing a sense of, 116
  support, and parenting, 92
Social–exchange theory of aging, 309–310
Socialization:
  in childbirth, 55
  impact of television on, 127–128, 130
  kinds of, 5
  and moral development, 143
  in middle childhood, 153
  occupational, 234
  and the school setting, 144–149
  through modeling, 125
  as transmission of norms, 6–7
Social–learning theory, 171
  and moral development, 117, 140–141
Social Security, 310, 327
Social work practice:
  with adolescents, 215–216
  with the elderly, 336–337
  and events surrounding birth, 64–65
  and infant development, 97–99
  with school and parent, 149
  and middle adulthood, 292–294

Social work practice (*cont'd*)
  and middle childhood, 170–171
  with preschoolers, 128–129
  for young adults, 256–257
Socioeconomic status:
  and defined delinquency, 208
  and values of adolescence, 187
Spatial orientation, 133
Specht, R., 44, 46, 48, 54, 57, 84, 111, 125,
  167, 168, 180, 181, 188, 244, 246, 266,
  272, 279, 307, 321
Special education, 167
Speech development, 75–76
Stable growth, 133
Stabler, J. R., 163, 164
Stages:
  formal operations (adolescence), 183
  in the human life, 11, 32
  in the life–span perspective, 27
Stage theory (Piaget), 13
Stagnation in middle adulthood, 273–274
Status (*see also* Peers; Socioeconomic status):
  and language, 111
  in middle childhood, 161
Stevens–Long, J., 239, 283
Stress:
  and birth of a child, 54
  and divorce, 285
  in the fetal environment, 52–53
  and involuntary unemployment, 287–288
  in middle adulthood, 295
Structural theory and ego psychology, 10
Structure of behavior, 16
Studies, longitudinal, 25
Substance abuse in adolescence, 210–211, 218
Sudden infant death syndrome (SIDS), 63
Suicide:
  in adolescence, 211–212, 218
  rate for Asian Americans, 328
Sullivan, H. S., 155, 156
Superego:
  development of, 116
  and moral development, 140
Support system parental, 127
Surrogate motherhood, 41

Tanner, J. M., 180, 181
Tasks, *see* Developmental, tasks
Taylor, N. B., 51, 52
Tay-Sachs disease, 46
Teenage pregnancy, 206–207
Television, impact of, 127–128
Temperament innate, 61
Teratology, 49
  and fetal development, 66
Theory, defined, 7
Theory of Data (Coombs), 2
Thomas, A., 25, 61, 314
Three–generation families, 252
Time–lag design, 26
Time sampling, 22
Toxemia, 50

Transactions, ego and environment, 32
Transition:
  adolescence, as a state of, 179
  adulthood for men, leading to, 275–276
  birth as, 27
  death as, 329
  from home to school, 145
Transmission of norms, 6–7
Trust of infants in the environment, 78
Tulkin, S., 76, 77
Twins, 45

U.S. Bureau of the Census
  1976, 199, 253
  1978, 214, 269, 285
  1983, 30
U.S. Department of Health, Education and
    Welfare, 207

Vaillant, G. E., 230, 233, 272, 275, 277
Value orientation, developmental types of,
    142–143
Values:
  in adolescence, 186–188, 198, 217
  change in parenthood, 255
  traditional, and problems with, 160, 250
  women's, 276, 277
  and work, 235, 287–288
Vance, A. K., 146, 147
Vander Zanden, J. W., 50, 51, 63, 70, 71, 72,
    75, 136, 311

Venereal disease, 52
Vinick, B. H., 286, 335
Vogel, S., 194, 200

Walters, R. H., 117, 141
Weinstein, K. K., 282, 322
White, Robert, 12–13, 32
  the preschool years, 114–115
  competence in middle childhood, 154–156,
    195–197, 198
  competence in infant development, 81
Widowhood, 285–287, 338–339
  in older years, 333–335
  groups (types) of, 334–335
Williams, J. E., 163, 164
Wills, living, 331
Women:
  and careers, 288–289
  the older years, 328–329
  role of, in young adulthood, 237
Work:
  in middle adulthood, 290–292
  role of, 232–235
  and self–esteem, 319
  as socialization, 257
  environment in young adulthood, 235

Yeakel, M., 181, 225, 226, 256, 336
Young adulthood, 29–30, 225–258
  role expectations of, 256
Young Mothers Educational Development
    program, 206